Governor Livingston High School
Instructional Media Center
175 Watchung Blvd
Berkeley Heights, NJ 07922

ICONS OF TALK

ICONS OF TALK

The Media Mouths That Changed America

Donna L. Halper

Greenwood Icons

GREENWOOD PRESS
Westport, Connecticut · London

Library of Congress Cataloging-in-Publication Data

Halper, Donna L.
Icons of talk : the media mouths that changed America / Donna L. Halper.
    p. cm. — (Greenwood icons)
  Includes bibliographical references and index.
  ISBN 978-0-313-34381-0 (alk. paper)
  1. Television talk shows—United States.   2. Radio talk shows—United States.
I. Title.   II. Title: Media mouths that changed America.
  PN1992.8.T3H35 2009
  791.45'6—dc22   2008028515

British Library Cataloguing in Publication Data is available.

Library of Congress Catalog Card Number: 2008028515
ISBN: 978-0-313-34381-0

First published in 2009

Greenwood Press, 88 Post Road West, Westport, CT 06881
An imprint of Greenwood Publishing Group, Inc.
www.greenwood.com

Printed in the United States of America

The paper used in this book complies with the
Permanent Paper Standard issued by the National
Information Standards Organization (Z39.48-1984).

10   9   8   7   6   5   4   3   2   1

Contents

List of Photos

Steve Allen (page 81). Allen was such a talented jazz musician that he was chosen to play big band legend Benny Goodman in a movie. In this 1955 photo, Goodman (standing) is giving Steve a few pointers. (AP Photo)

Johnny Carson (page 93). After an amazing thirty-year career, Johnny Carson was about to retire. Here, he is shaking hands with long-time sidekick and friend Ed McMahon, as they taped their final *Tonight Show* in late May 1992. (AP Photo/Douglas C. Pizac)

James Dobson (page 105). One of the most influential Christian conservatives, Dobson is an inspirational speaker, both on his radio show and in his many live appearances. (AP Photo/Mark J. Terrill)

Don Francisco (page 117). Francisco is the energetic and enthusiastic TV host of *Sábado Gigante*, a weekly variety show that has been on the air since the 1960s. Here, he is shown gesturing to the audience, undoubtedly asking them to sing along or to applaud. (AP Photo/Lynne Sladky)

Herb Jepko (page 127). Jepko's listeners adored him and eagerly joined his radio family called the *Nitecaps*. Seen here in the KSL studio, Herb did a show that avoided anger and controversy. (Courtesy of Professor Joseph Buchman)

Larry King (page 137). King has had a career of more than 50 years as a celebrity interviewer. With his trademark suspenders and a show that attracts the biggest newsmakers, there is no one quite like Larry King. (Courtesy of CNN/Photofest)

Jay Leno (page 147). In addition to being a successful stand-up comic and the popular host of the *Tonight Show*, Leno has written several books for children. His first, from 2004, was called *If Roast Beef Could Fly*. (AP Photo/Ric Francis)

broadcasts are tasteless, or even obscene, his fans continue to love his outrageousness and his willingness to push the envelope. (Courtesy of Photofest)

Jerry Williams (page 271). The man who introduced the call-in talk show to Boston, Williams was first a liberal and later a populist, but he always knew how to make his audience feel like he was on their side. (AP Photo/ Steven Senne)

Oprah Winfrey (page 283). She is among the world's most influential and beloved celebrities, and also one of the world's wealthiest. In fact, according to *Forbes Magazine*, there are only ten women who are self-made billionaires, and Oprah Winfrey is one of them. (AP Photo/Dima Gavrysh, File)

Series Foreword

Worshipped and cursed. Loved and loathed. Obsessed about the world over. What does it take to become an icon? Regardless of subject, culture, or era, the requisite qualifications are the same: (1) challenge the status quo, (2) influence millions; and (3) impact history.

Using these criteria, Greenwood Press introduces a new reference format and approach to popular culture. Spanning a wide range of subjects, volumes in the Greenwood Icons series provide students and general readers a port of entry into the most fascinating and influential topics of the day. Every title offers an in-depth look at a number of iconic figures, each of which capture the essence of a broad subject. These icons typically embody a group of values, elicit strong reactions, reflect the essence of a particular time and place, and link different traditions and periods. Among those featured are artists and activists, superheroes and spies, inventors and athletes, the legends and mythmakers of entire generations. Yet icons can also come from unexpected places: as the heroine who transcends the pages of a novel or as the revolutionary idea that shatters our previously held beliefs. Whether people, places, or things, such icons serve as a bridge between the past and the present, the canonical and the contemporary. By focusing on icons central to popular culture, this series encourages students to appreciate cultural diversity and to critically analyze issues of enduring significance.

Most importantly, these books are as entertaining as they are provocative. Is Disneyland a more influential icon of the American West than Las Vegas? How do ghosts and ghouls reflect our collective psyche? Is Barry Bonds an inspiring or a deplorable icon of baseball?

Designed to foster debate, the series serves as a unique resource that is ideal for paper writing or report purposes. Insightful, in-depth entries provide far more information than conventional reference articles but are less intimidating and more accessible than a book-length biography. The most revered and reviled icons of American and world history are brought to life with related sidebars, timelines, fact boxes, and quotations. Authoritative entries are accompanied by bibliographies that make these titles an ideal starting point for further research. Spanning a wide range of popular topics, including business, literature, civil rights, politics, music, and more, books in the series provide fresh insights for the student and the popular reader into the power and influence of icons, a topic of as vital interest today as in any previous era.

Preface

When I was growing up in Boston, I was a devoted fan of top-forty radio. I loved rock-and-roll, and I wanted to be a disc jockey. But I also enjoyed talk shows. My parents would watch David Susskind, whose syndicated television program was shown in Boston in the mid-1960s, and I recall how we would discuss the topics or comment on what a particular guest had said. It made me feel very much like an adult to be part of these conversations.

Boston was also an excellent talk radio market. In the early 1960s, when station WMEX was a popular top-forty station, I listened to it every night because that's when my favorite dj, Arnie Ginsburg, did his *Night Train* show. At the end of his show, the station suddenly transitioned into talk, with an issues-oriented program featuring Jerry Williams. I didn't realize at the time that Williams was a nationally known talk host, sometimes referred to as the "dean of talk radio." I became a faithful listener to The Jerry Williams Show, and I learned a lot from it. (I can still remember the rules that Williams gave to potential callers, what he called his ABC's: "Be accurate, brief, and concise.") Even though I was undoubtedly not in the target audience Williams was seeking, and even though I was not twenty-one—callers had to be at least twenty-one—I tried to call on several occasions, and I even got on the air once with my comments. I never forgot it.

The Boston airwaves were the home to many great radio talk hosts over the years. Jerry Williams was probably the best known when I was growing up, but there were others, too: Bob Kennedy, Larry Glick, and Paul Benzaquin come to mind. From the 1980s until his untimely death in 2004, there was erudite and literate conversation on the *David Brudnoy Show*. I found many of these talk shows very informative. While the host sometimes became involved in a heated exchange with a guest, the shows themselves were seldom as one-sided or partisan as many talk shows are today. The talk shows then rarely deteriorated into shout fests; the emphasis was on debate rather than character assassination.

When I got into radio myself, I started out as a dj and music director, but I never forgot my love of talk shows. I even hosted a few during my on-air days, and I found that doing an interesting interview and keeping the show moving was much more difficult than it seemed. That realization made me appreciate the genre even more. When I became a radio consultant, I had the privilege of training a number of local talk hosts, and to this day, I am occasionally called on to work with aspiring talkers, helping them to find the right balance between being entertaining and being informative. As I said, this balance is not as easy to find as the best talkers make it seem.

All of this is why I am pleased to write *Icons of Talk: The Media Mouths That Changed America*. The talk show genre has had a profound influence on American life, and this book examines why the genre has endured. Whether it's the television talk show where the host and the guests and the audience interact or the radio talk show where the host and the listeners debate and discuss, there are talk shows that appeal to just about every point of view. The term *talk show* is generally understood to mean a show that has a host (or hosts), guests, and some audience participation, whether listeners call in or the TV host interacts with the studio audience. There are some wonderful interview shows, including those hosted by Bill Moyers and Charlie Rose and the late Tim Russert, but they are not talk shows per se because there is no audience participation. One element that explains the success of talk shows is that they enable listeners or viewers to feel as if they are part of the experience, what the sociologist Benedict Anderson called an "imagined community." So while interview shows are certainly worthy of mention, this book focuses on those shows not only where the host and the guests talk to each other, but where the audience can also get involved.

Icons of Talk examines talk shows from several different perspectives. From the historical point of view, talk shows have a surprisingly long history, going back to the 1930s on radio. Talk moved to the new medium of television in the early 1950s, but radio talk was far from over. The talk show experienced a major resurgence in the late 1980s and is still one of radio's most listened-to formats. Another way to analyze talk shows is from the popular culture perspective. The hosts have certainly become iconic figures, frequently quoted and capable of inspiring intense opinions—not just about the topics discussed, but about the hosts themselves. Talk show hosts have helped to make or break political candidates, they've inspired trends or called attention to causes, and their larger-than-life personalities have earned them millions of fans (as well as more than a few enemies).

In the pages of *Icons of Talk*, you'll find entries on twenty of the best-known exemplars of the talk show host, past and present, along with shorter accompanying sidebar entries about personalities and issues that have influenced talk shows. Appendix A is a timeline of events that have been discussed by talk hosts from the 1920s to the present, and Appendix B gives brief profiles of sixteen other talkers who should be remembered. Also included is a bibliography of useful resources for those who want to learn more about talk show history.

Throughout *Icons of Talk*, I discuss the techniques that the best talk hosts have used to motivate (and sometimes aggravate) their audiences, and I look at why the talk format has been so successful. Talk has proved itself to be a very flexible format, winning new fans as it branched out into sports talk, religious talk, political talk, and celebrity talk. And since this book contains social history, each chapter puts the talk format and its hosts into historical context. The book also addresses such questions as: How did the most important talkers affect or change society? What were the issues they became famous for talking about? What reaction did they get—from listeners and from critics? How were talk hosts able to persuade people to vote for particular candidates or support certain causes? Which hosts were considered controversial and why? How did some friendly and companionable hosts manage to remain popular when so many others preferred confrontation? How did the best-known hosts become famous, and why are many of them still remembered? And finally, what does the future hold for talk shows?

While a number of local and national hosts are discussed (as well as the controversies that have surrounded some of them), the book focuses on the following icons of talk:

1. Steve Allen. A TV talk show pioneer, Allen inspired both admiration and criticism (depending on which side you were on) for his relentless critique of the vulgarity of popular culture. A skeptic with a quick wit, he was the first host of TV's *Tonight* show.

2. Johnny Carson. Carson was late-night TV's best known host, taking the *Tonight Show* to new heights during his long tenure there from 1962 to 1992. An estimated fifty million viewers watched his final broadcast.

3. James Dobson. Dobson, an Evangelical Christian talk show host, has put Christian radio and conservative Christian causes on the map over the past several decades. His show, *Focus on the Family*, is listened to by millions weekly, and his books and Web site attract even more attention from his large and vocal audience

4. Don Francisco. If there is a Hispanic version of Oprah Winfrey, it's either Don Francisco (real name Mario Kreutzberger), a European refugee whose family settled in Chile, or Cristina Saralegui. For decades, Don Francisco's weekly variety show, *Sabado Gigante*, has been watched by Latinos and Latinas of all ages.

5. Herb Jepko. Jepko wasn't controversial, and he wasn't rude. He was companionable and friendly, and his listeners adored him. His late-night show was based in Utah, but he was heard all over the western United States. His Nitecaps club had thousands of faithful members. He is typical of a time when talk radio was a best friend rather than a spiteful adversary.

6. Larry King. He is often referred to as the "King of Celebrity Talk" and with good reason. His CNN show "Larry King Live" is his network's most

popular program. He got his start on radio, where his very successful overnight talk show on the Mutual Radio Network combined celebrity chat with calls from listeners. King has continued to do the same on his TV show at CNN.

7. Jay Leno. Leno, an affable talk show host, is known as one of the hardest-working comedians in show business. When Johnny Carson retired in 1992, Jay was chosen to replace him, and since then, Jay's observational humor has skewered politicians and celebrities alike, keeping the show's ratings high. A man who truly loves to perform, Leno continues to do his act as often as possible, performing in clubs as much as 300 days a year and seldom taking a day off.

8. David Letterman. Everyone thought Letterman would be named Johnny Carson's successor, but the Indianapolis-born host with the often ironic sense of humor lost out to Jay Leno. Letterman left NBC and carved out his own niche at CBS, where his late-night talk show has remained popular, especially with younger viewers, since its inception in 1993.

9. Rush Limbaugh. On the air on over six hundred stations nationwide, this conservative talk show host revitalized AM radio, rescuing it from oblivion in the late 1980s. Often controversial but always interesting, Limbaugh has maintained number one ratings among radio talkers for several decades, and is credited with influencing the populace to embrace conservative causes.

10. Joe Pyne. By most accounts, Pyne was the father of the abrasive, nasty, and confrontational style of talk that is so well known today. His success on both radio and television proved that there was an audience for angry and outraged talk.

11. Randi Rhodes. Rhodes is one of the first liberal/progressive talk show hosts to appear in the top ten in *Talkers* magazine, as the top ten have been overwhelmingly conservative (and male) since the annual poll began. A former "shock jock," she is also one of the best-known (and most controversial) women in a format historically dominated by men.

12. Cristina Saralegui. Saralegui was named the "Queen of the Airwaves" by *Time* magazine in 2005 for her great influence on the Hispanic female audience. One of the few women on Spanish-language TV with a successful talk show, she has hosted *El Show de Cristina* for nearly twenty years, championing women's causes in an often machismo culture.

13. Laura Schlessinger. A proponent of tough love, Schlessinger has taken a genre often reserved for women (advice giving) and made herself the queen of this type of talk show. Her advice is often controversial, but her ratings keep her in the top five most listened to talk show hosts nationally year after year.

14. Ed Schultz. The highest-rated and most successful progressive/liberal talker, Schultz has refused to move his show to New York City or Los Angeles, instead broadcasting *Straight Talk from the Heartland* from Fargo, North Dakota. Ed is syndicated on a hundred stations, and is among the most influential talk hosts in the United States, according to *Talkers* magazine.

15. Tavis Smiley. One of the most respected and visible African American talk show hosts, Smiley has been on both radio and TV and in print journalism as well. Known for his interviewing skill and his ability to motivate his audience, Smiley's commonsense message resonates in the black community.

16. Tom Snyder. Snyder pioneered the late-late-night TV talk/interview show, the kind that was so popular on radio and later became a staple of TV thanks to him. The *Tomorrow Show* appeared after the *Tonight Show*, and Snyder became so well known that *Saturday Night Live*'s Dan Aykroyd did a parody of his style.

17. Jerry Springer. Like Springer or hate him, his often outrageous and voyeuristic examination of popular culture on his daily syndicated TV show has earned him the scorn of pundits and clergy, but that hasn't stopped his audience from growing. Springer continues to garner huge ratings, and his show is a "guilty pleasure" for many fans.

18. Howard Stern. Nobody has pushed the envelope more and nobody has been the object of more controversy (or more FCC fines) than Stern. He may be on satellite radio now and not subject to FCC supervision, but he hasn't stopped being controversial.

19. Jerry Williams. A libertarian and an opinionated host, Williams dominated the local talk genre in every city where he worked. Williams was often called "The Dean of Talk Radio" because of his success with call-in talk beginning in the 1950s. He motivated audiences in Boston, Chicago, Philadelphia, and Washington, DC, even getting several local laws reversed.

20. Oprah Winfrey. Winfrey is the undisputed queen of daytime talk. Her longevity, her popularity, and her transformation of the advice-giving and celebrity-chat genre are unparalleled in popular culture.

Acknowledgments

Given how important a role talk shows have played in my own life, and given how many millions of fans radio and TV talk shows have, I am very grateful to Kristi Ward and the other editors at Greenwood Press for agreeing that a book about the talk show deserves to be written. While many people helped me with my research, I can't say enough good things about the wonderful reference librarians I consulted, especially those at the Boston Public Library; the Thomas Crane Library in Quincy, Massachusetts; the Emerson College Library; the University of Massachusetts–Boston Library; and libraries in cities and towns all over the United States, from Springfield, Massachusetts, to Kenosha, Wisconsin, to Fargo, North Dakota, to Salt Lake City, Utah. Librarians are too often taken for granted in our Internet world, but I for one don't know where I'd be without their tireless efforts. My appreciation to Dr. Joseph Buchman, who helped with the Herb Jepko piece; to Gabe Hobbs of Clear Channel Communications for his input on Rush Limbaugh; and to Ira Apple, who provided me with access to several talk radio pioneers. I also want to thank media critic extraordinaire Dan Kennedy of Northeastern University for his insights and Professors Michael Keith of Boston College, Christopher Sterling of George Washington University, and Jarice Hanson of the University of Massachusetts–Amherst for their interest in the history of broadcasting. Of the former journalists who provided their recollections, Bill Buchanan was especially helpful. Internet list-servs were another wonderful resource, and I thank Barry Mishkind, Scott Fybush, Dan Strassberg, Garrett Wollman, and Len Zola for their contributions to my research. My husband, Jon Jacobik, could not have been more supportive during the months when I was preoccupied with this project. And above all, I want to dedicate this book to the memory of David Brudnoy, one of the last talk hosts in our contentious age who understood that talk radio should be about ideas rather than about insults.

Part I

How the Talk Show Was Born: The History of a Genre

Americans love talk shows. In a typical week, more than fourteen million Americans listen to Rush Limbaugh, whose syndicated radio show is carried by about six hundred stations. On television, Oprah Winfrey's syndicated television talk show is seen by an estimated thirty million viewers a week. Talk hosts like Limbaugh and Winfrey are among the most influential figures in American popular culture. Their names are so well known that what they say on the air is often discussed around the water cooler at work or commented on in Internet blogs and on fan Web sites.

Most contemporary radio talk shows can be found on the AM dial. At one time, AM stations simply played music; in fact, in the 1950s and 1960s, the hit-oriented format called *top-forty* was king on AM. Today, what is heard on AM tends to be various kinds of talk shows, and the success of this genre has kept many AM stations profitable. Rush Limbaugh is emblematic of that success. Thanks to his expertise in the political talk format, he has profited; in 2000, Limbaugh's base salary was reported by *Forbes* magazine to be $33 million a year, and when that contract was renewed in 2008, it was up to $40 million. In addition to his financial success, he has become a flashpoint for comment and controversy. Limbaugh is generally regarded as the man who put political talk radio on the map, and the many stations that carry his show have done well with it over the years. Like the politics of the majority of radio talkers (more than 95 percent according to some studies), his are conservative. Left-wing or "progressive" talk hosts are far less prevalent, but a few have achieved considerable success. The best known is Ed Schultz, who is heard on about a hundred radio stations nationally. In early 2007, Schultz was named one of the top five most influential talk hosts in the United States by *Talkers* magazine.

While political talk may have turned some hosts into media stars and pundits, other kinds of talk shows also deliver big audiences for AM radio. One is the sports-talk show. Call-in sports shows have become as popular as political talk shows. Whether concentrating on professional or college sports, this format creates a sense of community among its listeners, allowing fans to comment on their favorite team and to second-guess the decisions of the coaches and managers without ever leaving the comfort of home.

Also popular is Christian talk, a genre where well-known religious leaders like James Dobson offer their listeners advice and guidance in accordance with New Testament principles. Dobson was one of the pioneers of the Christian talk format, starting with one local show in 1977. Today, his *Focus on the Family* is heard not only in the United States but in over 160 other countries. He and his guests discuss current events, morality, and ethics; and like the political talk format, the Christian talk format tends to come from a conservative perspective.

Unlike radio, where specific formats like political talk and sports talk predominate, on television many of the most popular talk shows are much closer to what used to be called a variety show, where a high profile host and a number of celebrity guests sit and chat. Oprah Winfrey's show is a good example.

Oprah has a larger than life personality and her fans adore her, but she also fills her daily program with interesting guests from just about every political viewpoint. Some guests are famous movie stars talking about their new film or celebrities with a cause they believe in, but some guests are just ordinary people who have done something that Oprah considers worthy of media attention. The same can be said of popular Latina talk host Cristina Saralegui, who has done a similar type of program for several decades, and whose fans believe she is every bit as important as Oprah.

The most common type of talk show revolves around a host (or in some cases, several hosts) chatting about particular issues (current events, sports, religion, cooking, etc.). The host is often joined by invited guests who are experts on the topic at hand. On many radio talk shows, listeners take part in the discussion by calling in with questions or comments. A few hosts don't take calls and basically do an extended monologue, talking about whatever subject interests them that day; but most shows do allow for some audience participation. On television, the majority of the talk shows are presented to a live studio audience, and while these viewers may not be able to ask any questions directly, they do express themselves by applauding or booing. This is especially true for programs where the host gives relationship advice, such as the *Dr. Phil Show*. As psychologist Phil McGraw counsels the people who have asked for his help, the studio audience often reacts to the admissions and revelations that are made. On some TV talk shows, audience members occasionally have a chance to ask the guests questions, or the host may select a studio audience member to offer an opinion, but on most variety shows, the emphasis is on the host and the guests, many of whom are celebrities. Even though the members of the studio audience, like the people watching at home, serve primarily as spectators, loyal viewers still feel included. Studies have shown that these devoted fans see themselves as part of an extended family, and thanks to online Web sites and fan magazines, they do form a sort of community, sharing with other fans a love of their favorite talk show and its host.

Talk show fans often show their devotion to their favorite host by becoming involved in the causes the host seems to prefer, and supporting the advertisers on their favorite show. A good example of this loyalty is the way shock jock Howard Stern's fans have stood by him. Stern, the self-described "King of All Media," has generated lots of controversy over the years for his often vulgar on-air antics. Despite the criticism of politicians and clergy, his many fans have continued to support his show; during his long career on so-called "terrestrial radio," from 1978 to 2004, his Arbitron ratings consistently placed him among the top ten most-listened to announcers nationally. When in 2006 his show moved to Sirius, a satellite radio service, millions of his fans subscribed and bought the necessary equipment so they could continue to hear his show. Oprah Winfrey receives similar adulation from her fans, many of whom see her as a woman they want to emulate. Her viewers identified with her when she struggled with her weight, and some even dieted along with her or wrote her letters of encouragement. In addition, Oprah's Book Club has influenced her viewers' reading habits. When she recommends a book, an unknown author may become a best-selling writer. As for the influence of the political talkers, Rush Limbaugh has repeatedly demonstrated his ability to get listeners to call their representatives in Congress and even to vote for a certain candidate. And whether the host's style is friendly or confrontational, the fan base for talk shows continues to grow.

There have been many theories about why talk shows have remained so popular for so long. Among the most widely accepted explanations is that talk shows provide one of the few opportunities for working-class men and women to have a voice. Most educational programs and even most panel discussions feature experts and scholars, but talk shows feature what Boston's famous talker Jerry Williams used to call "Joe Average." Murray Levin, author of *Talk Radio and the American Dream*, has suggested that especially on radio, talk shows succeed by making people angry or by allowing them to vent their frustration. Even on the more friendly radio and TV talk shows, those that promote a sense of community, the target audience is the average working person. The hosts of these programs sometimes make dreams come true by giving away prizes, like home makeovers or vacations (Oprah has given her studio audience new cars). But above all, the most popular hosts make their audience feel as if somebody cares about them.

How the talk show developed and how it became so influential is an interesting story; the talk show genre, and the hosts who are its stars, did not suddenly emerge one afternoon. In fact, while much of the comment (and controversy) about talk show hosts has intensified since the 1980s, the evolution of this genre had two earlier "golden ages": the 1930s and the 1960s.

THE BEGINNINGS OF TALK RADIO IN THE 1920S AND 1930S

When most people think of talk shows, they think of something relatively modern. While it is certainly true that the talk show format achieved some of its greatest success beginning in the 1980s and 1990s, there were popular talk shows as far back as the mid-1930s. The first program that could be called a talk show was probably *America's Town Meeting of the Air*, which is discussed later. But if we want to discover how the talk show developed, we have to go back even further, to the early 1920s, the formative years of commercial radio. The first stations, including 8MK (later WWJ) in Detroit, 1XE (later WGI) in Medford Hillside, MA (near Boston), and KDKA in Pittsburgh, relied on music more than on talk. Because radio programs were broadcast live (audiotape had yet to be invented), stations used professional orchestras; vocalists from local music schools also performed. But even in radio's formative years, it was not unusual to hear all kinds of talk: college courses by radio, sermons about current issues by major clergy of many denominations, speeches by advocates of certain causes, and of course, politicians trying to get votes. President Franklin Delano Roosevelt's 1930s "Fireside Chats" are well known, but before them, in the early 1920s, presidents and former presidents were being heard on the air. For example, President Warren G. Harding was a big fan of radio and gave several radio talks himself in 1922. When he died suddenly in August 1923, many radio stations announced his death to the public, and some of them went silent on the day of his funeral, while others went on the air only to broadcast his memorial service. Former president Woodrow Wilson gave a radio talk about foreign policy in November 1923, and then, President Calvin Coolidge paid tribute to the late President Harding in a radio speech in December of that year. Thus, even in the early 1920s, an opportunity to hear the news from Washington directly from the president himself was now a part of life for anyone with a radio. (President Coolidge's taciturn personality had earned him the nickname "Silent Cal," but when it came to radio, he was very willing to talk. He made a number of appearances throughout the 1920s and maintained his sense of humor when critics made fun of his New England accent or said that his radio speaking style was imperious.)

It is doubtful that radio listeners were upset by the speaking styles of famous people. Hearing newsmakers on the air was amazing to the average person, and fan letters sent to radio magazines usually expressed excitement and gratitude. Radio was the first mass medium to bring the listener to an event as it was actually taking place, something newspapers, magazines, and movies could not do. Better still, radio was a very inclusive medium. Not everyone could afford theater tickets (and sad to say, many theaters were segregated), but a radio broadcast was available to anyone. Radio was also more user-friendly than a newspaper or magazine, since not everyone was able to read. It was thanks to the radio that the public first heard the actual voices of newsmakers and celebrities. People may have seen them in a newsreel at the movies, but since "talking pictures" had not yet been perfected, there had been no way to hear them speaking until radio came along. We take all of this for granted today, but in an era when long-distance travel was still expensive and slow, and the only way to hear the newsmakers was to go to see them, radio brought the world right into the listener's home.

In radio's beginning years, people with a background in engineering built their own sets, but as radio listening swept the country, manufacturers began mass-producing receiving sets in a wide variety of prices and styles. Some radios came with ornate cabinets and were so beautifully designed that they were treated like expensive furniture. A new magazine called *Radio in the Home* featured photos of celebrities and members of the upper class showing off their radios and their "radio room."

Although in radio's formative years, many of the performers were eager volunteers rather than professionals, there were soon vocalists and musicians who became popular, as well as announcers whose voices were especially pleasant. But while the performers gave their names, it was difficult to know who the announcers were because of a custom that came from amateur (ham) radio: station managers only allowed early announcers to use their initials. Thus, theater critic (and later radio executive) Bertha Brainard of station WJZ in Newark, New Jersey, was known to her audience as ABN (Announcer Brainard from Newark), and even station owner John Shepard III, who sometimes went on the air from his Boston station WNAC, did so as JS. Popular demand changed this custom because listeners came to enjoy certain voices and wanted to know the names of the people who were speaking. By mid-1922, a number of stations had begun to identify themselves with clever slogans, so that the listeners would remember where they had heard a program they liked. Of course, not every program was interesting to everyone, and listeners liked their freedom to accept or reject any program by turning the dial. They had no such freedom when attending a lecture or seeing a movie or stage show; their only recourse was to disturb others by leaving early.

At first, people were content with the novelty of radio. But by mid-1922, listeners were seeking ways to participate, rather than just sitting back passively and listening. Fans began writing to the editors at the local newspapers and radio magazines. Their most common complaint was that there was too much interference in the atmosphere: static and Morse Code messages from ships at sea often interfered with their enjoyment of their favorite programs. They also expressed their desire to hear more of some performers and less of others. They began writing to their favorite stations, and to the people they heard on the air; in fact, stations were suddenly receiving so much fan mail that they hired extra help to answer it. Some stations printed up postcards called "applause cards," so that fans could vote on which entertainers they liked best. (Entertainers also made their own applause cards available, so that fans could let the station management know how much they enjoyed particular programs.) Some listeners formed clubs where they discussed what they had been listening to, and advocated for better programming.

As more stations went on the air in the United States (there were fewer than twenty-five in 1921, but by the summer of 1922, there were more than two hundred), debates about the future direction of broadcasting began to take place. Newspapers and a growing number of radio magazines joined the discussion, and many articles were written about what radio ought to be doing. The biggest debate was whether broadcasting should be used mainly for bringing education and culture to the public, or whether it should concentrate on entertainment. Related to this was a debate about whether radio should play mainly "good music" like opera or dance music, or focus on the popular hits. And then there was the issue of sponsorship: Should radio be noncommercial, run as a public service; or should it be run for profit, with programs supported by advertisers? Among those who opposed allowing commercials on the air was Herbert Hoover, then Secretary of the U.S. Department of Commerce and later president of the United States. He believed that commercials would drive listeners away, and he even said that permitting what was then called "direct advertising" would kill broadcasting. Broadcasters disagreed. They wanted a way to finance the increasing expense of keeping their stations on the air, and they saw commercials as a good solution. Not much was resolved in these debates, although broadcasters did finally persuade the Department of Commerce (a precursor of the Federal Communications Commission) to allow advertising. The fact that these debates had reached the highest levels of the government proved how important radio was; it seemed to be on nearly everyone's mind, and it was creating a national conversation.

Of course, in those early years, broadcasting, which was first referred to as *radiophone*, was very different from what it is now. Stations seldom had more than 100 watts of power (some had as few as 10), and being on the air twenty-four hours a day was unheard of; most stations were on the air for only one or two hours a night. Radio station signals were able to travel long distances on the AM (amplitude modulation) band, the only one then available; it was not unusual for an East Coast station to be heard in the South or Midwest. What were called "radio talks" were not the sort of interactive communication we take for granted today. Call-in shows did not exist, since the technology for putting phone calls on the air was still in a primitive state, and on the few occasions when it was tried, the sound quality was poor. Also, in the early 1920s, the U.S. Department of Commerce didn't think it was a good idea to allow announcers and listeners to talk directly to each other; this kind of communication was reserved for amateur ham radio. Commercial radio was supposed to have mass appeal.

Radio talks were easy to produce, requiring only the speaker, a microphone, and an engineer. The best speakers, those who weren't intimidated by the microphone and were able to relate to the "invisible audience," won a following and were invited back to give more talks. Among those who adapted fairly quickly were professors and members of the clergy, who were accustomed to public speaking. However, these educators and clerics were quite surprised when they began receiving fan letters. Typical of this response was what happened to Rabbi Harry Levi, who never expected to become a local celebrity when station WNAC asked him to be one of the Boston clergy giving inspirational radio talks. After a few weeks, listeners began showing up at his synagogue to ask for his autograph, and he became so popular with people of all faiths that he had to publish two books of his sermons. Radio is well known for having turned small-town entertainers into national stars, but what is often overlooked is how it also turned local men and women who were good speakers into respected "experts," making them famous in their community.

WHY RADIO TALKS MATTERED

In an era when most people did not attend college, radio gave listeners access to information they might not have heard otherwise, and the best-known experts often delivered that information themselves, from scientific genius Albert Einstein to baseball great Babe Ruth to the much-loved Queen Marie of Rumania. As a result, radio equalized the social classes, giving the poor and the middle class the opportunity to hear performers and newsmakers, access previously available only to the wealthy. Sometimes, radio introduced perspectives the average person would not have heard. In the era before ecumenism and interfaith cooperation, many American Christians had never met a Jew. Most major cities asked at least one rabbi to participate, along with priests and ministers, in giving inspirational radio talks. As the popularity of Boston's Rabbi Harry Levi demonstrated, being able to hear what a rabbi had to say helped to gradually eradicate some of the culture's stereotypes about Judaism. Similarly, because America in the 1920s and 1930s was still racially segregated, and the average newspaper seldom covered the black community in a positive way, many white Americans were unfamiliar with the issues that concerned people of color. Unfortunately, for all too many white Americans, their view of blacks was influenced by the popular radio comedy *Amos 'n' Andy*; first aired nationally in 1928, it featured white performers portraying stereotypes of uneducated black people. But on the other hand, radio also broke down some barriers, by providing black entertainers the opportunity to be heard by a mass audience. And radio did much more than popularize the musical skills of performers like Duke Ellington, Count Basie, and Ethel Waters. A few radio stations also put black educators and advocates on the air. On their weekly programs, these community leaders were able to discuss important issues as well as talk about black history and the many achievements of African Americans.

Not all the radio talks were about serious subjects. As today, there were shows about celebrity gossip, shows about cooking, and about sports and physical fitness. There were also radio charlatans like the notorious "Doctor" John R. Brinkley, who promised amazing medical cures, which he promoted over his own radio station in Milford, Kansas. Increasingly, as the networks were formed and the quality of the talent improved, talks were not needed as much (in the early days, they had frequently been used to fill up airtime); but radio talks didn't vanish entirely. Religious talks survived, as did talks about politics. Many candidates conducted their campaigns by radio, effectively reaching more potential voters than they could reach by renting a hall. But political coverage created a new set of problems for radio. Some candidates found they were not welcome on the air. In May 1926, Socialist Party presidential candidate Norman Thomas accused New York radio stations of censoring his views by not permitting him to deliver an address. Similarly, in March 1936, a number of stations, including seven affiliates of New England's Yankee Network, refused to air a speech by the Communist Party's general secretary, Earl Browder. And it wasn't just political ideologies that were considered too controversial by a station or a network: who was to be allowed to speak and who was not became an ongoing debate. A 1937 book,

Not To Be Broadcast, by columnist and critic Ruth Brindze, discussed in great detail how station executives, especially at the networks, had become so determined to be inoffensive to sponsors and listeners that they banned certain political views and entire topics (racism, birth control and family planning, criticism of capitalism) from the airwaves.

There were newscasts on radio from the earliest days, since one of the pioneer stations (8MK, later WNJ) was owned by a newspaper (the *Detroit News*); among the station's first broadcasts were the state election returns, and it also joined the much better-known KDKA in Pittsburgh in broadcasting the presidential returns in early November 1920. A number of the pioneering stations quickly linked up with a local newspaper so they could have reporters come in and talk about the news. These first efforts to provide newscasts were particularly appreciated by people who had difficulty reading a newspaper, especially immigrants and the blind. And although the technology and the lack of funds made it difficult for early radio stations to cover news on their own, there were a few news commentators as early as 1922, perhaps the most famous of whom was New York City's H. V. Kaltenborn, a well-respected journalist who went on the air at a time when print journalists saw radio as competition and tended to stay away. Kaltenborn's acceptance of radio paved the way for other commentators. Listeners were not able to call in to his program and give their reaction, but Kaltenborn received many letters and applause cards, as did other news commentators. Eventually, broadcasters would find ways to get the opinions of the listeners on the air; for example, as early as 1922, some stations made room for a studio audience. This would be especially useful in the 1930s when, after a panel discussion, the attendees were allowed to ask questions, an approach used to good effect on the talk show *America's Town Meeting of the Air*.

By the mid-1920s, radio was covering more events live. A good example was the efforts made by Chicago's WGN, which was aligned with the *Chicago Tribune*. At great expense (more than a thousand dollars a day for the landline charges), WGN provided live coverage of the trial of biology teacher John T. Scopes in Dayton, Tennessee, in July 1925. The trial concerned the controversy over the teaching of the theory of evolution in the public schools; Tennessee law forbade it, but Scopes felt it should be taught. The debate dominated the newspapers, and thanks to radio, people could listen to the trial and form their own opinions. By the end of the 1920s, radio was regularly taking its audience to major national events, from presidential inaugurations to reports on the first transatlantic flight of Charles Lindbergh. Though radio was well established as a commercial and entertainment-oriented medium by the late 1920s, the need for more educational programs continued to be a topic of discussion. College courses had been offered on the radio since 1922, but a number of educators wanted to devise courses aimed specifically at young people. In late 1929, Ray Lyman Wilbur, U.S. Secretary of the Interior, and John W. Cooper, U.S. Commissioner of Education, began working with a committee of high school and college educators to create something new in educational programs. The committee's members were aware that young people listened to the radio a lot, and their plan was to deliver informative courses in a way that wouldn't bore these young listeners. The lessons would be concise and interesting, using professional broadcasters and orchestras; the subject matter, like American history or English literature, would be presented in mini-radio-dramas; and guest experts would talk about science or give a demonstration of some aspect of music. Teachers and students would all be provided with lesson plans and other materials to complement the programs.

The *American School of the Air* was broadcast on the CBS network beginning in February 1930, and initial estimates by the Federal Radio Commission were that more than a million children heard it in schools nationwide. The idea had already worked well in Ohio, which had started its own radio school of the air in early 1929, and there were high hopes for a national version. *American School of the Air* also featured a civics and current events segment, and the students were encouraged to learn more about the news so they could discuss it in class. Subsequently administered surveys asking about the effectiveness of this new type of radio education showed that students seemed to like it. But unfortunately, CBS, although claiming to be in favor of this kind of programming, was not very pleased with the result. The problem was financial: *American School of the Air* was a noncommercial educational program, which meant the stations donated the time and derived no revenue from the show, despite the cost of producing it. And it was surrounded by lucrative sponsored programs, such as women's shows and soap operas. Ultimately, despite positive reactions from teachers and students, *American School of the Air* was canceled in 1940.

LETTING THE AUDIENCE SPEAK

On a few occasions during the late 1920s and early 1930s, engineers had been able to put phone callers on the air, but the process was still complicated, and the quality not always the best. Whenever callers were put on the air, the print media described the event as something special. For example, when Hugo Gernsback, editor of *Radio News* magazine, experimented with putting listener call-ins on his New York station, WRNY, in late April 1927, newspapers reported on his efforts, although the *Washington Post* referred to it as a "stunt." In another attempt in late January 1929, popular vocalist and pianist "Little" John Little was in St. Paul, Minnesota, on a midwestern tour and, during a visit to station KSTP, he took phone calls on the air from fans, one of whom called from as far away as Dallas, Texas.

With or without callers, radio was now a central part of American life, and people of all ages were talking about what they heard, as well as about where they had heard it or wanted to hear it. Throughout the early 1920s, articles had appeared in magazines like *Radio World* and *Radio News* about efforts to listen to the radio while riding in an automobile, usually by putting a tall antenna and a receiving set in the car and hoping for the best. As more listeners demanded a reliable way to listen in the car, in 1930 two companies began manufacturing car radios: Crosley, which also owned radio station WLW in Cincinnati, and a new company based in Chicago called Motorola. Because of the Depression, the purchase of car radios began slowly: In 1939 only 20 percent of new cars came with a radio.

Despite improvements in the technology, it was still a challenge for radio shows to involve their listeners regularly. The concept of a national program oriented to discussing current events seemed like a natural way to attract the public's interest. One of the first efforts at this kind of program was the *University of Chicago Roundtable*, which had been on the air locally since January 1931 and went on the NBC radio network in October 1933. On this show, three or four professors discussed, and sometimes debated, various issues of the day. But it was not until May 1935 that an audience was invited to take an active part in a discussion forum. The program that was the first "modern" talk show was NBC's *America's Town Meeting of the Air*, moderated by George V. Denny Jr., Executive Director of the League for Political Education. But unlike the stereotypically boring educational program, this show held the listener's attention, and generated thousands of fan letters a week. The setup of this radio town meeting was simple: Take a thought-provoking question, select panelists to represent the various sides, and let the conversation begin. Or as the program's introduction said, "Town meeting tonight! Come to the old Town Hall and talk it over!" The topic of the first broadcast was "Which Way America: Fascism, Communism, Socialism or Democracy?"

In addition to the compelling subject matter on the program, what was really new was the role of the studio audience. Since radio's early days, performers had insisted on a studio audience, people they could see as they were performing. Later, as radio stations became more able to cover distant events, the sounds of the public were also part of the broadcast. Thus, people at home heard the performer or speaker and also the crowd's reaction, whether it was applause or laughter or boos. What was different about *America's Town Meeting* was that the audience was part of the show: Attendees could challenge or question what the speakers had said; the only rule was that comments had to be brief. People listening at home could send in a question to be read on the air, or they might make a comment themselves. Within a year, NBC's engineers designed a system that put listener phone calls on the air live, from remote sites where they had gathered to listen to the program together. It was the active audience participation that added a new dimension to the show and provided an effective way to let members of the public express themselves on the topic at hand. Despite only a limited number of stations airing the first program, over three thousand letters poured in, making it obvious very quickly that this show was going to have an impact. In fact, Denny was surprised to learn that groups were being set up all over the country to discuss the topic he had chosen for that week and what the speakers on the air had said. As the show continued to be broadcast, it did not shy away from controversial subjects, nor did it pander to one ideology or another. Denny brought in experts and people with credibility, including famous authors like Pearl Buck and Langston Hughes; Frances Perkins, the first woman in President Roosevelt's cabinet; and a variety of scholars and educators. Among the topics discussed on *Town Meeting* were whether the United States needed the Social Security program; whether there was a free press in America; who was to blame for juvenile delinquency; and what could be done to solve the race question. And for those who wanted a more tangible view of the subject in that era before taping a show was possible, Denny held a forum in the pages of *Current History* magazine in the late 1930s and early 1940s: He would invite a group of experts to write their opinions on a question he had raised, and the magazine's readers could also join the discussion by writing their own short replies (no more than three hundred words), the best of which were printed.

The success of *America's Town Meeting*, which aired on Thursday evenings (rather than in the early Sunday morning slot often reserved for public service programs), proved that the average person would get excited about current issues, especially if the topics were presented in the style that *Town Meeting* used. The show's popularity was even more impressive given the many distractions available, such as gossip about movie stars, debates over the plot lines of soap operas, and discussions of the exploits of star athletes.

There was another successful network program that, while not strictly a talk show like *America's Town Meeting*, also knew how to involve its audience. The *Breakfast Club*, based in Chicago and starring Don McNeill, went on the air in 1933 on NBC's Blue Network (NBC owned two networks, called Red and Blue). McNeill believed that listeners would enjoy starting their day with a cheerful and up-beat radio program, and the popularity of the *Breakfast Club* proved he was right. At first, McNeill and his staff did the show themselves. Listeners were invited to gather around McNeill's imaginary breakfast table, where they heard friendly conversation and a combination of music and comedy. Listeners were also invited to contribute, and they sent poems, corny jokes, and inspirational stories for McNeill to read during the show. By 1938, McNeill added a studio audience, and began chatting with its members and even putting them on the air live. This technique of the host chatting with the audience was also later used with great success by TV talkers like Steve Allen in the 1950s.

As the Depression dragged on and the situation in Europe grew more serious, people turned to radio for escape as well as for information. While network radio had become known for soap operas, comedies, variety shows, and talent contests, there was a growing interest in hearing more news. But this presented radio executives with a dilemma. While they wanted to broadcast programs that were informative, the sponsors preferred shows that were entertaining. Like educational programs, news broadcasts were not sponsored at that time, and it was the sponsored shows that paid the bills. In addition to the financial issue, radio executives had one other problem that kept them from expanding their news departments. Since radio's earliest days, newspaper reporters were given more access to government spokespeople than radio reporters were. Newspaper owners insisted that radio was just entertainment, and they persuaded the government that only print journalists should get press credentials. This meant radio reporters were excluded from many locations where news was being made, including the press gallery of the U.S. Congress. By the early 1930s, the radio networks decided to protest their lack of access. As might be expected, newspaper owners resisted, but by the late 1930s, radio reporters were finally able to gain admission to the press galleries of their local legislatures and congress, making it easier to cover politics. Even though radio owners were pleased, there was still one other complication in their goal of providing more news-oriented programs. Audience surveys had begun in 1930 (the first ones by market researcher Archibald Crossley, and then, in 1935, a competitor, Claude E. Hooper), and shows that didn't get enough listeners were often canceled, no matter how much critics might like them. The question was whether or not news-oriented programs would attract enough of an audience to remain on the air. Thus, when CBS first took a chance on *The March of Time*, a unique newsmagazine show which debuted in March 1931, the network executives were concerned because at first, it received low ratings. They shouldn't have worried: *The March of Time* gradually built up a large audience. With its signature phrase "Time marches on," the show was designed to be a newsreel for the radio audience. *The March of Time* featured actors and actresses, along with talented sound effects technicians, who reenacted the top news stories of the week from the pages of *Time* magazine. By the mid-1930s, the show's Hooper ratings were impressive. Along with *America's Town Meeting of the Air*, *The March of Time* proved that radio could deliver programs that were both informative and interesting to the average person.

As radio reporters got more access and interest in current events increased, the networks began to add more news and commentary, giving their best-known anchors more airtime. For example, the Mutual Broadcasting System's Gabriel Heatter reported on the 1936 execution of Bruno Hauptmann, convicted of killing the infant son of aviator Charles Lindbergh. Heatter's in-depth coverage earned him praise from the public and the critics. Newscasts and radio reporting were done almost exclusively by men (among the names familiar in the mid-1930s were Boake Carter, John B. Kennedy, and Lowell Thomas; by the late 1930s, they had been joined by H. R. Baukhage and Edward R. Murrow), but several women commentators became popular. The best known were Dorothy Thompson of NBC, one of the few women announcing hard news, including reports on the rise of the Nazis; and Kathryn Cravens of CBS, who specialized in reporting what would later be called "human interest stories," relating how news events affected the lives of ordinary people. No matter who was doing the reporting—even if it was President Roosevelt, whose "Fireside Chats" about current administration policy began in March 1933—it was still rare for listeners to comment directly on what they heard. They might write a letter to their favorite newspaper or magazine, but their comments were seldom put on the air.

However, as technology continued to advance during the 1930s, especially with the development of smaller and more sensitive microphones, radio stations began to experiment with letting the listeners' voices be heard. A radio reporter would take a portable microphone to the street (or to a hotel lobby) and ask questions of passersby. This type of feature was called a vox pop (*vox populi,* or "voice of the people") show, and while it was considered a novelty at first, the stations that tried it found that people were eager to participate. Interviews with the man (or woman) in the street began in cities like Boston, New York, and Houston in the early to mid-1930s. Listeners loved the vox pop shows because they were spontaneous, and it was impossible to know whether the person being asked the question would say something brilliant or something bizarre. By the late 1930s, there was a network version of the vox pop on NBC, and local versions continued. But aside from the vox pop shows and *America's Town Meeting*, radio still did not provide many occasions for listeners to ask their own questions or express their own opinions. This did not change until after World War II, when audiotape had been perfected and long-distance telephone service was both reliable and affordable. Then the voices of listeners would be heard more often, as the first call-in talk shows were broadcast. After the war, there was also a new mass medium to challenge radio; television, and it too would let the audience participate.

WHO WAS TALKING DURING THE 1920S AND 1930S

While there were no call-in talk shows in the 1920s and 1930s, there were a number of well-known radio commentators. For news, the best known of the 1920s were New York City–based Hans Von (H. V.) Kaltenborn (1878–1965) and Frederic William Wile (1873–1941), based in Washington, DC. Both had come from print journalism, and when radio news was just beginning to establish itself, their presence on the air gave the new medium credibility. One of the best-known sports announcers, who also broadcast from the national political conventions and covered major news events for the newly created NBC, was Graham McNamee (1888–1942). The queen of the "radio homemakers" was Ida Bailey Allen (1885–1973), author of many cookbooks and hostess of a popular daily show for women on the CBS network.

By the 1930s, several other important announcers were on the air, giving advice about relationships or helping people in need. Among the best known of this genre was John J. Anthony (real name: Lester Kroll), whose popular program, the *Good-Will Hour*, began on the Mutual network in 1937; Anthony gave advice on love or marital problems, and while critics scorned him as a fake, at one point in the late 1930s he was heard on over seven hundred stations. In a similar vein was the *Voice of Experience*, another popular 1930s advice show in which "The Voice"—actually Marion Sayle Taylor, who was the son of a Baptist minister and was trained as a social worker—answered questions from thousands of desperate people and tried to solve their problems. According to a 1939 profile in *Time* magazine, in a typical week Taylor received six thousand letters. Also popular was women's show host Mary Margaret McBride (1899–1976), who did much more than chat about recipes and how to raise children. Her guests included some of the top newsmakers, as well as authors, psychologists, and businesswomen. And for news commentary, conservative listeners of the 1930s turned to Fulton Lewis Jr. (1903–1966) whose late 1930s broadcasts on Mutual attacked the policies of President Roosevelt and opposed America's entry into World War II; Lewis became known years later for his support of Senator Joseph McCarthy.

THE 1940S: THE WAR AND NEW TECHNOLOGIES

When the Japanese attacked Pearl Harbor in December 1941, debate about entering the war was replaced by the reality that the United States had to defend itself. With America now involved in World War II, a number of changes occurred on radio, with more newscasts and more coverage by the major correspondents. Edward R. Murrow of CBS distinguished himself for his wartime reporting from Europe, as did his colleagues Eric Sevareid, Charles Collingwood, and several other CBS reporters, who were collectively known as the Murrow Boys. There was also one woman in the group, a news photographer and broadcaster named Mary Marvin Breckinridge. As events in Europe unfolded and radio coverage expanded, most listeners probably weren't aware that there were now two new government agencies, the Office of War Information (OWI) and the Office of Censorship. The men who ran these new agencies were both former broadcasters: Elmer Davis at OWI and Byron Price at Censorship. Almost immediately, there was a tug of war between reporters (who wanted as much information as possible) and the military, which, perhaps understandably, wanted to keep as much off the air as it could. Both agencies were supposed to work with the press to manage the reporting of the news and resolve any conflicts that occurred. For example, Davis believed that OWI, created in June 1942, should act as a clearinghouse, working with the U.S. Army and U.S. Navy to make sure journalists got enough information from "authorized sources" so that they would not report anything that might unwittingly aid the enemy. In return for more military access, radio stations agreed to broadcast numerous programs produced by the armed forces, such as *This Is War* and the *Army Hour*. Also, all the networks (and many local stations) agreed to help with the sale of war bonds, devoting entire evenings to on-air bond drives. A typical example was a bond drive held by the Blue Network in late August 1942: it featured stars from radio, film, and sports, and lasted seven hours. Popular radio entertainers Eddie Cantor and Kate Smith even did their own marathon broadcasts for the war effort. Cantor did a "talk-athon" in late January 1944, during which he stayed on the air for 24 hours straight and raised more than $37 million. Smith did several on-air marathons in the mid 1940s; one of her longest was 21 hours and raised $39 million.

While some reporters were concerned that too many restrictions would be placed on their reporting, most cooperated without complaint. In fact, Byron Price told *Time* magazine in January 1942 that nearly 100 percent of U.S. radio stations had immediately agreed on the need for a code of censorship and were willing to comply for the good of the country. His office issued such a code, and while it was ostensibly voluntary, there wasn't much question that stations ought to obey it. The purpose of the code was to tell broadcasters what could and could not be reported without putting the U.S. troops in danger, referring mainly to matters like troop locations and movements, but it also included seemingly innocuous pieces of information such as weather reports. Among those shows suddenly forbidden were vox pop shows and any other programs on which listeners spoke spontaneously (in this era before the tape delay, the government feared an audience member might speak out inappropriately). Even announcements about lost pets were banned because they might contain coded messages. Journalists were also warned not to make statements critical of the way the war was being conducted. And stations were told to avoid anything the enemy could exploit and turn into anti-American propaganda. For example, reports of anti-Semitism or racial tensions were not to go on the air. Stations were instead encouraged to broadcast positive stories, stressing that America was a place where tolerance and harmony prevailed. Thus, the war afforded new opportunities for women and minorities, who were suddenly invited to write and produce programs about their achievements. The iconic figure of Rosie the Riveter came to represent the "can-do" spirit of American women. Throughout the 1920s and 1930s, announcers had been men (usually with deep voices). Now, because many of the men were serving overseas, a number of women were hired to be radio announcers and engineers. Radio also came through with some positive representations of African Americans, especially the 1942 NBC series *Freedom's People*, which offered dramatic portrayals of the lives of black scientists, artists, and inventors, and the 1943 CBS series *Heroines in Bronze*, about the role of black women in the war effort. (Unfortunately, as soon as the war ended, nearly all of the women announcers were replaced, and the minority-written programs were removed from the air.)

Radio broadcasters had already felt some frustration in 1941 when the FCC issued the so-called Mayflower decision, which said stations could not use their airwaves to editorialize or actively support political candidates. At the time, there was a growing fear that American stations might be used the way the Germans used theirs: to disseminate propaganda and manipulate public opinion. As the Nazis seemed to be winning in Europe, the American government wanted to make sure American stations remained neutral and fair. Many broadcasters objected to the legislation, saying the ruling was arbitrary, and a violation of freedom of speech; they believed they were quite capable of being unbiased without a government fiat. But the war prevented any organized effort to overturn the decision; it would not be rescinded until 1949. On the other hand, wartime censorship, while undoubtedly frustrating, was generally tolerated. Although broadcasters must have felt irritated when some information they wanted to put on the air was deemed too sensitive, or when they were told to avoid certain topics entirely, Byron Price correctly reported that there would be total compliance with the code; and the few stations that didn't comply were soon brought into line. Meanwhile, U.S. military authorities gave press credentials to over six hundred new reporters, radio commentators, and press photographers, all of whom certainly understood the parameters within which they would be working. As the war went on, a few reporters and commentators occasionally objected to what they felt were excessive or arbitrary restrictions, but for the most part, there was little overt protest from the media. Perhaps reporters didn't want to seem unpatriotic, or perhaps they feared losing their press credentials. Then again, they may have genuinely understood that the military's caution was about protection of the troops, which took precedence over journalists getting a news story first. So when Price participated in a panel discussion broadcast by the Mutual network in early March 1942 and gave his usual defense of wartime censorship, he got no disagreement from his fellow panelists, several of whom were journalists. And although the scripts of the newsmagazine programs like *America's Town Meeting of the Air* and *The March of Time* now had to be approved, both shows stayed on the air and did the best they could to keep the listeners informed. In fact, the war brought a dramatic increase in *The March of Time*'s ratings; in addition to covering as much news as possible, the editors at *Time* magazine had expanded the scope of the show to include more human-interest pieces about how the war was affecting the lives of average Americans.

As might be expected during wartime, all the mass media—newspapers, periodicals, radio, the movies, and the music industry—united to create and disseminate as much pro-American content as possible, to "sell" the war and keep everyone motivated. Patriotic messages and a mention of the troops were inserted into the plots of soap operas, the lyrics of songs, and the commercials for nearly every major product. In public service announcements and print advertisements, Americans were warned not to spread rumors, and to rely only on trusted sources for war information. Radio served as one of those trusted sources, not only providing entertainment that kept listeners hopeful even during the darkest days of the conflict, but also letting the American public hear from some of the war's newsmakers: General Douglas MacArthur's voice was first heard in a brief message in late March 1942; members of the Roosevelt administration like Secretary of the Interior Harold L. Ickes gave frequent addresses to inform the public of new policies and the reasons for them; and of course, President Roosevelt continued to speak on radio regularly.

On the other hand, there were puzzling omissions in the news coverage, most notably the networks' failure to cover the Holocaust. The ongoing story of the Nazi persecution of Jews was only occasionally mentioned during network reports and was usually buried among stories of all the other atrocities occurring in the war. Jewish organizations occasionally put together a relevant broadcast, such as a January 1940 program from the American Jewish Congress that aired on NBC, but the public remained generally uninformed with only occasional exceptions, such as a December 1942 broadcast in which Edward R. Murrow gave one of his first reports about what was happening to the Jews in the concentration camps. There was little follow-up to this emotional report, and by the time Murrow revisited the topic in an April 1945 report from Buchenwald after its liberation by U.S. troops, all of the damage had been done. Perhaps broadcasters felt that the Nazis' treatment of Jews fell under the dictum from the Office of Censorship not to discuss race riots or lynching or other manifestations of prejudice. After all, several black newspapers, such as the *Pittsburgh Courier* and the *Chicago Defender*, had launched campaigns during the war to protest segregation and demand better treatment for black soldiers, and those stories weren't covered more widely either. In effect, while Americans were kept informed about many important stories during the war, some that should have been discussed were not. In an era before the Internet and before opinion-driven journalism, it was much easier for certain stories and certain views to be suppressed.

Overall, radio did a commendable job in boosting public morale and giving Americans a sense of purpose whether they had family members fighting in the war or not. The biggest radio stars frequently took time to remind the audience of the necessity of rationing and the need for sacrifice, helping to foster an attitude that all Americans, from celebrities to ordinary citizens, were working together to win the war. The women's shows put an extra effort into giving practical and helpful advice. They offered homemakers tips for making interesting meals despite the limitations on sugar or fruit or canned goods, and they gave fashion advice about how to look stylish without fabrics like silk or wool and without nylon stockings. Sometimes, letters from listeners were read on the air, especially requests for songs or comments about recipes. And despite the ban on vox pop shows, a few stations found ways to let their listeners be heard. For example, singer and announcer George B. German of WNAX Radio in Yankton, South Dakota, went out on the road with his engineer, a disc recorder, and a generator. He talked to people about what was on their minds and then broadcast their comments during his weekday program.

While all the radio stations had to adapt to the rules put forth by the Office of Censorship, it was the women's shows that had to adapt the most. During the Depression of the 1930s, women had been told it was their duty to stay at home and be housewives, but now, in the early 1940s, the message was that their duty was to help the war effort by going to work, whether in factories or in auxiliary units of the military. The Women's Army Auxiliary Corps (later called the WACS) was created in 1942 after much discussion and debate. The women were all in noncombat positions, but many Americans had been opposed to the idea of women in the military, and it took a while for the general public to be persuaded. Women's shows helped to promote greater acceptance by inviting female members of the WACS, and their naval counterpart the WAVES, to talk about their work on the air; some shows even did some recruiting, bringing in political figures who discussed how important these women were to the war effort. Meanwhile, more radio and print advertisements depicted women in nontraditional jobs, doing their part to free the men to fight.

Women, especially those with loved ones serving overseas, regarded radio as their lifeline. Their favorite radio personalities were a source of encouragement, as well as a way to temporarily forget their troubles. But radio was truly a haven for millions of listeners of all ages, male as well as female, since it seemed nearly every American either had a family member in the service or knew somebody who was serving. Of course, broadcasters and celebrities couldn't bring their loved ones home, but radio provided comfort and made the listeners feel less alone. This sense of community continued later in the talk show audience.

During the war, development of new broadcast technologies came to a halt. That was bad news for Edwin Howard Armstrong, an inventor who had found a solution for one of the listeners' most common problems—poor reception. During the mid 1930s, he put what he called Frequency Modulation (FM) on the air. This new technology promised radio reception without any static or atmospheric interference, and just before the war broke out, a handful of stations and even one small New England network were already using it. People who owned the special receivers were very impressed by its clarity and fidelity, but the war delayed further FM growth.

Television was the other new technology in the 1930s. It had first appeared in the late 1920s in a form that was far from user-friendly. Mechanical television used a noisy scanning disc that produced a very poor picture. But by the mid-1930s, the picture was being transmitted electronically; RCA's Vladimir Zworykin in New York City and a West Coast competitor, an entrepreneuring inventor named Philo Farnsworth, had both worked hard to improve the technology, and their experiments continued throughout the late 1930s.

By 1938, a couple of experimental stations were broadcasting on a very limited schedule. No more than four brands of television sets were available at the end of 1938, although that number increased to fourteen in July 1939. RCA's president, David Sarnoff, announced plans to begin televising sporting events and presidential talks, and people who had seen the demonstrations of television at the 1939 World's Fair were impressed. But with a war on the horizon and not much programming available, Sarnoff's 1940 prediction that television was on the verge of becoming a big success was not fulfilled.

In early July 1941, two New York City TV stations prepared to take to the air: NBC's WNBT and CBS's WCBW. There would soon be another station in New York City, WABD (owned by engineer Allen B. DuMont), as well as stations in Philadelphia, Los Angeles, Chicago, and Schenectady, New York. But TV sets were very expensive and still very small (a nine-inch screen was typical), and programming was very limited. Still, when Pearl Harbor was attacked, TV broadcast pictures of the aftermath, and WCBW even did a documentary and some news bulletins. Despite the small audience, a handful of TV stations stayed on the air during the war, on a very limited schedule of only a few hours a week. Few people noticed, because there were perhaps eight thousand television sets in all of the United States. As might be expected, during the war the average person wasn't thinking about whether television (or FM for that matter) had a bright future; and the focus of American engineers and scientists was on military research. There was even a freeze on the manufacture of radio sets for civilians, and if a set broke, it was difficult to find replacement parts. Nevertheless, nearly 89 percent of all American families owned radios in 1945.

In a surprising 1941 ruling, the Federal Communications Commission decided that NBC could not own two networks (NBC Red and NBC Blue) and would have to divest itself of one. The ruling was upheld by the U.S. Supreme Court, and in October 1943, Edward J. Noble, a wealthy business executive who had founded the Life Savers Candy Company, completed the purchase of NBC Blue. It was temporarily called the "Blue Network" until 1945, when it was re-named the American Broadcasting Company (ABC).

Nineteen forty-five was an important year for several reasons. Above all, World War II ended. The war in Europe was won in early May, and Japan surrendered in early August after the atom bomb was dropped on Hiroshima and Nagasaki. The Allies had been victorious over the Axis, and celebrations broke out everywhere.

Before the end of the war, another event had deeply saddened the nation: On 12 April 1945, President Franklin Roosevelt died suddenly of a cerebral hemorrhage. He had guided the country through the Depression and had been the U.S. leader during wartime, and even his adversaries could not deny that he had been a very popular president—the only president who had been elected to four terms. His effective use of the media, especially radio, had made the public feel close to him. And when he died, radio honored him by suspending all entertainment programs and commercials for two days, broadcasting only news, eulogies, tributes, religious services, classical music, and spirituals. Roosevelt's funeral received intensive media coverage, and as might be expected, radio's best-known political commentators discussed what his death would mean for the future of the country, as well as what policies the new president, Harry Truman, would pursue.

When the war officially ended, so did wartime censorship, a welcome event for journalists, few of whom were aware that a new form of censorship, McCarthyism, was on the horizon. The good news for broadcasters trying to bring in revenue to their stations was that any earlier hesitation about sponsoring newscasts had ended; where only eleven news and commentary programs had been sponsored in 1940, by 1945 that number had grown to twenty-eight. Not all of the commentary was on news events. There were a growing number of sports commentators. Most were retired athletes, like Irving "Bump" Hadley, a former baseball pitcher who now did sports commentary for WBZ radio in Boston, and women's tennis champion Alice Marble, who did sports commentary for WNEW in New York City. An especially noteworthy sports commentator was Sherman "Jocko" Maxwell, who was one of the first African American announcers, having begun his radio career in Newark, New Jersey, in 1932. By the 1940s, he was a sports commentator for several New York City radio stations. Maxwell interviewed all the sports celebrities of his day, both black and white.

The best news for everyone was that millions of servicemen and some servicewomen, too, were now coming home to resume their civilian lives. There were new houses and cars to buy, and families to start. Optimism pervaded the country. During the war, the birthrate had been in sharp decline, but beginning in 1946, that trend was dramatically reversed. The children born in the postwar period were later known as baby boomers, and they would affect the culture in numerous ways. The first changes they inspired were related to marketing. Manufacturers quickly realized that the birth of so many children offered a golden opportunity to sell their parents baby clothes, toys, and furniture. The recording industry began to produce more children's records, and the late 1940s were a good time to do so, because the technology was undergoing a change. Since the early 1900s, recorded music had been played on 78-rpm records, which were heavy and easily broken. By the late 1940s, the 78 was being replaced by long-playing records (LPs), twelve-inch vinyl discs that played at 33 and 1/3 rpm. Their biggest advantage was that they held much more content than the typical 78. But record companies also let the public know that the new vinyl records were lighter, more durable, and offered far better sound quality. Also perfected was another kind of recording that played at 45 rpm. It was smaller than an LP (only seven inches in diameter, with a big hole in the center), and because it was easy to carry, it became the format of choice for hit singles. As the baby boomers grew, so did their collections of 45s. Meanwhile, as record companies began putting new hit songs mainly on 45s, radio stations made the switch away from 78s. By the late 1950s, youth-oriented stations were flourishing, and 45s were the technology of choice.

In the late 1940s, another important innovation that became available to radio was audiotape, an invention that would soon be used for talk shows. The arrival of this new technology was especially welcomed by radio singers and comedians. Although more stations were now playing recorded music, many still had live orchestras and live programs. Putting them on the air meant performing the same show two or even three times, for each of the major time zones in the United States. Although it had been possible since 1929 to record a show on what was called an electrical transcription, networks like NBC didn't want to use them because executives believed transcribed programs had inferior sound quality to live shows. But then, in the mid-1940s, star vocalist Bing Crosby was eager to record his shows, so that he wouldn't have to stay at the radio studio for hours. When NBC refused to let him record, he left them and signed with ABC. There, beginning in 1946, Crosby was allowed to experiment with prerecording his show, but the early results were not very good, and his ratings fell. Fortunately, Crosby's chief engineer was John T. "Jack" Mullin, who had been an officer in the U.S. Army Signal Corps during World War II. Mullin was an expert in recording technology, and thanks to his skill, by 1947, the quality of taped programs had improved to such a degree that few listeners could tell whether a show was live or taped. It wasn't long before Crosby's ratings went back up. This was also helped by the show's sponsor, Philco, which advised Crosby to add more big-name guests. The improved technology and the celebrity performers meant better ratings for the Crosby show. Mullin also found a way to add a laugh track and an applause track to the tape, so that the audience appeared to react positively to everything Crosby did. Bing Crosby's success with audiotape persuaded other performers to use it as well, and the concept of taping for delayed broadcast became more and more accepted.

Immediately after the war ended, radio continued to be the home of the famous performers, the best-known soap operas, and the most widely respected newscasters. (The interest in news and information continued to be strong; in one survey, 63 percent of the public said they relied on radio as their primary source of news.) Given the continued importance of radio, the FCC began to give out licenses for additional stations, and in 1946, the number of AM stations increased from 1,004 to 1,520. Interest in FM, which had briefly seemed promising, continued to languish. Few receiving sets were available, and there was little unique programming; most of the time, AM station owners who also had FM capability simply simulcast the same programs on both stations.

Television, however, at last seemed ready for success. The small number of stations in existence during the war were now broadcasting more regularly, with longer hours. The new medium found a niche almost immediately: It became known for children's programming, which was especially helpful to stay-at-home mothers seeking to entertain their offspring during the day. Among the best known of the early TV children's shows was *Howdy Doody*, which debuted on NBC in late December 1947, hosted by Buffalo Bob (Bob Smith), who had previously hosted a radio show called the *Triple B Ranch*. Another host with a long reputation in children's programming was Boston's "Big Brother" Bob Emery. After starring on the *Big Brother Club* on Boston radio from 1924 until the early 1930s, he had moved to New York City, where he did a children's radio show called *Rainbow House*. But with the arrival of television, he went to the DuMont Television Network in March 1947 with the *Small Fry Club*, a show named after the song he had used as his closing theme since his Boston days: "So Long, Small Fry" (*small fry* was a slang expression then used for children). One other children's show, which became as popular with adults as with children, was *Kukla, Fran, and Ollie*. Fran was Fran Allison, who had been a member of Don McNeill's *Breakfast Club*. On *Kukla, Fran, and Ollie,* she interacted with two puppets, Kukla and Ollie, plus a cast of other amusing puppet characters called the Kuklapolitan Players, all designed and operated by the extraordinarily original and creative Burr Tillstrom. The show started on local TV in Chicago in 1947, and by late November 1948, it was on NBC's midwestern network, moving to the rest of NBC in January 1949.

Although children's shows were some of the first to become staples on TV, the large numbers of women staying at home to raise their families wanted something to break up the monotony of housework. So television began to offer programs that would appeal to this large audience. Some of these programs were talk shows.

THE FIRST CALL-IN TALK SHOWS

The late 1940s were the last time that radio, especially AM radio, would not have to compete with television. It was in this era that call-in talk radio got its start. It is nearly impossible to determine who hosted the first call-in talk show, since few, if any, talk programs from that time have been preserved, and the claims of some of the hosts cannot be verified. We do know that one of the earliest hosts who took calls from listeners was Barry Gray, who was an overnight disc jockey at WOR in New York City. He later told interviewers that he first did a talk show in late 1945, but the actual date has been the subject of debate; some radio columnists who listened to him place the year as 1946. Another New York City announcer, Jack Eigen, also worked during the overnight hours in the late 1940s, at station WINS. Eigen's talk show began in 1947, broadcast live from New York's Copacabana night club. It was equal parts playing records, taking phone calls, and gossiping about (and sometimes with) celebrities. In the south, there was Alan Courtney, who began a talk show in Miami, Florida in June 1949 at station WGBS. Texas, in the late 1940s at station KRLD. Another announcer who claimed to have done an early talk show was Joe Pyne; according to some sources, he began taking calls from listeners in 1948 or 1949, in either Kenosha, Wisconsin, or Atlantic City, New Jersey. Few of the late-night hosts were talking politics yet, although Pyne would later claim to have done so. Usually, these announcers played records, took an occasional phone call, and chatted with celebrities who dropped by. (It was common for late-night hosts, especially in big cities like New York or Los Angeles, to do their shows from a nightclub, guaranteeing not only well-known guests but a studio audience.)

Celebrity gossip had long been popular on the radio; it was also lucrative for the men and women who provided it, like Walter Winchell, Louella Parson, and Hedda Hopper. *Time* magazine noted, for example, that in 1946, Winchell, a syndicated columnist and radio host, was paid seventy-five hundred dollars a week by his radio sponsor. But it wasn't until the advent of the late-night call-in shows that listeners at home, as well as members of the studio audience, had a chance to ask questions of a guest celebrity. Taking calls added a new dimension to late-night radio, but just as these shows were gaining in popularity, there was a new technological challenge, thanks to the Federal Communications Commission. The FCC ruled that as of mid-January 1948, radio stations had to use a device that emitted a beep every fifteen seconds, to let callers know their phone call was being recorded and broadcast on the air. Critics found this ruling somewhat odd: why else would people call a talk show if they didn't want their call put on the air? But despite complaints, the ruling stood, and talk show hosts had to follow it, leading media critics to begin referring to the announcers as "beeper jockeys."

In the late 1940s, it was radio where the talk show genre was developing, since there was not any late-night television yet. Some of the overnight radio hosts realized that TV had a bright future—by the summer of 1948, according to research from George Gallup, there were 354,000 TV sets in use in the United States, a dramatic increase. Barry Gray and Jack Eigen were two of the radio talkers who decided to give TV a try, hosting televised daytime or early evening versions of their late-night shows; Gray was on New York's WOR-TV and Eigen was on WABD, the DuMont station in New York. They were not the only performers to make their TV debut. Women's show hosts on radio were also eager to see if television was right for them. Many of these women were skilled in interviewing, which meant they were at ease talking to celebrities. They were also able to deliver persuasive live commercials. While male critics liked to make fun of the women's shows, housewives considered them very informative. Among the first women's show hosts to be on both radio and TV was Boston's Louise Morgan, who had had a popular program on WNAC radio during the early and middle 1940s. By the late 1940s, she had also begun to do her show on WNAC-TV. In Cincinnati in 1949, Ruth Lyons of WLW radio took her *50 Club* (named for the size of her studio audience) to television's WLWT, where the studio audience was expanded, and the show was renamed the *50-50 Club*; it was simulcast on both radio and TV. Eventually, Lyons appeared exclusively on TV and even had a brief run in 1951 on the NBC television network. Lyons and Morgan made the switch with ease, but not all women's show hosts transitioned to TV successfully: New York City's Mary Margaret McBride was persuaded to do a TV show in the late 1940s; but the critics hated it, and although she did give TV one more try in 1957, she later admitted that she felt much more comfortable staying with radio. In September 1950, another popular radio show from the 1930s and 1940s, the *Breakfast Club* with host Don McNeill, tried a TV version. The *Breakfast Club* had long been an NBC radio staple, and it was still broadcast from Chicago. But it failed in its attempt to transfer to television. Perhaps the show's magic and the chemistry of the cast worked best in a medium where listeners had to imagine what McNeill's breakfast table was like, rather than watching the performers eating breakfast. The television version lasted only until December 1951, whereas the radio version spent more than thirty years on the air, from 1933–1968. One of the most successful radio stars to make the move over to television and do a talk show was Arthur Godfrey. He had hosted a popular morning radio show on CBS, *Arthur Godfrey Time*, since the early 30s, and listeners loved his sense of humor, as well as his folksy, laid-back announcing style. His show featured a cast of well-known performers, but Godfrey himself was the reason people tuned in. And although many radio stars who tried TV found it daunting, when Godfrey did his first experiment with the new medium in 1944, he seemed to be a natural. By 1949, he was hosting two successful TV shows, one of which was a talent show (*Arthur Godfrey's Talent Scouts*) and the other of which was a talk and variety show, *Arthur Godfrey and His Friends*.

In the late 1940s, nobody could predict if or when TV would overtake radio as the most popular broadcast medium. But TV quickly developed its own big stars, most notably comedian Milton Berle, and it also offered a home to professional wrestling, which was surprisingly popular in a number of cities. Most of the radio networks were prepared for the possibility that TV would become a huge success. NBC, ABC, and CBS quickly acquired television affiliates, and knowing that current events were still on people's minds, the networks were able to offer a daily newscast (usually fifteen minutes long) almost immediately, using their radio reporters. By modern standards, the first TV newscasts were primitive: although audiotape was now readily available, videotape had yet to be perfected, so the newscasts were all done live. They featured the anchorman (and in those early years, the news staff were nearly always white and male) sitting in the studio, reading the top stories, and using filmed segments taken from newsreels. The news copy was also written as if it was for radio, with many descriptive words, since on-the-scene reporting was still very difficult. One of the first of the network TV newscasters was Douglas Edwards of CBS, who debuted on TV in mid-August 1948.

While daily newscasts sometimes suffered from slow pacing and not enough visuals, the transition to television was easier for other radio news shows, such as panel discussion shows with important guests, such as *Meet the Press*. Carried by NBC-TV, *Meet the Press* went on the air in early November 1947. But as NBC, CBS, and ABC expanded their TV offerings and used their radio talent to fill some of the TV time, the DuMont network was having problems. DuMont did not have a radio network behind it, and as a result, it had to develop its own talent and create its own programs.

But as the numbers from Gallup demonstrated, the future of TV was looking up in 1948. The networks were able to telecast from the 1948 Republican and Democratic national conventions. The Republicans met in June, the Democrats, in July, and TV was there for it all, offering extensive coverage. There was even a female reporter, Pauline Frederick, although she was expected to cover only the wives of the candidates. And unfortunately for all concerned, at neither convention was the hall air-conditioned; the old-fashioned TV lights were extremely hot, and the people who appeared on camera often looked as if they were in a sauna. Only nine cities saw the network coverage, but it was an important first step in developing TV as a national force in politics.

By the late 40s, TV sets were on sale in nearly every department store, and new designs made them aesthetically pleasing. Some even looked like fine furniture, rather than what a critic had once called "radio with pictures." Meanwhile, in 1948, the FCC got its first woman member, Frieda B. Hennock; formerly a New York attorney, she became known as a passionate advocate for educational and non-commerical television.

Just when it seemed that commercial TV was taking off, the FCC suddenly put a freeze on new TV station licenses in September 1948. This freeze slowed TV's growth immediately, since cities like New York, Boston, and Los Angeles, which already had stations on the air, were the only places where new television shows could be developed. The cities that didn't have stations on the air yet would not have them until 1952. Therefore it was not surprising that radio stars were still keeping their options open in the late 1940s and early 1950s. Since radio would still be a factor for a while, a number of popular vocalists and musicians from the 1930s and 1940s began their own shows, on which they not only sang but also played records.

THE 1950S: TALK SHOWS AND THE MCCARTHY ERA

In early June 1949, the FCC had finally repealed the Mayflower decision, and radio stations could now editorialize and give political opinions, as long as these opinions were identified as such and opposing viewpoints were sought. Some stations immediately began to put editorials on the air, choosing local issues that affected their audience. Although years later, broadcasters would complain about the FCC's Fairness Doctrine, as the new ruling came to be called, it turned out to be a surprisingly positive development. It didn't stifle free speech, as its detractors claimed; the airwaves were soon filled with talk hosts who could be as angry and outraged as they wanted to be, as long as the other side was given a hearing at some point.

However, radio and TV were about to have some unexpected problems as a result of what came to be known as the cold war. The euphoria that accompanied the end of World War II had been somewhat tempered by worsening relations between the United States and what was then known as the Soviet Union. The alliance of the United States and the Soviets during World War II was based primarily on having a mutual enemy: the Axis countries, and particularly Germany. Most Americans had a long history of disliking and mistrusting communism, and even in the 1920s and 1930s, people who were considered too far to the left in their views were accused of being "reds," a common epithet for people who were disloyal to America. In addition to the worsening relations between the United States and the Soviets, there was a further problem: War had broken out between North and South Korea, and in late June 1950, under United Nations auspices, President Truman sent troops to help the South repel the invaders from the North, who were being aided by China, by then a communist country. The Korean War turned into a costly three-year involvement. Many historians today regard the UN offensive as a mistake, but right or wrong, the war was more proof to those who believed in the dangers of communism that proponents of this ideology were bent on taking over the world, and the UN had to stop them.

As far back as the late 1930s, there had been government hearings in Washington, DC, led by a conservative Democratic representative named Martin Dies, who made accusations that certain left-wing groups were secretly supporting the communists; but his assertions did not gain much attention at that time. It wasn't until 1950 that conservatives gained a powerful and influential spokesman, Senator Joseph McCarthy. In February 1950, the Republican from Wisconsin suddenly made a startling assertion. He gave a speech in which he claimed to have a list of 205 members of the Communist Party who were working in the U.S. State Department. He followed up a week later by informing the press that he had written a letter to President Truman, demanding that the president fire 57 communists who, he believed, were actively shaping State Department policy. And as if that were not enough, J. Edgar Hoover, the head of the FBI, put forth the notion that America was being destroyed from within. He stated that as many as fifty-five thousand Communist Party members were secretly at work in the United States, and that even more Americans were sympathetic to communism. Up to this point, few Americans knew anything about Senator McCarthy, but during the next four years, he would command the media spotlight. His actions, and those of J. Edgar Hoover, would affect the lives of thousands of people: teachers, government employees, members of the movie industry, and many performers on radio and TV, all of whom were accused of being traitors. Thanks in large part to a June 1950 book called *Red Channels: The Report of Communistic Influence on Radio and Television*, which claimed to identify those in the media who were subversive or had direct ties to communism, a number of writers, entertainers, movie directors, and stars of movies, radio, and TV lost their livelihood; many had to leave the United States, and several committed suicide. Some of the entertainers who were accused had expressed a passing interest in communism, especially during the Depression, but many others were guilty of nothing more than having prounion or antiwar views, attitudes that conservative Republicans like McCarthy considered too liberal and therefore unpatriotic. Years later, the harm he caused to many innocent people and the fear he inspired lives on in the term *McCarthyism*, which has come to refer to using such political tactics as making false and inflammatory assertions about political opponents and attempting to stifle dissent by branding anyone who disagrees with the government as anti-American.

The House Committee on Un-American Activities (which came to be abbreviated as HUAC) had been created in the mid-1940s by Representative Martin Dies, who like McCarthy, believed that those on the political left, including socialists, communists, members of organized labor, and most liberals, were disloyal and unpatriotic. He also believed that communists had already infiltrated education, the labor unions, and the media, and that the American Civil Liberties Union was a communist front organization. (While the ACLU defended people accused of being communists, it would continue to deny that this proved the organization was supporting communism. As the ACLU saw it, the group's mission was to defend freedom of speech, even if the speakers espoused radical ideas.) This had not persuaded Dies, nor did it persuade McCarthy. Both men were convinced that if the subversive elements in America were not stopped, they would destroy U.S. democracy. From the Dies Commission, which had begun calling people to testify in September 1947, it was not a big leap to the passage of the Subversive Activities Control Act, which required loyalty tests for government employees. The reaction of the mainstream press to Hoover's and McCarthy's charges was somewhat muted. Perhaps radio and television news reporters and executives wanted to seem objective, or they may have been afraid to protest, for fear of being accused of pro-communist sympathies. And not everyone thought McCarthy was wrong: some radio commentators who did speak out approved of the campaign to root out alleged subversives. The two most vocal supporters of McCarthy were Walter Winchell and Fulton Lewis Jr. Both used their radio shows to support the activities of Senator McCarthy and HUAC. These nationally-known commentators gave credence to what McCarthy had claimed. And although neither Lewis nor Winchell was as influential in the 1950s as they had been in the 1940s, both still attracted considerable attention.

It did not take long for a climate of fear to pervade the country. Once "blacklisting" had begun, people who were accused of being communists often had no way to defend themselves from campaigns that seemed based on hysteria, exaggeration, and rumor. For entertainers, just having their name in *Red Channels* or on any of a number of other such lists was enough for sponsors to drop them. One of the first to whom this happened was Jean Muir, a former radio actress who in late August 1950 lost her job for allegedly being a communist. She had been hired to play the TV role of Mother Aldrich on NBC's *The Aldrich Family.* Like many others who were accused, she was not able to clear her name or get her job back. Perhaps the most tragic case resulting from the blacklist was that of Philip Loeb. Loeb was a popular actor on the stage before he was cast in the role of Molly Goldberg's husband Jake on the TV version of the longtime radio hit *The Goldbergs.* In 1950, after his name appeared in *Red Channels,* several witnesses testified before HUAC that they knew Loeb had been a communist, a charge Loeb always denied. The sponsor of the show, General Foods, told its creator and star Gertrude Berg that Loeb had to be fired. To her credit, Berg seems to have been unwilling to fire him, and she told the press that she believed Loeb when he said he had never been a communist. But at the height of McCarthyism, Loeb had few options and even fewer defenders. When *TV Guide* put a portrait of the cast on the cover, it simply included the new actor chosen to play the role, and no explanation was offered of what had happened to the original Jake. Loeb found that being accused was as good as being found guilty, and he reluctantly left the show. Gertrude Berg paid him a forty-thousand-dollar settlement, but for Loeb, it wasn't about the money. With his reputation in ruins, he would not be hired anywhere. In debt, and suffering from depression, he committed suicide in 1955.

There were a few radio talk shows on the air by the era of McCarthyism, but most continued to be oriented to entertainment, just as their late 1940s predecessors had been. Political talk would certainly emerge, but at this point, the majority of the shows tried to be clever or entertaining, rather than controversial, perhaps a by-product of living under war censorship and the Mayflower decision. As a result, the good and bad points of McCarthyism were seldom debated on the air. The one program on which such discussions might have occurred was *America's Town Meeting of the Air,* which, in addition to radio, was having a brief run on TV in 1952. Some critics think it is no accident that the show was suddenly canceled from TV, given its tendency to invite speakers perceived by the McCarthyites as "liberal." In most cases, during the early 1950s, radio and TV preferred to avoid the subject, just as they avoided discussing segregation or anti-Semitism. As historian Stephen J. Whitfield remarked, it was as if both radio and TV had hung out a "Do Not Disturb" sign and waited for the red scare to end. It would take the efforts of a few courageous print journalists in periodicals identified as left-wing, like *The Nation* (and those journalists, it turned out, were under surveillance themselves), and the equally courageous investigative work of TV journalist Edward R. Murrow to cast sufficient doubt on McCarthy to diminish his effectiveness.

Murrow alone did not discredit McCarthy, nor was Murrow the only journalist to speak out, but today his efforts have a mythic quality about them. Having returned from his World War II coverage in Europe, Murrow was doing a public affairs program on radio called *Hear It Now*. In mid-November 1951, he took the show to TV, where it became *See It Now*. At first, the show wasn't especially controversial, but then Murrow took on Senator McCarthy. As he was doing his exposé of McCarthy during shows broadcast in March and April 1954, ABC and DuMont had started to telecast the Army-McCarthy hearings, which were ostensibly about exposing subversives in the military, but which finally provided the public with repeated opportunities to see how McCarthy bullied witnesses, made accusations, shouted, and tried to intimidate anyone who disagreed with him. Murrow's TV critiques of the senator on *See It Now* provided an effective one-two punch. At the end of the 9 March episode, Murrow's final words were these:

> We will not walk in fear, one of another. We will not be driven by fear into an age of unreason if we dig deep in our history and doctrine and remember that we are not descended from fearful men, not from men who feared to write, to speak, to associate and to defend causes which were for the moment unpopular. We can deny our heritage and our history, but we cannot escape responsibility for the result. There is no way for a citizen of the Republic to abdicate his responsibility. (Media Research Library)

Critics would later say that *See It Now* helped to demythologize McCarthy by letting the public see what a demagogue he was. And coupled with the broadcasts of the Senate hearings, the visual images were so damaging to McCarthy that his assertions were no longer taken seriously, except by a handful of "true believers." When all was said and done, Senator McCarthy was censured by the Senate in December 1954; ironically, for all of his claims and all of the people he accused, he never produced any list with the names of the "205 known Communists" (which sometimes became "57 known Communists") he often said he possessed.

MORE TALK SHOWS THAN EVER

During the 1950s, the entertainment-oriented radio talk show, complete with listeners calling in, began to appear in city after city. Most were friendly, with a host or hostess (or both), some guests, some interesting topics, and some good conversation. Perhaps the best known in the Midwest was *Party Line* on KDKA in Pittsburgh, featuring husband-and-wife team Ed and Wendy King. Although the show promoted good feelings of a party, the name was reminiscent of the shared telephone line still used by many people who did not have their own individual phone service. From January 1951 through November 1971, *Party Line* made listeners feel connected, and with KDKA's massive signal, the show was also heard in many cities other than Pittsburgh. What was unique about the show was how Ed handled callers. When people called in, their voices were never heard on the air. Instead, he would paraphrase what they had just said. And every night, many listeners called. There were also contests and a prize or two if a caller could answer the "Party Pretzel," which was a quiz question. Wendy King later remembered how many letters the show had received from all over the world, and in an interview for this book, she wondered why talk shows had all become "filled with people who are angry. It's not uplifting at all." She recalled that *Party Line* was always about the listeners having a good time.

Ed King's was only one of the various approaches to having other people's voices on the air. He was not the only one to use the paraphrase technique; some sources say that early in his career, Joe Pyne did too. It wasn't just that these talkers disliked the 15-second beep. While it was now easier to put callers on the air live, many announcers were concerned that one of them might say something obscene, and the FCC was very strict about acceptable language. Airing something vulgar, even accidentally, could result in fines or put the station's license renewal in jeopardy. Larry Keene, a producer who worked for Joe Pyne, recalls that when Pyne took callers in the mid-1950s, it was his responsibility to make sure nothing went over the air that would cause trouble for Pyne's show. The engineer or producer had to have very quick fingers and immediately hang up on any offending remarks. A few stations in the 50s were experimenting with some way to edit out crude language, but not until the 60s was a reliable system perfected. Called the seven-second delay, it recorded the caller on an audiotape loop, and then gave the producer or host seven seconds to delete an inappropriate comment before it went on the air. Because two-way talk shows were unscripted, a good host had to think fast and be ready for anything. There was no predicting who might call, and some callers were inarticulate, or opinionated, or misinformed. Joe Pyne had his own way of handling the callers. He had a quick wit and was a master of insults and putdowns. Where Ed and Wendy King tried to create a party, Pyne seems to have preferred a wrestling match.

By the late 1950s, there was another kind of talk show that was not getting much attention from the mainstream media, although it was already becoming influential. It started with a group of conservative Christians, mostly from Protestant denominations, who were interested in getting airtime on radio (interest in TV would come later). Led by a Fundamentalist preacher named Rev. Carl McIntire, they formed the National Association of Evangelicals in 1942, and from that group, another emerged in 1944, the National Religious Broadcasters. While church services of the mainstream denominations had been broadcast on radio since 1921, McIntire's group did not align itself with the mainstream Protestant National Council of Churches because McIntire believed the Council was much too liberal. A few Evangelical Christian preachers had occasionally managed to do an "old-time revival hour" on the

Mutual network, but in general, the Fundamentalist denominations felt radio was excluding them, so McIntire and another preacher named Billy James Hargis became advocates for getting their point of view on the air. Hargis and McIntire did not see eye to eye on every subject, but shared the belief that America was too liberal and was under threat from communist infiltration. McIntire even objected when President Dwight D. Eisenhower gave a speech in late August 1952 during which he spoke of his hope for a "brotherhood of man." McIntire wired the president, reminding him that the idea of a universal brotherhood was one that was popular with communists and socialists, and not something an American president should espouse. The reverend also gained media attention by offering himself as a pundit to broadcasters who were willing to air his controversial assertions, especially when he claimed the mainstream Christian churches were filled with communists.

Because radio was losing revenue to television in the early 1950s, some networks and individual stations decided to broadcast paid religious shows, even those produced by Fundamentalist churches. Thus, the Southern Baptists took to the air, as did some of McIntire and Hargis's members. From the late 1950s to the early 1960s, these preachers cobbled together unofficial networks, comprising mainly small AM radio stations in rural areas. Largely unregulated and unnoticed, McIntire's *Twentieth Century Reformation Hour*, with its message of ultra-conservative Christianity, anticommunism, antiliberalism, and anti-anyone-from-the-left was being heard on over five hundred stations by the early 1960s. McIntire had even created a tax-exempt foundation. For the most part, the mainstream media ignored these broadcasts. But in 1964, *The Nation*, one of the magazines McIntire hated for its liberal views, published an exposé of right-wing talk radio. It covered what McIntire had achieved up to that point and also noted that Rev. Hargis and his *Christian Crusade* was heard on fifty-five radio stations five days a week and was also seen on seven TV stations. That these men had gotten their shows on so many stations was not what bothered the author of the article, Fred J. Cook. It was the constant name-calling and insults, including the claim that President Kennedy and most of the members of his cabinet had been communists. When Kennedy was assassinated, the attacks switched to his successor, Lyndon B. Johnson. McIntire declared that the civil rights movement was communist-led and expressed his disdain for Catholics, while Hargis launched attacks on the entertainment media, particularly talk host Steve Allen and variety show impresario Ed Sullivan. Hargis also despised Eleanor Roosevelt and was opposed to integration. Sadly, such views had been heard on the radio as far back as 1927–1928, when the Ku Klux Klan briefly owned a radio station in Northern Virginia (WTFF, the Fellowship Forum), and station WHAP in New York City regularly aired talks that slandered Jews and Catholics. But such bigotry was always regarded as the exception; the broadcast networks prided themselves on being fair to all religions and ethnic groups. However, the same could not be said for some of the programs on small, independent stations.

And thanks to freedom of speech, the hosts of these shows could be as bigoted or as outraged as Joe Pyne, or his successor Morton Downey Jr. The big difference was that the press was very aware of what Pyne and Downey were saying, while the assertions of McIntire and Hargis were seldom reviewed in the mainstream media. It wasn't until the FCC issued a ruling on the so-called Red Lion case, in June 1969, that the average person became aware of these broadcasts. (The Red Lion case concerned a ruling that Rev. Hargis had in fact slandered Fred J. Cook during a broadcast and that the station which aired the program should have offered Cook equal time to reply.) McIntire, too, would lose an FCC decision, but McIntire and Hargis and others with similar attitudes continued to broadcast and acquire more affiliates throughout the 1950s and 1960s.

While radio shows continued to migrate to TV, and TV was beginning to air talk/variety shows like *Today, Home,* and *Tonight,* the baby boomers fell in love with top-forty music and stayed with radio. Many AM stations became hit-oriented stations with disc-jockeys who were best friends and heroes to their audience. FM still wasn't a factor for a number of reasons, but AM was now split between the younger and older audiences. AM talk shows were far from dead, however. Certain star talkers continued to get good ratings, among them Jerry Williams, whose career had begun in Bristol, Tennessee, in 1946, before he moved to stations in Camden, New Jersey; Philadelphia; Boston; and Chicago. It was in Boston that Williams made a name for himself as a talk show host, starting in 1957. He was hired by WMEX, a station that played top-forty music until about 10 p.m. After the teens had gone to bed, Williams made the late-night shift his own and won impressive ratings doing local talk in a city where politics is a religion. A liberal about many issues, but a populist when it came to government waste or political corruption, he could influence his callers to deluge their legislators with angry phone calls, a trait a number of talk hosts of the 1980s and 1990s became famous for.

Another popular talk host of the late 1950s was John "Long John" Nebel. His shift was overnight at WOR in New York City, where he became known for his offbeat choice of subjects to discuss, including astrology, conspiracy theories, and UFOs. Fans found him unique because they never knew who was going to be a guest. It might be a celebrity like Jackie Gleason or it might be somebody who believed aliens had visited him. While Nebel frequently had guests (and callers) who believed in UFOs, he also invited well-known skeptics like James "The Amazing" Randi to debunk such claims.

Nebel was also among the few in the 1950s to use a tape delay, which would become common by the late 1960s. Nebel's engineer set up his own version of the seven-second delay, and it proved helpful in purging bad language from the airwaves. Jerry Williams was one of the talkers who was influenced by Nebel. Williams was working in the Philadelphia market when he heard Nebel's show one night; WOR was a big-signal AM station that was heard in a number of cities. When Williams heard Nebel putting callers on the air, he wanted whatever device Long John was using because, like most talkers of the mid-1950s, Williams was still paraphrasing callers, and he found this technique increasingly awkward. A tape delay would let him put calls directly on the air. By the time he got to Boston in September 1957, Williams made sure he had a tape delay system.

Late-night talk radio continued to be popular throughout the 1950s and 1960s, and fans couldn't seem to get enough of the strange and the weird. Another unique talker in New York was Jean Shepherd. He held down the overnight shift, entertaining his "Night People," as his devoted fans were called, on station WOR beginning in the mid 1950s. A master story-teller, Shepherd never used a script, didn't have guests, and his show was comprised of what a critic for the *New York Times* described as "original and unorthodox comments on a wide range of subjects." On the West Coast, a popular late-night host was Ben Hunter, who was a mentor to Herb Jepko before Herb became a successful talker in Salt Lake City in the 1960s. Hunter did a late-night show called the *Other Side of the Day* on KFI in Los Angeles during the 1950, and even the critics found him worth staying up for. As on Long John Nebel's show, it was hard to know what Hunter might do next. He created a listeners' club called the Night Owls, and he involved his audience by assigning topics and asking the designated listener to be ready to lead an on-air discussion about that topic. Among the subjects were astrology, astronomy, sculpture, art, sports—any topic that would produce an interesting discussion. Hunter had a long history with two-way talk. As far back as 1949, he had tried putting some KFI callers directly on the air, with mixed results: on several occasions, vulgarities got on the air, leaving Hunter to question the wisdom of letting the listeners talk. But he stayed with the talk format, and his show remained popular until he left radio for TV in the early 1960s.

Another kind of talk show popular in the late 1950s and early 1960s was part of a new format that revolved around not just talk but also news and sports. One of the founders of this type of radio was Robert Hyland Jr., a St. Louis native who, according to many accounts, was the originator of what came to be known as "full service radio," an information-oriented format targeted to adults between the ages of 25 and 54. He called this radio format *At Your Service*, and it debuted on St. Louis radio station KMOX on 28 February 1960. Prior to that date, the station was still playing some music, but Hyland believed KMOX listeners were much more interested in what was going on in the world than they were about the latest hit songs. He put together a blend of shows that featured celebrity interviews, sports (and sports talk), advice, subjects of interest to homemakers, and increased coverage of the news, both local and national, which provided the station's hosts with plenty of topics to discuss. In the next decades, full service radio was emulated by many radio stations.

With a large number of women staying at home raising children, the women's shows that had been so popular on radio found a similar niche on TV during the 1950s. In Cincinnati, for example, Ruth Lyons, one of Cincinnati's most successful women's show hosts during her years on radio had returned to doing her successful local television show, after a brief time on network TV. Lyons was still able to book big-name guests like Bob Hope and Jimmy Durante, and she was also known for her charity work. Lyons was known for getting her viewers involved in causes that helped children. And like many women's show hosts, she was an outstanding promoter of her sponsors' products. She remained on the air on Cincinnati's WLWT until 1957. Although TV was changing, Ruth Lyons exemplified the traditional women's show host: always impeccably dressed, always enthusiastic, always relaxed and at home in front of her studio audience, who adored her.

It would have been as unthinkable for Ruth Lyons to say anything vulgar or suggestive as for Joe Pyne to be civil, but not every TV talk show fell into one of those extremes. Because TV was still relatively new, there were some interesting experiments with talk. One was *The Author Meets the Critic*, which had come to television from radio in the late 1940s and was still on the air on the DuMont network through October 1954. The show itself was a debate between two critics, one who liked a book and one who did not. A panel then joined the discussion. While this format may sound dull, the show was actually very entertaining, thanks in large part to opinionated panelists who might be radio announcers or politicians or musicians. *The Author Meets the Critic* got a surprising amount of mail, much of it disagreeing with one critic or the other.

In October 1958, four years after the end of *The Author Meets the Critic*, one of the more literate and articulate talk show hosts, David Susskind, made his TV debut with a syndicated program called *Open End*. Susskind's tone was so civil and courteous that his show was broadcast on some educational stations. At his best, he provided some of the most stimulating conversation on TV. (At his worst, and it often depended on the guest, critics said he could put anyone to sleep.)

Most TV critics agreed during the mid- to late 1950s that the television talk show was in a period of transition. In the late 1940s and early 1950s, the majority of the TV talkers were former radio hosts who came to TV and mostly continued what they had done on radio. Sometimes this worked out well, as with Arthur Godfrey, who made the transition from radio to television with ease. But more often than not, what had sounded good on radio did not work as well in a visual medium. A good example of this was Tex McCrary and his wife Jinx Falkenburg. The two had done a popular morning show on New York radio, during which they chatted with each other as well as with celebrity guests; but when they tried a TV version of the show on NBC beginning in 1947, the camera seemed to inhibit them, and they had difficulty building the same rapport with their guests. *New York Times* TV critic Jack Gould noticed that their show seemed disorganized; they had problems with fitting in the news bulletins or commercials. Tex and Jinx returned to radio, but decided to give TV one more try in 1957. Unfortunately, once again, they had difficulty relaxing in front of the cameras. As talented as they were, their radio success never translated to TV.

One host who was adapting to television in the 1950s was Mike Wallace, a former radio announcer who first came to television with his then-wife Buff Cobb as co-hosts of the *Mike and Buff Show*. Broadcast on WCBS-TV beginning in 1951, the show had an interesting premise: the two pretended to have a disagreement on that day's issue, and after debating it, they brought on some guest experts to discuss it with them. Later, as a solo host, Wallace enjoyed considerable success with an interview show called *Nightbeat*. Although he took a slight detour and briefly hosted a game show called *The Big Surprise* in 1956, throughout much of the 1950s, Wallace was known as an interviewer who asked tough questions and didn't let his guests give evasive answers. He also became known for tackling controversial subjects like integration; but unlike Joe Pyne, he didn't scream at his guests or create a conflict. And although 1950s was a very conservative era, Wallace did a series of programs on controversial topics, including whether the government and pressure groups had too much influence on American society.

Edward R. Murrow also had an interview show, called *Person to Person* during the 1950s. The show's premise was that Murrow would visit that week's guest in his or her home; on-location interviews were unusual in TV's formative years because the cameras were large and very cumbersome to take out to a remote broadcast. But Murrow made the show work, as he demonstrated his skill as an interviewer. Because of his stature at CBS, he had no trouble finding interesting newsmakers, and while he was known for reporting on hard news, *Person to Person* featured as many celebrity interviewees as political figures. There were guests like Cuba's Fidel Castro and John F. Kennedy, who was still a senator at that time; but one of Murrow's most-watched programs was the interview he did in April 1955 with movie star Marilyn Monroe.

Unfortunately, the networks sometimes proved to be rather nervous about the content of TV talk shows. Each network had its own censors, with whom the talk hosts had ongoing battles. One such battle occurred in June 1958, when Mike Wallace interviewed former NBC president Sylvester "Pat" Weaver, who took network executives to task for not doing enough public service and for other policies with which he disagreed. At least, that is what Weaver reportedly wanted to say, but the viewers never heard him say it. The network censors deleted those portions of the interview—which was taped ahead of time—that were deemed too controversial. (Videotape had finally arrived in April 1956, and for a while, it was a mixed blessing. Now that some shows were being taped, the censors could look them over and tell the host what had to be removed.) Another thing the networks were nervous about was offending sponsors. Although the American Cancer Society had issued a report in late June 1954 that men who smoked had a 75 percent higher death rate than men who did not, *New York Herald-Tribune* critic John Crosby, himself a smoker, noted that neither NBC-TV nor DuMont reported the story at all. NBC radio's one woman commentator, Pauline Frederick, did NBC's only report, and although both CBS and ABC also did a report, Crosby was puzzled about why this news was downplayed. He concluded that the cigarette companies' annual advertising budget of $30 million in radio ads and $70 million on TV ads had affected how this story was covered.

Throughout the late 1950s, TV was developing its own set of talk stars; some of the most popular hosts had learned the talk format while on radio but were now known exclusively for their video work. One good example was Art Linkletter, host of *House Party*, which had been on CBS radio in the mid-1940s; it debuted on CBS-TV in early September 1952, and by the mid 1950s, it was among TV's most popular daytime shows. (*House Party* remained on the air until 1969, making it one of TV's longest-running shows.) Like Arthur Godfrey, Linkletter too made a smooth transition from radio to TV. *House Party* featured contests, games, and chat, targeted to the stay-at-home mom. Linkletter was especially known for his spontaneous interviews with children, who tended to say amusing things when the genial host asked them questions. Some of Linkletter's most humorous moments with his young guests became the subject of a 1957 best-selling book, "Kids Say the Darndest Things."

As television's talk stars continued to make a name for themselves, there was a battle to see who would get the best ratings. Steve Allen, the comic genius who was so skillful with the ad-lib, was now in fierce Sunday night competition with variety show legend Ed Sullivan. In 1957, Allen had left *The Tonight Show* and he was replaced by an equally quirky personality, Jack Paar, who brought a far different style to late-night TV. Paar got his start filling in for comedian Jack Benny in the summer of 1947, and by September, he had been offered a show of his own. Like many young radio comics, he made the move to TV, and by 1954, he had become a morning-show host for CBS in a shift that turned out to be problematic for him. He was much happier and, critics agreed, more suited to late nights, and when he took over *The Tonight Show* in July 1957, it was expected that his "urbane and witty" personality would increase the show's ratings. Paar also proved to be more willing to talk about politics than Allen had been, and more willing to give his own opinions, rather than couching them in a comedy routine.

THE 1960S AND EARLY 1970S: TALK RADIO'S FIRST GOLDEN AGE

In the mid-1960s, there was a sudden proliferation of radio talk shows. Most listeners were unaware that talk was an expensive format to do well. It seemed simple enough, with a host and a microphone, but increasingly, the hosts were becoming big stars and demanding bigger salaries. Talk shows also required a producer to select and book the guests, and often an engineer, who made sure the tape delay and other equipment worked properly and that the technical quality of the phone calls was up to standards. A disc jockey show was much less complicated to produce, but radio stations found that talk shows got them a large number of listeners and much attention. They also received unfavorable commentary from the critics. It seemed that each city had at least one talk show the critics called vulgar and contentious. It may be a surprise that critics were complaining about the content of some talk shows even in the 1960s; broadcasting was still operating under the Fairness Doctrine, and despite the media coverage that the hippies and 1967's so-called "summer of love" received, the culture remained rather traditional. The critics, and many of the older listeners, still expected radio announcers to display a certain amount of decorum. But increasingly, radio stations carried angry talkers, who insulted listeners in the style of Joe Pyne, and talk hosts who discussed subjects that had previously been taboo, such as sexual problems in relationships and whether marijuana should be legalized. The seven-second delay became more common in the 1960s, which helped stations to make sure that the conversation remained intense but free of offensive language. But that didn't stop the critics from lamenting how radio was much more polite in the good old days.

By the late 1960s, talk radio reached new heights of success. The genre sounded very different from the talk shows of the late 1940s, when announcers like Jack Eigen sat in a night club, telling the occasional joke, playing records and chatting with celebrity entertainers. Most of the talk shows of the late 1960s followed a particular pattern. They featured a well-known and opinionated host, some equally outspoken guests, and large numbers of outraged callers. The typical talk show started with the host doing a monologue about a current political controversy, such as a recent vote in Congress. If there was no "outrage du jour," the host focused on a guest, perhaps the author of a provocative new book or an expert on some aspect of current events. Some nights, there was neither a major crisis nor a special guest, and the host opened the lines to callers who wanted to express their opinion on whatever subject concerned them.

But something that was happening in the United States had begun to affect radio talk shows: a growing generational clash based on the emerging civil rights and women's rights movements and on increasing U.S. involvement in Vietnam; like the Korean War had been, the war in Vietnam was now a source of controversy. The divide between the pro- and antiwar factions continued to escalate, and was a frequent subject of discussion on talk shows. The quality and intensity of the discussions varied. In some cities, the conservative hosts regarded as unpatriotic and cowardly the actions of students in the antiwar movement. These hosts railed against the protesters, and callers expressed their dismay at student demonstrations. In other cities, a more nuanced set of talk shows featured guest experts and pundits who tried to shed some light on issues like the antiwar movement, and who discussed the war more objectively. On such shows, the intent was to help the audience learn about and understand the current changes in society, rather than just to hurl insults or to find somebody to blame. Perhaps as a result of the Fairness Doctrine, most major stations that did call-in talk shows had an equal number of conservative and liberal talk hosts, so that the station would not be perceived as too one-sided. A good example of this tendency was found in Los Angeles, where media critic Don Page praised both KLAC and KABC for being balanced. He noted in a 1968 article that KLAC, which aired the conservative Joe Pyne show, also aired liberal host Joel Spivack; and KABC had both conservative Ray Briem and liberal Michael Jackson.

Who was listening to talk radio in the late 1960s? Some stations were doing research to learn more about their audience. In Los Angeles, in the spring of 1967, talk station KLAC hired David Martin, a sociologist at the University of Southern California, to study its talk show audience and try to learn more about who listened and why. The stereotype was that all talk listeners were either hostile or emotionally unstable, a myth undoubtedly perpetuated by the angry talk show hosts who encouraged callers to rant about whatever grievance they had at that moment. The professor found that current talk radio was not just for the perpetually disgruntled, however. Many fans of the format saw themselves as concerned citizens who wanted to discuss current events with others who shared their interests. It was becoming obvious to media critics and educators that talk shows were a form of catharsis for the average person. These shows provided people who felt ignored by the politicians and the powerbrokers with a safe place to air their opinions, as well as a place to learn useful information about the issues of the day. These shows also sometimes provided them a chance to call in and talk to a celebrity, and to the format's growing number of fans, the hosts themselves were regarded as celebrities.

Talk radio in the 1960s was including black listeners more than at any time in the past. While there had been efforts as early as 1930 to put a black station on the air, not until the late 1940s were there radio formats directed at what was then called the Negro audience. In fact, until the mid-1940s, African Americans were generally ignored by broadcasting. Although a few radio programs had black characters, the Negro press frequently complained that these characters either played a minor role or were portrayed stereotypically. Some network programs featured black musicians (bandleader Duke Ellington had his own show, for example, as did vocalist Ethel Waters), and there were even some public affairs or educational shows that featured black educators and scholars discussing black history, but black appearances on radio were sporadic, usually connected with what was then called Negro History Week. The media were de facto segregated. There were some well-known black newspapers that served the minority community, but in general, when blacks were mentioned in the mainstream press, it was usually because they had been accused of a crime, or because they were famous entertainers or athletes. With very few exceptions, the announcers on the networks were white, as were the reporters, and nearly all the major dramatic actors and actresses on the soap operas. And network reluctance to upset a sponsor or offend a southern affiliate meant that news stories about lynchings or race riots often went unreported in the mainstream media.

Then, in late October 1948, WDIA in Memphis, Tennessee, changed to an all-black format. The owners were white, but the majority of the staff was African American, and the programming was designed to appeal to the large black population in Memphis. The station programmed primarily music, but there was also a women's show, the *Tan Town Homemakers Show* hosted by Willa Monroe, and an advice giver named Aunt Carrie (actually a local educator, Carlotta S. Watson), along with public service shows and an increasing amount of news. As more black stations went on the air in the 1950s (by 1953, the number had increased to 270), they provided a perspective that many white-run stations did not. The airing of this perspective would be especially important during the civil rights movement, when Martin Luther King Jr. used black radio to inform the audience of meetings that would be held, and the djs would encourage people to attend. Among the first African Americans to do an issues-oriented talk show was Wesley South of WVON in Chicago; on his late-night show *Hotline*, which debuted in 1964, he spoke out about civil rights and gave the audience a place to talk about their own experiences and frustrations. He also gave them the chance to hear the newsmakers. His show attracted a number of celebrities, including jazz great Duke Ellington, pioneering baseball player Jackie Robinson, and even Martin Luther King Jr. himself. Another well-received talk show for the black audience was *Night Call*, a national call-in show that debuted in June 1968. After only three weeks on the air, it had picked up 38 affiliates and was heard in 17 states. Hosted by Del Shields, *Night Call* won critical acclaim for giving black listeners a chance to question major newsmakers and discuss issues like poverty, racism, and the war in Vietnam. During the turbulent days of the late 1960s, the black radio stations were a lifeline for people in the community, especially when King was assassinated. And while there would not be a black television host seen nationally until September 1970, when NBC signed comedian Flip Wilson to do a variety show, at least a growing number of local radio talk shows were available to the black audience.

THE IMPACT OF TELEVISION

During the mid-1960s, talk radio enjoyed great popularity in cities like Boston, New York, Chicago, and Los Angeles, but it was television that had the most dramatic effect on American society. A good example is the now-famous debates between John F. Kennedy and his opponent, Richard Nixon, in September and October 1960 during the presidential campaign. Kennedy seemed relaxed and confident, whereas television made Nixon seem ill at ease.

The differences between the two media, television and radio, were noteworthy: Those who had listened to the debates on radio believed that Nixon was the better speaker, and their conclusion was that he had won them. But Nixon had made a bad visual impression on those who watched the debates on television, and that perception took precedence over what he said. The TV viewers believed that Kennedy had won the debates. To this day, the Kennedy-Nixon debates are studied in college media criticism courses, as an early example of how television coverage could make or break a candidate.

If Franklin Delano Roosevelt was known as the "radio president," Kennedy was considered a "television president," who knew how to use the visual medium effectively. So did his equally photogenic wife Jacqueline and their two attractive children. The nation came to feel close to the First Family, without discerning whether Kennedy was a good leader or not. It was an era when certain subjects were still taboo, and the president's personal life was one of them. He was able to guard his image against prying members of the media, who, despite knowing (or at least suspecting), that the president was unfaithful to his wife, never reported it. Years earlier, President Roosevelt had a similar agreement with the press, although in his case it was about his health: the press agreed that he would never be shown in a wheelchair (Roosevelt had been a victim of what was then called infantile paralysis), nor was his disability mentioned. When people saw him, he was always standing at a podium or seated at his desk or riding in an official car; although the public was aware of his paralysis, he looked strong and healthy. President Kennedy was also able to exert his influence over the kind of media coverage he received. Decades later, questions about marital infidelity would plague President Bill Clinton and there was no lack of reporting about the subject; but the media of the 1960s considered Kennedy's extramarital relationships off-limits, and nothing was said about it to the public. When the TV and radio pundits discussed the Kennedy administration, they discussed only policy. His private life was revealed only in the officially controlled coverage of his stylish wife Jackie and the latest cute behavior of young John Jr. and Caroline. On 22 November 1963, newscaster Walter Cronkite interrupted a soap opera with a bulletin that the president had been fatally shot in Dallas, Texas. Cronkite, known for being cool under pressure, was briefly choked up before continuing with the announcement. Just as an earlier generation had been comforted by nonstop radio and print coverage when President Roosevelt died, in 1963 television held the country together, providing the news and the images that helped the nation to mourn, and ultimately to move on. Of course, radio talk shows were a part of the coverage, letting the listeners express their concerns and fears about the death of the president. But it was on television where Americans were able to watch live coverage of the funeral procession, seeing in real-time world leaders paying their respects, and the Kennedy family saying their good-byes. The black-and-white images were powerful (color was not yet widely available, so most TV programs, especially news shows, were still broadcast in black and white); years later, many Americans would still remember where they were when they heard the news that President Kennedy had been shot.

Television also helped to bring other major events home to the viewer. While radio and early TV had been hesitant to discuss racism, some of the key events of the civil rights movement were too momentous to ignore. Beginning in 1954 with the U.S. Supreme Court's decision in *Brown v. the Board of Education of Topeka* (the Court ruling that finally made segregation illegal), followed by coverage of the clashes that resulted when schools were desegregated, TV was there to bring the pictures into the homes of average Americans. In the 1950s, it was much easier for radio to cover news events, because TV reporters were still forced to carry cumbersome and heavy equipment around, and there was still no videotape. But in the 1960s, as reporters became more experienced with remote broadcasts and equipment became smaller and lighter, TV covered more breaking news. Both TV and radio were on the scene to cover the civil rights movement, including the marches in Selma, Alabama, in March 1965. The public was horrified by the TV images of peaceful protesters being attacked by vicious police dogs; later, some critics would say that these images of police brutality increased popular support for passage of the Voting Rights Act in August 1965.

As might be expected, black radio stations were following these events very closely, but the civil rights movement was discussed by some white talk show hosts, too: Barry Gray was known for his support of civil rights and had talked about racism with black guests for years, and Jerry Williams was another of the hosts who supported civil rights and discussed it on his show. But in the formative years of television, the talk shows tended to avoid this sort of discussion. The first TV talk shows featured music and celebrity guests rather than discussions of controversial issues. Steve Allen showed his views about integration by frequently having black performers on his show, as did Arthur Godfrey. It wasn't until November 1956 that popular black vocalist Nat "King" Cole became the first African American to host his own TV show. It was actually a typical TV variety show, with little, if any, controversy, but Cole immediately ran into the kind of racism that was still pervasive in America. No national sponsors wanted to be associated with his show, for fear that southern viewers would boycott their products. Cole's friends and colleagues did their best to keep his show on the air by making guest appearances, but without a sponsor, *The Nat "King" Cole Show* was ultimately canceled. Because it was the mid-1950s, there was no outcry and little outrage, except in the black press; what had happened to Cole was barely mentioned by the mainstream media. Racism was still a subject nobody at the TV networks wanted to acknowledge.

A further example of network timidity occurred in September 1961, when ABC-TV offered a documentary called *Walk a Mile in My Shoes*, about racism in six American cities. At least eleven of ABC's southern stations found excuses not to broadcast it.

The early 1960s continued to be a transitional period for television talk shows, and especially for the women's shows. The radio hosts from the 1940s who had moved to TV, with varying degrees of success, had now retired, and the question was what the woman of the 1960s wanted from a daytime talk show. Whereas in the 1950s the expectations of women were more traditional, many women were now going to work (and their daughters were going to college rather than marrying immediately after high school). There were still some stay-at-home moms, but as author Betty Friedan noted in her best seller *The Feminine Mystique*, a number of these homemakers felt a malaise that they had been told not to feel. Society's message to women in the 1950s had been that the home and the family were all that mattered, and the women's shows (on radio and then on TV) had reflected that view. Even on the shows with guest authors or politicians, the general theme involved being in the home and taking a break for a few minutes of interesting chat. But by the 1960s, the female audience was becoming more fragmented. One of the hosts who found a way to entertain them was Virginia Graham. Her TV show, *Girl Talk,* went on the air in 1963 and was nationally syndicated. Graham, a former journalist in Chicago, was known for her bouffant hairdo and her diverse guests. In fact, by 1968, *Time* magazine, which seldom said anything good about women's shows, described *Girl Talk* as having the "brightest female panel discussion in television." (On the other hand, the article was entitled "Cackleklatsch," using a derisive reference to female journalists, who were often called "news hens" by the predominantly male media of that era.) Graham's guest list read like a who's who of successful women, including authors, educators, humorists, political figures, and, of course, celebrities. By 1968, the show was being seen in eighty-three cities, and at its highest point, it reached an average audience of two million people. While the panel was known for its intelligence, the conversation wasn't always intellectual. Sometimes the guests seemed to dislike each other, and sometimes Graham was sarcastic, but she was an excellent interviewer and knew how to bring out the best in the people who were on her show.

Of course, even in an era when TV was trying to avoid controversy, some hot-button issues did get on the air. Not all of the TV talk shows were based on the variety model. As mentioned earlier, from the 1950s on there were some popular interview shows where the host sat down with a guest, or with several guests, and chatted about a number of current issues. The occasional controversy arose because advocacy groups, often affiliated with a particular religion or political party, were very vocal in their objection to speakers with what they called "radical" views. As far back as the 1930s, some stations refused to broadcast radio talks that were critical of capitalism, or that espoused the need for family planning. And in the television age, network executives remained cautious about offending these advocacy groups. An example of this occurred when Margaret Sanger of Planned Parenthood was a guest on *Mike Wallace Interviews* in September 1957. Because Sanger was an outspoken proponent of birth control at a time when obtaining contraceptives was still illegal in a number of states, there had been pressure from Catholic clergy to keep Sanger off the air. During the interview, Wallace repeatedly asked her what she thought about Catholicism, but Sanger was not interested in criticizing any specific faith and refused to be baited by Wallace. Rather, she focused on explaining why she felt birth control should be legal. By all accounts, Sanger, who was seventy-eight at the time and inexperienced with TV, held her own with the often abrasive Wallace.

In the 1950s and early 1960s, the angry and outraged talk shows had not yet taken over, especially on television, and few hosts were eager to have a spontaneous conversation with a controversial guest because it could lead to problems: listeners might send letters of complaint to the FCC or deluge the station's management with protests. To avoid that sort of trouble, when CBS decided to revisit the still contentious subject of birth control in November 1959, executives did not leave the content to chance. They taped separate interviews with Catholic and Protestant clergy, rather than having any dialogue. The program was presented as educational, in the accepted TV and radio tradition of turning to "responsible spokesmen" from various causes and letting them be the experts.

Family planning was not the only subject considered unsuitable for TV. Sponsors and clergy pressured the networks to keep other topics off the air as well, especially any mention of homosexuality. The Daughters of Bilitis was a lesbian advocacy group in the 1950s and 1960s. Along with its male counterpart, the Mattachine Society, the group had started to campaign for equal rights in an era when gay men and lesbians were subject to arrest and were referred to as deviates by the mainstream media. In late June 1964, talk show host Les Crane planned to do an interview with several DOB members, but ABC's legal department ordered him to cancel the show, and he did. CBS broadcast a documentary about homosexuality in March 1967, but it had taken over two and a half years to get on the air. What is especially ironic about television's hesitation is that by now, Joe Pyne and others on radio were regularly insulting and making fun of homosexuals, without anyone's complaining to the FCC.

TV TALKS SHOWS AND THEIR NICHE

Throughout the rest of the 1960s, TV talk shows were in a state of flux. Most of the hosts of these shows were veterans, the majority of whom had originally been nightclub entertainers. Even though society was changing around them, their shows continued to resemble a nightclub performance from the good old days, with singing, dancing, jokes, and only an occasional mention, usually hidden in a joke, of current events. Comedian Joey Bishop was a good example; in 1967, he was host of a late-night show on ABC, one of the many that tried to defeat Johnny Carson over the years. Bishop's sidekick was Regis Philbin, who in the 1980s became a well-known talk show host in his own right on *Live with Regis and Kathie Lee*—later re-named *Live with Regis and Kelli,* as Kathie Lee left and was replaced by Kelli Ripa; Philbin also became the host of the hit game show *Who Wants to Be A Millionaire?*. As for Joey Bishop, despite good reviews and a very impressive guest list, his show was canceled after only two seasons. Ironically, Bishop later became a popular fill-in for Johnny Carson when Johnny was on vacation from *The Tonight Show.*

The traditional variety format continued to be popular on TV throughout the 1960s, and there were a number of syndicated shows. One of the most successful was the *Mike Douglas Show.* This syndicated daytime talk show was first seen in 1961; by 1967, it was on the air in more than 150 cities. A former radio singer, Douglas often performed on his TV show, much as Steve Allen had when he hosted *The Tonight Show.* What made the *Mike Douglas Show* unique was the use Douglas made of cohosts. It was Douglas's custom to ask a guest to cohost the show, sometimes for as long as a week. Douglas was genial and easygoing, and his show was synonymous with family-friendly entertainment. However, one week in February 1972 that changed. Douglas invited former Beatle John Lennon and his wife, Yoko Ono, to serve as cohosts. During the same week, he invited as guests some members of what was then called the counterculture, including Black Panther Bobby Seale and antiwar activist Jerry Rubin. Known for nonthreatening family entertainment, Douglas suddenly found himself in the media spotlight as a result of his unexpected choice of guests.

Actually, what Mike Douglas did that week in 1972 had been heard on radio since the late 1960s, although many of the radio hosts were not as civil and courteous as Douglas. Interestingly, as the next generation of talk hosts came to TV in the 1960s, they were being pulled in two different directions. There was a new openness and an interest in subjects previously considered taboo, such as racism or divorce. A number of talk radio hosts were addressing these so-called "hot button" issues in a contentious manner, and the question was whether TV talk shows would follow the kinder gentler model of Mike Douglas or the outrage and controversy that was getting good radio ratings. Among the hosts who chose to resist the trend toward controversy was Johnny Carson. Carson had taken over as host of NBC's *The Tonight Show* in October 1962, and like the original host, Steve Allen, he preferred being clever to being crude. Some of his ongoing skits, like "Carnac the Magnificent," relied on puns, and the "Mighty Carson Art Players" performed parodies of movies, commercials, and current events. Despite the occasional double entendre, nothing qualified as vulgarity.

Another host who tried to avoid the confrontational style was Dick Cavett, who started on the air at ABC-TV in March 1968 as a daytime host and, in May 1969, was put opposite Carson (without much success). The *Dick Cavett Show* became a favorite of the critics, who admired Cavett's insightful interviews and thought he was more intelligent than many of the other hosts on TV.

There was also the *Merv Griffin Show*. Like Johnny Carson, Merv Griffin had been a game show host at one point in his career. After a failed attempt at TV talk in 1962, Griffin returned in 1965 with a syndicated daytime talk show that was celebrity-oriented; this time, he was much more successful. According to some reports, Griffin got his guests to reveal embarrassing things or to speak off-the-cuff by giving them cocktails before they taped the show. While Griffin did address some of the titillating themes that the new freedom of the 1960s permitted, talking about transsexuals and even incest, his show was generally not known for being outrageous, nor did it focus only on sexual topics. Griffin was a very capable interviewer, and in addition to talking with newsmakers, movie stars, and hit vocalists, he also interviewed intellectuals like philosopher Bertrand Russell and historians Will and Ariel Durant. Griffin is probably best remembered for having created the game show *Jeopardy*, but he hosted the syndicated version of his talk show through 1969 and then was hired to do a late-night talk show on CBS in yet another attempt to compete with Johnny Carson's *The Tonight Show*. This CBS show suffered the same fate as that of Dick Cavett, Joey Bishop, Les Crane, and many others who tried to defeat Carson. Griffin's show was canceled in early 1972.

One other popular TV talk host had an interesting career prior to becoming a talker. Dinah Shore was a successful vocalist who had numerous hit songs during the 1950s. Host of her own musical variety program, *The Dinah Shore Chevy Show*, sponsored by Chevrolet, she was famous for her constantly cheerful personality, as well as for singing the sponsor's theme song ("See the USA in your Chevrolet") and then throwing a big kiss to the audience. But beginning in August 1970, Shore proved she could do more than just sing. She began hosting *Dinah's Place*, a syndicated chat show that featured what *Washington Post* media critic Lawrence Laurent described as ". . . a pleasant mixture of conversation, exercise, cooking, sewing, art appreciation, home decorating, dieting information and music . . . " While it may have looked like just another women's show, Shore provided some unique touches, helped by having made many celebrity friends during her long career in both radio and TV. Among her guests during the early 70s were politicians like Senators Hubert Humphrey and Barry Goldwater; boxer Joe Frazier and tennis star Billie Jean King; Dean Burch, the chairman of the Federal Communications Commission; and a number of entertainers, from rock star James Brown to actor Peter Ustinov. Another interesting element of her show was her ability to get the celebrities into the kitchen to show off their cooking. In one segment, vocalist Frank Sinatra made spaghetti, while in another, Vice President Spiro Agnew demonstrated his recipe for linguini. The show got a new name, *Dinah!*, in 1974, and it remained on the air until 1980.

Dinah Shore was known for being non-confrontational, and even though all around her, talk was focusing more on outrage and controversy, she was not the only one to resist that trend. In the late 60s, Aline Saarinen, a former art critic turned NBC news reporter, hosted *For Women Only*, a show where a panel of interesting guests chatted about issues ranging from the so-called "generation gap" (the widening divide between what adults and their children thought about contemporary issues), to changing attitudes about women's role, to the latest fads in fashion. The show was praised by critics for being intelligent and thought-provoking when it was first seen on New York's WNBT-TV in 1969. By 1971, however, Saarinen was replaced by another of NBC's rising stars, Barbara Walters. Walters had once been the "Today Girl" on NBC's *Today Show*: one of the few jobs for women in early television, it mainly required beauty and a willingness to be helpful to the male host. Walters, however, worked her way up to reporting on human interest features and doing on-camera interviews, and now she was going to moderate her first talk show. She re-named the program *Not for Women Only*, and began including men as guests in the panel discussions; but like her predecessor, Walters moderated a show where the conversation remained courteous. On radio too, there was a new group of talk hosts who rejected the idea of arguing with the callers and talking about only one side of an issue. They felt that some hosts had gone too far, and they wanted to bring a more friendly and inclusive style to the genre. One of the best proponents of this style was Herb Jepko, who began a show called the *Nitecaps* on radio station KSL in Salt Lake City in February 1964. Among the rules of the show was that no controversial subjects (like politics or religion) were allowed. The audience, which became a loyal extended family, was at the heart of the show; listeners called to talk about their day, to read poetry, or just to ask what other listeners were up to.

Another of the younger breed of talkers was Les Crane, previously mentioned, who had hosted a successful call-in radio show on San Francisco's KGO and a TV version on KGO-TV in the early 60s. Handsome and personable (one critic said he looked like he could be a movie star), he arrived in New York City in late August 1963 and promised that his show would deliver hard-hitting interviews and stimulating conversation, without rudeness or vulgarity. *Night Line*, debuted on WABC-TV in mid-September 1963 in the 1 a.m. time slot. A live overnight talk show was new: television executives still believed there was only a minimal audience available for late night TV, and that time period was usually reserved for old movies. Crane was determined to make the show worth staying up for: he not only talked to the guests and interacted with the studio audience, but he also took calls from viewers and put them on the air, letting them directly question a guest or take issue with something Crane had said. Critics found this format an interesting innovation but were dismayed by the large number of commercials on the show, which interrupted every good discussion. And one reporter described the special microphone Crane used to do his interviews and take calls as resembling a hunting rifle; when he pointed it at an audience member, "It looks as if he is about to shoot a spectator." Critics praised Crane for bringing some youthfulness to the talk show genre, but his show never attracted a large enough audience, even when he experimented with controversy and then backed off.

Night Line was canceled in August 1964, but ABC liked Crane enough to give him one more try. Crane's new program was now called *The Les Crane Show*, and it was unique for having an unusual set: Crane sat on a stool in the center of the stage, and the audience sat in bleachers surrounding him. The show was now on the air from 11:20 p.m. to 1 a.m., yet one more talk show trying to compete with Johnny Carson. During his time on the air in New York, Crane became known for his liberal views, and for his ability to get big-name popular culture icons to appear on his show, including singer-songwriter Bob Dylan and British rock group the Rolling Stones. He was one of the earliest talkers to interview an openly gay man, an activist named Randy Wicker, in January 1964. But the topic evidently made his network uncomfortable, because when Crane attempted to do a show about lesbianism a few months later, and invited spokeswomen from the Daughters of Bilitis, a lesbian advocacy group, ABC ordered him to cancel the show, and he complied. After a number of tries at TV talk and only minimal ratings, Crane finally left New York City in 1968, going back into radio at KLAC in Los Angeles. In 1971, he had a spoken-word hit record, "Desiderata," an inspirational song which reached the top-10 on the *Billboard* magazine Hot 100 chart.

TALKING ABOUT SEX

Attracting younger viewers and listeners was not the only challenge facing talk shows in the 1960s and early 1970s. How best to present controversial themes was on the minds of both the TV and the radio talkers. The Federal Communications Commission was very responsive to complaints from the public, and stations were trying to figure out how far they could push the envelope before they received unwanted FCC scrutiny. As mentioned earlier, not every host wanted to be angry and confrontational, and some like Herb Jepko on radio and Dinah Shore on TV carved out their own niche just by being warm and friendly. Yet, increasingly, Americans seemed to be living in angry times. As political division over the Vietnam War deepened and even newscasters like Walter Cronkite went from supporting the administration's position on Vietnam to opposing it, many hosts seemed unable to avoid the tendency to use opposing views as a way of creating an exciting show. This style would become even more popular in the 1980s and was identified with hosts like Jerry Springer, but the truth is that the airwaves first became contentious in the late 60s, and not just on the Joe Pyne show. Critics noted the developing tendency of radio talk hosts to let bigoted callers spout their views uninterrupted before finally screaming at them and then hanging up. "The radio dial [is] oozing hatred, distrust, disgust, and verbal violence," wrote Don Page, the radio/TV critic of the *Los Angeles Times* in a 1968 column, noting with disappointment that even Les Crane had become more confrontational.

As talk show hosts found that controversy equaled higher ratings, they still had to be cautious. They were well aware that the FCC periodically cited stations for airing obscene language or excessive (and vulgar) sexual content. Beginning in the mid-1950s, as rock music became more popular, complaints about allegedly dirty lyrics had increased, and by the late 1950s, disc jockeys were being fined by the FCC for making remarks that today would be considered tame, but were seen as overly suggestive for that era. As talk shows gained in popularity and subjects like changing sexual mores were on people's minds, the hosts had to find a way to talk about human sexuality without being considered obscene. It was a fine line, and often a very arbitrary one, based on how many listener complaints the FCC received. And as the line kept moving, some hosts tried to move it even further. Bill Ballance is the man generally credited with starting all of the sex talk on radio with his *Feminine Forum* in 1971. (Joe Pyne and other controversial talkers discussed sex at times, but Ballance made an entire program out of it.) Ballance, who had once been an announcer in Chicago and not controversial in any way, went to Los Angeles because he wanted a warmer climate, and by all accounts, his dj shows at KNX were considered witty but not crude. But by the late 1950s, at rock station KFWB, he was gradually becoming known for using more double entendres and making suggestive comments, to the point where the FCC once asked to review his tapes. After his successful time as a top-forty dj, the music changed and so did the personnel at the station where he worked. He had trouble finding a job but found a way to reinvent himself and become relevant again. It was at KGBS in Los Angeles where he started what came to be called "topless radio." It was surprising to critics how many women were willing to call a middle-aged man and talk with him about their sex life, but call they did. He referred to them as "fillies" and "chicklets" (unless he found out they were overweight, and he then called them "porkers"); he expressed disdain for feminism. And yet he told a reporter for *Newsweek* in 1972 that he believed his show was therapeutic: "They communicate with me because they can't communicate with their husbands." And listeners, who perhaps felt like the auditory version of voyeurs, seemed fascinated by what the callers confessed to or wanted to discuss. The show and its subject matter stayed on the right side of the obscenity line, but (no pun intended) just barely. And it led to a number of clones, with versions of the show in cities like Chicago, Washington, and Dallas. It also led to endless complaints to the FCC, which stated in March 1973 that it had received over two thousand letters from people who were irate about this sort of programming. It may have got stations impressive ratings, but attracting the attention of the FCC was soon to change all of that. The Chicago version, known as *Femme Forum* and airing over station WGLD, featured graphic discussions of oral sex, and the FCC decided that the topless-radio format and this particular version of it had gone too far. Fines were issued, and stations broadcasting such programs were put on notice. Most stations did the prudent thing and canceled the shows, although a few owners expressed displeasure with what they saw as a freedom-of-speech issue. And although it seemed at the time that talking about sex was not worth the aggravation, by the 1980s, these shows had returned, with similar results: critics complained and wrote to the FCC, but the shows persisted, as talk hosts like Howard Stern became popular by saying outrageous things, and making crude jokes about sex. Controversial announcers like Stern were helped by changes in cultural attitudes, but also by media deregulation, which diminished the watchdog role of the FCC. Many critics believed that Stern's success paved the way in the early 1990s for the man often considered the king of TV talk show vulgarity, Jerry Springer.

What is interesting about that first golden age of talk radio is how many precedents were set that are still used in today's broadcasting. For one, there was the angry and confrontational talker upset about all sorts of things. In the 1960s, the hosts were irate about "long-haired hippies" who used drugs and refused to go to Vietnam; crime in the inner city; the vulgar lyrics of rock music—the list was endless, and if the host didn't rant, the guests did. Also getting a surprising amount of attention back then was sex, with hosts acting like what we might today call "shock jocks," making suggestive remarks and encouraging people (usually women) to reveal intimate personal details. One other very common aspect of radio in the 1960s was the host who had ultra-right-wing conservative views. Some of these hosts were religious and some were secular, but they all believed that anyone who disagreed with them was a traitor. Perhaps they were reacting to the changing norms in society. The 1960s were an era when some young people dressed in nontraditional styles, refused to defer to authority, and protested the war in Vietnam; it was also an era when movements for civil rights, women's rights, and even gay rights emerged. A few of the talk hosts expressed liberal viewpoints, and some created their shows as comfortable places where no rage was allowed. Some even preferred to be called "communicasters," as if to say that they were communicators as well as broadcasters. But then as now, the majority of the hosts seemed to hold conservative political views, and they genuinely disliked where society was going. When today's talk listeners think of the history of the talk show, it is doubtful they associate the 1950s and 1960s with hosts who behaved like shock jocks or hatemongers, but those hosts were there, and many were developing a large following, especially on late-night radio. While the critics continued to lament the vulgarity and the vitriol, that didn't stop people from listening. In fact, by the late 1960s, the talk show had become such a popular form that listeners couldn't wait to find out what the hosts would say next.

TALK SHOWS REINVENTING THEMSELVES

The early 1970s brought about some major changes for talk radio. Where in the late 1960s the genre seemed to be everywhere and people were excited about it, by the early 1970s the FCC had clamped down on topless radio and seemed more willing to enforce the personal-attack rule of the Fairness Doctrine, which meant that stations had to be careful how vitriolic a host might get. The newly elected president, Richard Nixon, and his vice president, Spiro Agnew, gave the impression that they regarded the media as their enemy and both disliked popular culture. None of this stopped radio talk hosts from discussing controversial subjects, but as in the 1950s, the country seemed to be going through a conservative period politically, and being perceived as too outspoken didn't seem like a good idea. Americans remained very much divided on the conflict in Vietnam, and Nixon and Agnew believed it was the media that were turning people against the war. Vice President Spiro Agnew gave a widely publicized speech in mid-November 1969, in which he vehemently criticized the TV networks for what he felt was biased coverage. It was one of many attacks on the press that occurred in the late 1960s and early 1970s. But war criticism on radio was now coming from a new direction: college radio.

Until the mid-1960s, there was little original programming on FM. Although frequency modulation was a technology that offered better audio quality as its inventor Edwin Howard Armstrong had demonstrated in the mid-1930s, by the early 1960s FM still hadn't caught on. Few Americans owned FM radios, and those FM stations that were on the air either played classical music or simulcast what was on the AM station that owned them. Then, in August 1965, the FCC ruled that AM stations could no longer simulcast the same programming on their FM stations. Delays in implementation stalled the actual change, but by 1967, there were some new FM stations on the air, some playing what was then called "underground music," long album tracks (as opposed to three-minute hit singles) that were often about hot-button issues. Where AM music tended to be safe and often formulaic, FM music took chances and mentioned subjects that were taboo on AM top-forty radio: racism, drug use, and Vietnam War protests. By the late 1960s, FM stations like KSAN in San Francisco, WNEW-FM in New York City, and WBCN-FM in Boston were speaking out, sometimes using music and sometimes using announcers, including news reporters. The style of underground (later called progressive rock) radio was not objective. Strong feelings were expressed about the direction of the country. This style of radio also began emerging at some FM college stations, where students who opposed the war, as well as the injustices they saw in society used radio to express their point of view. (For more about the history of FM underground radio, see Michael C. Keith's 1997 book *Voices in the Purple Haze*.) Perhaps as a result of the new choices available on FM, sales of AM/FM radios showed a dramatic increase beginning in 1970.

On 4 May 1970, four unarmed antiwar protesters were shot dead by National Guard troops on the campus of Kent State University in Kent, Ohio. The first story given to the media was that the protesters had fired on the soldiers, but it was quickly found that there was no evidence to support that; some students did throw rocks in the direction of the National Guard, but a debate immediately broke out over whether the soldiers should have used lethal force. Conservative talk hosts rose to the defense of the Guard, representing the protesters as an out-of-control mob, but the FM underground stations and college radio stations presented a different side, talking about how even generally peaceful protests were being suppressed. Leading this side were musicians. The popular rock group Crosby, Stills, Nash, and Young recorded a song called "Ohio" that blamed President Nixon for what had happened. FM stations played it immediately, and surprisingly, so did many (though not all) AM top-forty stations. The song reached the top fifteen in late June 1970. FM broadcasters had begun giving regular air play to antiwar folk and rock songs as part of their strategy to use the airwaves to protest the president's policies.

Student talk shows were also created during this era, and these shows discussed a wide range of subjects, all from a perspective not heard on AM talk radio. In the past, some AM hosts had tried to get young people to listen, but attempts to make the traditional talk shows more relevant had not succeeded. (Then, as now, typical talk listeners were in their forties or fifties.) The FM underground and college talk shows found a niche, however, and while their audience was never large, it was very loyal. After the tragedy at Kent State, a number of FM college stations were convinced that the mainstream media were not providing accurate coverage of the antiwar movement, so they decided to do something about it. Stations at Boston University, the University of Chicago, Duke University, New York University, and other schools created an unofficial network and sent their own reporters to cover major antiwar demonstrations and report back about what was happening. By the mid-1970s, in addition to shows that used both music and talk to protest the war, there were radio shows that explored what was then called the women's liberation movement, as well as gay rights, civil rights, and other issues of social justice. The stereotype of college stations was that they were a haven for disgruntled hippies who used drugs, but as someone who was on the air during that time, I saw firsthand how passionate college broadcasters could be when using radio to promote positive social change. On the other hand, college and noncommercial stations were also eager to push the proverbial envelope by challenging what they saw as efforts by the FCC to restrict freedom of speech on the airwaves. On 30 October 1973, one station, WBAI-FM in New York City, played a comedy routine by George Carlin called "Filthy Words." It contained seven words not permitted on the radio because they were considered obscene. A parent heard the broadcast and complained to the FCC, which fined WBAI. The station's management appealed, and the case went all the way to the U.S. Supreme Court, which finally decided in 1978 that the FCC did have the power to fine stations or restrict the times when they could play material containing offensive language.

Meanwhile, the president and the vice president, who already had been vocal in their dislike of the media, seemed especially displeased by what was happening at these underground stations, and many of the announcers who opposed the war were convinced that the administration wanted to stifle them. Their beliefs were reinforced by a surprising FCC ruling in early March 1971, which said that radio stations must stop playing any songs that promoted or glorified the use of drugs. The ruling seemed to be directed specifically at the music played on FM radio, some of which advocated all sorts of rebellious behavior. But the wording of the ruling was so vague that it could have been applied to the lyrics of even the most innocuous songs, depending on how someone interpreted them. Long before Nixon became president, there had been songs considered too controversial to be played. For example, in 1966, Janis Ian's song about an interracial romance, "Society's Child," was banned from a number of stations. But an FCC policy about what music could and could not be played troubled even conservative broadcasters, who disliked government censorship. It also troubled one of the FCC commissioners, Nicholas Johnson, who was convinced the ruling had been inspired by pressure from the vice president, and he went to the press to say so. The resulting furor ended in April with the FCC backing down, admitting that it had no power to determine what songs radio stations did or did not play. And once again, a cultural issue provided fodder for talk show hosts nationwide.

With the divide widening between what was on AM and what was on FM, TV talk shows were also divided. Some, like Johnny Carson, preferred to ignore the cultural issues and focus on noncontroversial entertainment. Others, like Dick Cavett and David Frost (a British-born talk host, first seen in the United States on a satirical TV review of the news called *That Was the Week That Was*, and now broadcasting a syndicated interview program), were quick to gravitate toward the newsmakers on both sides of the issues, so there was frequent competition for guests who could discuss not just Vietnam but other current topics like the ecology and integration.

Meanwhile, on AM talk radio, while some hosts continued their very successful policy of inspiring outrage, other hosts sought out guests who could shed some light on current problems, rather than just ranting about them. Veteran talkmaster Jerry Williams was a good example. He had spent part of the 1960s on the air in Chicago and was now back in Boston, on powerful AM station WBZ, discussing everything from Vietnam to the energy crisis. While it was a truism that the talk hosts in New York City and Los Angeles got the biggest guests, Williams had a reputation for talking with the most important people, no matter what city he was in. During the presidential campaign of 1972, he interviewed the Democratic candidate, Senator George McGovern, with whom he discussed how polarized America had become about the war, how corrupt the Nixon administration was (and why Americans didn't seem especially upset by the corruption), and whether McGovern felt his antiwar message was resonating with the public. McGovern insisted that it was, but evidently it didn't resonate enough, as he lost in a landslide. Still, this conversation was typical of the style of talk show that clarified the issues rather than generating angry calls.

In his January 1972 interview with Jerry Williams, Senator McGovern briefly mentioned allegations that the Republican Party had been spying on Democrats, but what would come to be known as the Watergate scandal (named after the hotel-apartment complex where the Democrats had their national headquarters) was still unfolding. Throughout 1972, new revelations continued to emerge. Print journalism was widely credited with pursuing the Watergate story to its finish, led by the page one reporting of Robert Woodward and Carl Bernstein of the *Washington Post*, beginning in mid-June 1972. The president continued to deny any wrongdoing, but questions from the media grew more insistent and led to several well-publicized confrontations between CBS-TV reporter Dan Rather and President Nixon. The president tried to get Rather fired and accused the TV networks of bias (and asked the U.S. Justice Department to investigate them). He also tried to stop the two *Washington Post* reporters from doing further digging, but the damage had been done. As the scandal widened and evidence was presented that Nixon operatives had also spied on a number of people perceived to be political enemies, the focus kept shifting between print and television, which covered the Nixon press conferences as well as the investigations into the president's actions. In fact, it was TV coverage of the Senate hearings in May 1973 that made the story impossible to ignore. President Nixon finally resigned in disgrace in August 1974. Much has been written since then about the Watergate scandal and its effect on the nation; suffice it to say that talk show hosts on both radio and TV followed the events closely, allowing the public to be part of an important news story as it was happening.

Although radio and TV talk shows were briefly slowed by the FCC's scrutiny of their content in the early 1970s, there were plenty of subjects to talk about. Any show about the culture wars generated phone calls and ratings, as people continued to have deeply felt opinions on the war, on sex, and even on the role of the media in their lives. The early to mid-1970s were also a good time for celebrity news. Newspaper heiress Patty Hearst was kidnapped, aging tennis star Bobby Riggs was defeated by Billie Jean King in a so-called battle of the sexes, and Johnny Carson moved *The Tonight Show* from New York City to Burbank, California, as part of a parade of TV shows that left New York City for studios on the West Coast. There were also economic issues like the energy crisis of 1973, the result of an embargo by the Organization of Petroleum Exporting Countries (OPEC), which temporarily halted those countries' exports of oil to the United States. Suddenly, there were long lines at gas stations, many of which had no gas to sell, along with a dramatic increase in the price of fuel. Frustrated consumers besieged talk shows with calls, and many radio stations tried to help by organizing car-pools and suggesting ways to save energy. The crisis would return with a vengeance in 1979, and President Jimmy Carter's perceived inability to deal with it was one reason he was not reelected. That same year, another issue that dominated public discussions was the Iran hostage crisis. The shah of Iran had been overthrown and replaced by a theocratic regime led by the Ayatollah Ruhollah Khomeini. Anti-American fervor led some of his supporters to invade the U.S. embassy in Tehran and take all of its employees hostage. As the crisis continued, ABC newscaster Ted Koppel began a late-night report called *America Held Hostage*, which evolved into the successful newsmagazine show *Nightline*.

CHANGES IN THE MEDIA MIX

As one crisis after another took center stage during the 1970s, there was a new participant in the discussions: cable television. Cable technology wasn't really new. It had been around since the latter part of the 1950s, but a pay cable television service didn't get started until late 1972. Gradually, cable TV became financially viable, offering viewers programs they could not see on "free" television. In 1975, only 15 percent of all U.S. homes had purchased cable, but that was a much larger percentage than in the previous several years. One reason for the increase was that Home Box Office (HBO) was now the first cable channel to deliver its signal via satellite, making it possible to instantly broadcast sports and news events from distant locations as they were happening. In fact, radio also began putting satellite to good use when in 1978 Mutual Broadcasting employed it to make its new late-night talk show with Larry King available nationwide.

There was also an event in the popular culture that saddened millions of baby boomers in August 1977. Elvis Presley, often called the king of rock-and-roll, died. Rock music had been part of the cultural change of the 1950s, and Presley had been the first major rock star. Throughout the 1960s and into the 1970s, popular music continued to evolve, and as the baby boomers got older, new radio formats were created to appeal to them. In the 70s, the FM band was now the home of such new formats as urban radio, which featured the dance music then called "disco" and catered to the black audience; album-oriented rock, a more mass-appeal and hit-oriented version of what the underground stations of the early 1970s had played; and "oldies," the hits from the early years of top-forty radio.

The debate over the supposedly negative effect of popular music (and popular culture) on children had died down, but on talk radio, social issues continued to generate controversy. The same was true on television, as talk hosts, in an effort to be competitive and increase their ratings, scheduled interviews with leaders of such controversial groups as the Ku Klux Klan and the American Nazi Party. There was also another new kind of talk show that generated intense emotions, but without bigotry or rage: sports talk. There had been sports commentators, usually former athletes, on the air since the 1930s, but as more telephone talk shows went on the air in the 1950s and 1960s, not all of them focused on politics, current events, or religion. By the late 1960s and early 1970s, a growing number of stations had begun sports-talk shows and had found them very popular, especially with thirty-five- to fifty-four-year-old men. Among these stations were WBZ in Boston, which in July 1969 debuted *Calling All Sports*, hosted by station sports director Guy Mainella. In San Antonio, Texas, Station KBAT had a Sunday night show with Johnny Moore in 1971, and in Miami, the *Superfan* show with Alan Minter started on public TV station WPBT in 1972 and then moved to radio on WINZ. On these and other call-in shows, the hosts tended to be people who loved sports, and not necessarily former players.

Meanwhile, the late-late-night talk show, which had not been successful when Les Crane tried it in the mid 1960s, was about to make a comeback in the 1970s. On NBC, host Tom Snyder did his first *Tomorrow* show in mid-October 1973, as critics wondered whether anyone would stay up past 1 a.m. to watch. People did, and the show remained on the air until early 1982, when it was replaced by a talk show hosted by a promising new comic, David Letterman. Another 1970s TV innovation debuted in October 1975: a new show that mingled political satire, comedy skits, and musical guests. It was called *NBC's Saturday Night* (later known as *Saturday Night Live*), and it would pave the way for other shows that took a comic (and often caustic) look at current events and popular culture. At a time when most American TV was taped ahead of time, *SNL* was broadcast live from New York and aimed at the young adult audience. It featured a different guest host each week, a musical performance by an up-and-coming or already well-known pop star, and a cast of talented performers who were jokingly known as the "Not Ready for Prime Time Players." While *SNL* was at first described as a variety show, its political humor and parodies of pop culture were like nothing else on TV. *SNL* was fearless in poking fun at the famous and the popular. For example, Chevy Chase depicted President Gerald Ford as clumsy, and Dan Aykroyd portrayed chef Julia Child as an eccentric old lady. The cast also parodied the typical TV newscast, with Jane Curtin as an anchor trying to maintain control while the guests and pundits caused chaos all around her. Other variety shows had tried to attract the baby boomers, with mixed success, but *SNL* became a cultural phenomenon, the forerunner of many political satire shows of the 1990s like the *Daily Show*.

In October 1970, what had originally been called National Educational Television and was famous for its award-winning children's show *Sesame Street* was re-named the Public Broadcasting Service (PBS). PBS programmed more than just children's shows. With so many important news stories to cover, people were seeking additional outlets besides CBS, NBC, and ABC. PBS was able to provide an alternative source of information. Liberal commentator

Bill Moyers and conservative commentator William F. Buckley Jr. had their own programs on PBS, beginning in the early 1970s. Another respected PBS news program was *Washington Week in Review*, a roundtable discussion that featured four top journalists discussing the week's political events. *Washington Week* had debuted as a local TV show on WETA in Washington, DC, in February 1967 and was added to the NET/PBS roster in early 1969. In 1977, PBS debuted a new program for viewers who wanted more in-depth and less sensational coverage: the *McNeil-Lehrer Report*. In its original incarnation, it focused on one story per show. In 1983, it was renamed the *McNeil/Lehrer News Hour*.

While known for its television shows, PBS had begun to offer a radio service called National Public Radio (NPR) in 1970. One of its best-known daily news shows, *All Things Considered*, went on the air in early May 1971, covering antiwar protests in Washington, DC, and sending its reporters out to talk to the demonstrators. By early 1972, Susan Stamberg was the show's cohost, the first woman to anchor a national news program. The show was accused of "liberal bias," but it also won a number of prestigious awards for coverage of current events, and it proved that radio news, even on the FM dial, could attract a loyal audience.

In the 1970s, radio was changing in another way. Proving that everything old is new again, radio advice givers returned. In the days of the traditional women's shows, there was often a guest who was known for solving the average homemaker's problems. The role of the female advice giver experienced a resurgence in the mid-1970s, starting with Toni Grant, a clinical psychologist who advised callers on Los Angeles station KABC. Grant had been the resident psychologist on Bill Ballance's *Feminine Forum* in the early 1970s, but now she became a star in her own right. By 1980, she was making what *Time* magazine called a "five-figure salary" and was among the highest-rated hosts in her time period.

Another female advice giver with a style that was somewhat more direct (her critics would later say caustic) was Laura Schlessinger, who had begun her career as a guest pundit on the Bill Ballance Show. By July 1976, Schlessinger had her own show on KWIZ, Santa Ana. She was soon to become a national talk radio star.

In New York City, another unique talk show host was giving advice on sexuality. As mentioned earlier, the early 1970s shows that upset the FCC had been crude and voyeuristic, and by the early 80s, a few announcers, most notably Howard Stern, were using sexual innuendo on a regular basis. But when Dr Ruth Westheimer talked about sex, she was unlike Bill Ballance (or Howard Stern). Her broadcasts were friendly and informative. A New York City professor and sex therapist with a heavy German accent and a speaking voice that comedians soon parodied, she had a Sunday night program, *Sexually Speaking*, which debuted on WYNY-FM in 1980 and almost immediately became very popular. But NBC, which owned WYNY, was worried. Given how controversial the subject matter was (Dr. Ruth discussed such topics as contraception, impotence, and masturbation), NBC was concerned about what callers might say. At first, Westheimer was not allowed to have listeners call in and was told to focus on guest experts. That policy was soon changed, thanks to the existence of a good tape-delay system. With the focus of the show on the callers and their need for reliable advice on sexual topics, Westheimer's show quickly became a success, and a cable television version debuted on Lifetime in 1982.

As the 1970s drew to a close, some new talk hosts were being introduced, including Jay Leno, a stand-up comic who frequently performed on *The Tonight Show* and was also a frequent guest on David Letterman's show. Johnny Carson was rumored to be leaving, due to a contract dispute, and people were trying to guess who would host the show if he decided to leave. One person suggested was David Letterman, who had first appeared as a guest on Carson's show in late November 1978, and was getting favorable reviews from the critics for his sly wit and off-beat sense of humor. Carson didn't leave, but the question of who would replace him some day kept critics and talk show fans wondering. And throughout the 1980s, the two up-and-coming comics, Leno and Letterman, developed a friendly rivalry, each one hoping he might be chosen as the next host of *The Tonight Show*.

Meanwhile, in Baltimore, an African American woman named Oprah Winfrey was coanchoring the news at WJZ-TV. By her own admission, she was not a very good news anchor, but when she was given a chance in 1978 to cohost a local talk show on WJZ-TV, she found her calling and began what would be a very successful career as a daytime talk host. There had been few African American talk show hosts on the networks, but Oprah's success proved that talent and personality were more important than race or gender.

Sports was making its debut on a new cable television network called ESPN, and while at first not many people watched it, by the early 1980s announcers like Chris Berman were making their presence felt. Berman, who joined ESPN a month after it went on the air, was known not only for his thorough knowledge of sports, but for the playful way in which he reported the stories. He liked to use clever catch phrases, which usually involved puns on the athletes' names.

In politics at the end of the 1970s, a new advocacy group began to show its influence. It was called the Moral Majority, and it became one of the most powerful conservative Christian lobbying groups in America. While it had positions on a number of hot-button issues, such as wanting the *Roe v. Wade* decision overturned, one of the Moral Majority's main concerns was eliminating what its members saw as smut and vulgarity on TV. Led by Rev. Jerry Falwell, already well known as a televangelist whose *Old Time Gospel Hour* was carried on more than 370 stations, the Moral Majority soon aligned itself with the Republican Party and was credited with helping Ronald Reagan get elected president in 1980.

CHANGES BROUGHT BY MEDIA DEREGULATION

As the 1980s began, things were looking up for cable television. A new invention from Sony had made covering breaking news stories much easier. It was a portable device called the camcorder, which was introduced in 1981, with a consumer version in 1983. This device led to the era of electronic news gathering (ENG). Reporters could now go to an event and record it on video, which could then be quickly put on the air.

Now that cable was offering more channels and more interesting programming, the number of homes with cable had risen to 20 percent, and those numbers were on the verge of another big increase. What would have an impact on that number was the creation in June 1980 of the Cable News Network (CNN), the first twenty-four-hour all-news network, and in August 1981, the debut of Music Television (MTV), which featured rock and pop music videos and interviews with celebrities.

An even bigger change occurred when Republican presidential candidate Ronald Reagan defeated the incumbent, Jimmy Carter. Reagan was a big believer in deregulation, and he appointed Mark Fowler as the new chairman of the FCC, encouraging him to do away with regulations felt to be too burdensome to broadcasters. One regulation station owners had long disliked was the Fairness Doctrine, but there were other past decisions about how much news or public affairs stations had to carry, that were now believed to be unnecessary. Before Fowler was confirmed, one of the most conservative members of the FCC, Robert Lee, served as acting chairman, and among the changes made between January and mid-April 1981 was the elimination of the requirement to broadcast public service programs. (Since the Radio Act of 1927, stations had been expected to air a certain number of programs on behalf of charitable and nonprofit groups that served the community.) Also, the FCC allowed stations to broadcast more than eighteen minutes per hour of commercials and shortened the license renewal form so that stations no longer had to document how they had operated in the public interest. Then the FCC increased from three to seven the number of years between radio stations' required license renewals; for TV stations, that period was extended from three to five years.

In 1983, the FCC revisited the "equal-time" rule that if a station had given airtime to one political candidate, it had to provide time to his or her opponents. With the new version of the rule, stations did not have to give equal time to all the candidates. This was the beginning of a process by which radio and TV executives, using poll numbers, decided who were the viable candidates and then excluded from broadcast debates those candidates they felt couldn't win. Some critics believed that this process created an impossible situation for the newer candidates, who, without media exposure, couldn't get their message out and increase their poll numbers. Now that neither radio nor TV had any obligation to give free time to these candidates, the public would have no opportunity to decide whether they had something worthwhile to say. (All candidates could purchase commercial time, of course, but a 30 second advertisement wasn't the same as being included in broadcast debates.) Unfortunately, there was not much public discussion of these and other new FCC policies, and it is doubtful that the average person was aware of what had changed.

Even bigger changes were still to come. In 1984, the FCC eased the rule that one company could own only seven AM stations, seven FM stations, and seven TV stations nationwide. A rule that had been intended to maintain diversity of ownership and prevent any one company from becoming too dominant was now being gradually eliminated. The new limits were twelve AMs, twelve FMs, and twelve TV stations, and soon, those numbers, too, were raised. The rules were increasingly different from the rules in the 1940s, when NBC had had to divest itself of one of its two networks. By 1985, a number of media mergers had begun. General Electric purchased RCA and NBC. Capital Cities Communications purchased ABC, and Mutual Broadcasting was bought up by Westwood One, a network that produced and syndicated radio programming nationwide. An Australian-born newspaper magnate named Rupert Murdoch bought six American TV stations and created a new network, Fox. And more mergers were on the way.

The biggest change occurred in 1987, when the FCC abolished the Fairness Doctrine. For those broadcasters who opposed having to present both sides of an issue (and some actually did, seeing this as a freedom-of-speech issue that should not be regulated by the government), this was good news indeed. The abolition of the Fairness Doctrine led to a major shift on talk radio, as the airwaves became more polarized, and more conservative in political orientation. Among the first to put the new freedom to good use was a former dj turned talk show host, Rush Limbaugh. At a time when AM listening was dropping, his newly syndicated national show, which began in August 1988, was credited with bringing listeners back to AM. Limbaugh became the leading figure in the conservative dominance of talk radio.

Despite the influence of the Moral Majority (also called the Religious Right), efforts to keep controversial programs off the air usually failed. If a show had sponsors, it generally remained on the air. The radio host who generated the most outrage during the mid-1980s was shock jock Howard Stern, who horrified his critics and delighted his fans with his morning radio show. He was brash, crude, and vulgar; he talked about his sexual fantasies; he used words like *penis*; and he pushed whatever limits he could. His audience tended to be young males, and they thought he was extremely humorous. The FCC did not find him amusing, however. Even though it fined him, and several stations fired him, all the notoriety that surrounded Stern only caused his listenership to grow.

If shock radio wasn't enough to frustrate profamily traditionalists (and many moderates as well), TV now had its own version of shock, called trash

TV. Throughout the 1980s and into the 1990s, daytime TV talk shows kept pushing the envelope, choosing subjects that were increasingly outrageous. On trash TV, no topic was off-limits, not even bestiality, satanism, or incest. The hosts explained they were simply trying to be educational, so that the audience would have a better understanding of these subjects. Trash TV featured the most dysfunctional families, who put their foibles and troubles on display before a cheering or screaming studio audience. The master of this genre was Jerry Springer, whose show debuted in 1991 in a comparatively tame form, but it grew increasingly more outrageous as time passed. Springer's was the most volatile of the trash TV shows, with guests who frequently got into shouting matches and fistfights onstage. Other tabloid TV shows of the 80s and 90s were done by Sally Jessy Raphael, Geraldo Rivera, Maury Povich, Jenny Jones, and Morton Downey Jr., all of whom seemed to compete to see who could come up with the most bizarre topics.

Raphael, who had been a radio talk host, went on the air with her syndicated TV talk show in 1983. There were days when her show was more soap opera than trash, with guests who cried and told stories of traumatic incidents in their lives. Raphael did episodes about black children adopted by white parents, victims of crimes, and people who were morbidly obese. On other episodes, she was as voyeuristic as any of the tabloid TV hosts, talking to conjoined twins or men who were afraid to have sex.

Geraldo Rivera, a former ABC news correspondent, put his syndicated show on the air in 1987, with topics he never would have covered when doing the news. On one very well-publicized show in November 1988, entitled "Young Hatemongers," a brawl erupted between skinheads, white-power advocates, black-power advocates, and Jewish advocates. The fight went so far out of control that Rivera suffered a broken nose.

Morton Downey Jr. was the most angry and confrontational of the trash TV hosts. His show went on the air in 1987, and while it initially got a lot of interest, his often bizarre behavior scared away sponsors, causing the show to be canceled in 1989.

Critics hated trash TV and clergy protested to the FCC about the language and the subject matter, but most of the shows got good ratings and got enough sponsors to stay on the air. While sponsors in the 1940s and 1950s had avoided controversy, by the 1980s and 1990s, the higher the show's ratings often meant the sponsors would purchase air time, whether they personally liked the show or not.

Two events reminded talk hosts of the dangers of inflaming an audience. One took place in June 1984, when Denver, Colorado, radio talk host Alan Berg, the confrontational and abrasive host of a morning show on KOA, was shot dead in front of his home. Berg, a liberal on many social issues and an outspoken foe of racism in society, often referred to himself as "the last angry man." He had numerous enemies, and some circumstantial evidence linked his death to a white supremacist group called the Order, but no one was ever prosecuted for his murder. The other event occurred as a result of an episode of the Jenny Jones television show. Jones's show, which debuted in 1991, was similar in many ways to the other trash TV shows, although Jones always disliked the comparison, insisting her show was much more lighthearted and not as confrontational. In early March 1995, the topic of the show was secret crushes. Jones invited a young man named Jonathan Schmitz to find out who had a crush on him. Schmitz, who assumed it would be a woman, was stunned and upset when at the taping it turned out that a man, Scott Amedure, was the one who had a crush on him. Several days later, Schmitz shot Amedure to death, a crime for which his sentence was twenty-five to fifty years in prison. Amedure's family also sued the *Jenny Jones Show*, saying the producers should have been prepared for some kind of outrageous reaction, given that Schmitz had a long history of drug and alcohol abuse as well as mental illness. The family won a large judgment that was later overturned on appeal. As for the *Jenny Jones Show*, its ratings had already been in decline, and this tragedy provided affiliates with an excuse to cancel it, ending the show in 2003.

While television was immersed in trash and gossip, on talk radio there were always news events that could outrage the audience. Two from 1984 were typical of the kinds of hot-button issues that resulted in large numbers of calls. One topic was school prayer. Ever since the U.S. Supreme Court had banned it from the public schools in 1963, there had been attempts by conservative politicians from both parties to bring it back. In the early 1980s, President Reagan himself got involved. Keeping a promise he had made to the religious Christians who had helped to elect him, he proposed a constitutional amendment that would restore school prayer, and on 25 February 1984, he devoted his weekly radio address to why the amendment was a good idea. Congress was soon to vote on it, and many talk radio fans were in agreement with the president, and not just those on Christian radio stations. In mid-March, Congress voted down the amendment, and the continued ban of school prayer resulted in more outraged calls to the talk shows. Talk shows often stirred up the outrage by booking guests who were identified as atheists. In the 60s, the most controversial of these guests was Madalyn Murray (later Madalyn Murray O'Hair), an outspoken foe of all public prayer, and sometimes called "the most hated woman in America." Her appearances always generated lots of irate calls. She continued to be a guest on both radio and TV talk shows even into the 1980s.

Another event that got nationwide attention began as a local New York City story. In late December 1984, a white New Yorker named Bernhard Goetz shot four young black men who were trying to rob him on the subway. One of the would-be muggers suffered severe and permanent injuries. Goetz was charged with attempted murder, and he claimed self-defense. There were reports that he had uttered racially charged remarks while shooting, and two of the young men had been shot in the back, so it seemed that they had been running away from him, yet the public still seemed to regard him as a hero.

Some even suggested that he run for New York City mayor. There were also local talk show hosts who defended him, including conservative talker Bob Grant of WABC in New York, who made the remark that Goetz hadn't done the job right, since the young men were still alive. Dubbed the "subway vigilante" by the media, Goetz was soon the subject of talk shows all over the country. People who had been victims of crimes spoke out, expressing their anger over courts they perceived as too lenient and judges who often let criminals go free. A majority of the callers said Goetz had done the right thing. Evidently, that sentiment prevailed when Goetz's case came to trial, as he was acquitted of attempted murder.

Another issue that came to the forefront in the 1980s was one that the media weren't sure how to handle: acquired immunodeficiency syndrome, or AIDS. Because this new illness was originally considered a gay disease at a time when homophobia was still rampant in society, it was not discussed much in the early 1980s. Then, several celebrities, notably movie star Rock Hudson, acknowledged having the disease. When the news of Hudson's illness broke in July 1985, it led to a desire for more factual information. One other story that put a more sympathetic face on the illness was that of Ryan White, a thirteen-year-old hemophiliac from Kokomo, Indiana, who had contracted AIDS from a blood transfusion. There was little reliable information about AIDS. Nobody knew how contagious it was, and people didn't want to take chances. Suddenly, Ryan White's school barred him from attending. ABC-TV's *This Week With David Brinkley* was among the first shows to talk about AIDS and provide as much accurate information as was then available. In mid-September 1985, Brinkley had a panel discussion featuring educators, doctors, and Ryan White's attorney. Continuing media coverage of Ryan's situation followed him as he finally was allowed to go back to school, but his classmates refused to sit near him and parents kept their kids at home rather than be where he was. Two years later, there was sufficient knowledge about AIDS that when he attended a new school, he was welcomed. He was also the subject of an educational program on New York City's WNET, produced by the Children's Television Workshop. The program featured Ryan discussing how AIDS had affected his life and answering questions from New York City schoolchildren. Unfortunately, there were few discussions about how AIDS affected gay people, and it would take some time for most TV talk shows to tackle the subject. Notable exceptions were Phil Donahue and Geraldo Rivera, both of whom had talked about it in the early 1980s, a time when few radio or TV shows even mentioned its existence. By the 1990s, Oprah Winfrey, Latina talk show host Cristina Saralegui, and numerous others were doing heroic work to raise awareness. But in the mid-1980s, for the most part, talkers came to rely on Ryan White when they wanted to discuss AIDS. In early April 1990, Ryan died at age eighteen. More than fifteen hundred people, many of whom had seen him on TV, attended the memorial.

Another example of how the culture was changing was that more shows were featuring minorities. The Spanish-language network Univision was being watched by a growing number of viewers, and two of its most popular shows were talk, *Cristina*, hosted by Cristina Saralegui and *Sábado Gigante*, hosted by a veteran variety show star who used the pseudonym Don Francisco. Then in January 1989, Arsenio Hall, a talented African American comedian, got a new syndicated show on late night TV, the *Arsenio Hall Show*. Hall had been one of the hosts on Fox Television's *Late Show*, when the network made its debut in the mid 1980s, but few people watched. However, his talent attracted enough attention so that he co-starred in a movie with comedian Eddie Murphy, "Coming to America," and now he had his own show, something he had dreamed about since he was a child. Hall was stylish, young, and not crude like the trash TV hosts. Eloquent and personable, he could also be sarcastic or talk in the language of young people, who started watching his show and began to emulate some of his expressions. When he wanted applause for a guest, for example, he would say, "Give it up for ___," and when he wanted people to cheer loudly, he would raise his fist in the air and make a circular motion, while uttering a sound that resembled "woop, woop, woop." Politicians who wanted to reach the young audience started dropping by, including presidential candidate Bill Clinton, who played the saxophone on Arsenio's show in 1992. At its height, Hall's syndicated show was seen on more than 150 stations before it was canceled in 1994.

While people who listened to talk radio in the late 1980s and early 1990s might not have known the reason, the fact remained that the end of the Fairness Doctrine had led to a proliferation of opinionated and entirely one-sided talk shows, most of which were conservative. Media critics and scholars wondered why talk radio had embraced the conservative viewpoint. One study from the Times Mirror Center for People and the Press determined that compared to liberals, "conservatives [were] more likely to listen to talk radio and more likely to call talk shows." And exit polls from the 1992 presidential election showed that frequent listeners to talk radio voted overwhelmingly for Republicans. Other studies suggested that conservatives perceived themselves as the "little guy" fighting against an uncaring bureaucratic government. That "us versus them" way of looking at the issues worked well for talk hosts; they encouraged listeners to tell their story and express their frustration, as others who felt the same way nodded in agreement. It was easier to do right-wing talk radio, according to this theory, since conservatives preferred to discuss issues in black and white, whereas liberals had a more nuanced viewpoint. Where talk stations of the 1960s and 1970s had both right wing and left wing shows, by the mid 1990s, more than 95 percent of talk hosts were identifiably conservative. Interestingly, studies showed that most listeners to talk radio in the 1980s and 1990s were convinced that the mainstream media were dominated by liberals, an assertion that was repeated over and over by the right-wing talk hosts.

But not all talk radio was political. More and more AM radio stations were finding that sports talk was a big success for them. In early January 1992, the now-successful cable TV network ESPN launched a radio network, featuring some of the most popular hosts from ESPN-TV. Among the unique personalities who broadcast on ESPN radio was Nancy Donnellan, better known by the name of her alter ego the "Fabulous Sports Babe." She was one of the few women doing sports talk, and at the height of her success in the mid-1990s, her syndicated show was heard on about two hundred stations nationally.

The 1990s were an excellent time for both local and syndicated sports talk. Stations doing the sports talk format usually broadcast the games of at least one of the major local teams and also gave fans the chance to voice their opinions on both local and national sports, whether college or professional. A number of stations changed to this format. For example, in Dallas–Fort Worth, there was KTCK ("The Ticket"), which began broadcasting sports talk in 1994. The station's popular morning show, featuring longtime friends George Dunham and Craig Miller (also known as "The Musers"), debuted in 1995 and was still getting excellent ratings in 2008. Given how passionate fans are about sports, they often develop a strong bond with certain hosts. Radio has historically been known for replacing announcers after only a short amount of time, so it is remarkable that some sports talkers have remained at the same station for years. Another good example of this longevity is Sports-Radio WEEI, the first station in Boston to use the sports-talk format, beginning in 1991. Among its most popular programs is the *Big Show*, featuring former Boston Celtics basketball play-by-play announcer Glenn Ordway and a regular cast of sidekicks, sports journalists, and guests, as well as a feature called the "Whiner Line" (where fans call in to make humorous comments and complaints about the games or the athletes). Ordway joined WEEI at its inception in 1991 and created the *Big Show* in 1995. In 2008, the show was more popular than ever. On several occasions, Ordway has been nominated for a Marconi award, given annually by the National Association of Broadcasters to the best announcer in each format.

As the 1990s continued, so did the mergers. In late July 1995, the Walt Disney Company purchased Capital Cities/ABC, and Westinghouse Electric was ready to buy CBS, which got FCC approval in December. By mid-June 1996, Westinghouse was about to purchase Infinity Broadcasting, giving the rapidly expanding company more than eighty stations. What happened next surprised media historians. In late 1997, Westinghouse, a company that had been around since the birth of commercial broadcasting in 1920, changed its name to CBS Corporation. A company that had once been a manufacturer of radio receivers, with plants and studios located in Pittsburgh, Chicago, Springfield, Massachusetts, and Newark, New Jersey, was now a major conglomerate with a new name and nationwide reach. And its acquisitions were not finished. In 1998, CBS Corporation purchased American Radio Systems, giving it ninety more stations. While all of these mergers and acquisitions were good for shareholders and broadcast executives, media critics worried that permitting so many mergers was leading to the death of local radio. To effectively serve a local community cost money, and some companies believed it would be much cheaper to use big-name syndicated hosts from other cities. During the 1990s, that was exactly what happened in many cities. Also worrisome to critics of deregulation was that practices like "voice tracking" had become common; instead of a live on-air disc jockey, new technology allowed the giant companies to save money by having announcers at one station record the stations breaks and other chat, and then transmit all of it to numerous other stations. Voice tracking gave the illusion of live personalities when in fact everything was recorded ahead of time, in another city.

Congress moved ahead to deregulate broadcasting even further. The Telecommunications Act of 1996 eliminated many of the remaining ownership rules and paved the way for behemoths like Clear Channel Communications to own over a thousand stations nationwide. As critics accused the conglomerates of further eliminating local programming, this turned out to be good news for the talkers, especially those whose specialty was sports or politics. While many of their shows were syndicated (at one point, Rush Limbaugh was heard on more than six hundred stations nationwide), at least they were usually live, and most had a toll-free number so that listeners from anywhere could call in. In fact, syndicated talk had been growing, with the addition of new networks such as TRN, the Talk Radio Network, which began offering its predominantly conservative lineup in 1993.

In early October 1996, the Fox News Channel, the first identifiably right-wing television network, went on the air. Using the slogan "fair and balanced," it presented itself as an alternative to the allegedly biased liberal media, especially CNN. Since its inception in 1980, CNN had become both profitable and respected. Once jokingly called the Chicken Noodle Network for its low-budget in its early years, its conservative critics later called it the Clinton News Network for a perceived bias in favor of Bill Clinton and the Democrats. CNN always denied this bias, insisting its coverage was objective and accurate. The network pointed with pride to its outstanding coverage of the first Gulf War, Operation Desert Storm, in 1990–1991, when reporters like John Holliman, Peter Arnett, and anchor Bernard Shaw were often the only newspeople with access to the story. After CNN had had no real competition for years, the arrival of Fox News was regarded by critics as something that would make both news networks better. Few predicted that Fox, with its visibly conservative slant, would overtake CNN and come to dominate the cable news ratings the way conservative talk hosts had come to dominate radio. And while nearly every host on Fox was conservative, there was one who was liberal—Alan Colmes. A veteran radio talk host in New York who once thought about a career as a stand-up comic, Colmes was paired on Fox News with an unabashed conservative, Sean Hannity. Hannity had grown up listening to radio talkers like Barry Gray, but it was the rise to power of

Ronald Reagan that influenced him the most. He began doing conservative-oriented talk, first working in the South, and ultimately returning to New York City (like Colmes, Hannity had grown up on Long Island). He developed friendships with major stars in the Republican party, and being able to get them for interviews on his talk show helped advance his career. In addition to the successful Hannity and Colmes TV show that debuted in 1996, both men also began doing solo radio talk shows.

The 1990s saw the arrival of a number of new talk hosts, as well as a few old ones who reinvented themselves. Two of its most respected veteran hosts were on PBS, which remained a haven for viewers who wanted literate talk shows without celebrity gossip—Bill Moyers and Charlie Rose. A political liberal and a vocal advocate for issues involving social justice, Moyers, had once been the press secretary for President Lyndon Johnson. His long career included first joining PBS in 1970, leaving for CBS news in 1976, and then returning to PBS in the late 1980s. He won critical acclaim for his in-depth investigative reports on *Bill Moyers Journal*, focusing on such topics as poverty in America, political corruption, and presidential politics. As a talk show host, he did a number of PBS specials on current events during the 1980s, and in early 1990, hosted a talk and interview program called *A World of Ideas*, and continued to do award-winning specials for PBS before hosting a controversial newsmagazine show in 2002. *Now with Bill Moyers* featured harsh criticism of President George W. Bush and his administration, and while liberals felt the show was courageous and factual, conservatives attacked it for being biased.

For a while in the mid-1970s, Moyers's executive producer had been Charlie Rose, who first hosted a talk show while working in Dallas, Texas, in the early 1980s. Rose, a veteran reporter and political correspondent, continued to host TV talk shows during the mid-1980s, but they were low-rated and few people were aware of his work. That changed in early 1993, when he finally got a show that won him a sizable group of fans. Known for his erudite style, Rose debuted on a late night PBS show, *Charlie Rose*. Actually, more of an interview show than a talk show, it still showcased the host's ability to ask tough questions while remaining courteous to his guests.

But neither courtesy nor civility were hallmarks of the new breed of radio talkers. They continued to be opinionated, controversial, and usually conservative. In addition to the previously mentioned *Sean Hannity Show*, one of the most successful, as well as one of the most controversial conservative talkers was Michael Savage. He was already a best-selling author of health books under his real name (Michael Weiner), and his radio show *Savage Nation* went on the air in San Francisco as a fill-in in early 1994. By January 1995, he had his own show, and by 1999, he was syndicated nationally. Savage has consistently been accused by his critics of being a bigot, a homophobe, and a hatemonger. He has also been a fierce opponent of liberals, authoring a 2005 best-selling book entitled *Liberalism is a Mental Disorder*.

Another talker who had a long career on the air had once been considered a liberal. By the mid-1990s, Tom Leykis was known mainly as a shock jock whose specialty was misogyny. His blunt and often crude show, which was syndicated from Los Angeles by Westwood One, was aimed exclusively at men: *Leykis 101* had the attitude that women served one purpose and only one—sex. Leykis presented techniques for men to use to persuade women to have sex, and he expressed the belief that because women are a distraction to a man's career, there is no reason for men to ever get married. Leykis has used as his slogan "He says what you're thinking."

As for other shock jocks, the 1990s were still looking good for Howard Stern. He had left AM radio once and for all in the mid-1980s and had been hired by the New York City FM station WXRK. Before long he was being heard in syndication in Washington, DC, and Philadelphia, and by 1991, his morning show was syndicated in Los Angeles as well. In each market, he far exceeded expectations, although he continued to upset his critics with his vulgar language and the sexually suggestive content of his show. At one point in 1992, his parent company, Infinity Broadcasting, was fined six hundred thousand dollars by the FCC, but he remained such a money maker for Infinity that company president Mel Karmazin seemed completely unconcerned. He told a reporter that the FCC's efforts to clamp down on Stern were simply making more people tune in to see what the fuss was about. A one-minute commercial on his show cost three thousand dollars, and advertisers were lining up. In the early 1990s, Stern remained number one in New York, with the largest audience of any morning show. In 1997, stations in Toronto and Montreal experimented with broadcasting his syndicated show, but their efforts ran into trouble. Canadian indecency laws were much stricter than in the United States, and that caused his show to be canceled.

Another interesting change seemed at first to have nothing to do with radio or TV. In 1990, a British computer engineer named Tim Berners-Lee created what came to be known as the World Wide Web. Computers had been used for military communication since 1969, the inception of ARPA-NET, the Advanced Research Projects Agency, which was developed by the U.S. Defense Department. Since then, there had been ongoing efforts to create a network that allowed anyone, not just members of the military, to communicate by computer, but before the mid-1980s, no-easy-to-use system was available to the average person. The term *Internet* came into use around 1974, and thanks in large part to the work of computer scientist Vinton Cerf of Stanford University, it enabled the general public to begin logging on, although in the 1970s and most of the 1980s, the vast majority of users were at universities. It was Berners-Lee whose innovations allowed general usage, including sharing graphics, browsing Web pages, and other activities that seemed amazing in the mid-1990s in the same way that radio had seemed amazing in 1920. By the mid-1990s, average people who knew nothing about computers were able to "surf the Web," as home computer use had risen from single digits in the mid-1980s to forty percent and climbing at the end of 1995. Home computers and personal Web pages continued to proliferate, and it seemed that everyone was sending e-mail. By 1998, many radio and TV stations had created their own Web pages. The web had become a promotional device, used by media companies, advertisers, and individual announcers, as well as a way of keeping in touch with the audience, as stations started to have polls and contests to encourage audience response. Many stations also began to use streaming audio, which meant that people could listen to a program on their computers.

With the growing popularity of the Internet came concerns that children might be exposed to indecent material. The Communications Decency Act was passed by congress in early 1996 It was a bipartisan effort to regulate indecency and obscenity online, based on a belief that Internet pornography was on the rise and readily available to children. Despite its good intentions, the bill seemed to criminalize language: If a novel that contained curse words was posted to the Internet, was the person who posted it guilty of transmitting obscene material? The definition of indecent material appeared to be open to interpretation, so it became a freedom-of-speech issue, and the American Civil Liberties Union sued to have the law overturned. The U.S. Supreme Court agreed that the law was excessively vague, and struck it down, but the battle over indecency has continued.

In the 1990s, political satire was enjoying new freedom, thanks to cable TV. *Saturday Night Live* was still on the air, having endured many cast changes yet continuing to reinvent itself. An interesting new trend in talk shows emerged in the late 1990s: Comedians whose specialty was social satire began to do "fake news" shows. These shows offered political commentary similar to that on *Saturday Night Live*, but the emphasis was entirely on current events. In a mock-serious style, the hosts covered the big stories as if they were actually doing a newscast, except they used humor—parody, irony, and sarcasm—to make their point. Since these fake news shows were on cable TV, which didn't have to worry about the FCC's supervision as the broadcast networks did, the material could be more controversial. And it often was.

The best known of the fake news shows is the *Daily Show* on a cable channel called Comedy Central. The *Daily Show* made its debut in July 1996, hosted by Craig Kilborn, but it began achieving its continuing success when a former stand-up comic and MTV host named Jon Stewart took over in early 1999. With his team of fake correspondents, who do satiric impressions of "typical" news reporters and pundits, Stewart also does a nightly segment during which he interviews newsmakers. The *Daily Show* makes fun of the excesses of both political parties and takes on subjects like the war in Iraq and the presidential elections. The show also uses parody to name individual segments. During the 2000 presidential campaign, the coverage was called "Indecision 2000" many local and network news shows had begun referring to their presidential election coverage as "Decision 2000." The coverage of the war in Iraq is headlined "Mess O'Potamia", referring to the consensus that the war has been badly handled, and making a pun on the historical name of the region, Mesopotamia. Known for his sly and ironic sense of humor, Stewart is especially popular with the eighteen- to twenty-four-year-old demographic that advertisers eagerly seek. Research studies have shown that young adults, who have not generally been interested in traditional newscasts, find the *Daily Show* both amusing and informative.

One of Stewart's correspondents, Stephen Colbert, left the *Daily Show* in 2005 to host his own program of fake news. His program is called the *Colbert Report* (with the *T* at the end of both words silent and pronounced in a faux-French style, *Col-BAIR Re-POR*). He models his character on a traditional right-wing conservative host; many fans are sure he is doing a parody of Fox News host Bill O'Reilly. Unlike Stewart, who generally does a conversational interview with the guest, Colbert stays in character, often badgering or criticizing guests whose views are "too liberal."

On the late-night talk shows, the question about who would replace Johnny Carson was finally answered. It was Jay Leno who took over the show when Carson retired in 1992. Leno's comedy rival and then-friend David Letterman believed the job should have been his, and after more than a decade with NBC, he left for his own show on CBS in 1993. By all accounts, Leno and Letterman stopped being friends at this point. In other TV talk changes, NBC's late-late show went to Conan O'Brien in September 1993. O'Brien is a former writer for *Saturday Night Live*, *The Simpsons*, and other TV shows, and while his show was slow to build an audience, it gradually improved and by the early 2000s, it was doing so well that O'Brien was being suggested as the next *The Tonight Show* host, when Jay Leno retires.

Another popular talk show on TV made an immediate impression when it went on the air in August 1997: *The View* is a daytime talk show on ABC-TV, similar to Virginia Graham's 1960s show *Girl Talk*. (Barbara Walters said that show was one of her influences.) *The View* features what *New York Times* critic Nancy Hass described in 1998 as "an unscripted kaffeeklatsch with five bright, brash women, representing different generations . . . " Led by the veteran interviewer and former newswoman Barbara Walters, every day the ladies, along with their guests, sit around a table talking—about their lives (including their sex life), about current events, about movies they have seen, and so on. Viewers cannot predict which direction the conversation may take. Meanwhile, Oprah Winfrey had established herself as the dominant daytime talk show host, having begun a syndicated show in 1986 and never looking back. By the late 1990s, she had had so many successes—as a movie and TV producer and actress, a philanthropist, an advocate for children's issues, and the host of her highly rated program—that she was considered one of the most influential women in the United States. She keeps her finger on the pulse of society, adapting her show to every new trend, anticipating what her viewers want, and reinventing the show when needed.

Also good for the talk shows were some events that evoked a very strong response from the audience, among them the revelation of a sexual affair between President Clinton and an intern named Monica Lewinsky in early 1998 and the subsequent effort by the Republican-controlled House of Representatives to impeach the president. Despite the best efforts of conservative talk radio to demonize Bill Clinton, opinion polls showed that he remained very popular with a majority of Americans, although certainly tainted by the scandal.

The contentious subject of race was also in the news and on the talk shows on a number of occasions. In March 1991 a black motorist named Rodney King was beaten by Los Angeles police officers who said he was resisting arrest. A bystander with a video camera recorded the incident and sent the video to the media, which replayed it constantly. Black viewers, and many white viewers as well, believed it showed clear evidence of police brutality, but in April 1992, an all-white jury acquitted the four officers, saying they had been justified in subduing King.

Another polarizing case that generated much discussion was the 1995 trial of former football star O. J. Simpson, accused of murdering his wife, Nicole, and her friend Ron Goldman, and found not guilty despite what many people felt was overwhelming evidence against him. This verdict showed that America was still divided along racial lines, with most whites believing he had gotten away with murder and most blacks believing he was really innocent.

Teenage violence was also a subject of discussion, especially after the 1999 school shooting at Columbine High School in Littleton, Colorado, when two students, Eric Harris and Dylan Klebold, went on a rampage, during which they murdered twelve and wounded twenty-three others before killing themselves. Talk shows, as often happens after such a tragedy, brought out the experts, who blamed everything from video games to bad parenting to bullying (the two killers had been bullied at school) to easy access to guns. The truth was that nobody truly understood youth violence, but talk show discussions seemed to provide some catharsis for the public.

Another story from the 1990s that wasn't about race or sex or teen violence but had a profound effect on the public conversation: the death of Great Britain's thirty-six-year-old Princess Diana, Princess of Wales, in an auto accident in August 1997. She had been the object of celebrity watchers for years, due to her marriage to Prince Charles; their wedding in 1981 had been presented as fairy-tale, but when the marriage later fell apart, amid rumors of Charles's infidelity, the public became aware of how unhappy Diana had been. More than just a princess in a failed marriage, Diana became a media celebrity, an object of public fascination: wherever she went, whomever she dated, photographers persisted in following her, as any details of her life were scrutinized and discussed on the entertainment shows. Diana was an important figure in the popular culture. She was often called the "people's princess" because she was approachable, and became known for her charitable work. When she died, every U.S. network and most talk shows covered the unfolding events, from the investigation into the car crash to the lavish funeral ceremony. When she was laid to rest, an audience of two billion people worldwide watched.

Of course, the 1990s were not just about matters of life and death. As mentioned earlier, it was during the 1990s that sports talk really came into its own. It may never be known which radio station did the first all-sports-talk format, but most historians credit the arrival of New York City's WFAN ("The Fan") in July 1987 with bringing sports talk to the forefront. The 1990s saw a dramatic increase in the number of sports-talk stations, especially on AM radio. If Rush Limbaugh had helped to bring the audience back to AM, the sports-talk format did its share as well. In 1992, for the first time, a team from Canada, the Toronto Blue Jays, won baseball's World Series, a feat they repeated in 1993. Unfortunately, a baseball strike in 1994 weakened fan support, but it also gave the sports-talk stations plenty to discuss. The epic home-run race in 1998 brought the fans back in a major way: Mark McGwire of the St. Louis Cardinals and Sammy Sosa of the Chicago Cubs were two power hitters trying to beat Roger Maris's record of sixty-one home runs in one season. Both did, with seventy for McGwire and sixty-six for Sosa. A few years later, there would be accusations about the use of steroids and other performance-enhancing drugs, but in 1998, baseball fans were delighted to see so many home runs.

People were also talking about an amazing record that had nothing to do with sports: John Glenn, the former astronaut and U.S. senator, returned to space in 1998, at the age of seventy-seven.

As the century came to a close, more people were online, and the Internet became a major factor in how people communicated. It seemed that the world was in fact getting smaller. As sociologist Marshall McLuhan had once predicted, it was more of a global village, with satellites and twenty-four-hour news and the World Wide Web making it possible for people from all over the world to be in touch. But few Americans could predict that the next several years would be among the most turbulent in America since World War II.

9/11 AND ITS AFTERMATH

In a country that had become very polarized since the Republicans took over congress and Bill Clinton was nearly impeached, the outcome of the presidential election of 2000 was highly controversial. Vice President Al Gore, a Democrat, won the popular vote, but George W. Bush claimed to have won the electoral vote, in an election marred by accusations of voter fraud and a lingering belief on the part of Democrats that Gore had been cheated out of the presidency by Republican "dirty tricks." Many books and journal articles were written after the election, dissecting what had taken place, but in the end, it was the U.S. Supreme Court that stopped the recount of the votes in Florida (the state whose electoral votes decided the election) and awarded the presidency to Mr. Bush. Because the governor of Florida was Bush's brother Jeb, and because there were some documented irregularities in counting the votes, Democrats were never satisfied with those results, but there was nothing they could do.

The Congress and now the presidency were in Republican hands. Conservative talk shows were understandably jubilant, but the mood in America was about to change unexpectedly, due to the events of what came to be called 9/11. On the morning of 11 September 2001, nineteen Muslim terrorists hijacked airplanes and perpetrated the largest terrorist attack on American soil. In a coordinated suicide mission, they crashed the airplanes into the twin towers of the World Trade Center in New York City, while a third airliner hit the Pentagon in Washington, DC. A fourth airliner did not reach its destination (which was assumed to be the White House) because some passengers fought with the hijackers and brought down the plane in a rural area in Pennsylvania. All nineteen hijackers died, as did close to three thousand Americans. For several days after the attack, radio and TV suspended regular programming for news and talk. Even music-oriented stations cut back on entertainment to concentrate on conversation. The result was very much like an ongoing town meeting of the air, and it provided some catharsis for millions of Americans. It was soon determined that Osama Bin Laden, a radical Muslim with a hatred of the West, had orchestrated the attacks through an organization called Al Qaeda. Fifteen of the nineteen hijackers were from Saudi Arabia, two were from United Arab Emirates, and one each was from Egypt and Lebanon. None were from Iraq.

At the time of the tragedy, the world reached out to America. Countries that had been considered America's enemies expressed regret at what had happened. Candlelight vigils were held, and prayers were said worldwide. People in the United States who disliked President Bush or thought he had won the election unfairly rallied around him as the commander in chief. America was united. But the unity would be brief.

As patriotic fervor swept America, people awaited the response to those who had perpetrated the tragedy. Believing that Al Qaeda was operating from Afghanistan, the president and a coalition of international forces went into that country and removed the Taliban, a dictatorial and repressive government that had been been in power. The goal was to capture Bin Laden and bring him to justice. To that point, most Americans were comfortable with what was being done. But at the same time, the Bush administration declared a War on Terror and, in doing so, began to implement policies that led to what his critics believed were a drastic curtailment of Americans' civil liberties. At first, caught up in the shock and horror of the events of 9/11, most people gave the president the benefit of the doubt. But something else was happening: Members of the Administration were starting to make remarks about Saddam Hussein, the Iraqi dictator, trying to link him with 9/11. The mainstream media would later be accused of failing to challenge the president's assertions. Conservative talk radio didn't challenge them either. On the Internet, a new phenomenon was slowly emerging, but it was too new to be much of a factor in 2001: It was called blogging (*blog* was the short version of *Web log*, a sort of Internet diary), and it would gradually make an impact on talk radio.

In mid-March 2003, the president began the invasion of Iraq, allegedly because Saddam Hussein had weapons of mass destruction, as well as because the administration, especially Vice President Cheney, linked him with 9/11, an assertion for which there had never been credible proof. Only the British were part of what was called the Coalition of the Willing, although a few other countries offered minimal numbers of troops for the invasion. Unlike the first Gulf War in 1991 which was widely supported, this war was puzzling, since the hijackers were from countries that America didn't try to penalize at all. The conservative talk shows cheered the president on, but the few dissenters, mostly from what were considered "left wing" magazines and a few liberal Web sites, had no effective way to express themselves. In fact, dissenters were being called traitors, and some music stations even went so far as to remove all antiwar songs from their playlists. Saddam Hussein was deposed quickly, and many who had suffered under his brutal regime were happy. But an unanticipated resistance movement arose, and suddenly, it looked as if American troops were in the middle of a civil war, both factions being resentful that a foreign (Western) power was occupying their land. As American and British soldiers were being killed by suicide bombs and roadside explosives, what had been justified to the American public as a quick and painless war of liberation became a long and dangerous stay that seemed to allow no easy way out.

At first, the mainstream media had been supportive of the invasion. Now there were bloggers and liberal web commentators, part of what was being called the "alternative media," since they provided what they felt was an opposing viewpoint to that of the mainstream media. Web sites and Web magazines were all suggesting that the president had misled the American people. A number of possible reasons for attacking Iraq were offered, but what all on the political left agreed on was that they needed some talk shows of their own. Of course, forgetting the successful talk hosts from the 1960s who were liberal and had good ratings, the common wisdom insisted that liberal talk shows had never succeeded. In addition, the Democrats had realized far too late how important talk radio could be, and by the time they did realize, most of the major stations were dominated by right-wing hosts. Still, a number of liberals (some of whom preferred to be called *progressives* since the right wing had demonized the word *liberal*) decided to pool their resources and put a liberal network on the air. Some of the planning began in 2003, but the network did not come to fruition until 2004. It was named Air America Radio, and it debuted on 31 March 2004.

The best known performer on the new network was Al Franken, a comedian who had been a writer and performer on *Saturday Night Live* during its formative years (1975–1980). Air America hoped to provide what its founders felt was a much-needed alternative to the right-wing point of view. Unfortunately, there were problems almost immediately. The new network was able to get its programming on a number of stations; however, the majority of these stations had either weak signals or were in smaller cities. Most of the hosts had no radio experience, even though they had been performers. Also, the original owners didn't have the money they had said they had, and rumors of paychecks bouncing were leaked to the media. Needless to say, the conservative talkers found all of this amusing. But for those who had long been waiting for talk show hosts who shared their point of view, the arrival of Air America, even with its problems, was very welcome.

Air America continued to experience growing pains, but several of its hosts, notably Rachel Maddow, Randi Rhodes, and Al Franken, developed a following, getting interesting guests and providing the audience with a forum for discussing everything they felt was wrong with the Bush administration. Meanwhile, another group of Democrats and progressives had decided to try to put their own liberal programming on the air. They held some tryouts for a talk show host they could develop and then syndicate, and they chose a former conservative from Fargo, North Dakota, Ed Schultz. Deciding not to put a network on the air, they found a syndicator: the Jones Radio Network. Schultz, a moderate with strong liberal leanings on issues like workers' rights, did his first progressive talk show on 5 January 2004. He began on only two stations, but by October 2005, he was on nearly a hundred. An experienced talk show host who also had a background in sales, he did not experience some of the growing pains that beset the Air America hosts, and within a year, his show was turning a profit, something the right-wing talkers had insisted could never happen.

As the war in Iraq dragged on, and as many of the policies of the Bush administration began to be questioned even by some on the right, progressive talk lasted longer than its detractors thought it would. Air America, with a number of personnel changes, was still on the air, and the Jones Radio Network had picked up several other progressive talk hosts to syndicate, although most of its lineup remained overwhelmingly conservative. Ed Schultz had far exceeded expectations, even becoming sufficiently well known to be called on by CNN and other networks to be a pundit; Rachel Maddow of Air America made a similar impression and was also frequently seen on TV talk shows when a liberal counterbalance to the conservative point of view was being sought. By 2008, she had been named a regular commentator on cable network MSNBC, where she provided critiques of current administration policy.

Although it took time for the nation to get back to some sense of normality, talk shows had been a big help during the most difficult time after 9/11, and in the remainder of the decade, there would be a number of controversial events involving talk. One was an on-air feud between right-wing commentator Bill O'Reilly of the Fox News Channel and his arch rival Keith Olbermann, a liberal commentator on MSNBC. Olbermann had been a sports reporter before finding himself radicalized by what he felt was unfair treatment by

Republicans of President Clinton. He was further outraged by the actions of the Bush administration and began doing a nightly news and commentary show called *Countdown*, during which he sometimes presented extended opinion pieces called "Special Comments." These editorials were caustic and highly critical of the administration. He was also highly critical of O'Reilly, who had a large and passionate following, and whom Olbermann regarded as a right-wing shill and a hypocrite. O'Reilly vehemently disagreed with that assessment; he saw himself as an independent populist, someone who was unafraid to tell the truth, no matter who was in power. By all accounts, the two genuinely dislike each other, and their sniping at each other on the air during their shows has been good for the ratings of each of them. The 2000s were also when one well-known TV talk host decided to put his successful news and opinion show on radio: historically, most radio stars migrated to TV, but Lou Dobbs of CNN decided that a radio version of his show could work, and in late 2007, he announced that he would do a syndicated radio show as of early 2008. Doing both a TV and a radio show has also been successful for several talkers: the previously mentioned Sean Hannity, and another Fox News star, Bill O'Reilly. The *O'Reilly Factor* gets big ratings for Fox, while a radio show called the *Radio Factor* is syndicated by Westwood One.

While most radio and television talk shows are well rehearsed, sometimes there are unscripted moments of controversy. One such incident erupted on *The View*. The popular women's show had already experienced several changes of personnel, which were not unusual for talk shows. But the arrival of comedian (and former talk show host) Rosie O'Donnell in 2006 changed the dynamics of the show. Rosie wanted to talk politics much more than previous participants, and she was very outspoken. A vocal critic of the Bush administration, she was immediately at odds with Elisabeth Hasselbeck, whose politics were conservative and who, as a born-again Christian, often found Rosie vulgar and tactless. The early years of the twenty-first century had seen the growth of YouTube, a popular site where fans could post video to be seen by people all over the world. Some YouTube video was homemade, with a would-be star lip-synching to a dance hit or pretending to be Spiderman, but equally common were snippets from the talk shows, especially controversial snippets. A number of interactions between O'Donnell and Hasselbeck were played over and over on YouTube, such as a segment in which O'Donnell seemed to be attacking organized religion. This received a lot of attention, and not necessarily the kind Rosie wanted. She became the topic of conversation on the right-wing talk shows and blogs. The show's ratings went up, but the constant controversies took a toll, and in late May 2007, Rosie asked to be let out of her contract.

Another TV talk show that made an impact early in the new century starred comedian Ellen DeGeneres, the first lesbian to host a television talk show. (Ellen had revealed her lesbianism while a guest on the Oprah Winfrey show in 1997.) It was a sign of how moderate society had become that neither viewers nor sponsors were at all deterred by DeGeneres's open lesbianism. (On the other hand, Rosie O'Donnell, who had done her own syndicated TV talk show from June 1996 to May 2002, did not discuss her lesbianism until she published a memoir in 2002 called *Find Me*, after her talk show had ended.) Ellen's show debuted in September 2003 and got good enough ratings to be renewed for another year, and since then, the show has become increasingly popular. Audiences find Ellen amusing and entertaining. Like Dinah Shore from 1950s she often does a song-and-dance routine, and like Dinah, she seems to be a woman who genuinely enjoys entertaining the public.

Sports-talk shows have also continued to be as popular on TV as they are on radio. One influential show is on ESPN: *Jim Rome Is Burning* (formerly called just *Rome Is Burning*), which went on the network in early May 2003, featuring sports talk, opinion, and guests. Rome is known for being outspoken and for using his own set of expressions and phrases, called *smack*, to express his views on certain players. For those who are new to his show, his Web site has a "smacktionary," which lists some of his most popular phrases, such as referring to a certain baseball manager as "Chernobyl" because of his explosive temper and tendency to "melt down," or referring to a male basketball player by a female name, indicating that the player doesn't act sufficiently tough and whines too much. Rome also has a nationally syndicated ESPN radio show, which is heard on over two hundred affiliates.

Since the early 1920s, talk shows have shaped America's public discourse, giving people something to think about or exposing them to new perspectives. They have created a sense of family, making people feel included by letting their opinions be heard. Whether it's the kind of show where an opinionated host stirs people up, a show where people can hear what the rich and famous have to say, or a show where people discuss what bothers them, talk shows continue to matter. Society may change, the issues may change, but the need to talk it all over remains constant, year after year.

FURTHER READING

Brooks, Tim, and Earl Marsh. *Complete Directory to Prime Time Network and Cable TV Shows, 1946–Present, 9th ed.* New York: Ballantine Books, 2007.

Gwinn, Alison, Ed. *Entertainment Weekly: The 100 Greatest TV Shows of All Time.* New York: Time-Life Books, 1998.

Hilmes, Michele. *Only Connect: A Cultural History of Broadcasting in the United States.* Beverly, MA: Wadsworth, 2002.

Klinenberg, Eric. *Fighting for Air: The Battle to Control America's Media.* New York: Metropolitan Books, 2007.

Media Research Library, University of California at Berkeley. Transcript of broadcast. Available at http://lib.berkeley.edu/murrowmccarthy.html.

Munson, Wayne. *All Talk: The Talkshow in Media Culture.* Philadelphia: Temple University Press, 1993.

Sterling, Christopher, and John Michael Kittross. *Stay Tuned: A History of American Broadcasting*, 3rd ed. Mahwah, NJ: Erlbaum, 2002.

Part 2

The Icons

AP Photo

Steve Allen

It wouldn't be an exaggeration to call Steve Allen the father of late-night television. At a time when late-night TV shows were almost unheard of, Allen's pioneering work on *The Tonight Show* in the early 1950s set the standard for
future hosts. Some of his innovations, such as the opening monologue and
walking around with a microphone to talk to the audience (and even going
outside to talk to strangers), would become staples of late-night comedy shows.
But Steve Allen did them first. He came to television as a comedian, having first
performed on radio in Phoenix and Los Angeles during the late 1940s. But it
was his work as a TV talk show host that would later be emulated by other
talk show hosts such as Jack Paar, Johnny Carson, and Jay Leno. With his talent for the quip and the one-liner and his ability to parody almost anything in
popular culture from a song to another TV show, Steve Allen made his audience
think as well as laugh. And at a time when network executives doubted that a
late-night show could be profitable, the *The Tonight Show* quickly developed a
large and loyal following. After he left *The Tonight Show* to host other network
variety programs and even do an award-winning educational series for PBS,
Allen continued to be a popular vocalist, a songwriter, an actor, and an author,
in a career that lasted more than fifty years.

EARLY YEARS

Steve Allen's real name was Stephen Valentine Patrick William Allen, and he
was born in New York City on 26 December 1921. His parents, Carroll
"Billy" Allen and Isabelle Donahue (known professionally as Belle Montrose),
were both entertainers who had worked in vaudeville as a comedy duo. His
father died when Steve was only eighteen months old, and his mother went
back out on the road as a performer. Steve was raised by his mother's family,
whom he later described as "sarcastic, volatile, sometimes disparaging, but
very, very funny" (Severo, 2000, p. B13) And to make matters even more interesting, sometimes his mother would come back and take him out on the road
with her. Among his babysitters while she performed was comedian Milton
Berle. Allen's childhood was never dull, but it wasn't very stable either: By the
time he was in high school, he had attended at least sixteen different schools.
   It was while Allen was attending high school in Chicago that some early
indications of his talent first surfaced. He wrote poetry, and the *Chicago Tribune* published several of his poems. He also developed a love of jazz and
became a fan of such big-band stars as the Dorsey Brothers and Benny Goodman (later in his career, Allen would portray Goodman in a movie biography). After graduating from Chicago's Hyde Park High School in 1941, he
briefly studied journalism at Drake University in Des Moines, Iowa, but
because he suffered from asthma, he needed a warmer climate. In 1942, he
and his mother moved to Arizona, where he attended Arizona State Teacher's
College (today known as Arizona State University) in Tempe. Performing was

in his blood, however: He dropped out of college to go into radio, taking a job as an announcer at KOY in Phoenix. His radio career was interrupted by World War II; the army drafted him in 1943, but due to frequent asthma attacks, he was given an early release. Recalling that period of his life, he wrote in 1960 that he had been "a pampered, sickly beanpole, too weak for athletics and too asthmatic for the army" (Severo, 2000).

Being asthmatic turned out to be a blessing in disguise. Having served only five months in the military, he could get back to doing radio again. He returned to Phoenix, where he married his college sweetheart, Dorothy Goodman, and resumed his on-air career at KOY. It was a good time to be a radio announcer (in the early 1940s, the term *disc jockey* was beginning to gain popularity, but it didn't really apply to Allen, who was never just a record spinner). He became known for his quick wit and ability to make his audience laugh. He also developed a following as a comedian, performing his comedy routines in local clubs. His success as an entertainer led him to Los Angeles, where he became part of a syndicated comedy show called *Smile Time*. By October of 1946, he had been hired to do a late-night radio show on station KNX. Allen was always much more than the typical dj; he was an entertainer, who told jokes, played the piano, and sang. (Some of the songs were his own compositions: A prolific song-writer, over the next several decades he would go on to write more than a thousand songs, several of which became hits.) He also interviewed celebrity guests, interacted with the studio audience, and made comedic observations about society and the popular culture. When the critics began to take notice of his show, they liked what they heard. Syndicated gossip columnist Hedda Hopper gave him a brief mention in the *Los Angeles Times* on 28 June 1948, telling her readers to "give him a listen. He's good." In her 18 April 1949 column in the *Times*, she was even more effusive, saying, "Steve Allen has built up a fabulous reputation as a midnight disc jockey." She praised his ability in ad-libbing and relating to his devoted fans. She concluded, "He's by way of being sensational."

NEW YORK BECKONS

By mid-1950, Allen's show had created enough of a buzz to be carried on the CBS radio network as a summer replacement for the popular comedy *Our Miss Brooks*. Knowing that he would be heard by a national audience, even if it was only for several months, Allen wanted to make a positive first impression. His guests for that show included some big names, among them Eve Arden, the star of the show he was temporarily replacing; Groucho Marx; and Jack Benny. His offbeat sense of humor, his satirical way of poking fun at society's foibles, and his skill as an interviewer continued to win him new fans.

Then on 16 November 1950, Walter Ames, the radio/TV critic of the *Los Angeles Times*, reported some big news: "Steve Allen Leaving for New York

Video Show." His last late-night show from Los Angeles would air 9 December. CBS wanted him to come to New York and do his show there. Said Ames, "What a Christmas present for easterners. . . . He says he'll use the same format on TV that he did on his radio show." Other critics took note as well. On 1 December 1950, syndicated columnist Walter Winchell, writing in the *Washington Post*, reported on Allen's impending arrival in New York. He told readers that Steve Allen was supposed to be "a very glib guy . . . sort of a 'refined' Groucho Marx. He will be 29 next month, and never works from a script." That was something else that was unique about Allen. He was accustomed to thinking on his feet and had long been known for his ability to ad-lib. This ability would soon be a major plus for him when he moved from radio to television. In those early years of TV, most shows were scripted, and announcers, determined to do things the right way, took few chances. But Allen changed that: He was spontaneous and seemed to be having fun. Soon his style was imitated by other hosts.

In New York, Allen continued to be a hardworking host, except now he was doing the *Steve Allen Show* five nights a week, at 7 p.m. on WCBS-TV, and critics began to take note of his appearance as well as his ability. Although he was known for his comedy routines, the large tortoise-shell eyeglasses he wore gave him a look of "owl-like solemnity," said a *New York Times* critic, who also marveled at how serious Steve was about perfecting his craft. Allen wasn't afraid to take chances; he would read some of his mail on the air or wander into the studio audience and chat with the fans. Then he got a big break: Arthur Godfrey, the popular host of *Talent Scouts*, was the victim of a flight delay and couldn't get back to New York in time to do his show. Allen, who up to this point had done only local TV, was asked to fill in for Godfrey, a big star with a nationally televised program. Godfrey's audience was favorably impressed, and in early January 1951, when Godfrey had to take a refresher course in the naval reserve, Allen was called on again. This time, he hosted for several weeks.

When his guest-hosting duties on Arthur Godfrey's show ended, Allen returned to local television again, hosting the *Steve Allen Show* on WCBS-TV in New York, but his friends who were radio/television editors didn't forget him. Both Larry Wolters of the *Chicago Tribune* and Walter Ames of the *Los Angeles Times* kept Allen's many fans up to date on how he was doing in New York. Ames noticed that one aspect of Allen's show was being especially well-received: "He does a 5 minute ad-lib at the beginning of his show that ha[s] the audience in stitches," Ames wrote on 22 January 1951. That ad-lib was later known as the "opening monologue," and many television hosts emulated it. Allen missed the West Coast, and several times, he flew out to Los Angeles to visit friends and family; he had been reluctant to move his wife and children to the East Coast, since he had hoped he could persuade CBS to let him do the show from LA. Unfortunately, CBS had not completed its nationwide hookup yet, so what Steve wanted couldn't be done. Reluctantly, he finally moved his family east in February 1951.

HOSTING A LATE-NIGHT TALK SHOW

That wasn't all the moving in Allen's life. CBS decided to move his show, as of 26 March 1951. He had started in the early evening, but now CBS wanted him on from 11:30 a.m. to 12:30 p.m. The good news was that Steve's dream of being seen nationally would finally be realized, although he still had to do the show from New York. But CBS had even more plans, and they were a result of the many changes daytime television was undergoing. TV was still relatively new, and many of the popular radio shows were gradually moving over to the visual medium. Daytime dramas (better known as soap operas) had been a huge success on radio, and Procter & Gamble wanted to sponsor a couple of them on CBS. In August 1951, *Love of Life* and *Search for Tomorrow* took part of what had been Steve's slot. Fortunately, the company also wanted to sponsor Steve, although he would not have an hour any longer. He was moved to 12:45–1:15 p.m.

Meanwhile, changes were about to take place at NBC that would affect Allen's career. On 14 January 1952, the president of NBC, Sylvester L. "Pat" Weaver,

Arlene Francis and Home

Home was billed as a women's magazine of the air when it debuted on 1 March 1954. NBC-TV's president, Sylvester "Pat" Weaver thought *Home* would complement both his new morning show, *Today*, and the new late-evening show being developed, *The Tonight Show.* The choice for hostess (or "femcee" as the print media called her) was Arlene Francis, a versatile performer who had spent years as a radio star and a stage actress and was now a regular panelist on the TV quiz show *What's My Line?* She was so popular that *Newsweek* magazine put her on its cover on 19 July 1954. On *Home*, Francis was the host and the managing editor, so she had a say in what features the show broadcast.

A traditional women's show, *Home* focused on fashion, cooking, and child raising. Francis had regular "experts" who gave advice or demonstrated new products. At first, there was little about news or current events, and the show had so many commercials and product mentions that the critics complained. Gradually, more news was added, delivered by veteran print journalist Esther Van Wagoner Tufty. Although the show remained mostly about homemaking, Francis was a capable interviewer who chatted with authors, politicians, and newsmakers. She also took *Home* out on the road, to cities like San Francisco and Washington, DC, and distant locations like Japan and Paris.

Home taped its last show on 9 August 1957. To this day, questions remain about why it was canceled. Some media historians blame sexism, while others blame power struggles within NBC after Pat Weaver left. *Home* was an experiment that failed, but Francis won critical acclaim for her work as its host.

put a new show on the air. It was called *Today* and it was unique. As TV had continued to expand, Weaver believed the time was right for a morning show, with newscasts, weather reports, interesting guests, and humor. Radio had done very well with this type of show, so why not put one on TV? A former radio personality from Chicago named Dave Garroway was chosen to host the new program. Of course, the critics wondered if anyone would watch morning TV, and when the show made its debut, it was not an immediate success. But NBC stuck with it. In fact, CBS put on its own version of it, called the *Morning Show.* The name wasn't exciting, and neither was the show; critics and viewers found it much too serious for that early an hour, and CBS eventually had to revamp it and make it somewhat lighter. Meanwhile, *Today* was finding an audience. Eventually, Garroway even inherited a new sidekick, a chimpanzee called J. Fred Muggs. The concept may sound strange to us today, but in the early 1950s, morning TV was still in its experimental phase. The audience liked Garroway and they adored the chimp, who even got fan mail.

As for Steve Allen, he had come to the conclusion that NBC would offer him better opportunities. So, in early 1953, he changed networks and got back his preferred late-night shift in the process. At first, he was still only on WNBT in New York, but he continued to enhance his visibility by performing onstage and guesting on other TV variety shows. One of his regular appearances was as a panelist on the CBS quiz show *What's My Line?* where contestants with unusual occupations tried to stump the panel. While all of this was happening, his personal life was in the midst of some change. His marriage to Dorothy Goodman had ended in divorce in 1951. Subsequently, he fell in love with television star Jayne Meadows, who was a panelist on *I've Got a Secret* as well as a stage actress. They married in late July 1954. Throughout the rest of his life, he would repeatedly credit Meadows with being a source of inspiration and encouragement, and by all accounts, they had one of those rare celebrity marriages that was both happy and stable.

Meanwhile, there were rumors that Pat Weaver wasn't finished with his plans for expanding NBC. By the spring of 1954, the newspapers were announcing that the network would soon offer a new late-night variety show; it would be live and would be called *The Tonight Show*, the name chosen to complement that of the morning show, *Today.* Steve Allen had a different recollection of how the show got its name. Years later, he told reporters that his own local TV show in New York had been called *The Tonight Show.* The local newspapers didn't use that name, however; they listed it as the *Steve Allen Show.* But whether it was Weaver or Allen who first came up with the name, what would become known as *The Tonight Show* debuted on the NBC network on 27 September 1954, with Steve Allen as the host. He had enjoyed great success doing his late-night radio show in Los Angeles, and now he was getting the chance to show that late-night television could work just as well.

To modern viewers, the idea of a late-night variety program probably doesn't seem as fascinating as it did in that era, when TV was only a few years old. Back then, TV stations seldom had live programming after the 11 p.m. news. Stations that didn't sign off entirely showed old movies. Therefore many people were curious to see if this experiment with live programming would work. One thing that was guaranteed to get the attention of potential viewers was a program's promising big name celebrities. *Tonight* was going to feature some of the best-known stars of radio, movies, theater, and nightclubs. Thanks to his years as a performer and songwriter, Steve Allen had a lot of friends in show business, and that may explain why a surprisingly large number of viewers began watching; they were eager to see if Allen was as funny as the critics said he was, and they hoped their favorite celebrity would make an appearance on his show. *The Tonight Show* made an immediate impact on one young fan in particular. Jay Leno, who many years later become the host of *The Tonight Show*, later recalled in a 2000 tribute to Allen, "Some of my earliest memories of TV are of watching Steve Allen. The first time I ever stayed up and saw the clock strike 12 midnight, I . . . saw him on TV." The young Leno marveled at how clever Allen was. As he told *Time* magazine in a 2000 tribute when Allen died, "He did *The Tonight Show* live, so it was spontaneous. Every mistake and every flaw and, of course, every brilliant ad-lib . . . was right there in front of your eyes."

BECOMING A STAR

The charm of *The Tonight Show* was its unpredictability. Even some of the critics who liked the show had trouble explaining what made it so interesting. The show usually opened with Allen seated at the piano, playing and singing a song (often one that he had written). He would then walk over to a desk and begin a monologue, touching on as many subjects as crossed his mind that night. As for what would happen next, viewers could never be certain, and that's what made the show unique. In his 1992 memoir Allen recalled, "What crazy nights there were on the old 'Tonight' show, what crazy ad-lib routines. . . . [One] of my favorites was to open the back door [of the studio], walk quickly into the night dressed in some particular costume and engage strangers in extemporaneous conversation." One night, the costume he chose was a realistic-looking policeman's uniform. Allen "charged into the street and began stopping automobiles. I had no idea what I was going to say to the drivers but figured that just the sheer, insane idea of stopping actual cars on live TV and saying anything would be unusual enough." His prop that night was a "3-foot Hebrew National salami," and he ordered a taxi driver to take this large salami to Grand Central Station. The taxi driver complied, although we can only guess what he did once he got there. But the crowd thought the stunt was hilarious (Allen, 1992).

Television critics found Allen's performance uneven; some nights he was much funnier than others. And yet, there was something about him that made the critics continue to watch, as if they were afraid they would miss something. The *New York Times*'s veteran TV columnist Jack Gould used words like "engaging" and "intriguing" to describe *The Tonight Show*, saying that Steve's comic observations were "rooted in an amusing appreciation of the immaterial, irrelevant, and unimportant." As he had in his local version of the show, Allen loved to interact with his audience, seeking out people who were offbeat or eccentric, or who had something unusual to say. He also began doing interviews with ordinary men and women on the street, something that talk show hosts do even today. But while he liked to find people who were in some way unique, he was not an insult comic. Rather, as Gould noted, Steve could take even the most ordinary event and find humor in it.

The Tonight Show was a vehicle that showcased Allen's many talents. He was onstage through much of the show, bantering with his sidekick, Gene Rayburn; introducing the guest celebrities; playing the piano; and sometimes performing the crazy stunts. Alas, these were still the formative years of television, and sometimes props didn't work right, or a stunt didn't go as planned; but Allen seemed to know how to recover and keep the show moving. As Gould and others observed, night after night, Steve Allen could make an hour and a half pass quickly. He was also doing something that had worked well for him when he was a radio star: performing his own compositions. He enjoyed some of his greatest success as a songwriter during this period, and several of his songs even became hits, the best-known being "This Could Be the Start of Something Big."

Another interesting aspect of *The Tonight Show* was its egalitarianism. In 1954, part of the United States was still segregated, and *Brown v. the Board of Education* had not yet been implemented. Certain southern affiliates had expressed dismay over programs that featured integrated casts. Governor Herman Talmadge of Georgia had complained about this numerous times in the early fifties, pointing to variety shows like Arthur Godfrey's as offensive to southern viewers. But like Godfrey, and like Ed Sullivan, Allen was going to feature the best talent, no matter what color that talent was. On his first show, for example, he featured a white TV star named Wally Cox, star of the TV situation comedy *Mr. Peepers*, and a popular black vocal group called the Ink Spots. Because he was a longtime jazz aficionado, Allen especially enjoyed having jazz stars on his show, giving them national exposure in front of a mass audience. Among the big-name jazz performers he invited were Erroll Garner, Count Basie, Art Tatum, Teddy Wilson, and Lionel Hampton. Allen also booked such well-respected black performers as vocalists Ethel Waters and Lena Horne, baseball star Willie Mays, and the always-entertaining singer and dancer Sammy Davis Jr. One of Sammy's appearances led to a miniscandal that today would be entirely unremarkable, but in 1956 it caused one of those moments that made some affiliates nervous. *The Tonight Show* cast member Pat Marshall, a successful actress who was white, gave Sammy Davis Jr. a kiss. She and Sammy were appearing together on Broadway in *Mr. Wonderful*, but her friendly gesture caused switchboards all over America to light up. Because of his efforts on behalf of black (or Negro, as they were called then) performers, Steve Allen was given a Russwurm Award in 1956 by the National Newspaper Publishers Association; the NNPA was a group of owners and publishers of black newspapers in America, and the award was for "unbiased and forthright use of talent regardless of race or religion."

Allen's love of jazz and his talent as a musician also earned him a movie role. He was asked to star in a film about big-band great Benny Goodman, one of the earliest bandleaders to integrate his orchestra, in 1935. (Critics also said Allen bore a facial resemblance to Goodman.) Allen temporarily relocated *The Tonight Show* to the West Coast in June 1955, so he could continue to host the show while also shooting the movie. Although he jokingly told an interviewer that he considered himself a lazy person, the truth was that he kept up a pace that was nearly nonstop, doing five shows a week live, starring in a movie, doing guest appearances on other TV shows, and still finding time to spend with his wife and children.

By today's standards, *The Tonight Show* didn't have a lot of political discussions, although every now and then, Allen would find a way to deliver a quip on a current topic. In his personal life, he was not afraid to champion causes that mattered to him; he spoke out against capital punishment, for example, and later in his career was especially vocal about how vulgar he thought television had become. But on *The Tonight Show*, in a much more conservative era, he mostly poked fun at the popular culture, especially current trends and fads. His self-deprecating humor also allowed him to make fun of his own show, and to answer questions from the studio audience. Jay Leno, who took over *The Tonight Show* in May 1992, has called him the first modern talk show host because, until *The Tonight Show*, hosts tended to be clowns or song-and-dance men. Allen made people think. And as for his influence on the talk genre, one critic wrote in his obituary that "Allen was credited with establishing virtually all of the conventions of late-night television, through Carson to Jay Leno and David Letterman—the opening monologue, chatting with the bandleader, and relying on a lineup of regular characters" (Post, 2000).

AFTER *THE TONIGHT SHOW*

In April 1956, NBC announced that Steve Allen would be cutting back from five nights to three nights, another host taking over the two nights he was off. But it wasn't a demotion. It was perhaps the biggest challenge of his TV career. NBC wanted him to go up against Ed Sullivan, host of Sunday night's top-rated variety show. Given how popular Allen was, NBC assumed that if anyone could defeat Sullivan in the ratings, it was Steve Allen. And so it was that on 24 June 1956, the Sullivan/Allen Sunday-night feud began, and it would continue through 1959. The critics were fascinated, writing numerous columns about who had the better guests. Allen was able to get Elvis Presley before Ed Sullivan did, and although Allen was contemptuous of rock music and was quite patronizing to Presley, the show got huge ratings. On that show, Allen did defeat Ed Sullivan. But most of the time, both shows were able to get so many celebrities that frustrated viewers often switched back and forth between the two in the era before the VCR or TIVO enabled fans to tape one of the shows for later playback. Ironically, neither Allen nor Sullivan became the ratings champ. While Sullivan's show normally defeated Allen's, both shows were finally beaten by the western *Maverick*.

As for Steve Allen, the Sunday night show only further enhanced his reputation. He acquired the nickname "Steverino" from one of his regulars, comedian Louie Nye. He showed that he could continue to be topical, satirical, and improvisational. He perfected his "Man on the Street" interviews and, with his regular cast members, developed a number of characters that frequently appeared in skits. Then, in mid-January of 1957, he announced that he would leave *The Tonight Show*. When he cut back to three nights, comedian Ernie Kovacs had filled in for him on the other two nights. But when his tenure on *The Tonight Show* ended, the new host was Jack Paar, a well-respected comic who had built up a big audience with guest appearances on both radio and TV. Where Steve Allen had done more of a variety show, Paar would transform the program into the kind of traditional talk show that is still around, in which the host chats with some of the biggest newsmakers of the day. There was still comedy, still celebrity entertainers, but Paar was also a brilliant conversationalist and did memorable interviews. Once Allen had left, each subsequent host would bring his own unique style to what became *The Tonight Show*, but none of the show's success would have happened without Steve, who proved that there was an audience for late-night TV.

LATER YEARS

After he left *The Tonight Show*, and after his Sunday night show ended, Allen did another variety show that ended in 1961, but his career was far from over. He went on to appear on other people's variety shows, and he did one more of his own, the short-lived *Steve Allen Comedy Hour* in the summer of 1967. From 1964 to 1967, he was the host of *I've Got a Secret* on CBS. He also appeared on several comedy specials throughout the 1970s and did a short-lived syndicated show called *Steve Allen's Laughback* in 1976. In 1980, he did a comedy special called *The Big Show*, and a show once again called the *Steve Allen Comedy Hour* aired occasionally in 1980–81. But one series he was especially proud of had nothing to do with comedy: In January 1977, along with Jayne Meadows, he wrote and produced an award-winning series on PBS called *Meeting of Minds*, which depicted some of the great names in world history discussing what they had done and why.

By this time, Allen had become active on the Council for Media Integrity, an organization that advocated for "balance in scientific reporting in the media" and that also debunked pseudoscience. Always an independent thinker, Allen began to write more books that expressed his skeptical side and encouraged readers to do critical thinking—even about religion. He wrote several books about the Holy Scriptures in which he advocated reasoned and rational discussion about how much of the Bible is literally true, also encouraging tolerance of different interpretations and belief systems. For fans who expected only comedy, Allen showed he had a serious side and was willing to take on even the most contentious issues. Of course, he never stopped writing books about humor. Some of them recycled his old jokes, but others were about the process of becoming a successful comedian. Over all, he wrote fifty books. And he never stopped writing songs; his widow told an interviewer that during his lifetime, he had written more than four thousand songs.

Allen's many contributions to the talk show genre were acknowledged in 1986 when he was inducted into the Academy of Television Arts and Sciences Hall of Fame.

In the last stages of his life, Steve was becoming increasingly frustrated by what he felt was a general coarsening of the popular culture; his last books were about that subject, including the one he was working on when he died, *Vulgarians at the Gate: Trash TV and Raunch Radio*. The man who was known as a skeptic about religion found himself embraced by right-wing conservatives, who agreed with him that rock and rap music, video games, and many TV shows were violent and crude. His outrage about popular culture puzzled some of his fans, who didn't like to think of him as a conservative scold, especially when he aligned himself with the Parents' Television Council, an organization that was highly critical of shock jocks like Howard Stern. He also became an advisory board member of the Dove Foundation, a nonprofit organization that promoted family-friendly movies and TV shows. Yet, in spite of his disgust with current popular culture, Steve was not an ideologue, and he continued to advocate for a wide range of causes, both liberal and conservative. He remained an active participant in the Center for Inquiry, a secular humanist organization that promoted and encouraged science and critical thinking. While he took considerable criticism for his attacks on popular culture, he never abandoned his interest in science, and he never stopped promoting better education in the public schools of America.

Allen died of a heart attack on 30 October 2000 at the age of seventy-eight. To this day, he is remembered as the innovative comic who first made late-night TV a success.

STEVE ALLEN TIMELINE

1921: born in New York
1941: graduates from Chicago's Hyde Park High School
1942: moves to Arizona and briefly attends college

1943: drafted into the military but released early due to health problems; becomes an announcer at KOY in Phoenix

1946: hired by KNX in Los Angeles to be a late-night disc jockey

1950: leaves Los Angeles to work in local TV for CBS in New York

1951: fills in several times as host of Arthur Godfrey's *Talent Scouts*; hosts a talent show for songwriters called *Songs for Sale*

1953: leaves CBS to work for the local NBC TV station in New York

1954: hosts the first episode of *The Tonight Show* on NBC; one of the many songs he wrote, "This Could Be the Start of Something Big," becomes a hit

1956: hosts the *Steve Allen Show*, a Sunday-night variety show on NBC

1964: hosts the TV quiz show *I've Got a Secret*

1967: hosts the *Steve Allen Comedy Hour*

1976: hosts a syndicated show called *Steve Allen's Laughback*

1977: with his wife, Jayne Meadows, begins hosting an innovative educational program on PBS called *Meeting of Minds*

1992: publishes an autobiography, *Hi-Ho Steverino! My Adventures in the Wonderful Wacky World of Television*

2000: dies of a heart attack, at age seventy-eight

FURTHER READING

Allen, Steve. *Hi Ho Steverino! My Adventures in the Wonderful Wacky World of Television*. Fort Lee, NJ: Barricade, 1992.

Ames, Walter. "Steve Allen Leaving for New York Video Show." *Los Angeles Times*, 16 November 1950, p. 30.

Christy, Marian. "Steve Allen Unveils His Secrets of Success." *Boston Globe*, 9 July 1989, p. A12.

Horn, John. "Mr. Allen: Gentleman of Owl-Like Solemnity." *New York Times*, 2 September 1951, p. 59.

Kurtz, Paul, "A Tribute to Steve Allen." *Skeptical Inquirer*, January–February 2001, pp. 5–7.

Leno, Jay. "Eulogy." *Time*, 13 November 2000.

Massing, Michael. "Children and the Demons of Pop Culture." *New York Times*, 25 August 2001, p. B9.

Oliver, Wayne. "Show Biz Comes Naturally to Allen." *Washington Post*, 25 February 1951, p. 4L.

Post, J. Y. "Comic, Songwriter, Author Steve Allen Dies; Pioneer of 'Tonight' Show in 1953." *Washington Post*, 1 November 2000, p. B7.

Severo, Richard. "Steve Allen, Comedian Who Pioneered Late-Night TV Talk Shows, Is Dead at 78." *New York Times*, 1 November 2000, p. B13.

Wolters, Larry. "A Man Going Everywhere." *Chicago Tribune*, 1 March 1959, p. H16.

AP Photo/Douglas C. Pizac

Johnny Carson

Johnny Carson has been called the king of late-night television. He took over as host of *The Tonight Show* on 1 October 1962, and at the height of his amazing thirty-year reign, more than fifteen million viewers watched him every night.

Carson was a master of topical humor, and like Steve Allen, who had hosted the show when it first went on the air, he could always find something in the popular culture to joke about, whether it was parodying a song or making fun of a bad movie. Also like Allen, he was a skeptic, and he held psychics up to ridicule with his character "Carnac the Magnificent." But unlike Allen, Carson was willing to do a certain amount of political humor. He was not a partisan; he was just as quick to satirize the Republicans as he was the Democrats, but commenting about political figures was quite a change for late-night talk shows. *The Tonight Show* had come on the air during the Senator Joseph McCarthy era, and while Steve Allen had his own personal views about politics, he seldom mentioned them directly because of his network's fear of offending sponsors or politicians. Carson, on the other hand, had few sacred cows. He became known for his ability to point out the foibles and foolishness of everyone from celebrities to ordinary people, and his opening monologue often contained his humorous assessment of current events. Johnny Carson exerted such a great influence on popular taste that a guest appearance on his show could launch someone's career. He had an eye for talent. For example, Oprah Winfrey first appeared on his show in December 1985, when few people outside Chicago, where she did a local show, had ever heard of her. When Carson chose you, that was a sign that you were someone with potential, and the national press began to take notice of Winfrey as a result. Carson was also a mentor and an inspiration to many up-and-coming comedians, including Joan Rivers, Jay Leno, and David Letterman. But while he became one of TV's most popular late-night hosts, he had originally wanted to be a magician.

GROWING UP

John William Carson was born in Corning, Iowa, on 23 October 1925. His mother, Ruth, was a homemaker, and his father, Homer, was employed by the Iowa-Nebraska Light and Power Company as a lineman. Because of his father's job, the Carson family frequently moved, settling in Norfolk, Nebraska, when Johnny was eight. It was in Norfolk that he spent the rest of his childhood, and he graduated from Norfolk High School in 1943.

One event in Carson's youth seems to have profoundly affected him. He encountered a copy of a *Hoffmann's Book of Magic* and became immediately interested. He sent away for a magic kit, so that he could learn how to do some of the tricks he had read about, and he began practicing faithfully. When he was fourteen, he was ready for his first performance, at the Norfolk Rotary Club. He called himself "The Great Carsoni," and to help him look professional, his mother embroidered that name on the cloth that he draped over the table when he did his act. He was paid three dollars for the performance, and his career as a magician began. In spite of being shy, Carson found he was confident whenever he performed, so he continued to do stage magic throughout his high school years. He also began learning ventriloquism and discovered he had a talent for doing comic monologues. All of these skills later helped him to earn extra money while he was trying to break into show business (Severo and Carter, 2005).

A major influence in Carson's life was radio. He grew up in the era just before television, when some of the biggest names in entertainment could be heard on the NBC, CBS, and Mutual networks. He especially liked a radio comedian named Jack Benny and wanted to emulate him. Years later, when he had become a success, Carson acknowledged how much he had learned about timing and how to "sell" a joke from listening to Benny when he was a growing up. He ultimately had the opportunity to do some comedy routines with his idol, and there is no doubt that was a gratifying experience. Years later, comedians like David Letterman felt the same way about what they had learned from watching Carson.

FROM JOHN TO JOHNNY CARSON

After he graduated from Norfolk High School, Carson went into the military. During World War II, he served as an ensign in the U.S. Navy for two years, and according to the naval publication *All Hands*, he sometimes entertained his fellow sailors by doing magic tricks and comedy routines to keep their morale up. After his discharge in 1946, he continued his education. He studied broadcasting and drama at the University of Nebraska, in Lincoln, where he received his BA in radio and speech in 1949. While he was studying, he was working as a magician to pay the bills, and he was also able to find some work at KFAB radio, a station that had studios in both Lincoln and nearby Omaha; in addition to announcing, he also wrote scripts for some of KFAB's live radio shows. After graduating from college, Carson worked at Omaha's WOW, and when WOW-TV began in 1949, he did his first television show, called the *Squirrel's Nest*. At that time, he was "John Carson," rather than Johnny, but whatever he might have been called, few people saw his new show, as only a handful of people in Omaha owned television sets. Still, doing the *Squirrel's Nest* gave Carson valuable experience in preparing a daily comedy show, telling jokes, and doing skits that would amuse the local audience.

Carson stayed in Omaha until 1951, but it was obvious the major hubs of the television industry were New York and Los Angeles. He decided to take his chances in LA, where he became a staff announcer at KNXT-TV. There wasn't any comedy involved—just telling the viewers what the movie was or giving the station identification—but he persuaded the management to give him a

Sunday afternoon program, which he called *Carson's Cellar*. It didn't pay much—about twenty-five dollars per show—but again, the key was getting experience and, this time, in a much larger city. He knew he wouldn't have a big audience; even in Los Angeles, television was still relatively new, and most people watched at night rather than on a Sunday afternoon. But Carson's quirky humor attracted one famous comic, Red Skelton, who even offered to be on the show. Skelton's appearance led to that of another famous comedian, Groucho Marx, and then of Carson's childhood hero, Jack Benny himself. These performers knew they wouldn't get paid for being on Carson's show, but they recognized an up-and-coming talent, and they wanted to help him out.

Despite the guest celebrities, KNXT had no plans for *Carson's Cellar*, nor for Carson, but luckily, he had impressed Red Skelton; the Redhead had a weekly variety show on CBS-TV, and he hired Carson to be one of his writers. Then, one day in late August 1954, Skelton sustained an injury during rehearsal and couldn't host his show. Carson, by now officially known as "Johnny," got the call, and when he stepped in to do the *Red Skelton Show*, he impressed everyone who watched. CBS network executives liked his performance so much that they soon offered him a show of his own. And so it was that Johnny Carson got his first shot at network stardom. He briefly served as master of ceremonies for a quiz show called *Earn Your Vacation*, and then in late June 1955, he was given a variety show of his own, which aired on Thursday evenings, from 10 to 10:30 p.m. It was not a big hit. Although Carson showed flashes of the brilliance he would later become famous for, the critics felt the show was inconsistent and it didn't get good enough ratings. The main sponsor, General Foods, canceled, and the show was replaced by the *Arthur Murray Dance Party*.

But Carson had shown he had the talent; all he needed was the right vehicle. His next opportunity was as the host of a quiz show on ABC television beginning in September 1957. The show had begun as a Tuesday night program on CBS called *Do You Trust Your Wife?* but by the time Carson was offered the job, it had been renamed *Who Do You Trust?* and was picked up by ABC, which moved it to daytime. While the new title wasn't grammatical, the show became very popular and brought Carson some of the success he had hoped for. He had a good team of writers, the ability to ad-lib when necessary, and a wry sense of humor, and he also had another element that helped make the show popular: a sidekick. Ed McMahon, who had made a name for himself in Philadelphia TV, was hired to be a combination straight man, announcer, and whatever else Carson needed him to be. McMahon was flexible; he could tell a joke or feed Carson a line so that Carson could get the laugh. McMahon genuinely liked and believed in Carson, and whenever Carson said something amusing, McMahon laughed enthusiastically. There would be times when the two clashed, but for the most part, their on-air relationship and off-air friendship endured for more than four decades.

JOHNNY ON *THE TONIGHT SHOW*

Hosting *Who Do You Trust?* was the boost Carson's career needed. The show was broadcast from New York, and since he was now living there, he was able to do some live theater, costarring on Broadway as a replacement with Marsha Hunt in *The Tunnel of Love* in early 1958. But he loved doing television, and it wasn't long before he was getting ABC some of its best daytime ratings. The critics liked his sense of humor, and they also liked the chemistry between him and Ed McMahon. Everyone who knew the TV business saw Carson as a rising star; the consensus was that one day, he would be doing something far more important than hosting a game show, even a popular game show like *Who Do You Trust?* As it turned out, when the next opportunity came along, it was definitely something major: the chance to host *The Tonight Show* on NBC. It was 1962, and Jack Paar was about to retire. Paar had been known for his storytelling ability, as well as his skill at interviewing. The critics wondered what kind of host Johnny Carson would be. Carson immediately made the show his own, complete with Ed McMahon's effusive introduction, "Heeeeeeeere's Johnny!" Interestingly, what bothered the critics, even those who had liked Paar, was that *The Tonight Show* had too many commercials, making it difficult for even the best comedian to shine.

Jack Paar

Jack Paar began his broadcasting career in 1946 as a summer radio fill-in for comedian Jack Benny. A talented comedian with a sly sense of humor, he guested frequently on numerous radio shows throughout the late 1940s. By the summer of 1952, Paar was hosting his first television show, an NBC game show called *Up to Paar* and based on current events. His big break came in 1954, when he was asked to host CBS-TV's morning show, which was competing with NBC's *Today* and not doing very well. The show continued to lag behind *Today*, but Paar received a lot of critical notice. In 1957, when Steve Allen left *The Tonight Show*, Paar got the job as host. There would later be some debate about whether Allen or Paar was the true father of late-night talk, but it cannot be denied that Paar's vision for *The Tonight Show* was different from Allen's. Paar loved to talk politics, and some of the biggest newsmakers sat on his couch and chatted with him. But in addition to being witty and articulate, he could also be moody and emotional. In one famous example, in February 1960, NBC censored a joke of his, and Paar walked off the set, refusing to continue. Even a personal plea from the president of NBC couldn't persuade him to come back for three weeks. With his catch phrase "I kid you not," Jack Paar could be outspoken and unpredictable, but he was never dull. From 1957 to 1962, he ruled late-night TV.

Johnny Carson took over as host of *The Tonight Show* on 1 October 1962; he would have started sooner (Paar left at the end of March), but ABC wouldn't let him out of his contract. It wasn't his first time on the show; in fact, in the spring of 1958, he had been a guest host on *The Tonight Show*, just on the strength of getting such good ratings on *Who Do You Trust?* Paar had thought that Carson showed some talent and later recommended him to host *The Tonight Show*. When Carson began hosting *The Tonight Show*, NBC gave him a starting salary of $100,000 a year. In addition to bringing Ed McMahon to play the role he had played before, Carson decided to use the current NBC Orchestra leader, Skitch Henderson. That would later change.

Critics noticed right away that Johnny Carson didn't look like the stereo-typical talk show host. He was slim and baby-faced, and his speaking style wasn't "Hollywood": He avoided the most common television-host clichés and was not loud or boisterous. He also didn't shout at the guests. He might give his loyal sidekick a dirty look or appear horrified by something, but it was all part of the act that he and McMahon had been doing for the past few years. Viewers never knew what Carson had planned. He might set Ed McMahon's script on fire, as he did on quite a few occasions, or he might calmly sit with a famous celebrity and do an insightful interview. And when a skit didn't work out, which often happened on comedy shows, he or Ed had a one-liner ready to save the skit and make a transition into something else. As people had said about Carson since he first became the Great Carsoni, he genuinely seemed to enjoy being onstage.

As already mentioned, Carson was unlike Steve Allen, the first host of the show: Allen preferred singing and making wry observations about the human condition, while Carson wasn't reticent about telling political jokes. In fact, his topical humor became an important part of the show. Viewers regarded him as a pop culture barometer: What he talked about at night would become watercooler conversation at work the next day. And as with any highly rated show, getting invited to be a guest was good for a person's career. After Carson had retired, somebody counted up how many guests had been on the show during his three-decade reign: not counting the many animal acts that had appeared, more than twenty-two thousand human guests had been seen on his show. And for those who wondered, there had been over two hundred animal guests as well. But it was the Carson monologue that fans tuned in to watch. Carson was not afraid to skewer anyone, from political leaders to corporate CEOs. His main interest was the idiosyncracies of the powerful and the famous, whether they were Democrats or Republicans or apolitical. Among those he took a poke at were members of whichever party was in power (he was on the air during the terms of seven presidents), as well as polluters, tax evaders, corrupt politicians, criminals who seemed to get too light a sentence, and celebrities behaving badly. Night after night, he and his writers came up with between sixteen and twenty-two jokes for the monologue. Carson made it look easy.

From his first show in 1962, he got the important guests. He started with legendary comedian Groucho Marx, and that night, viewers also saw actress Joan Crawford, singer Tony Bennett, comic Mel Brooks, and crooner Rudy Vallee. Over the years, he would launch many careers; he was especially known for helping up-and-coming comedians get much-needed exposure. Among those who benefited from appearing on *The Tonight Show with Johnny Carson* were stand-up comic Jerry Seinfeld, and another young comedian who later became a talk show host, David Letterman. And appearing on Carson's show often provided a boost that helped an older comic to get back into the spotlight. This was certainly true for both Don Rickles and Buddy Hackett, who found renewed interest from the public once they had performed on Carson's show. Writer and comic Woody Allen (later also a major movie director), comedians Steve Martin and Jay Leno also found their appearances on Carson's show very helpful, even though Leno admitted later that he was so in awe of Carson that it was difficult to relax and do a good comedy routine on his show. (Despite that, Leno was still named as Carson's replacement when Johnny retired.) Comedienne Joan Rivers found public acclaim from appearing on *The Tonight Show* beginning in the mid-1960s; she went on to appear on many other TV variety shows, and became so popular that Carson frequently chose her to serve as his guest host when he was on vacation. (Unfortunately, their friendship came to a bitter end when Rivers had the chance to host her own show, directly opposite Carson, in the late 1980s. Carson prized loyalty, and by all accounts, he felt Rivers had been disloyal in accepting the offer without first letting him know.)

Rivers's show was no more successful than a number of others in putting a dent in Carson's ratings. Over the years, many entertainers would try to knock Carson out of the number one slot, but to no avail. In addition to Rivers, among those who tried were Joey Bishop, Merv Griffin, Mike Douglas, Alan Thicke, David Frost, Les Crane, and Dick Cavett. But once Carson became the most highly rated late-night talker, he remained impossible to dethrone. Many theories were offered for the show's success, but it all came down to the many skills Carson brought to the show. He became well known for the continuing cast of characters that he portrayed, some of which were Floyd R. Turbo, a stereotypical ultraconservative who had an opinion about everything; Aunt Blabby, an elderly woman who liked to gossip; and his most popular character, the turbanned Carnac the Magnificent, an all-knowing psychic. Carson had been a magician for years and felt that psychics were phonies; he enjoyed debunking them and refuting their claims. One of his frequent guests was James "The Amazing" Randi, a fellow magician and skeptic who also had little tolerance for the phony claims of psychics. The Carnac skits gave him a chance to poke fun at the idea of a wise man who is so clairvoyant that if he is given a hermetically sealed envelope with an answer inside, he can "see" what the question is supposed to be. With much fanfare, McMahon would hand him an envelope (which he reminded the viewers had been "hermetically sealed"); in it were the answers to questions that Carnac supposedly had never seen. Carnac would then miraculously reveal the questions that were supposed to go with the answers. Of course, it was all played for laughs: The answers were serious, but the questions involved puns, parodies, and sly putdowns. For example, one "answer" was "A, B, C, D, E, F, G." Carnac looked up, as if to "see" the question and then responded, "What were some of the earlier names of Preparation H?" (The fact that the product he mentioned was a well-known cream for hemorrhoids probably made the joke even funnier.) In another example, his answer was "Catch-22." If the audience was expecting something about the Joseph Heller book of that title, they instead got a commentary on how poorly the local baseball team was doing and their troubles in the field: "What do the Los Angeles Dodgers do with 100 pop flies?" In addition to Floyd, Aunt Blabby, and Carnac, Carson was a featured member of the "Mighty Carson Art Players," which did parodies of movies, television shows, and other examples of popular culture.

THE PERSON VERSUS THE PERFORMER

By May 1967, Johnny Carson was on the cover of *Time* magazine. He would be on the cover of other magazines, too, over the years, including rock music publication *Rolling Stone*, which put him there in March 1979. In the case of *Rolling Stone*, the occasion was Carson's consenting to do an interview with journalist Timothy White. It was not a myth that Carson was very shy in his personal life, and it was well known that he disliked being asked personal questions. He preferred to be the one doing the interviews. In 1978, Kenneth Tynan of the *New Yorker* was also able to interview him, but over the years, very few celebrity magazines got sit-downs with Johnny.

Throughout his career, Carson exerted great control over how much people were allowed to know about him. For example, in a 1979 interview with Mike Wallace on *60 Minutes*, he acknowledged that early in his career, he had had a drinking problem, and that because drinking too much brought out the worst in him, he no longer drank much anymore. But his problems with alcohol had seldom been mentioned up to that point, even by the gossip columnists. And when he was arrested and charged with drunk driving in March 1982, he briefly mentioned it on *The Tonight Show*, then subsequently pleaded no contest and paid a fine rather than endure the bad publicity of a trial. One thing that helped Carson with damage control was his TV sidekick and longtime friend Ed McMahon. McMahon was always very protective of his boss, never talking to the tabloids about Carson's personal habits and defending him if he was asked. Even after Carson's death, McMahon remained loyal. In his 2005 book, *Here's Johnny*, he wrote about the fun they had had at clubs and parties but gave no details that would make Johnny look bad and insisted that Carson was not an alcoholic.

However, although specific details of Carson's personal life were often a closely guarded secret, it was certainly obvious that he had difficulty letting even those he loved get too close to him. He had three broken marriages. The first, to his college sweetheart, Jody Wolcott, ended in divorce in 1963. He then married Joanne Copeland, but they were divorced in 1972. His third marriage, to Joanna Holland, ended in divorce in 1985. And his fourth marriage, which by all accounts was the one that seemed to be successful, was to Alexis Maas, to whom he remained married until his death. Carson did make some jokes about all of his divorces, but for the most part, he preferred to poke fun at the foibles of others.

If his personal life didn't get much media attention, some of the unique guests Carson managed to get certainly did. Carson and his producers knew how to keep a finger on the pulse of pop culture. For example, it was on the Carson show that the eccentric "Tiny Tim" decided to get married. Tiny Tim was a tall, long-haired older man with a prominent nose, who sang in a high falsetto while playing a ukelele. He had a novelty hit with "Tip-Toe Thru the Tulips" in 1968, and in late 1969, his wedding to "Miss Vicki" earned *The Tonight Show* its highest ratings to that time; some estimates said more than fifty million viewers tuned in. Another important episode of the show took place in August 1973, when self-described psychic Uri Geller was a guest. Geller had earned much publicity from what seemed to be an ability to psychically bend spoons and perform other feats of mind power, but Carson, with his years of experience as a magician, was convinced that Geller was a clever trickster rather than a psychic. With some help from fellow magician and skeptic James "The Amazing" Randi, Carson was able to debunk Geller's alleged psychic powers on national television.

CARSON'S LASTING INFLUENCE

Because of his popularity, critics and network executives closely watched whatever Carson was doing. He was seen as a trendsetter, capable of influencing the entire entertainment business. For example, in May 1972, he relocated *The Tonight Show* from New York to Los Angeles; that move provided other shows with the incentive to do the same. New York had been the center of television broadcasting, but now that center shifted to the West Coast. Carson preferred to tape his shows rather than broadcast them live; again, other variety and talk shows began to follow his lead.

Carson did get some negative publicity from his tendency to make demands on NBC and then threaten to quit if those demands weren't met. His ratings were so outstanding that NBC eventually capitulated to what he wanted.

And when he wanted to cut his show back from ninety minutes to an hour in 1980, that's what happened. When he wanted time off, he got it. And if his demands seemed egocentric, NBC management understood his value. After all, *The Tonight Show* was the biggest moneymaker on NBC, and Carson had succeeded beyond anyone's wildest expectations. It was his great success as an entertainer that probably explains why he was selected to host the Academy Awards in 1979. The committee wanted somebody well known, and even though Carson was not a movie star, he was such a household name that choosing him made sense. In addition, he understood the medium of television and never seemed flustered by anything, a useful skill when one is hosting a four-hour TV show filled with big names and big egos. He did such a good job that he was chosen as host on four other occasions and turned down numerous other requests from the Academy.

When Johnny Carson finally announced his retirement, he was earning about $25 million a year. From 1962 to 1992, he had been synonymous with late-night entertainment. He was admired by both the veteran comics and those who were up-and-coming. After he died, a number of comics—including Jerry Seinfeld, Gary Shandling, Roseanne Barr, Ellen DeGeneres, and Ray Romano—said they thought of him as a mentor or as somebody they admired. And when he did his final show on 22 May 1992, more than fifty million viewers tuned it.

After Carson retired, he became almost reclusive, spending time with his fourth wife, traveling, and trying to relax. One thing few people knew was that he still tried to keep active in comedy: He wrote jokes for David Letterman, and often Letterman used those jokes. Interestingly, a bitter rivalry had sprung up between Jay Leno and Letterman over which man would take over from Carson. Leno won, and Letterman left NBC. But Carson, who still respected Letterman's talent, would send him jokes for his late-night CBS show.

Throughout his life, Carson had been a heavy smoker. When smoking on TV was still permitted, it was common to see him interviewing a guest while smoking a cigarette. All of that smoking over the years was undoubtedly a factor in Carson's contracting emphysema in his later years, which contributed to his death on 23 January 2005. He was seventy-nine.

After Carson's death, the University of Nebraska, his alma mater, announced that he had donated $5.3 million in 2004, an endowment for the Johnny Carson Fund for Theater, Film and Broadcasting. On his death, his estate donated another $5 million, and the university renamed its department of theater arts the Johnny Carson School of Theatre and Film.

In a world where there are twenty-four-hour news channels, the Internet, and various other media, it is doubtful that any talk show host will ever be as influential as Johnny Carson was. Even when his audience had declined due to media fragmentation, he was still attracting twelve million viewers a night, an amazing feat. It is no wonder that he is remembered by fans of the talk show genre as the king of late-night TV.

JOHNNY CARSON TIMELINE

1925: born in Corning, Iowa

1943: after graduating high school, serves in the U.S. Navy

1949: graduates from the University of Nebraska

1951: does a comedy-variety show, *Carson's Cellar*, on KNXT-TV, Los Angeles

1954: fills in for comedian Red Skelton

1955: hosts a variety-comedy show on CBS

1957: host of quiz show *Who Do You Trust?* on CBS

1962: becomes host of *The Tonight Show*, replacing Jack Paar

1969: *The Tonight Show*'s highest ratings with the wedding of Tiny Tim and Miss Vicki

1979: hosts the Oscars for the first time

1992: retires from *The Tonight Show*

2005: dies of emphysema, at age seventy-nine

FURTHER READING

Brioux, Bill. "Hail to the King of Late Night." *Toronto Sun*, 24 January 2005, p. 38.

Hinckley, David. "Farewell to Johnny. Carson Ruled Late-Night TV for 3 Decades." *New York Daily News*, 24 January 2005, p. 35.

Ludwig, Charles L. "The Carson Connection." *All Hands*, April 2005, p. 40.

McMahon, Ed. *Here's Johnny*. New York: Berkley, 2005.

Ouzounian, Richard. "Johnny Carson, TV's King of Late-Night Comedy, Dies at 79." *Toronto Star*, 24 January 2005, p. A1.

Pastorek, Whitney. "Choice Moments in the Late-Night King's Career." *Entertainment Weekly*, 4 February 2005, p. 14.

Severo, Richard, and Bill Carter. "Johnny Carson, Low-Key King of Late-Night TV, Dies at 79." *New York Times*, 24 January 2005, p. A1.

Timberg, Bernard M. *Television Talk: A History of the TV Talk Show*. Austin: University of Texas Press, 2002.

Tynan, Kenneth. "Fifteen Years of the Salto Mortale." *New Yorker*, 20 February 1978, pp. 47–8, 81.

White, Timothy. "Interview: Johnny Carson." *Rolling Stone*, 22 March 1979, pp. 38–48.

AP Photo/Mark J. Terrill

James Dobson

James Dobson is one of the most influential talk show hosts in America. His syndicated column has appeared in over five hundred newspapers, and in 2007, his syndicated talk show reached 220 million listeners daily, on over seven thousand stations in 160 countries. But James Dobson is not just a typical pastor: He is one of the most polarizing figures in American life. To conservative Christians, Dobson is a hero, a man who is not afraid to defend America's Christian heritage. They admire his efforts as an advocate for government policies that reflect traditional Christian values, and they respect the advice he gives in his best-selling books about parenting. Because he has had the ear of President George W. Bush, he has often been able to move the conservative Christian agenda forward. To his detractors, Dobson is a man of faith who has too much power in the secular world, someone whose influence over the president and Congress has even affected nominations to the Supreme Court. To moderates, liberals, and non-Christians, Dobson is a theocrat, a man whose opposition to the separation of church and state has harmed our democracy. But what both sides agree on is that James Dobson cannot be ignored.

IN THE BEGINNING

James Clayton Dobson Jr. comes from a long line of Nazarene evangelists. His father and grandfather were preachers, and a deep Christian faith was a part of his life from his earliest years. In fact, he claims that he was able to pray before he was able to talk. That claim does not seem like hyperbole to those who know him because Dobson's religious beliefs continue to affect every part of his life.

Dobson was born in Shreveport, Louisiana, on 21 April 1936 to Myrtle and James Dobson. His father and mother took him along when Pastor Dobson went out to preach, and young "Jimmie Lee," as he was called then, was exposed to evangelism throughout his childhood. He later said that he had given his life to Jesus at the age of three, after an "altar call" by his father. Following the traditions of the Nazarenes, his mother deferred to his father in all major decisions, and if James was rude, he was immediately disciplined. Nazarene belief teaches that there should be no dancing, no going to movies, and a lot of time spent in church. There is no evidence that Dobson rebelled against any of this; in fact, he became a proponent of parents taking a strong stand with their children, and letting them know that it was the parents who were in charge.

When Dobson was in high school, his father was given the opportunity to pastor a Nazarene church in San Benito, Texas, near the Mexican border. Dobson graduated from San Benito High School in 1954. While his father had not gone to college, Dobson was encouraged to go. Interestingly, given all of the preachers in his family, he did not want to enter that occupation. Instead, he felt called to study psychology. This was a very unusual choice, since in the 1950s and 1960s, most Evangelicals regarded psychology with suspicion, but young Dobson was convinced that God was calling him to become a Christian counselor or perhaps a Christian psychologist. He did his undergraduate work at a small Nazarene school, Pasadena College in Pasadena, California, and then entered the graduate program at the University of Southern California (USC), where he studied child development and educational psychology. He received his PhD in 1967 and became a professor of pediatrics at USC's School of Medicine. He also spent seventeen years at Children's Hospital in Los Angeles, where he was in the Division of Child Development and Medical Genetics. His area of interest was research on the causes of mental retardation.

Dobson also embarked on a career as an author of advice books for parents. He had already published several journal articles while completing his PhD, so he knew how to get his work into print. In 1970, he published his first book. At the time the liberal child-rearing theories of Benjamin Spock seemed to be everywhere, and James Dobson provided conservative parents with an antidote: *Dare to Discipline*.

DOBSON'S GROWING INFLUENCE

The late 1960s and early 1970s were a turbulent era, when many young adults refused to accept the customs that conservative society imposed. Parents wondered what to do about young men with long hair and young women who didn't want to get married and stay at home. It seemed that long-observed societal strictures were being replaced by "do your own thing," and individuality was all that mattered. Dobson repudiated the teachings of Spock and gave parents permission to be strict, like his own parents. The feminist movement was giving young women more choices, including choices Dobson considered bad ones, and he recommended that parents reimpose traditional gender roles. Because he blamed parental permissiveness for the perpetual state of rebellion of so many young people, he encouraged parents to set rules and boundaries. He said the key to preventing another generation of disobedient and rude young people was asserting parental authority from the time the child was little; in fact, under certain circumstances, spanking might be necessary. While the book was about parental authority, Dobson's style was friendly and conversational, rather than heavy-handed or preachy. Those parents who had longed for a return to the traditional values of the 1950s were delighted that they now had a child-rearing manual they could use. *Dare to Discipline*, which was put out by Tyndale Press, a Christian publishing house, sold about three million copies; in fact, it remained so popular that in 1996, it was reissued and updated as *The New 'Dare to Discipline.'*

Dobson's success as a child psychologist led to numerous speaking engagements. Although he had not become a pastor, it was mainly church groups that sought his guidance, and he was ministering to hundreds of anxious parents. In subsequent books about family life, such as the 1975 *What Wives Wish Their Husbands Knew about Women*, he continued to use Scripture as the source of family values, while teaching his readers rules to improve their lives. Again, his was a kinder, gentler conservatism. He was a strong opponent of feminism and believed sincerely that like his own mother, the woman should defer to her husband. And yet, he did not believe husbands should be tyrants. He encouraged them to be nurturing and loving, and he even recommended that husbands and wives learn to be more open and honest with each other. Of course, the gender roles were to remain in place, with the man as the head of the home and the woman his devoted assistant, just as he believed God had intended.

By 1977, Dobson was making so much money from speaking engagements, books, and educational materials that he was able to leave USC. He told his wife, Shirley, that he felt he was being called to create a radio ministry and an organization of his own, both of them to foster the traditional family, which he believed was under attack. She was, by her own admission, somewhat nervous about his going out on his own, with her and their two children to support. On 26 March 1977, Dobson debuted his new radio program, *Focus on the Family*. It was a twenty-five-minute show, once a week, and when it started, only about thirty-six stations carried it, few of them in large cities. Dobson was determined to create a professional business to syndicate the show and market educational materials, and on 7 June 1977, the organization Focus on the Family was officially incorporated. He had a small office in Arcadia, California, and a staff of two. By 1997, the radio program was being heard on several thousand American stations, and the small organization had grown to 1,330 employees on a large corporate campus located in Colorado Springs, Colorado.

THE IMPORTANCE OF *FOCUS ON THE FAMILY*

Focus on the Family was different from most religious programs of the 1970s. As in his books, Dobson maintained a warm and conversational tone, dispensing biblical truths and solving family problems in a manner that was much like that of a trusted friend. Most average Americans who didn't listen to Christian radio were probably unaware of the show, but Christian listeners loved the show and the host. Within a year, Dobson had produced a seven-part series of films about the family that was available to church groups, and during speaking engagements, he showed the films and answered questions, the way a counselor might. One of his most well-received films was *Where's Dad?* This 1981 production stresses the importance of fathers in child rearing. Like all of his films, it was professionally done, and it even made careful use of certain elements of popular culture. Dobson has said in interviews that he enjoys some soft-rock music, and in this film, he used a hit song by Harry Chapin, "Cat's in the Cradle," about a father who has never had time for his son and realizes too late that his son has grown up to have no time for his dad.

Meanwhile, the radio program was picking up more affiliates in more cities. By 31 March 1980, a fifteen-minute daily show complemented the twenty-five-minute once-a-week broadcast. And by June of that year, he was being heard on a hundred stations.

The growing number of stations was significant: The larger the number of people who heard him, the larger the number who got in touch, calling or writing to the show. They told their friends, and his audience continued to increase. His was an activist audience, one that believed in him, bought his merchandise, applied his teachings, and was willing to speak up on his behalf. For example, for a White House Conference on the Family in the summer of 1980, Democratic president Jimmy Carter, an evangelical Christian, was seeking advisers for the task force. Dobson mentioned on the air that he wanted to be one of those advisers and urged his listeners to nominate him. Jimmy Carter's staff received more than eighty thousand letters and phone calls on Dobson's behalf, and he was appointed. Carter later issued a letter of commendation to him for all of his work.

Carter was not the last president Dobson would advise. In 1982, Republican president Ronald Reagan named him a member of the National Advisory Commission to the Office of Juvenile Justice and Delinquency Prevention (see the Focus on the Family Web site). These early efforts put Dobson in direct contact with some of the most important political figures in America. While he was not known for political advocacy at that point, he soon began to use his influence to make government officials more sensitive to what Christian conservatives wanted.

As he served on presidential councils and spoke at more events, it became obvious to Dobson that an advocacy group was needed to direct attention to what Christian conservatives felt were the important issues. Because he was now on even more radio stations and regularly heard from his audience members, he was well aware of what concerned them. In 1983, Dobson founded the Family Research Council (FRC), a think tank and lobbying organization. According to its mission statement, it "shapes public debate and formulates public policy that values human life and upholds the institutions of marriage and the family." Its first leader was Gerry Regier, who had served in the Reagan administration's Department of Health and Human Services, but the organization rose to prominence under the leadership of Gary Bauer, who had served as a policy adviser to President Reagan and came to the FRC in 1988.

As Dobson used his *Focus on the Family* radio show with its expanding network of affiliates, the FRC worked to make both Congress and the administration aware of what mattered to millions of conservative Christians, most of whom felt ignored by a government they believed had become too secular. Among the issues that were important to the FRC was overturning *Roe v. Wade*, the 1973 U.S. Supreme Court decision that had legalized abortion, and restoring prayer in the public schools, which the Supreme Court had ruled unconstitutional in 1963. The FRC also promoted a federal law banning gay marriage and pushed for other legislation it believed was supportive of traditional morality.

DOBSON AND POLITICS

While media consolidation changed mainstream talk radio and hosts like Rush Limbaugh became passionate advocates of Republican policies and politicians, Dobson was becoming an increasingly powerful force in the Christian media. He, too, had aligned himself with the Republican Party, although he would later deny that affiliation to reporters. But how much power he had and how close he was to Republican presidents was a source of debate, his detractors believing he was trying to tear down the wall of separation between church and state, and his supporters saying he was one of the few true spokesmen for traditional Christian values.

As the 1980s ended, Dobson forged more alliances with Republican members of Congress, as he and his organization continued their advocacy (detractors would call it "pressure"). He served on presidential commissions on gambling and pornography, and his view that there was a link between viewing pornography and becoming a criminal was reinforced by his interview in late January 1989 of serial killer Ted Bundy, just before Bundy's execution. In that interview, Bundy claimed to have become a Christian and blamed his criminal behavior on an addiction to pornography. Critics felt that Dobson had been conned by a master manipulator, but to Dobson's followers and to Dobson himself, what Bundy said was a fact. This interview once again put Dobson and his ministry in the spotlight. He may not have been a pastor, but he certainly filled that role in a number of ways, whether giving advice through his radio show or reaching out to people in trouble, including a serial murderer like Ted Bundy.

The election of Bill Clinton to the presidency truly mobilized Dobson's members of FRC and Focus on the Family. Clinton was much more liberal than his predecessors, Reagan and George H.W. Bush, and his own personal morality was sometimes called into question. Members of the Christian right wing were alarmed by Clinton, whom they associated with all the ills of secular society. The attitudes they attributed to him stood in marked contrast to those of Dobson, who friend and foe alike acknowledged had never had a hint of scandal in his life. He had been happily married to the same woman for many years, had two children who were as involved as he was in outreach to the Christian conservative community, and was generally regarded as consistent in what he said and what he did.

Christian Radio and Television

There have been Christian preachers on the air since broadcasting's earliest days. Most have been uplifting and inspiring; for example, in the early 1950s, Archbishop Fulton J. Sheen's TV program, *Life Is Worth Living*, appealed to Christians of all denominations. But there have also been preachers who stirred up controversy. Father Charles Coughlin, a radio priest in the 1930s, had a message that was populist but sometimes anti-Semitic. During the 1950s, Rev. Billy James Hargis and his contemporary, Rev. Carl McIntire, brought an extreme right-wing form of Fundamentalist Christianity to the radio. In the 1960s, Christian broadcasting began to reach a wider audience, due in large part to Marion G. "Pat" Robertson, founder of television's Christian Broadcasting Network, and host of the *700 Club*. On radio, the number of preachers increased as well, and by 1977 there were more than two thousand, serving over 114 million listeners. Another influential figure in Christian broadcasting was Jerry Falwell, who founded a lobbying group called the Moral Majority. Falwell made good use of broadcasting on his *Old Time Gospel Hour*, which started on radio in the mid-1950s and eventually moved to television, where it was seen for more than four decades. TV preachers, or "televangelists," proliferated throughout the 1970s and 1980s. Sex scandals tarnished the careers of Jimmy Swaggart, Jim Bakker, and several others, but the popularity of Christian religious broadcasts has never diminished. Today, Christian preachers can be seen and heard on hundreds of radio and television stations. There are also Christian radio stations, some of them broadcasting only sermons and scriptural talks, while others offer Christian music, news, talk shows, and inspirational messages.

When the so-called "Republican Revolution" occurred and the Republican Party took back control of Congress in the 1994 midterm election, Dobson and his empire were actively involved, and it is no exaggeration to say that Dobson had an empire. By 1991, he had moved his organization to Colorado Springs, Colorado, where it took up eighty-eight acres; Dobson and *Focus on the Family* was receiving so much mail that he was given his own zip code. He had never expressed an interest in running for political office himself, but he was perceived by many to be similar to a political leader. By mid-decade it was a truism that no Republican politician, especially one running for office in a conservative state, could ignore him; getting his endorsement meant contributions of time and money from millions of Dobson's supporters, who trusted him to point them in the direction of the candidates who would be "family-friendly." Dobson led a large voting bloc. Before the 1970s, many evangelical Christians had shunned politics, but now they were voting and taking strong stands on issues they felt needed to be addressed. And Dobson's name was getting into the mainstream media more often. Whereas before the 1990s, he had been known mainly to the conservative Christian audience, by the end of the 1990s he was the subject of intense discussion among liberals and moderates, who worried about his growing influence. By February 2005, *Time* magazine named him one of the "25 Most Influential Evangelicals" who were directly responsible for the election of George W. Bush to the presidency.

It was during the administration of President Bush that Dobson came into the public eye most often, but he had become a powerful force in Republican politics even while President Clinton was still in office. In March 1998, for example, Dobson held a meeting with two dozen congressional Republicans during which he chastised them for not supporting all of the policy items that his Christian conservative supporters expected, and for being less than enthusiastic in moving that agenda forward. He warned them that his group would hold them responsible if they didn't pass "profamily" legislation. That he could hold such a meeting showed how important Dobson was: He and his supporters had been working hard to elect Republicans and defeat Democrats, and he wasn't exaggerating when he said he could mobilize millions of supporters.

When President George W. Bush took office in 2000, Dobson's political influence had not diminished. He had been widely credited with leading the electoral fight that cost longtime South Dakota senator Tom Daschle his seat in 2004. Daschle, the Senate Minority Leader, had earned Dobson's ire for refusing to vote to confirm the appointment of federal judges that Daschle felt were too conservative, as well as for refusing to support a constitutional amendment to ban same-sex marriage by defining marriage as a union of one man and one woman. In addition, Dobson and his supporters wanted U.S. Supreme Court justices who would overturn *Roe v. Wade*, and he vowed to defeat any politician who disagreed. Dobson was even quoted in a 2005 *New York Times* article warning Democrats that they would "be in the bulls-eye" in the next election, as Daschle had been.

While Dobson had always been opposed to same-sex relationships, the 2004 decision by the state of Massachusetts to legalize gay marriage horrified him. One of his priorities became making such marriages illegal. The constitutional amendment he was seeking did not materialize, so he worked closely with Bush's adviser Karl Rove to get such a ban onto state ballots, most notably in Ohio, a battleground state in the 2004 presidential election. Getting a law that would ban gay marriage onto the ballot ensured a large turnout of conservative Christians, who would presumably vote Republican. The strategy worked. President Bush was reelected, and Dobson's efforts in mobilizing large numbers of white, conservative Christians were a major factor. Dobson then became a strong advocate for the president's two conservative Supreme Court nominees. After his confirmation, one of them, Samuel Alito, wrote Dobson a thank-you note that appeared to promise that Alito would support the policies Dobson wanted. Dobson denied any such collusion in the media, saying the note had just been a harmless thank you, with no quid pro quo intended.

DOBSON TODAY

These days, while Dobson remains as popular as ever with his supporters, he undergoes more scrutiny by his detractors, especially about consultations with the White House and his influence on conservative members of Congress. His most vocal critics are liberals and civil libertarians, members of such groups as People for the American Way and Americans United for the Separation of Church and State. Dobson's views on social issues have remained unchanged: He is a strong proponent of school prayer, favors the teaching of intelligent design (a theory offered by those who deny Darwin's theory of evolution), believes that any course on sex education should teach abstinence only, and is opposed to gay marriage, abortion, and euthanasia. He supports candidates who share his views and encourages his listening audience to be "values voters," meaning that they should vote for those who share traditional Christian beliefs on social issues. In 2003, he stepped down as the president of Focus on the Family, although he continued to take an active role in the organization he had founded. While other Christian advocacy groups like the Moral Majority have long since disbanded, Focus on the Family remains a prosperous and influential organization with a worldwide reach.

Dobson also remains a prolific writer. He is the author of more than thirty self-help books for the Christian audience on such themes as how to be better parents or spouses, how to cope with life's problems, and how to maintain traditional values in a secular world. His love of writing seems to run in the family: His wife, Shirley, has been his coauthor on several of his titles, and their daughter, Danae, has written more than twenty children's books. James Dobson's endorsement of political candidates can still carry a lot of weight, and he can still mobilize large numbers of his listeners and supporters to write letters or to work on behalf of a cause. As a result, politicians still seek him out.

Dobson has slowly embraced new technologies, learning how to use them to to get his message out. Friends have expressed amusement over how long he resisted word processors and computers: Until the late 1980s, he wrote all of his books in longhand. But Dobson has always adapted. Once he saw that the world was going online, he did, too, and today Focus on the Family has a multimedia Web site that not only keeps supporters up-to-date but also markets Dobson's numerous books and audio- and videotapes.

In *Time* magazine's 2005 profile of influential evangelicals, it referred to Dobson as a "Culture Warrior" who continues to fight against what he sees as the excesses of secularism. Some critics say Dobson no longer commands as much influence as he once did. For example, when he endorsed former Arkansas Governor Mike Huckabee for president in the 2008 election, Huckabee still had to drop out of the race; and although Dobson expressed doubts about John McCain, it was McCain who became the Republican nominee. In 2008, as recognition of his enduring popularity, Dobson was inducted into the Radio Hall of Fame. There is no denying that James Dobson remains a revered and important figure among members of the Christian right.

JAMES DOBSON TIMELINE

1936: born in Shreveport, Louisiana

1967: receives his PhD from the University of Southern California

1970: publishes his first book, *Dare to Discipline*

1977: debuts his new radio program, *Focus on the Family;* incorporates his new advocacy organization

1980: *Focus on the Family* heard on over one hundred stations

1982: appointed by President Reagan to the National Advisory Commission of the Office of Juvenile Justice and Delinquency Prevention

1983: founds a think tank called the Family Research Council

1991: relocates to an eighty-eight-acre site in Colorado Springs, Colorado

1998: holds meetings with key congressional Republicans, demanding that "profamily" legislation be passed

2003: steps down as head of Focus on the Family

2004: credited, along with his supporters, by many political observers with President Bush's reelection

2005: named by *Time* magazine as one of America's twenty-five most influential Evangelical Christians

2008: inducted into the Radio Hall of Fame

FURTHER READING

Apostolidis, Paul. *Stations of the Cross.* Durham, NC: Duke University Press, 2000.

Asay, Paul. "Nearly 70, James Dobson Still Focused." *Colorado Springs Gazette*, 9 April 2006, p. 56.

Burlein, Ann. *Lift High the Cross: Where White Supremacy and the Christian Right Converge.* Durham, NC: Duke University Press, 2002.

Gilgoff, Dan. *The Jesus Machine: How James Dobson, Focus on the Family, and Evangelical America Are Winning the Culture War.* New York: St. Martin's Press, 2007.

Heilbrunn, Jacob. "The Gospel of Dobson." *New York Times*, 27 May 2007, p. 17.

Kirkpatrick, David. "Evangelical Leader Threatens to Use His Muscle against Some Democrats." *New York Times*, 1 January 2005, p. A10.

Stepp, Laura Sessions. "The Empire Built on Family and Faith." *Washington Post*, 8 August 1990, p. C1.

Van Biema, David. "The Top 25 Most Influential Evangelicals in America." *Time*, 7 February 2005, pp. 34–45.

Vogrin, Bill. "In 20 Years, Focus on the Family Has Grown in Size and Influence." *Colorado Springs Gazette*, 30 March 1997, p. A3.

The Web site of the Family Research Council is www.frc.org. The Web site of Focus on the Family is www.focusonthefamily.com.

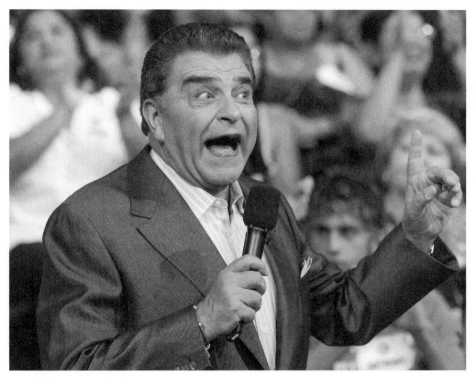

AP Photo/Lynne Sladky

Don Francisco

When most Americans think of television talk show hosts, names like David Letterman or Jay Leno come to mind. But one of the most popular personalities on TV for nearly thirty years may not be familiar to the average American who doesn't speak Spanish. For the Spanish-speaking audience, the name Don Francisco is as familiar and beloved as Letterman or Leno. The jovial and charismatic host of *Sábado Gigante* seems to have unlimited energy as he presides over a variety show that is a throwback to another era. Somehow, even new generations of viewers find his show so entertaining that they don't want to miss it. By some estimates, he has over 100 million viewers in thirty countries who faithfully watch him every Saturday night. But when he was growing up, Don Francisco never thought he would go into television. In fact, his family didn't even own a set, and he never watched a TV show until he came to America to attend school.

BECOMING DON FRANCISCO

The man whose TV alter ego is Don Francisco was born Mario Luis Kreutzberger Blumenfeld on 28 December 1940. His parents, Erich and Anni, were Holocaust survivors. His mother had planned to have a career in opera, but in Nazi-dominated Germany, where she had gone to study, such a dream became impossible. However, her desire to have a music career influenced her son; in his 2001 autobiography, Don Francisco stated that his mother's thwarted aspirations were one reason he had decided he should become a performer.

After Don Francisco's parents escaped from the Nazis, they ultimately settled in Chile. Don Francisco was born in Talca, about 160 miles south of Santiago. His father moved the family from the small town to the bigger city when Mario was four and opened a men's clothing store in Santiago. As Mario grew, his father assumed that his son would one day enter the family business, so after Mario finished high school, he suggested that Mario go to New York City because back then, it was still an influential part of the fashion industry. His father's plan was to have Mario learn the business by studying how men's clothing was manufactured. Around this time, Mario had already begun to do a little performing, but not yet for any career goal, just as a means of self-preservation. Painfully shy and having to confront anti-Semitism at school, he began to use humor and performance to win people over. And although he had his doubts about whether the clothing business was his destiny, in 1960, he followed his father's wishes and went to New York to observe and prepare for running the family clothing store.

It was while he was in New York City studying that Mario discovered television for the first time. He had never seen it in Chile, and from his very first encounter, he became convinced that it was the wave of the future. When he went back to Chile in 1962, he was able to speak some English, but that wasn't the only thing that changed. He got married, and although working in his father's store full-time would undoubtedly have been more stable, he had fallen in love with television and decided he would rather be an entertainer than sell men's clothing. He created a comic character called Don Francisco, a portly, boisterous man who loved to tell jokes, and much to his father's displeasure, he finally talked the management at Santiago's Channel 13 into giving him a chance to perform on TV. Unfortunately, because television was very new in Chile, his first job didn't pay much, nor did it offer him a permanent position, so he continued working for his father. But as soon as he was able to concentrate entirely on television, he did so. Being an entertainer was where his heart was.

He first did a show on Sundays. After it was canceled, he got an idea for a new style of variety program, similar to those he had seen in the united States. The show that he created went on the air on 8 August 1962 with the name *Sábados Gigantes* (Gigantic Saturdays), and at first it was an incredible eight hours in length but was soon modified to three hours, a much more typical duration for a variety show. In agreeing to do the show on a Saturday night, he was actually being asked to take quite a risk; at that time television in Chile did not usually broadcast on Saturday, and the management wondered if anyone would watch. But the new show changed Chilean viewing habits, making Saturday nights an important time to be in front of the TV set. Then as now, the show featured a mix of comedy skits, talented singers and dance bands, interviews, live ad-libbed commercials, contests, and attractive models dressed in sexually alluring outfits, and everything revolved around the energetic personality known as Don Francisco. As time passed, the show became so popular that its host became a national celebrity, admired and respected throughout Chile. Even when there was political unrest in Chile, people had come to rely on Don Francisco: The show was fun and entertaining and kept people's minds occupied, no matter what their political views might be. But Don Francisco had to deal with some political realities. In 1973, Chile was taken over by the brutal dictator Augusto Pinochet, who wanted Don Francisco to announce to the nation that the previous government had been overthrown. The *Sábados Gigantes* host tactfully declined, using the excuse that a comedian, even a popular comedian, shouldn't be the one to announce a military coup. Instead of having political discussion on his show, Don Francisco turned to a safer but very necessary topic: philanthropy. He used his celebrity status to raise money for a number of worthy causes; the telethon he started in 1978 to help handicapped children raised $2.5 million its first year; several decades later, it was still an important annual event for Chile, just as the Jerry Lewis telethon for Muscular Dystrophy was in the United States.

CONQUERING THE UNITED STATES

For two decades, Don Francisco had been a well-known personality in Latin America, so it was not surprising when he decided to try his luck in the United

States, where there was a large Spanish-speaking population. He moved to Miami and approached a fellow Chilean who now worked there, Joaquin Blaya, general manager of Miami's WLTV, and by mid-April 1986, he was doing a local version of his show. WLTV was affiliated with what was then called the Spanish International Network (SIN), which also had stations in other cities. Although Don Francisco's program was only one hour long and was seen only in Miami, Blaya liked what his friend was doing, and within a year, it was decided to put the show on the network. (A self-proclaimed workaholic, Don Francisco also continued to do the show in Chile as well, flying back and forth between the two countries. Thanks to videotape, he was able to tape part of each show and still not miss his plane.) In November 1987, the U.S. version of what was now called *Sábado Gigante* began to air on SIN, which not long after was renamed Univision. Today, Univision is the largest Spanish-speaking network in the United States, and *Sábado Gigante* is its longest running show, having remained on the network for more than twenty years. It is seen in more than twenty-five countries and has estimated viewership of 100 million. In 2003, the *Guinness Book of World Records* announced that the show had been certified as television's longest-running variety show. It has no summer reruns, and Don Francisco has been the show's only host since the first night it went on the air in 1962.

As a youth in Chile, he had said he wanted to be a performer, and on *Sábado Gigante*, that is exactly what he is. As master of ceremonies of a program that features a fast-moving amalgam of music, celebrity guests, contests, special features, and lots of commercials, Don Francisco is not confined just to announcing the acts. He is an active participant, often dancing with a contestant or looking disappointed when he sees the Jackal (a character who appears onstage with his trumpet when someone in the talent show segment is about to be eliminated). He bounces around the stage, exhorting the audience to applaud more loudly (for viewers who don't speak Spanish, one of the phrases his viewers hear him utter repeatedly is "un aplauso!"—a round of applause). He also encourages the audience to sing along with a sponsor's jingle, and they always do so with enthusiasm. Since his show is international, his guests may perform in the musical genres popular in Puerto Rico or Venezuela or Mexico or Chile; Don Francisco stays abreast of what is popular in each country. He even acts in some of the comedy skits, wearing ridiculous costumes designed get a laugh from the audience. And then there are the numerous commercial breaks; he still reads many of the commercials himself, while others are read by his regular sidekicks. Sponsors want him to endorse their product because he is seen as a credible spokesperson, and because he knows how to generate excitement about a product.

Although *Sábado Gigante* has become an international hit, there are some critics who dislike the show. They see it as a relic of another era, too fake, too glitzy, too reminiscent of the 1950s variety programs on which all the performers made fools of themselves. The show's many commercials and Don

Francisco's enthusiastic plugs of every sponsor remind some critics of a late-night infomercial. But he isn't upset by the criticism. He has told interviewers that he has good reason to spend extra time plugging his sponsors: He remembers when *Sábado Gigante* was first proposed to U.S. businesses, and they all rejected it. Potential advertisers failed to believe that a variety show aimed at a Hispanic audience would be successful, and they seemed to stereotype all Hispanics as poor. Don Francisco had to use his powers of persuasion to win over the corporate executives who could make or break his new show. Even now, he feels he should go the extra mile for his sponsors, and he does.

CONTROVERSIES AND SUCCESSES

Over the years, Don Francisco has also been criticized for not taking a stand on politics, and especially for not using his considerable influence to speak out against the Pinochet regime in Chile. He responds that opposing the dictator would have put his family's life in jeopardy, and it was better for him to be perceived by the government as nonthreatening. To this day, while he has newsmakers of every political ideology as guests, he never lets his show become contentious—arguments about politics are not appropriate for an up-tempo, high-energy variety show. There is one other criticism he sometimes hears: He has been accused of sexism by those who believe he treats the scantily clad young female models on *Sábado Gigante* like sex objects. It probably came as no surprise to these critics when in 1994, Don Francisco was accused of sexual harassment by one of the models, a charge he denied. The case was settled out of court. In *Life, Camera, Action* he attributed the charge to cultural miscommunication, saying he came from a culture where men are very flirtatious around women but mean no harm. On the other hand, not everyone believes that Don Francisco is a sexist: While he does admit that he likes to look at beautiful women—the reason he has so many gorgeous models on his show—he has used *Sábado Gigante* as a forum to promote causes that affect women. His guests have discussed spousal abuse, addiction, and the need for reconciliation between family members.

People seem to feel they can talk to Don Francisco, that he will understand. Of course, he can't solve every problem, but like Oprah, he enjoys doing special things for his studio audience. For example, the show has a number of contests, and the prizes are sometimes new cars, or new home appliances, or even cash. He also likes to bring together family members who haven't seen each other for a long time. Many of his viewers are people who came to the United States to make a new life, and the rest of the family is still in the old country. Don Francisco may approach an audience member and ask him or her to talk about a family member he or she misses very much. As the story is being told, suddenly everyone sees a video greeting from that person in the old country. In most cases, the video marks the first time the audience member has seen the relative in a long time, and the reaction is very moving. But Don Francisco isn't done yet. The video was only part one. Suddenly, the family member emerges in person, having been flown to the United States for an emotional reunion, as the studio audience loudly applauds.

Don Francisco is also skilled in giving a human touch to current events that relate to the Hispanic audience. In one segment about illegal immigrants, he interviewed a Mexican couple whose daughter had died in the desert while trying desperately to cross the border and enter the United States. And whenever the Hispanic community suffers the loss of someone famous, it is often Don Francisco who helps his viewers to cope with the situation, as in 2005, when Latina singing sensation Selena was murdered by her former fan club president. Selena was one of the most popular young stars of that time, and Don Francisco hosted a tribute concert in her memory and even tried to comfort Selena's mother.

Sábado Gigante has evolved over the years. It was at first almost entirely focused on entertainment, but now time is allowed for advice-giving and problem-solving features. There have been other changes as well, and Don Francisco has benefited from them. As he explained to reporter George Winslow in 2004, Spanish-language TV in the United States has matured since he inaugurated the U.S. version of his show. "In the beginning, it was very low quality, and we had very poor production facilities," he recalls. But these days, *Sábado Gigante* is as flashy and professionally produced as any other U.S. show. Further, Don Francisco has seen the available audience grow, as more immigrants from Spanish-speaking countries have arrived in the United States, augmenting Americans of Hispanic descent who want to keep in touch with their heritage. "When I came on the air [in 1987], there were 12 million [Hispanic] viewers. Now there are 40 million" This larger audience has certainly benefited his network, Univision, and it has also benefited *Sábado Gigante*, giving the show new viewers while continuing to keep the old ones happy.

Although there are still critics who don't understand his show's enduring popularity, Don Francisco has continued to attract new generations of fans. Like the old variety shows of the 1950s, *Sábado Gigante* has something for viewers of all ages. It is not surprising that in 2001, Don Francisco was awarded a star on Hollywood's Walk of Fame, and in 2005, the National Academy of Television Arts and Sciences praised his longevity and gave him an Honorary Trustee award. He has also continued to do in the United States what he did in Chile: mobilize his audience to help during times of crisis. He raised funds for people left homeless during Hurricane Andrew in 1992, spoke out against hatred and violence after the attacks of 11 September 2001, and has donated his time to a number of causes related to children's health, literacy, and cross-cultural understanding, including being a goodwill ambassador for UNICEF. His ongoing fund-raising for the National Telethon in Chile each year has raised more than $160 million since he started the telethon in 1978, and it has resulted in the construction of seven new hospitals. One other organization to which he has donated considerable time is the Pan American Health Organization (PAHO), which gave him an award as a Champion of Health of the Americas in 2002 for his advocacy of childhood vaccination and better prenatal care. In December 2003, the government of Chile awarded him the Gabriela Mistral Order of Merit for his contribution to the country's culture and society.

Because Don Francisco is trusted by the Hispanic community, his show is an important stop for political candidates, including non-Hispanic candidates for political office. Both the 2000 and the 2004 U.S. presidential candidates (George W. Bush and Al Gore in 2000, and President Bush and John Kerry in 2004) made appearances on *Sábado Gigante*. Appearing on the show has also helped to launch several careers, most notably those of vocalists Enrique Yglesias and Thalia. And like the traditional variety shows to which *Sábado Gigante* has been compared, each week the show hosts some of the best-known performers are seen on the show—from pop stars like Marc Anthony, Jon Secada, Gloria Estefan, and Ricky Martin to salsa legend Celia Cruz to talk show host Cristina Saralegui.

Don Francisco also has a travel segment, for which he flies to interesting places all over the world to tape segments. Among the places he has visited are Russia, Jordan, and China.

Because his is such a well-known face, it is understandable that sponsors want him to endorse their products, even if some are somewhat uneasy about the seminude models seen on the show. A 2008 article in *Adweek* noted that sponsors who generally avoid shows perceived to be sexist make an exception for Don Francisco's show, because of his reputation as a trusted source. He became the national spokesperson for the Puerto Rican–based Banco Popular in 1999, when the company introduced its new credit cards. He has also commercially endorsed such products such as Mazola Corn Oil, Ford automobiles, as well as doing testimonials for companies like American Airlines and State Farm Mutual Auto Insurance. Because Don Francisco is multilingual (he speaks English, Spanish, and German fluently), he is very persuasive in selling videotapes to help his Spanish-speaking viewers learn conversational English.

THE MAN BEHIND THE TV PERSONA

While most viewers know him as the jovial and boisterous character he plays on TV, in real life Mario Kreutzberger is quite different from Don Francisco. People who have interviewed him find him affable but somewhat shy. Like many entertainers, he seems most comfortable when he is performing. For all his furious activity onstage, in his personal life he doesn't even like to go dancing. And negating all the controversy over his attitude toward women, he and his wife, Teresa, have been married for more than forty years. They have a daughter, Vivian; two sons, Patricio and Francisco; and nine grandchildren.

It is his daughter Vivian, better known as Vivi, who has been hosting the Chilean version of *Sábado Gigante* since the late 1990s, so that her father doesn't have to make as many trips between the two countries, and Vivi has become a TV star in her own right. Don Francisco admits the life they lead hasn't been easy for his wife. He has joked with reporters that he is really a bigamist, since he married his wife and television at the same time. Although he says that he has slowed down somewhat, his career as an entertainer still dominates his life, along with his ongoing efforts to raise money for causes he supports. It's difficult to escape from being Don Francisco.

Of course, as he gets older, he may have to face a time when somebody else hosts the show that he made famous. When asked by a reporter whether he had ever missed a performance, he said that the only time he could recall was when his mother died in 1974, an amazing record for more than forty-five years as a talk show host. An older man in a genre that caters to youth, he even admits to having had some cosmetic surgery so that his face will continue to be telegenic. But he is philosophical about the day when he will have to retire and sees it as a transition. After all, shows that he enjoys and admires, like *The Tonight Show*, have continued after their star—whether Steve Allen or Jack Paar or Johnny Carson—retired. But it's difficult for most fans to imagine *Sábado Gigante* with any host other than Don Francisco.

The Chilean immigrant who fell in love with TV the first time he saw it is now a wealthy celebrity, but his deep appreciation of the talk show genre remains unchanged. In 2002, he began doing a solo interview program every Wednesday night called *Don Francisco Presenta* (Don Francisco Presents). In addition to interviewing celebrities, he also chats with interesting guests who have done something unique or unusual. By 2004, the show had become one of Univision's most highly rated shows. Don Francisco has told reporters how much he was influenced by American talk shows. He admired Johnny Carson, and he is also a fan of Jay Leno, Carson's replacement. When time permits, he likes to watch David Letterman and Oprah Winfrey, but the success of Jerry Springer puzzles him: He can't understand why Springer's guests are so violent toward each other. However, no matter how famous other hosts may be, he doesn't try to imitate any of them. He has his own persona, and there is still nobody quite like him on television. Talk show hosts have come and gone, but to maintain success for more than four decades like Don Francisco is an achievement that may never be equaled.

DON FRANCISCO TIMELINE

1940: born in Talca, Chile
1962: debut of his variety show, then called *Sábados Gigantes*, on Chilean TV
1978: inaugurates a national telethon to raise money for handicapped children
1987: debut of U.S. version of *Sábado Gigante* in Miami

2001: awarded a star on Hollywood's Walk of Fame

2002: inaugurates a talk show called *Don Francisco Presenta*

2003: *Sábado Gigante* certified by the *Guinness Book of World Records* as the longest-running variety show on television

2005: given an Honorary Trustee award by the National Academy of Television Arts and Sciences; does one thousandth taping of *Sábado Gigante*

FURTHER READING

Brennan, Bryna. "Don Francisco Gives Back." *Perspectives in Health*, vol. 7, no. 3, 2002, online at www.paho.org/english/dpi/Number15_article4_4.htm.

DeLafuente, Della. "Lust in Translation: T&A Is a Hallmark of Spanish Language TV. Are Marketers OK with That?" *Adweek*, 4 February 2008, p. S1.

Dominguez, Robert. "Mr. Sabado Night." *New York Daily News*, 20 May 2006, p. 75.

Hill, Lee Alan. "Giant of Spanish TV First in U.S. Production." *Television Week*, 30 May 2005, p. 26.

Kreutzberger, Mario (Don Francisco). *Life, Camera, Action.* Miguel Hidalgo, Mexico: Grijalbo, 2001.

Lush, Tamara. "Señor Saturday Night." *St. Petersburg (FL) Times*, 21 August 2005, p. 1E.

Martin, Lydia. "Spanish Language TV Host Don Francisco Was Hispanic before Hispanic Was Cool." *Miami Herald*, 5 February 2000.

Rohter, Larry. "For 100 Million, He Is Saturday Night." *New York Times*, 2 June 2002, p. 32.

Wides-Munoz, Laura. "After 20 Years in U.S., Don Francisco Still Rules." Associated Press release, 13 October 2006.

Winslow, George. "Mario Kreutzberger: For 42 Years, 'Don Francisco' Has Hosted Sabado Gigante." *Broadcasting and Cable*, 8 November 2004, p. S26.

Courtesy of Professor Joseph Buchman

Herb Jepko

In the mid- to late 1960s, as talk radio began to change and hosts became more angry and confrontational, Herb Jepko was regarded by his fans as the proverbial breath of fresh air. His talk show style was the style of years before: He refused to discuss hot-button issues like religion or politics, he never shouted, and his focus was on creating an extended radio family. When listeners called the *Nitecaps*, as his program was titled, to chat, whether about something trivial or some exciting personal news, every caller was treated with courtesy and kindness. Herb's unique late-night show brought comfort and companionship to millions of listeners for nearly two decades. Critics didn't like the show and accused it of being boring, but the late-night audience of college students, shut-ins, shift workers, and long-distance truckers considered Herb Jepko their best friend.

EARLY YEARS

Herbert Earl Jepko was born in Hayden, Colorado, on 20 March 1931. His birth name was William Parke: At the time, having a child out of wedlock was considered shameful, and his birth mother, Mary Irene Parke, gave her son up for adoption. The baby's early years were difficult. He was adopted by Metro and Nellie Jepko of Prescott, Arizona, who renamed him Herbert, but their marriage was not saved by the arrival of a child, and the couple split up. To make things worse for young Herb, after the divorce his adoptive mother left, and then his father, a wounded veteran from the World War I, took ill and had to be hospitalized. As a result, Herb ended up in a number of foster homes, sometimes reunited with his father but then sent to foster care again. By the late 1940s, his father was healthy enough to gain custody, and the two of them moved to Phoenix. Herb finished high school and briefly attended Phoenix College, a two-year community college. He was thinking about eventually becoming a doctor, but he ran out of money and had to drop out before graduating.

At the age of nineteen, Jepko was drafted into the army, during the Korean War. Fortunately for him, he wasn't sent overseas to fight; the army wanted to train him for work in broadcasting. And so it was that he found his calling. He became chief of radio-television operations for the First Armored Division, which was stationed at Camp Roberts in California. His duties included writing and producing eighteen weekly radio shows and at least one television show, as well as producing army training films.

When his military service ended in 1954, Jepko stayed on the West Coast and sought work in radio. Like most newcomers, he worked at several small stations in order to gain experience; among them were KVNA in Flagstaff, Arizona, and KCKY in Coolidge, Arizona. As often happens at small stations, his duties varied: he was an announcer, sold advertising, and also performed some management functions. In his spare time, he participated in such service organizations as the Lions Club and Kiwanis International. That interest in community service would later become an essential part of his *Nitecaps* radio show, but in the late 1950s, Herb was still finding his way in commercial broadcasting; he didn't have a regular radio show, and much of his work was behind the scenes, where he learned all he could about the business side of radio.

Then, in 1959, Jepko got a job that had a profound influence on his life: He became the promotion director of KFI in Los Angeles. As part of his duties, he helped with all of KFI's publicity, and that meant working closely with one of the station's most popular announcers, Ben Hunter, who did a late-night program called the *Night Owl Show*. It was a very interactive program; Hunter took phone calls from listeners, a format that was still relatively new. At the time, such an announcer was called a beeper jockey, after the special phone line that stations used to put callers on the air; it emitted a beep tone every fifteen seconds. Hunter also had a club that his listeners could join; he called it the Night Owl Club, and local chapters were called roosts. Thanks to KFI's strong signal, the club had members from many distant cities. The way Hunter ran his overnight show influenced some of what Jepko later did on the air. Meanwhile, while working in California radio, Herb met Patsy Little Brown, who became the love of his life. Both had been married before, and both had children from those previous marriages, but this marriage was a strong one. Patsy soon became an integral part of Herb's radio success.

THE BIRTH OF *NITECAPS*

By 1961, Herb and Patsy had decided to move their blended family of six children to Salt Lake City, Utah, where Patsy's parents lived. Herb found on-air jobs at KCPX, playing jazz late at night, and at a new station, KANN in nearby Ogden, where he did the afternoon shift. Then, in 1962, the most influential station in the area, KSL, offered him an on-air midday position. By April 1963, he had been moved to mornings. But while he was at the top station in Salt Lake City in a very visible time slot, Herb was puzzled about something: KSL went off the air at midnight. It seemed like a waste of possible airtime for a station with such a powerful signal, and Herb, who had enjoyed being on the air late at night, decided to suggest an all-night show to KSL's management. He was convinced there was an audience out there, and he believed he could attract it. Management was skeptical, so skeptical that they told him he'd take a pay cut if he wanted to do that shift, and he was given six weeks to prove the show could be successful. Herb took the challenge, determined to show them that he could get KSL a late-night audience.

On 11 February 1964, Herb's new show debuted. It did not yet have a name and was simply referred to in the radio listings as *The Other Side of the Day*. The show's new name may have been chosen by a listener contest, or it may have been influenced by Ben Hunter's *Night Owl Show*, a name that had impressed Herb when he was doing KFI's publicity. Whichever way it happened, within a year, Herb Jepko's *The Other Side of the Day* program became known as the *Nitecaps*, although newspapers often referred to it as "The Night-caps Show," and fans of the program began to call themselves Nitecaps. By any name, Herb's show immediately stood out from other programs on radio at that time. The Nitecaps Show was an extended conversation; listeners could call and talk about anything, as long as it wasn't a controversial subject. As Jepko often told interviewers, he took pride in never embarrassing or insulting a listener. Jepko's listeners seemed to appreciate how he treated them: Even if they hadn't called for a while, he always remembered their names, and he seemed genuinely interested in how they were doing. Perhaps his audience, many of whom were elderly, became the family he had never had as a child.

At first, Jepko didn't get a lot of calls, but within months, the phone lines were busy all the time, even at 3 or 4 a.m. And because the station had a powerful 50,000-watt signal, the *Nitecaps Show*, just like Ben Hunter's *Night Owl Show* at KFI, could be heard in many distant cities, regularly receiving calls from hundreds of miles away. Today's toll-free phone lines and Internet phone technology make Herb's receiving calls from distant cities seems less than amazing, yet in that era of expensive long-distance calls, hundreds of people waited patiently to get through, just to chat with their radio friend Herb Jepko. In addition, while it is now taken for granted that large numbers of people are up late listening to radio or watching TV, in the media environment of the 1950s and the 1960s, many stations still signed off at 1 a.m., convinced that there was no need to stay on all night. Herb Jepko proved to KSL that he was right about late-night radio: it could develop a devoted audience, it could make money, and it could attract a lot of positive media attention.

A UNIQUE RADIO SHOW

Although his on-air persona was friendly, Herb still understood the basics of good radio. To make sure the conversation didn't drag, he had a device known as Tinkerbell, a music box that played the theme from the movie *Never on Sunday*. One of the show's rules was that a caller got a maximum of five minutes, and then Tinkerbell would remind the caller that time was up. There were other rules, too, such as being allowed to call only once every two weeks. After a slow start (on his first show, he had fewer than twenty calls), Jepko soon had no trouble finding enough callers, and all of the radio station's phone lines were busy all night long. His audience seemed to comprise shut-ins, truckers, shift workers, and lots of insomniacs, all of whom were eager to talk to Jepko and the other Nitecaps. Some had poems they wanted to read. Some tried to sing. Some had recipes to share or chatted about their grandchildren. Critics found the show puzzling, perhaps because it seemed to have no central theme, no excitement, no feuding guests. And yet, listening to it became like a religion for *Nitecaps* fans.

Herb Jepko, a nonpracticing Catholic, would probably not have described himself or his show as religious in any way, and yet his vision for the show involved such themes as doing good for others and helping those less fortunate. He wanted the *Nitecaps Show* to have a lasting effect, beyond the time he was on the air. Since his listeners regarded the show as a community, his next step was to create a club for fans of the show. Thus, the Nitecaps International Association (NIA) was born, and by late July 1965, the date of the first annual NIA convention in Salt Lake City, there were over twenty-five thousand active members. Nitecaps also organized into local groups, called Nitestands, and in addition to having monthly meetings, each Nitestand devoted itself to a particular charitable endeavor. For example, the Ogden, Utah, Nitestand made regular visits to a local hospital, where they read to patients and talked with the elderly.

The *Nitecaps Show* had its own theme song, "We're the Nitecaps," a cheerfully upbeat song written by devoted fan Della Dame Edmunds in 1965, and recorded by local musician Don Ray. Jepko had held a contest for fans to write an original theme song for the show, and Edmunds's song was declared the winner by *Nitecaps* fans at that first annual convention. The NIA also had membership cards, and there was a Nitecaps pledge, which became part of each Nitestand meeting. It stated, in part, "I hereby pledge myself to the building and support of the Nitecaps International Association (NIA), its founder, Herb Jepko, this Nitestand and every sincere Nitecap. I will seek and exalt the good I find in all persons and seek to overlook their errors and weaknesses, just as I trust others will accept me with my strengths and weaknesses. I will do all in my power to help build the Nitecap organization and to carry out all its projects designed to lend friendship, comfort and pleasure to all persons, particularly the ill, aged and unfortunate."

In addition, the *Nitecaps Show* had an official magazine, *The Wick*. In its pages were some of the same features as on the show, including recipes and chatty news from regular callers and NIA members, and news from the various Nitestands. *The Wick* also had inspirational messages from Herb about the goals of the NIA, as well as insights into what the show meant to him. In August 1965, he wrote about who comprised the show's audience:

A Nitecap is a person who finds a measure of pleasure in being awake during the dark hours . . . and turns to "The Nitecap Program" in search of companionship, intelligent discussion, story telling, and general, wholesome fun. A Nitecap might be a mother who awakens to care for the baby during the night and finds herself unable to return to restful sleep; a trucker on the highway at night who turns on the radio to ward off the drowsiness of motion; a student up late studying for an examination; a teacher up late grading the previous day's test papers; an all-night service station operator; an early-rising milk man, farmer or swing-shift worker. A Nitecap might be a nurse, a waitress, a motion-picture projectionist, a young man coming home from a late date. . . . Yes a Nitecap may have any number of occupations, but the one thing all Nitecaps have in common is the bond of friendship and understanding that shines like the brightest star in the night.

Besides the messages from Jepko, which also included cheery news about his own family, readers of *The Wick* enjoyed seeing the photographs each issued contained. In that pre-Internet era, such pictures were eagerly anticipated, because members in each city wanted to see what other members looked like. A wide variety of show-related merchandise was also advertised in *The Wick*. For example, from the November 1966 issue, fans could purchase Nitecap Stationary (100 sheets of paper and 50 envelopes, 2 for $5.00). There were "Herbie" Nitecap pins in silver for $2.25 or in gold for $3.00 (both for $5.00). The Don Ray Nitecap theme song was also for sale, on a 45-rpm record for $2.00 each or 6 for $10.00. Herb (whose listeners often called him Herbie) and his wife (known to radio listeners as Pat) filled all the orders themselves. Herb certainly knew how to promote his show, and there was always a demand for new Nitecaps items.

While Herb spoke about creating a nationwide Nitecaps movement that would do good for society, he was also a businessman. As much as he may have enjoyed hosting his giant radio family, he still had to make the show financially viable or it would go off the air. Because he had been in radio sales earlier, he knew how to get sponsors. And he was especially skilled in "direct-response advertising," that is, commercials that ask the listener to call a number or send a letter in order to receive the product. Herb sold many supplemental life insurance policies this way. He also had a few traditional sponsors, such as Icy Hot, a topical pain reliever. Whatever Herb asked listeners to send away for, it was Patsy who answered the lion's share of the mail.

As the *Nitecaps Show* grew in popularity, Herb and Patsy planned trips and tours for the members, all as part of Herb's mission to encourage Nitecaps to meet each other and become friends. And whenever possible, he went to the cities where there were Nitestands to do a remote broadcast of his show. In late September 1967, for example, he took the annual Nitecaps convention to Desert Hot Springs, California, and seven hundred fans attended. The city council was delighted to have such a prestigious event. Wrote Councilwoman Mae O'Harra in the *Desert Sentinel*, "Jepko can be called 'Mr. Success.' . . . He is the leader to more than 90,000 card-carrying Nitecaps, 27,000 in California. . . . Herb has received calls from every part of the globe, even ships at sea." In fact, wherever Herb did a broadcast from a remote location broadcast, large and enthusiastic crowds showed up.

By early 1968, Jepko had begun doing some syndication, putting the *Nitecaps* on several other radio stations in addition to KSL. The first was KXIV in Phoenix, Arizona, and then a handful of others followed, including KVOO in Tulsa, Oklahoma. A few stations stayed with the show, while others tried it and then dropped it; but Herb was proving that his show could get listeners even outside the greater Salt Lake area. In fact, according to an article in the March 1969 issue of *The Wick*, there were now about 119,000 Nitecaps nationwide. And according to a September 1971 Associated Press article, among the show's fans were a few celebrities, including then-governor Ronald Reagan of California and singer Pat Boone. By this time, critics were acknowledging that while they might not understand the show's appeal, Herb Jepko certainly had his finger on the pulse of Main Street USA.

MAKING HISTORY

The *Nitecaps Show* continued to grow, and by early 1975, Jepko had more than twenty phone lines in his studio to handle all the calls. He had been picking up more stations, including some with big signals like WHAS in Louisville, Kentucky, and WBAL in Baltimore. His staff, mainly his wife and himself in 1964, now numbered twenty-five. He had become enough of a phenomenon that in 1975, both the *Los Angeles Times* and the *New York Times* carried features about his unique radio show. Given his higher profile, it was not surprising that Mutual Broadcasting System, a national radio network, became aware of him and asked him to put his show on its affiliates. Today there are many syndicated late-night shows; in 1975 there was one: Herb Jepko's. The *Nitecaps Show* went on the network on 4 November 1975 and was now heard coast to coast on more than five hundred radio stations.

Friendly Voices in the Night

These voices were on local AM stations during the overnight shift, but because their stations had powerful signals, their voices carried. One of the most admired was Jean Shepherd, affectionately called Shep by his fans. He was a storyteller and humorist who talked to his *Night People* on the Jean Shepherd Show on WOR in New York City from 1956 through the mid-1970s. He never used a script, yet he kept audiences fascinated by his observations about the news, people he knew, and life in general.

In Boston, there was Larry Glick, who spent twenty years on WBZ Radio, where people in more than thirty states thought of themselves as "Glickniks." Larry had a quirky sense of humor. He played novelty songs, read weird news stories, talked about hypnotism (he performed at nightclubs), and took calls—if you got through, you might get a "Glick University" T-shirt, but if you weren't very interesting, he had a sound effect to "shoot you off the air." If you were a trucker in the 1970s, perhaps you listened to Buddy Ray on WWVA from Wheeling, West Virginia. His show was not strictly talk, since he played some country music, but he was known as the truckers' companion, taking calls from guys who missed their family or sending out the road conditions in other states. Buddy knew many of the truckers by name, and sometimes he'd go to a truck stop and do a remote broadcast for them.

The network affiliation should have been the start of something big for Herb, but unfortunately, it turned out to be a disaster. There was tension right from the start, with Mutual executives growing increasingly uncomfortable about the show's folksy and nonconfrontational style. According to an interview Herb did with the *New York Times*, demands were made that he make the show more controversial. There were also requests that he move closer to the corporate headquarters in Arlington, Virginia. As he told *Times* reporter John S. Crewdson in that 1977 interview, he said no to both. But the real problem was sales. Mutual had never broadcast an overnight show before, and its sales force had no idea how to sell all-night radio, especially radio aimed at an older audience. In years past, Herb had handled the sale of advertising, an area where he felt he had expertise; but the deal he signed with Mutual gave the network total control of sales, and in the end, the number of commercials was too small to generate sufficient revenue. Mutual canceled the *Nitecaps Show* on 29 May 1977.

The cancellation was a disappointment for Jepko, but a bigger one for his audience. He continued to work at KSL in Salt Lake City until August 1979, but then this station, too, canceled his show. His listeners refused to give up on the *Nitecaps Show*, however. A group of Nitecaps fans in San Diego got together and helped Herb get back on the air in June 1981, broadcasting from KMJC radio in El Cajon, California, as well as on a few other small stations. That experiment did not last, nor did a subsequent effort in October 1982. The era of the Nitecaps was over.

FINAL DAYS

For a while, Jepko worked for the Humane Society in Salt Lake City and also tried to get back into radio; as late as 1990, he did an air shift at a local station, KTTK, but he was never able to recapture his previous success. It was a difficult period for him: He still loved radio, but there was no longer a place for him in broadcasting. Undoubtedly affected by the death of his son Herb Jr. of AIDS in 1992, he became increasingly withdrawn and depressed. As Patsy Jepko later told reporters, Herb's depression was exacerbated by his own declining health (he suffered from severe arthritis) as well as the loss of his radio show. On 31 March 1995, Herb Jepko died of liver failure. He was sixty-four.

His fans never forgot him. Web sites were put up in his memory, and in June 2003, a plaque was awarded posthumously to him by the Utah Association of Broadcasters Hall of Fame. The inscription on the plaque, which resides at the University of Utah, reads:

> Over the span of three decades, Herb Jepko used radio and a soothing voice to connect thousands of listeners throughout the country. His Nitecap radio show began in 1964 and tapped into a segment of the elderly population that often

went unheard. From midnight till 6:00 am, Herb and his listeners discussed everything from the weather to the watermelon crop, but never politics or religion. This controversy-free environment created loyal audiences on KSL and other stations including stints on national networks. Herb Jepko's *Nitecap* show pioneered national talk radio and he created a culture served by his magazine and conventions as well as a lasting impact until he signed off in 1990.

Long after Herb had died, fans continued to remember what the show had meant to them, as they posted their recollections of him on nitecaps.net, a Web site started by Joseph Buchman, a professor of communication who became a friend of the Jepko family and wanted to preserve a history of the Nitecaps. Buchman also collected every issue of *The Wick*, so they could all be posted on the site. Thus, the words of Herb Jepko live on, letting him speak for himself about the phenomenon that was the *Nitecaps Show.*

ACKNOWLEDGMENT

Special thanks to Joseph Buchman for giving me access to issues of *The Wick*, and for creating the Herb Jepko tribute Web site www.nitecaps.net.

HERB JEPKO TIMELINE

1931: born in Hayden, Colorado; adopted by Metro and Nellie Jepko of Prescott, Arizona

1949: graduates from North Phoenix (Arizona) High School

1952: drafted into the army, where he becomes head of his division's radio-television department

1959: hired as publicist and promotion director at KFI, Los Angeles

1961: moves to Salt Lake City, where he is hired at KCPX

1962: hired at powerful KSL-AM

1964: begins doing his overnight *Nitecaps Show*

1965: first convention of the Nitecaps International Association held in Salt Lake City

1968: begins syndicating his show on several other stations

1975: show syndicated by Mutual Broadcasting System to a nationwide audience

1977: show canceled by Mutual, causing his fans great consternation

1979: local version of the show canceled by KSL

1990: attempts a comeback at station KTTK

1995: dies of liver failure at age sixty-four

FURTHER READING:

Bapis, James. "Utah Radio Program Rekindles Human Values, Listeners Say." *Ogden Examiner*, 25 July 1965, p. 16.

Broder, Mitch. "Small-Talk Show Is Big Draw in Wee Hours." *New York Times*, 23 February 1975, p. D29.

Crewdson, John M. "Cut in All Night Radio Has Insomniacs Muttering in the Dark." *New York Times*, 18 July 1977, p. L14.

Keith, Michael C. *Sounds in the Dark: All Night Radio in American Life.* Ames: Iowa State University Press, 2001.

O'Harra, Mae. "City Side." *Desert Sentinel* (Desert Hot Springs, CA), 28 September 1967, p. 2.

Rose, Hilly. *But That's Not What I Called About.* Chicago: Contemporary Books, 1978.

Courtesy of CNN/Photofest

Larry King

Larry King is one of television's most visible hosts, with the longest-running interview program on CNN (Cable News Network). A quick look through the TV listings over the past two decades demonstrates his importance: Nearly every major newsmaker has at one time or another appeared on *Larry King Live*. Whether they're stars who have behaved badly and want to make amends or candidates who have an announcement about their campaign, *Larry King Live* is where they want to be. And when a movie or TV plot portrays a typical TV talk show host, Larry King is often used as the example. He has made guest appearances on such TV shows as *Law and Order: Criminal Intent*; he offered his recollections about baseball in Brooklyn for a documentary called *The Brooklyn Dodgers: The Ghosts of Flatbush*; and he even did the voice of a character (Bee Larry King) in the animated film *Bee Movie*. Larry King is such a prolific interviewer that by the year 2000, his forty-third year on the air, he estimated that he had done over thirty thousand interviews. In 2006, his network said that in fact, the number was closer to forty thousand. Whatever the actual figure, there is no denying the iconic status of Larry King.

But Larry didn't start out to be a talk show host. In fact, at one point in his life, he seemed headed for prison.

EARLY YEARS

Larry King was born Lawrence Harvey Ziegler in Brooklyn, New York, on 19 November 1933. His father, Edward, and his mother, Jennie, were both Jewish immigrants from Russia. Edward owned a bar and grill in a lower-middle-class neighborhood in Brooklyn, and while it never made him rich, the family lived comfortably In 1926, his parents had a son whom they named Irwin, but he died of a ruptured appendix at the age of six, a year before Larry was born. As might be expected, Larry's parents overprotected him, worried that something might happen to him, too. In 1938, his brother Martin was born, but there were no other changes in the King household until World War II broke out. Larry's father tried to enlist in the armed forces but was turned down because he was too old and had two young children, so he sold the bar and concentrated on doing defense work at a plant in New Jersey.

With Larry's father earning a good salary, the King family was eagerly making new plans for after the war, but in 1944, their lives suddenly changed: Edward King unexpectedly died of a heart-attack at the early age of forty-three. Larry was told repeatedly that he was now the "man of the house." He was only 11, and it was a responsibility he didn't want. Even with help from her extended family, Larry's mother, now the sole support of two young boys, and had to go on welfare (which was then called *relief*).

An indifferent student, King graduated from Lafayette High School in the Bensonhurst section of Brooklyn, but he had no plans for college. In fact, his heart was in radio: He had loved broadcasting since he was five, even pretending to be an announcer by "announcing" what he saw when looking out his window. He dreamed of one day being on the air, but wanting to help his mother with the bills, he took a variety of odd jobs, including making deliveries for United Parcel Service. One day, he accidentally met the chief announcer at CBS radio, James Sirmons. When he asked how to get a radio job, Sirmons told him to go first to a smaller city to get experience, suggesting Miami, where the small stations supposedly had openings. Deciding to follow his dream, Larry got on a bus for Miami one day in 1957; he had an uncle who lived there, and he was ready to try to get a radio job.

EARLY FAILURES AND SUCCESSES

Unfortunately, Miami was not the paradise King had expected, and instead of an immediate radio job, he ended up working as a janitor at one of Miami's smallest stations, a 250-watt AM station called WAHR. Then, as luck would have it, the morning disc jockey quit, and Larry offered to fill in. Before he did, the station manager told him his last name sounded "too Jewish" and suggested something non-ethnic, like King. Thus, in May 1957, the persona of "Larry King" was born. After a brief time at WAHR, Larry moved to a bigger station, WKAT. At that time, announcers often did their shows from clubs or restaurants, which guaranteed a live audience as well as the possibility that local politicians or celebrities would stop by. Doing live morning radio during the late 1950s, Larry began to hone his skills as an interviewer, and by late 1958, he was working for one of Miami's top radio station, WIOD. He did his morning show from a deli called Pumpernik's, where he sat in a booth and chatted with customers, tourists, and whoever dropped by. His first celebrity was singer Bobby Darin, and more celebrities soon followed. Larry's style was simple: He asked for information that he thought the average person might want to know. For example, he asked Darin about his real name and where the name Bobby Darin had come from. When interviewing an author, he did not read the book ahead of time; instead of talking about the book, he just engaged the author in conversation. Having grown up listening to radio, he admired the well-known network commentators, and now that he was doing his own show, he wanted to provide the audience interesting discussion.

King was becoming famous in Miami, with a newspaper column in the *Miami Herald* as well as his radio show and a local TV interview program about current events, called *Miami Uncovered*, on WPST. But it was on radio that he was happiest. Well-known performers who were in Miami stopped by to see him, including vocalist Ella Fitzgerald, comedian Don Rickles, and TV impresario Ed Sullivan. Even in his spare time, he began socializing with famous people. As he would later admit, he began living far beyond his means. A compulsive gambler, he soon found that the bills were piling up, as were the phone calls from bill collectors. Some accounts say he was as much as $300,000 in debt and also hadn't paid his taxes. In 1971, he was arrested for larceny, the result of some shady business deals that he had engaged in trying to get himself out of debt. Although the charges were eventually dropped, his reputation in Miami was ruined. Always the master of reinvention, Larry left Miami and spent some time on the West Coast, writing for magazines and trying to get back into radio. By 1975, he had returned to Miami, and WIOD hired him back. He was as popular as ever, and by 1978, he was ready for the next big career move.

Barry Gray, Talk Radio's Founding Father

We may never know who invented two-way talk radio, but many people believe it was Barry Gray. It began accidentally: Hired as a disc jockey at WOR in New York, Gray was doing his usual overnight shift one evening in 1945. He was discussing jazz star Woody Herman, when suddenly Woody called in, and Gray decided to put the call on the air. The rest is talk radio history, as Gray began having regular on-air conversations with celebrities.

In the late 1940s, Gray worked in Miami at WMIE and WGBS, where he shocked some listeners by talking to black musicians about their experience of racism. By mid-1950, he had returned to New York and was hired by WMCA. He remained there for thirty-nine years. Gray chatted with the stars of music and movies, but he also discussed contentious issues. It was on the *Barry Gray Show* that listeners learned that the famous Stork Club wouldn't admit black people. When Gray defended singer Josephine Baker, who had been refused service there, columnist Walter Winchell (who was friendly with the club's owner) began to feud with Gray; the feud lasted for several years. Gray repeatedly stood up for the underdog and took unpopular stands, such as criticizing McCarthyism in the 1950s. He was always on top of the action: He debated Malcolm X in March 1960, and in October 1964, he moderated the New York senatorial campaign debate between Kenneth B. Keating and Robert F. Kennedy.

Toward the end of his career, Gray returned to WOR, the New York City station where his radio career had begun. It was there that he did his last shows. He died on 22 December 1996, at age 79, and while few people today know his name, the success of talk radio is partly due to him.

Since 1977, the Mutual Broadcasting System had been experimenting with a national late-night radio show. The network had first tried the popular Salt Lake City announcer Herb Jepko, but the show had not produced enough advertising revenue, and Jepko's contract was not renewed. Then Mutual tried a New York City announcer named Long John Nebel, but Nebel was ill and nearly at the end of his career. After Nebel, Mutual was still trying to find the right announcer for a national late-night talk show, and a Mutual executive named C. Edward Little knew who that announcer might be. Little had been in upper management at WGMA Radio in Hollywood, Florida, for many years, and King had briefly worked at his station. Now, Little was the president of Mutual and, having heard Larry's work in the Miami market, was certain that Larry would be the ideal late-night host: He was a celebrity interviewer who would attract thirty-five- to fifty-four-year-olds, the demographic that advertisers wanted. So Little persuaded Larry to leave Miami and relocate to Washington, DC (Mutual's studios were in nearby Arlington, Virginia), to do a national all-night talk show. In late January 1978, Mutual put Larry King on the air, announcing in newspaper advertisements that this was a "coast-to-coast" radio show. It started with 28 affiliates and at the beginning didn't even have a toll-free number; yet people began calling in almost immediately. By early 1980, King was being heard on nearly 220 stations. As in Miami, Larry was able to get the good guests, including authors, comedians, and politicians, but he also sought out people he thought the audience would find interesting, such as lawyers who had been involved in high-profile cases or well-known professional athletes. Not everyone was an easy interview. Some guests began by responding just yes or no to Larry's questions, but more often than not, he was able to draw them out and get something interesting for his audience to listen to. In the show's usual format, King interviewed the guest during the first part, and then the listeners were invited to call in. And they did, in large numbers.

BECOMING A STAR

Cable news on television had come into its own in the early 1980s, and Ted Turner, then the owner of CNN, thought King's radio style would translate well to a television show. King had always joked that he had the perfect face for radio, but in June 1985, there he was on CNN, doing *Larry King Live* every week night at 9 p.m. Among his first guests were Mario Cuomo, then the governor of New York; actress Betty Davis; and singer Frank Sinatra. Because it was delivered by satellite, the show was seen live all over the world and was perhaps the first call-in talk show to be seen internationally. The premise was simple, as it had been on radio: There was no fancy set, nothing distracting, just Larry at a desk with a microphone, a telephone, and, of course, his guests for that evening. And just as on radio, the response was very positive. Larry talked to everyone, from Playboy bunnies to presidents of corporations. Critics accused him of asking "softball" questions, of being too deferential to his guests, but audiences liked his nonconfrontational and nonargumentative style, and guests liked him because he seemed genuinely interested in what they had to say. Just as in Miami in the late 1950s, King used his natural curiosity to ask the questions he thought his audience would want to ask.

Larry King Live became so well known that political candidates used the show to test the waters for their own campaigns. In mid-February 1992, Texas billionaire H. Ross Perot appeared on King's show to discuss a possible run for the presidency. His office was immediately deluged with phone calls from over a million people, offering to volunteer. The critics were divided about whether using television to test the waters for a presidential run was good for democracy, some worrying that political candidates would turn the race for president into a TV popularity contest rather than a serious discussion of the issues. But once the impact of Perot's appearance on the show became clear, it didn't take long for other politicians to guest on the show. In November 1993, Vice President Al Gore debated with Ross Perot on free trade and the proposed North American Free Trade Agreement (NAFTA), and 16.3 million viewers saw the show—a record for that time. What started in 1992–1993 became a fixture on Larry's show: From then on, numerous politicians and presidential candidates stopped by to take questions from him and the viewers.

King has also interviewed many international leaders, such as the Soviet Union's Mikhail Gorbachev and Jordan's Queen Noor. A 1995 series on the Middle East included conversations with Yasser Arafat of the Palestinian Authority, King Hussein of Jordan, and Israeli prime minister Yitzhak Rabin. In fact, there are few major political figures whom King hasn't interviewed during his long career. The same is true of celebrities, from sports stars like Michael Jordan and Mike Tyson to television superstars like Oprah Winfrey and Johnny Carson. Even many religious leaders have appeared on King's show, including the Reverend Billy Graham; Gordon B. Hinckley, at the time the head of the Mormon Church; and the Dalai Lama, the leader of Tibetan Buddhism. No matter how important the guest may be, Larry insists that he is not intimidated: "I approach them not as famous people, just as people—who probably have the same likes, dislikes, and feelings as the rest of us" (King, 2004, p. 74).

Of course, King's show is not always filled with serious topics. In fact, critics have taken him to task for giving airtime to psychics like John Edward and Sylvia Browne, who claim they can talk to the dead. He has also been criticized for spending too much time focusing on celebrity gossip and scandals, but he isn't bothered by the criticism. He believes his success is largely due to his being able to sign the guests that the average person is most curious about at any given moment, and while sometimes these people are celebrities who have behaved badly, just as often his guests are important newsmakers like former president Richard Nixon or former British prime minister Margaret Thatcher.

In early 1998, a month before her death, King interviewed Karla Faye Tucker, the first woman executed in Texas since the Civil War. At that time, Tucker's impending execution was outraging millions of death penalty opponents worldwide, and the debate intensified after Tucker experienced what seemed to her supporters to be a very sincere religious awakening and a commitment to the Christian faith. Religion and faith are frequent topics of discussion on King's show. While he has stated that he is totally nonreligious (he had a bar mitzvah but seems to have had few ties to organized Judaism since then), Larry has frequently invited some of America's best-known clergy of all faiths to discuss subjects like what the world's religions say about war or whether religious tolerance is possible since the events of 11 September 2001.

NEW PROBLEMS, NEW SUCCESSES

King's career as a celebrity interviewer has made him a very wealthy man; in 2006, his annual salary was $7 million. It has also earned him such respect that his awards could fill a museum, including ten CableACE awards for best interviewer and best talk show (*ACE* stands for "Award for Cable Excellence"; these awards were the early equivalent of the Emmys for cable TV); induction in 1989 into the Radio Hall of Fame; a George Foster Peabody Award for his election coverage in 1992; a 1993 Neuharth Award for excellence in journalism; and the Hugh Downs Award for communication excellence in 2007. *Talkers,* the Bible of the talk show genre, named him the fourth greatest radio talk show host of all time in 2002 and simultaneously named him the top television talk host as well. In 1997, he was given a star on the Hollywood Walk of Fame. In 2003, he was the master of ceremonies when the National Radio Hall of Fame held its awards ceremony in Chicago, and a portion of the event was broadcast on the Westwood One Radio Network. In 2007, he got his own city block, as the Los Angeles City Council voted to rename a city block near CNN's studio Larry King Square, in recognition of King's fifty years in broadcasting.

But with his radio and TV success came certain problems in Larry's personal life—a heavy smoker, he had a heart attack in February 1987 and required quintuple bypass surgery to save his life. He has since quit smoking and frequently covers issues related to good health. In 1988, he set up the Larry King Cardiac Foundation to help people who can't afford cardiac care. In 1989, he also wrote a book about his experience, *Mr. King, You're Having a Heart Attack.*

By his own admission, Larry King is still a very driven person, obsessively devoted to his work. This dedication may explain why he has been married six (some sources say seven) times. And although in late 1994, he stopped doing his radio show, he did not slow down. Well known for his involvement in philanthropy, he continued to raise money for worthy causes, including the Pediatric Epilepsy Foundation. He also donated $1 million to George Washington University's School of Media and Public Affairs in the District of Columbia, to provide scholarships for disadvantaged students. After Hurricane

Katrina brought destruction to Louisiana and Mississippi in 2005, King was an active participant in raising money for the victims. He hosted a three-hour special broadcast in early September that year, called *How You Can Help*. The broadcast not only raised money for the victims but also provided information to viewers about relief efforts and where they could contribute. A number of celebrities were seen live or via satellite, including singer Celine Dion and actor Bill Cosby.

While critics have continued to accuse him of doing softball interviews, his nonconfrontational style has brought guests to his show who generally avoid appearing on talk shows, such as Vice President Dick Cheney. And celebrities who are caught up in a scandal or political figures who need damage control frequently turn to *Larry King Live*, where they know they will be able to make their case before a huge audience. A good example occurred in January 2006, when Oprah Winfrey was under critical attack for having chosen the book *A Million Little Pieces* for her famous book club, and doing an enthusiastic interview with its author, James Frey, on her show. When the book, which purported to be a nonfiction memoir, turned out to be a fake, Oprah called in to Larry's show to try to explain and to defend her book club. King also had Frey on the show to discuss what was true and what was false in the book.

In 2007, CNN held a week-long celebration of Larry's fiftieth year in broadcasting. Among the celebrities who appeared during the week to pay tribute to Larry were Oprah Winfrey, former president Bill Clinton, and comic Bill Maher. CNN also announced that it was issuing a special three-disc DVD entitled *Larry King Live: The Greatest Interviews*. With his trademark suspenders and his seemingly unlimited energy, Larry insisted he wasn't even thinking about retiring, even though he would turn seventy-five in November 2008. However, something seemed to change in the spring of 2008: There were rumors in the press that King might indeed cut back on his hectic schedule, and this time, Larry did not refute those rumors, nor did CNN. Larry had already told Jacques Steinberg of the *New York Times* in 2007 that if somebody did replace him, he thought his friend Ryan Seacrest, a radio and TV talk show host who had gained fame as host of the highly rated TV talent show *American Idol*, would be a good choice. Seacrest, who also hosted a syndicated radio show, *American Top 40*, was an experienced celebrity interviewer, and he had filled in for Larry on a number of occasions. In April 2008, stories in the media suggested that CNN and Seacrest were in negotiations and that sometime in 2009, Seacrest would probably be named the show's permanent host. However, several months later, as CNN continued to deny the reports, media interest in what seemed to have been only a rumor faded.

As 2008 progressed, it became increasingly apparent that while King was willing to discuss his eventual retirement, he hadn't yet made any official decision to step down. He has not only continued doing *Larry King Live*, but he has also continued writing or cowriting books. Some are about his life and the celebrities he has met, such as a 2000 collection of anecdotes and recollections called *Anything Goes: What I've Learned from Pundits, Politicians and Presidents*, and others are advice books about how to be a better communicator, such as a book he originally wrote in 1994 that was so popular it was reissued ten years later: *How to Talk to Anyone, Anytime, Anywhere*. And while Larry is certainly young at heart, occasionally, his age does manifest itself: In a November 2006 interview with comedian Roseanne Barr, he startled his guest and his audience by admitting he had never used the Internet. But within a few months, he had established a Web site and was trying to send e-mail. Larry King has always been able to adapt. Perhaps that is why he has remained the best-known interviewer on television.

LARRY KING TIMELINE

1933: born Lawrence Harvey Ziegler in Brooklyn, New York

1957: first on-air radio job, using the name Larry King

1958-62: hosts an interview show on WIOD in Miami

1978-94: does nationally syndicated radio show on Mutual network

1985: begins doing nationally syndicated talk show, *Larry King Live!* on CNN

1987: has heart attack and needs quintuple bypass surgery

1989: inducted into Radio Hall of Fame

1992: announcement by Ross Perot of his candidacy for the presidency on *Larry King Live*

1997: gets a star on Hollywood's Walk of Fame

2002: named by *Talkers* magazine as one of the top five most influential talk hosts of all time

2007: celebrates his fiftieth year in broadcasting

FURTHER READING

Applebome, Peter. "Perot, the Simple Billionaire, Says Voters Can Force His Presidential Bid." *New York Times*, 29 March 1992, p. 1.

Garvin, Glenn. "King of CNN: Rags, Riches, Miami Roots." *Miami Herald*, 14 January 2007, n.p.

King, Larry, with Marty Appel. *When You're from Brooklyn, the Rest of the World Is Tokyo*. Boston: Little, Brown, 1992.

King, Larry, with Bill Gilbert. *How to Talk to Anyone, Anytime, Anywhere*. New York: Gramercy Press, 2004.

Laurent, Lawrence A. "Radio: Larry King." *Washington Post*, 14 December 1980, p. 38.

Meyer, Thomas J. "The Master of Chin Music." *New York Times Magazine*, 26 May 1991, pp. 20–21, 32.

Nye, Doug. "Larry King Still Can't Believe Success of his Television Show." *Augusta (GA) Chronicle*, 11 March 2000, p. B6.

Steinberg, Jacques. "Who's Talking about Retirement?" *New York Times*, 5 April 2007, p. E1.

Larry King's Web site is www.cnn.com/CNN/Programs/larry.king.live. The Larry King Cardiac Foundation is at www.lkcf.org

AP Photo/Ric Francis

Jay Leno

Jay Leno has been called one of the hardest-working comedians in show business. Beginning in 1969 when he was still in college, he continually performed his act as many nights as he could get hired, and even after becoming an established comedian in the 1980s, that relentless pace did not change. A 1983 profile of him in the *Washington Post* noted that in addition to making TV appearances, he performed in clubs every night of the year. By some accounts, even after he was named host of *The Tonight Show* in 1992, he still performed in clubs as many as three hundred days a year, and seldom took a day off. While many celebrities get into the tabloids for behaving badly, Jay Leno isn't one of them. He and his wife, Mavis, have that rare Hollywood marriage which, by all accounts, is both happy and successful. Leno is rich (his annual salary in 2004 was increased to about $27 million), he's famous, and in the fiercely competitive talk show industry, he's number one in the ratings. And yet his goals haven't changed: Ever since he was a child, Jay Leno has known that what he enjoys most is making people laugh.

EARLY YEARS

James Douglas Muir Leno was born on 28 April 1950 in New Rochelle, New York, but he and his brother, Patrick, were raised in Andover, Massachusetts, about thirty miles from Boston. Jay's mother, Catherine, was a homemaker, and his father, Angelo, sold insurance. Neither had a background in show business, but Angelo had a good sense of humor and often joked. Conversely, his mother tended to be more serious, and Jamie, as she called Leno, liked to try to make her laugh. In fact, from very early in his school life, Jay was the class clown, always trying to amuse people. By his own admission, he was an indifferent student, perhaps because he was mildly dyslexic. He often got C's, but an English teacher interested him in creative writing, and this interest gave him the idea of writing comedy scripts. He graduated from Andover High School in 1968 and then attended Boston's Emerson College, which has a strong program in performing arts and media. While in college, Leno began to work on comedy routines and started doing some performing. And although he graduated in 1973 with a degree in speech, he told reporters years later that he went to college only because he had promised his parents he would. On the other hand, one piece of advice his mother gave him would prove especially useful. She said that since he was dyslexic, he would always have to work twice as hard if he wanted to succeed. It was advice that he took to heart.

Breaking into show business isn't easy, and Jay Leno's early years as a new comedian were filled with the frustration and rejection every inexperienced entertainer endures. To make some money, he found a job at a Rolls Royce dealer as a mechanic; working on cars had always been one of his passions, and collecting and restoring them would later become a hobby. In 1972, the year before he graduated from college, he finally bought his first car, a 1955

Buick Roadmaster. He paid three hundred dollars for it, and in 2004, he was still taking it out for a drive. Once he fell in love with a car, he liked to hang onto it. Among his duties while working for the car dealer was driving some of the cars from Boston to customers in New York and New Jersey. Jay took this opportunity to keep an eye on who was performing at the comedy clubs in Manhattan, and even to try out his own act on amateur night.

The greater Boston area was not a mecca for comedy, so making contacts in New York City was very useful. Since Leno couldn't afford to stay in New York for long periods of time, he also tried to find places in the Boston area to get experience. They were often bars and strip clubs, where patrons were more interested in drinking or watching the dancers than in listening to a new comedian. He also performed at colleges, and even at carnivals. Wherever he went, he was honing his observational humor.

Leno is not movie-star handsome. His prominent chin would later be the subject of caricatures (and the joking title of his 1996 autobiography, *Leading with My Chin*). But he had a pleasant and expressive face and the comic persona of an average Joe who points out the puzzling, ironic, and foolish aspects of daily life. Unlike many comedians of the 1970s, he wasn't vulgar and he didn't make jokes about drugs. In fact, he didn't use drugs at all, nor did he drink or smoke. He was so focused on perfecting his comedic skills that he regarded the party scene as a waste of time. Jay's parents were supportive but puzzled. They couldn't quite understand his determination to be a professional comedian, but no matter how hard things got, nothing could change his mind.

Leno was finally able to work his way up to performing at a respected local club, Lennie's-on-the-Turnpike, where he was booked along with the hit rock group America. Unfortunately, there weren't enough of these opportunities, and it soon became obvious to Jay that he needed to be closer to one of the centers of the comedy profession, New York City or Los Angeles. While he was tuned to *The Tonight Show* one night, he came to the conclusion that his act was better than the one he was watching. Since *The Tonight Show* was taped on the West Coast, he decided that LA was where he should go. His goal was to become good enough to perform on Johnny Carson's show—Carson was one of Jay's comedy heroes. So in 1974, he packed up and moved to Los Angeles, where he began performing at local clubs. At times, he made so little money that he had to sleep in his car, but he had no regrets about his choice. He believed that if he worked harder than everyone else, he would ultimately become a success, and he was prepared to do whatever it took to build up his name.

MOVING UP

Among the clubs in Los Angeles where he began performing regularly was the Comedy Store, and while there, he met and worked with a number of young comedians, such as Jimmie Walker, Richard Lewis, and Elayne Boosler.

He also encountered another up-and-coming comic, a new one who had come to the Coast from Indiana: David Letterman. They became friends, and later, when Letterman got his own show, he invited Jay to be a guest. Meanwhile, throughout the mid-1970s, Jay kept performing, night after night. Some of the people he had worked with were cast in TV situation comedies, notably Jimmie Walker, whose sitcom *Good Times* became a hit on CBS, but Jay was told by one network executive that TV sitcoms weren't an option for him because he wasn't attractive enough. Jay was philosophical; he really wanted to do stand-up comedy, not be a character on a TV show. He did some script writing for *Good Times*, but he kept returning to his goal of being a star in stand-up comedy.

One of Leno's wishes did come true on a night in 1975. He was performing at a club called the Improv (short for *improvisation*) when Johnny Carson came by to watch the evening's acts. He critiqued Jay's performance and advised him to put more jokes into his routine, and Jay took his hero's advice to heart. He was also able to perform on two popular variety shows, the *Merv Griffin Show* and the *Mike Douglas Show*.

On 2 March 1977, Leno got the opportunity he had been waiting for: a chance to perform on *The Tonight Show*. He made sure he had plenty of jokes, and Carson must have liked what he heard because he invited Jay back for another appearance. Leno has said that each time he was on *The Tonight Show*, he felt in awe of Carson and never relaxed completely. Interestingly, he performed much better on his friend David Letterman's new show than he did on Carson's. Throughout the mid-1980s, Letterman had Leno as a guest about once a month, and thanks to those appearances, Leno became more confident. Evidently Johnny Carson had seen enough potential in Jay to stay informed of how the comic was progressing, and the regular appearances on Letterman's show made an impression. In September 1986, Leno was chosen as one of the two permanent guest hosts, along with Gary Shandling, to fill in when Carson had a day off or was on vacation. But Shandling was doing a comedy show on cable TV, and when it became a hit, he dropped out of guest hosting, leaving Leno as the only guest host on *The Tonight Show*, a role he filled from 1987 to 1992; during that time, he made more than three hundred appearances, which made the audience comfortable with him.

But behind the scenes, there was about to be a problem. Leno and David Letterman, his friend, were in competition to take Carson's place when he retired. The quirky and offbeat Letterman had developed a sizable following on *Late Night with David Letterman* on NBC. In fact, this show had followed Carson's *The Tonight Show* since February 1982, and Carson liked Letterman. But the rumor was that Carson was going to give the show to Jay Leno. Letterman's allies were lobbying hard for him, trying to persuade NBC that he would be a better host that Leno. Leno and his allies were doing the same on Leno's behalf. In the end, the competition for *The Tonight Show* became so intense and harsh that it cost Jay and Dave their friendship. By most accounts,

Dave Garroway and *Today*

Television was still fairly new in mid-January 1952, when NBC debuted a new morning program. *Today* offered the TV audience all the elements of morning radio: cheery announcers, news, weather, comedy, and celebrity guests. The host of the new show was Dave Garroway, a Chicago announcer who became one of the 1950s' most popular TV hosts.

Garroway first became involved in broadcasting in 1938, when he got a job as a page at the NBC studios in New York while attending the network's announcer school. He became a popular disc jockey at WMAQ in Chicago in 1939, and by 1949, he was doing a local TV variety show, *Garroway at Large*, that was syndicated by NBC. His style was relaxed and conversational, and he didn't take himself too seriously. His trademark was a bow tie, along with large horn-rimmed glasses. He looked like a professor.

NBC executives liked his work on Chicago television, so they relocated him to New York to host *Today*. Garroway was a likable host, but the show's ratings were slow to build. Then, in late January 1953, the show got a mascot, a chimpanzee named J. Fred Muggs. The viewers loved him. There is evidence that Garroway hated the concept, but it worked. *Today* became a successful morning TV show. However, behind the scenes, he and the chimpanzee never got along. Garroway also battled an addiction problem, but viewers would not have known that. On the air, he was genial and friendly and he made the early morning more bearable. After he left *Today* in 1961, he produced an educational program for PBS and later tried to host one more show of his own before he retired. Also unknown by most fans was that Garroway suffered from depression, and he ultimately committed suicide in July 1982. Dave Garroway is remembered for putting morning television on the map and proving that people would indeed get up early to watch TV.

they have not spoken to each other since. Johnny Carson made the announcement that Jay Leno had been chosen, and although NBC wanted Letterman to remain on the network, he sincerely felt that *The Tonight Show* should have been his. He ultimately left NBC for a show of his own at CBS, directly opposite his former friend.

Meanwhile, with much fanfare, Carson retired, and the torch was passed to Jay Leno, who did his first program as the new host on 25 May 1992. While he would later admit to being surprisingly nervous, Leno had other problems to contend with. For one, he was replacing a legend: Carson had done his last show just several days before, ending a thirty-year career. Critics wondered if Jay Leno would be able to make *The Tonight Show's* fans replace their love of Johnny with a love for Jay. And at first, Leno's future as a host didn't look very promising. While the ratings were acceptable, the reviews from critics were nearly all negative. One said Leno was like a robot, with not enough personality, while another said he was just a joke teller and paled in comparison to Carson. The general feeling of the critics was that NBC had made a terrible mistake. Then there was the public perception that Letterman had been cheated out of a job he deserved. It seemed to Jay that nearly every day, another negative story about him appeared in the media. Not generally considered a "bad guy" in show business, suddenly he was written about as the villain in the Letterman/Leno story. All he could do was try to ignore the negative publicity and keep working, but it wasn't easy. And then, to make matters even worse for the pro-Leno camp, when the new Letterman show took to the airwaves on CBS, it got better ratings than *The Tonight Show*.

The entire story of how Letterman and Leno fought for the job of *The Tonight Show* host was revealed by *New York Times* media critic Bill Carter in a 1994 book, *The Late Shift*, which also became a made-for-TV movie on HBO in 1996. It seemed that the public was endlessly fascinated by the rivalry between these two well-known talk show hosts.

LENO AS *THE TONIGHT SHOW* HOST

Most people didn't know how difficult that first year was for Jay. For one thing, his longtime manager, Helen Kushnick, who had alienated guests and staff alike, was fired by NBC. She may have had Jay's interests at heart, but she had become a polarizing figure. Among the reasons people disliked her were her insistence that guests commit themselves to appearing only on Leno's show and no one else's; her tendency to scream at people for the slightest reason; and the rumor that it was she who had originally planted stories in the press that Johnny Carson was too old and was about to be replaced. Jay, known for his loyalty, didn't want to be the one to make the decision, but once NBC fired Kushnick, some of the tensions on the set dissipated.

Another source of tension for Jay that first year was his mother's illness. In early 1993, Catherine Leno was dying of cancer, and Jay flew home every weekend to be with her. In June, she finally died, and the experience affected Leno deeply. He even mentioned it on the air, proving that there are times when even a comedian can't find humor in a situation.

But the biggest problem for Jay was finding his own voice, rather than being perceived as an imitation of Johnny Carson. As he later told Curt Schleier in a 1997 interview, "I think my big mistake was doing the show the way Johnny had done the show, which was fine for Johnny. But, obviously, if you move into somebody else's house, you can't live the way they do. You have to live like you do."

In mid-May 1993, *The Tonight Show* made its first road trip, doing a live telecast from Boston's Bull and Finch Pub to mark the final episode of NBC's hit program *Cheers*. And after some serious evaluation, in late September 1994, Jay decided to make some changes in the set, to give it more the look of a comedy club. He also changed some of the show's features: He made the opening monologue longer, and he hired a different bandleader, as Branford Marsalis departed and Kevin Eubanks joined the show. Eubanks was not as well known as Marsalis, but he is a talented musician with an engaging smile, and the banter between him and Jay is much more relaxed. In fact, the more Jay put his own stamp on the show, the better things went. By 1995, his ratings were on the rise. One incident that helped increase those ratings was actor Hugh Grant's appearance on 10 July 1995 to discuss his recent arrest for lewd conduct; the Los Angeles police had caught him in his car with a prostitute. Grant had a close relationship with then-model (and later, actress) Elizabeth Hurley, and fans were curious about how she would react to Grant's escapade. Leno was incredulous, asking Grant why he'd behaved as he had, and to Grant's credit, he responded honestly, apologizing for his bad behavior; he also praised Hurley for being so understanding. Celebrity scandals have always boosted the ratings of talk show hosts, and this one was no exception. Also helpful to Jay's ratings was some topical humor, a recurring comedy skit during the O. J. Simpson murder trial called the "Dancing Itos." It featured male dancers dressed in judge's robes, wearing beards and stage makeup so that they would resemble the trial's presiding judge, Lance Ito. The "Dancing Itos" did choreographed routines and were greeted enthusiastically by the viewers, who understood the skit's message: The trial had become a circus and the judge was not in control of the proceedings.

Topical humor became a large part of Leno's opening monologue. Coming from stand-up comedy, he had become accustomed to making observations about everything, including current events. Critics who had previously dismissed him praised him for his ability to tell jokes about even the latest-breaking news events. In fact, his opening monologue was said to contain "the largest number of topical jokes on any network late-night show" (Shales, 2005). Of course, doing topical humor is harder than it looks. For one thing, Leno was very careful not to align himself with any one political party. He skewered whoever was in in the news and played no favorites. He also understood that his role was to entertain, not to be polemical or ideological. He avoided jokes that would be too esoteric for the average viewer, not because he thought the average viewer was stupid but because many Americans didn't follow politics and current events very closely. Jay turned that lack of political awareness into a recurring feature, "Jaywalking," and a contest called "Battle of the Jaywalk All-Stars." The segment pokes fun at just how oblivious of the news some people are. It is a taped segment in which Leno asks ordinary people on the street to identify a big name or famous event in the news; in many cases, they have no idea what he is talking about, even when it is one of the biggest news stories of the day.

As the 1990s progressed, Jay Leno solidified his number one rating, continuing to attract big-name guests and win over new fans. He also had credibility with his sponsors. In fact, when computer giant Microsoft wanted to introduce its Windows 95 Operating System, they turned to Jay Leno to be a spokesperson. Microsoft has not been the only major company that wanted his services. Jay had long since overcome the perception that he was the bad guy in the Letterman/Leno feud. Both now hosted successful shows, and the feud was no longer on people's minds. Sponsors like Leno because he has a reputation for being easy to work with, and they also like the fact that his material isn't vulgar; he is a very family-friendly pitchman. And corporate executives who hire him are often surprised by how down-to-earth he is. Jay doesn't flaunt his wealth, and he doesn't expect sponsors to treat him like a big star. People who have known him for years say that he acts like the same "regular guy" he was when he was just starting out.

A MAJOR STAR

Despite being so successful, Leno has continued to work as hard as he did before he became the host of *The Tonight Show*. In addition to hosting, he still does his stand-up routine, except now he can be a headliner in Las Vegas and command the top fees for doing so. By early in the new century, it was estimated that he was making $17 million a year from NBC and another $12 million from stand-up performances. In 2004, he signed a new $100 million, five-year contract with NBC, and received a boost in salary to $18 million annually; with the additional money Leno earns from his frequent stand-up appearances, his total annual compensation would be somewhere between $25 and 27 million a year. Jay says that he enjoys doing stand up performances, because they keep him in touch with the audience, and help him write new material. As a result of his success, he and Mavis (they married in 1980) now own a beautiful home in Beverly Hills, California, and Jay has plenty of money to indulge in his favorite hobby, collecting and restoring classic cars and motorcycles. He still enjoys working with his hands, and by one estimate, he owns about 180 cars, trucks, and motorcycles, some of which date to as far back as the 1910s; he needs three garages to store them all.

But Jay does more than just fix up and display his unusual assortment of vehicles. In 1997, he announced that he would begin funding a scholarship for a student at a unique university in Kansas. McPherson College, located about an hour north of Wichita, has one of the few degree programs in classic car restoration. Since the first scholarship student, Jay has funded several more, with the hope that more young people will learn how to repair and restore antique automobiles.

Jay is also involved in a variety of charitable endeavors, most notably the Feminist Majority Foundation, where his wife has been a board member since

1997. While Jay avoids identifying with any one political party, his wife is very public about her support for liberal Democratic and feminist causes. The Feminist Majority Foundation worked in the 1990s to end prejudice against women in countries like Afghanistan, where at that time, the Taliban, a brutal regime, earned international scorn for its repressive policies. Mavis, joined by her famous husband, spoke out against the Taliban's oppression of women and girls, who were denied the right to even a minimal education, were not allowed to work outside the home, and were forced to cover themselves from head to toe in a thick, heavy garment called a burka. In 1998, Jay donated more than $100,000 to the cause and continued to support his wife's efforts to call attention to the plight of Afghan women. He has also donated to other charities, including the Lance Armstrong Foundation, which provides encouragement and empowerment to people with cancer; and Keep Memory Alive, a foundation supporting research to find a cure for Alzheimer's disease. And while he always tells interviewers that his wife is the literary one, Jay is a published author. In 1996, he wrote his memoir, *Leading With My Chin*, as well as two children's books, *If Roast Beef Could Fly* in 2004, and *How to Be the Funniest Kid in the Whole Wide World (or Just in Your Class)* in 2005.

Since its inception, *The Tonight Show* has always been a place for important celebrities to make appearances, and since Jay became the host, that hasn't changed. However, because he is interested in politics, he invites major politicians to visit, although they are warned ahead of time not to expect to give any speeches. If they want to present a more human face to potential voters, that's fine, but the rule, even for presidential candidates, is to be entertaining. A number of political figures have made the effort. In mid-February 2000, Vice President, and presidential candidate, Al Gore was on the show, and in late October of that year, the other candidate, then Texas governor George W. Bush, stopped by. In November 2003, Senator John Kerry brought his motorcycle onstage; both he and Jay enjoy riding a motorcycle, so they had something other than politics to discuss. One guest who proved controversial was movie star Arnold Schwarzenegger, who used his appearance *The Tonight Show* in early August 2003 to announce for the first time that he was running for the governorship of California. It later became a trend for prospective candidates to announce their intentions on a talk show, but at the time, a firestorm erupted because the other gubernatorial candidates felt they should get equal time on Leno's show. Also, some critics said Jay was being too easy on Schwarzenegger and not asking any tough questions. But Jay pointed out in his defense that his was not a serious interview show and that he rarely asked tough questions of anyone.

In late May 2007, Leno celebrated his fifteenth anniversary as host of *The Tonight Show*. During those fifteen years, the show has been nominated for ten Emmys for outstanding variety series, winning the award in 1995. In 2000, Leno was given a star on Hollywood's Walk of Fame, and in 2004, he was named *Television Week* magazine's Entertainer of the Year. Still as driven as he was in his earlier days, Jay sleeps only about four hours a night, hates to go on vacation, and rarely takes time off. He is also still known for being loyal to his staff, many of whom have been with him for his entire fifteen years as host of the show. What he still loves best is writing and telling jokes. And although his current contract runs out in 2009 and he has already agreed to pass the torch to NBC late-night host Conan O'Brien, most people who know Leno cannot imagine that he'll retire. In fact, he has hinted that retirement isn't in his plans. Some media critics have surmised that his leaving *The Tonight Show* in 2009 was NBC's decision, rather than Jay's; good ratings or not, he is getting older, and networks are constantly seeking a younger audience. NBC has denied this rumor, insisting that there are plans to find other opportunities for Leno with the network, but of course that remains to be seen. Whatever happens, few people who know him expect him to stop performing. He will undoubtedly continue to do his stand-up routine somewhere, and even though his contract won't permit him to be back on a competing network until January 2010, there are rumors that several networks are interested in hiring him.

The average Joe who was not expected to fill Johnny Carson's shoes has done very nicely since he left Andover, Massachusetts, to try his luck in Los Angeles. Jay Leno has proved to people who doubted him that he is a major force in late-night comedy and talk.

JAY LENO TIMELINE

1950: born in New Rochelle, New York

1973: graduates from Emerson College in Boston; begins doing comedy in clubs

1974: moves to Los Angeles to further his career

1975: seen by Johnny Carson performing at the Improv

1977: performs on *The Tonight Show* for the first time

1987: becomes Johnny Carson's permanent guest host

1992: becomes the host of *The Tonight Show*

2000: receives a star on Hollywood's Walk of Fame

2004: signs a five-year, $100-million-plus contract renewal with NBC

2007: celebrates fifteenth anniversary as host of *The Tonight Show*

FURTHER READING

Block, Alex Ben. "Jay Has a Few Things to Say." *Television Week*, 27 September 2004, p. 32.

Carter, Bill. "Behind the Headlines in the Leno-Letterman War." *New York Times*, 30 January 1994, pp. SM 28, 30, 32.

Gunther, Marc. "The MVP of Late Night." *Fortune*, 23 February 2004, p. 102.

Kornheiser, Tony. "Stand Up and Be Comic." *Washington Post*, 24 September 1983, pp. C1, C5.

Leno, Jay. *Leading With My Chin*. New York: HarperCollins, 1996.

Lipton, Michael A., and Pamela Warrick. "Funny Man at Work." *People*, 6 May 2002, pp. 64–68.

Manzo, Kathleen Kennedy. "Jay Leno Funds Antique Auto Restoration Scholarship." *Community College Week*, 5 May 1997, p. 8.

Mitchell, Elvis. "Jay Leno, Common Sense Comedian." *New York Times*, 22 November 1987. p. H35.

Santosuosso, Ernie. "Jay Leno Drops by the Old Corner." *Boston Globe*, 30 August 1987, p. B21.

Schleier, Curt. "Jay Leno: Sometimes Nice Guys Do Finish First." *Biography*, August 1997, pp. 38–44.

Shales, Tom. "Arnold on Leno and Other Shameless Plugs." *Television Week*, 13 October 2003, p. 33.

———. "Living Up to the Late Night Legacy." *Television Week*, 28 November 2005, p. 59.

Stengel, Richard. "Midnight's Mayor." *Time*, 16 March 1992, p. 58.

Wild, David. "The Anchorman." *Rolling Stone*, 4 March 2004, pp. 35–36.

———. "Rock and Roll Yearbook: Jay Leno." *Rolling Stone*, 11 January 1996, pp. 76–79.

Zeman, Ned, and Rebecca Crandall. "Call Off the Jay-Bashing." *Newsweek*, 29 June 1992, p. 56.

AP Photo/Mark J. Terrill, File

David Letterman

David Letterman has been entertaining network audiences since the early 1980s. Mentored by NBC's Johnny Carson, he was widely assumed to be Carson's successor. Instead, the job went to Jay Leno, and Letterman ended up at CBS, where he carved out his own niche. David Letterman has always been a survivor, overcoming a serious heart ailment, as well as greatly exceeding people's expectations of him. His critics said he wasn't handsome enough to be a TV anchor, and besides, he had an offbeat sense of humor. And yet, throughout his long career, Letterman has shown his critics that it's not a good idea to underestimate him. In fact, he has become successful because of his ability to do the unexpected.

GROWING UP IN THE MIDWEST

David Michael Letterman was born in Indianapolis, Indiana, on 12 April 1947, the only son of Harry Joseph Letterman, a florist, and Dorothy Letterman, a secretary at the Second Presbyterian Church; the Lettermans also had two daughters, Janice and Gretchen. David was by all accounts an awkward and insecure boy whose father seemed larger than life, a man with a very outgoing personality and a fondness for telling jokes. David admired his father's ability to be the life of the party. But Mr. Letterman also had ongoing health problems, and after he suffered a heart attack when David was still a little boy, it was always in the back of his mind that his father might become sick again. Sadly, a second heart attack did, in fact, kill his father, at age fifty-seven; David Letterman was just twenty-seven, and it took him a long time to get over his father's death.

Much of Letterman's childhood was typically that of a middle-class baby boomer. He lived right near the Speedway, where the Indianapolis 500 was held, so his uncle would take him there to watch the auto races. One of his hobbies was collecting model cars. He and a friend liked to watch the other neighborhood children participating in the soap box derby, but Letterman was happy to be a spectator and never wanted to compete. As a student, he was smart, but he didn't particularly like school. When he was old enough, he got an after-school job working at the local supermarket.

The entire time he was growing up, David loved to watch television. In fact, one of his earliest childhood memories was getting a set of Tinker Toys as a present and using them to build something that looked like a microphone, so he could pretend he was on the air. He was especially impressed by comedians like Johnny Carson and Steve Allen. Years later, he still recalled what a treat it was when he was just a boy and his parents would let him stay up late on Friday nights to watch *The Tonight Show*. Letterman liked the way Steve Allen did comedy; he was often silly, but it was obvious that he was having fun and didn't take himself too seriously. David Letterman was impressed by Carson for a different reason: Johnny Carson was a master at putting people down without cruelty and without hurting their feelings. When he was making fun of someone, he knew just how far to go. Because he admired Allen's and Carson's talent, Letterman decided he someday wanted to do what Carson and Allen did. Of course, because young David was somewhat lacking in confidence, he hadn't exactly formulated a plan, but his dream was that somehow, someday he'd be on TV.

Letterman attended Broad Ripple High School, a school that would later become known as a magnet school for students interested in the performing arts. He wanted to attend Indiana University, but fearing his grades wouldn't be good enough, he applied to Ball State University in Muncie, Indiana, and it was there that he attended college. While he was at Ball State, two things happened that affected his career plans. First, he discovered the campus radio station, WBST. It was just a 10-watt station and it played classical music, but he was able to do some announcing and even broadcast the news. Unfortunately, his "wise-guy" side was beginning to show itself, and according to the college radio station's Web site, he was fired for making sarcastic comments—or as the college Web site puts it, for being "irreverent" about the music. He then got involved with another campus station and continued his radio career.

The other major event that had a major impact had nothing to do with broadcasting but with his social life: He joined a fraternity. For the average person, this event might not have been a major one, but for somebody who lacked confidence, finding the right group of people to spend time with was important. Letterman found those people in Sigma Chi Epsilon, and being a member helped him to become more outgoing. He found, to his surprise, that there were people who liked his sense of humor, and who enjoyed being around him. Where the program manager at WBST hadn't appreciated his sarcasm, his fraternity brothers in Sigma Chi did appreciate his ability to use mocking or derisive humor to negotiate campus life. Even though this was the Vietnam era, and changes were taking place in society everywhere, Dave was, by his own admission, totally uninterested in politics. However, in an era of turbulence, he was the one who knew how to help people relax. His main interest was in clever pranks that made his friends laugh. Perhaps in some way he was trying to emulate his father's image as the life of the party, but whatever his motivation, his fraternity experience helped him gain the confidence he had lacked before.

BEGINNING A MEDIA CAREER

By the time he graduated from Ball State in 1969, Letterman had worked briefly at WERK in Muncie, and it didn't take him long to begin writing letters to famous entertainers, asking for their advice about how he could reach his career goals. Although he wasn't necessarily telegenic in the traditional anchorman sense (he had curly hair that often refused to behave, wore glasses, and had a gap between his two front teeth), David had a unique personality and was able to get a job as a news anchor and weatherman at Indianapolis station WLWI-TV (later known as WTHR-TV). Just as at WBST radio, and perhaps because he was bored by the rigid rules of being a news reader, he often inserted sarcastic comments, especially when giving the weather. In one example, he said there was "hail the size of canned hams." In another, he showed the audience a national weather map that was missing the state of Georgia and explained that the U.S. government had traded Georgia for the country of Iran. There was no telling what he might say or do next, and while some people thought he was amusing, the station's management wanted him to stop clowning.

After working in a number of areas of local TV, including hosting a children's show, Letterman felt he was not advancing. His wife, Michelle, a fellow Ball State student whom he had married in 1969, encouraged him to pursue a career in comedy, which is what he seemed to want to do most. His fraternity brothers agreed and also encouraged him to give comedy a try. And so, in 1975, like another young comedian, Jay Leno, David Letterman chose to go to Los Angeles so he could be close to his idol, Johnny Carson, and try to succeed as a comic or perhaps a comedy writer. It was well known that Carson came to the local comedy clubs to see new talent, and he sometimes selected a comedian to be on *The Tonight Show.*

At first, Letterman peddled some of his comedy scripts, but nobody seemed interested. So he began performing a stand-up routine at the Comedy Store, a popular Los Angeles club for up-and-coming comedians. It was there he met Jay Leno. Initially, Letterman was somewhat intimidated by Leno, feeling that Leno was a much better comic than he was. But gradually, Dave Letterman and Jay Leno became friends. Like Leno, Letterman sold some material to a couple of TV shows, such as *Good Times*, but mainly he worked on perfecting his stand-up routine. By late September 1978, he got his first major break: He became part of a CBS-TV variety show starring Mary Tyler Moore. *Mary* debuted with high hopes, but its ratings were so poor that it was canceled after only three shows. However, the work he did on *Mary* was enough to get Letterman noticed. By November, he had been invited to make his first appearance on Johnny Carson's *The Tonight Show*. He would go on to make more than twenty appearances, and he would also guest-host the show so many times over the next few years that critics assumed he was being groomed as Carson's successor. One critic, the *Chicago Tribune's* Larry Kart, even remarked on David's and Johnny's similar mannerisms and wry sense of humor, perhaps the product of their midwestern upbringing. Watching David Letterman on *The Tonight Show*, Kart continued, was like "watching Johnny Carson Jr."

Convinced that they had found a potential star, NBC's executives decided to give Letterman his own show. The original concept was called *Leave It to Dave*, but it never went on the air. And unfortunately, when Letterman was finally given his first hosting job, it was in the daytime, when the average viewer was expecting either game shows or soap operas. *The David Letterman Show* debuted in late June 1980; it was at first ninety minutes long, but within three months, it had been shortened to an hour. And while a couple of critics liked it—one even called David a "breath of fresh air"—the TV audience didn't seem to understand what he was trying to do. *The David Letterman Show* was also beset by internal problems, including losing its producer days before its scheduled debut. It was also broadcast live, so all the mistakes, including those caused by inexperience, stayed in. In the end, the show lasted only until the end of October and was canceled because of low ratings. But one good thing came out of it: the beginning of a feature called "Stupid Pet Tricks," which became so popular that Letterman has continued it for several decades.

Although Letterman's first experiment with doing his own show ended badly, the experience wasn't a total loss. NBC's president at that time, Fred Silverman, continued to believe Letterman was going to be a success, and he wanted to find another program for the young comedian to host. Concerned that they might lose him to another network, NBC's upper management decided to offer him a one-year contract for $625,000, just so that he wouldn't leave. He told reporters on several occasions that he had found it interesting to be paid a large amount of money to basically do nothing. The right opportunity did not present itself until early 1982, when Dave was chosen to replace Tom Snyder. While he was happy to get his own show again, the decision meant that somebody Dave admired was going to lose his job. He certainly understood that this was a business decision, but he had often watched Snyder's *Tomorrow* show and thought Snyder was very talented. Eventually, Letterman would be able to do a favor for Snyder, helping him to return to TV after he had been away from it for some time. But for now, as of 1 February 1982 *Late Night with David Letterman* was on the air, and Dave Letterman and his staff concentrated on making it work better than the 1980 show had.

DAVE LETTERMAN BECOMES A STAR

It didn't hurt that Letterman's time slot was right after Johnny Carson, at 12:30 a.m. Eastern Standard Time. It also didn't hurt that the majority of his staff had survived the first Letterman show and now had more confidence about how to make the most of David's skills. Where many late-night shows focused on celebrity interviews and musical guests, *Late Night* was mostly comedy, and some of it was quite different from the typical variety show. Viewers might see parodies of popular TV shows or watch "Stupid Pet Tricks" (one segment featured a dog trying to open the refrigerator to fetch a soda). Cast regular Larry "Bud" Melman (real name, Calvert DeForest) appeared in a number of skits—he was a genial older man who played a bewildered but endearing character. He dispensed well-meaning but erroneous advice in a feature called "Ask Mr. Melman" and was sent out to perform various bizarre tasks, such as going to the Port Authority Bus Terminal, in a 1983 segment, to hand out hot towels to arriving passengers and welcome them to New York. Many of the skits were developed by head writer Merrill Markoe, who was also Letterman's live-in girlfriend during most of the 1980s. It was she who developed such recurring segments as "Stupid Pet Tricks" and "Stupid Human Tricks," and she was also instrumental in the creation of another popular feature, the "Top Ten List." This feature, which made its debut in mid-September 1985, was a parody of the lists that popular culture magazines like *People* often compiled, for example, the ten most popular movies of all time. Letterman felt these lists were being overdone, so the *Late Night* writers came up with humorous top-ten lists. The first one was "The Top Ten Things That Almost Rhyme with *Peas*." Though at first just another occasional segment, it was so popular that it became a nightly part of the show. (And when Letterman moved from NBC to CBS in late August 1993, he immediately came up with "The Top Ten Things We Like about CBS.")

Talkers Magazine and Michael Harrison

After talk radio exploded in popularity in the late 1980s, a new magazine debuted, devoted to covering the format and the hosts. *Talkers* was created in 1990 by Michael Harrison, who felt that talk radio was such an influence on American popular culture that it deserved a publication of its own. Harrison knows the talk format from personal experience: He was an announcer and a talk show host himself. When he worked for KMET in Los Angeles, he did the first major talk show aimed at a young adult audience, beginning in the mid-1970s and continuing for ten years. Harrison has also been an editor at the broadcasting-industry publication *Radio & Records*, and he has been a station owner as well. *Talkers* isn't a fan magazine; its audience is mainly people in the business of talk shows, whether announcers, producers, syndicators, or station managers. One of the magazine's most frequently quoted features is the annual selection of the "Heavy Hundred," the one hundred most important talk show hosts nationally. In 2002, *Talkers* also compiled a list of the "Greatest Radio and Television Talk Show Hosts of All Time." (Rush Limbaugh was number one for radio; Larry King was number one for television.) Harrison is amused that some conservatives think *Talkers* is proliberal and some liberals think it's proconservative. He insists his magazine is neutral, and wherever the hot subjects and the hot personalities may be, *Talkers* is there to cover them.

Letterman's humor, often delivered in a sly or deadpan style, was well-suited to the late-night time period, when many of the viewers were college-aged students who appreciated that type of humor. The man who had once had only a cult following was now being seen by a much larger audience, and he quickly won them over. His show was different from other late-night shows, and the critics tried to put into words what made it unique, describing Letterman's comedic style as "glib," "silly," "cynical," and "ironic." However it was described, *Late Night with David Letterman* was a hit. One thing the audience liked was the show's unpredictability, and every now and then, one of the skits would really start people talking. A good example occurred in late July 1982, when Dave invited a professional wrestler named Jerry Lawler onto the show. Lawler had been challenged by comedian Andy Kaufman, who claimed he could beat any wrestler. Taunts were exchanged, and the two ended up in what looked like a very brutal fight in the studio. Viewers wondered if it was real, because it certainly looked real; in fact, it seemed as if Kaufman had been injured in the brawl. The segment got much publicity as people debated whether they had seen two guys out of control or something that had been preplanned. Much later, it was revealed that Kaufman and Lawler, who were friends, had staged the entire event.

And speaking of friends, once Letterman had his own show and it was going well, he invited his former Comedy Store colleague Jay Leno to be a guest. Where Leno, by his own admission, was nervous and awkward when he appeared on Johnny Carson's show (both Dave and Jay had great reverence for Carson and thought of him as a mentor), he was much more relaxed and much funnier when he appeared on Letterman's show. Dave had Jay on his show a number of times, and they had a good relationship. Unfortunately, that changed in 1991, when Johnny Carson announced that he was getting ready to retire and that Jay Leno, not David Letterman, would be his successor. Letterman was extremely hurt: Most people in the broadcasting industry had believed he would be the new host, and Leno's selection was a shock. Letterman believed that Leno had gone behind his back to lobby NBC's affiliates, winning them over and then persuading Carson that he was the better person for the job. By most accounts, once Leno became the official host of *The Tonight Show*, he and Dave never spoke again. The discord between the two former friends was undoubtedly exacerbated by the fact that after Dave left NBC to go to CBS, he got a show directly opposite Leno, but Leno's show usually got better ratings than Letterman's.

During his years with NBC, Letterman was seldom mentioned in the gossip columns and seemed to have a good relationship with his staff (although news reports frequently noted that he was extremely hard on himself, he didn't seem to be excessively hard on those who worked for him); but not all of his guests got along with him, mainly because of his tendency to have fun with the guests, some of whom felt he was mocking them. Letterman did not do the typical interview. Appearing as a guest on his show meant being prepared for unusual questions, or requests to do something foolish as part of a skit. Some guests went along with this agenda, finding it a refreshing change of pace to let their hair down and act silly. But some guests felt Letterman's attitude was insulting. Most notable among the guests who were offended was singing star and actress Cher, who, during her first appearance on the show in May 1986, became annoyed and called him a vulgar name. Eventually, the two resolved their differences and Cher came back as a guest on the show, but there would be other instances when guests objected to how Dave had treated them. There was also the much-hyped feud between Letterman and Oprah Winfrey. It was a feud that neither celebrity could entirely explain, but sometime in 1989, Dave had begun making occasional jokes about how Oprah hated him and didn't want to be on his show. Over the years, the jokes about Oprah became a recurring theme, as Dave told his audience that he had begged and pleaded, but Oprah absolutely refused to be a guest. At some point in 2005, it was decided to bury the hatchet, and in early December, Oprah Winfrey did in fact appear as a guest on Letterman's show, where the two admitted they didn't know what the problem had been and then chatted amicably, as if they had been friends for years.

Letterman's not taking the customs and traditions of the late-night talk show very seriously was probably his attraction for younger viewers. This demographic group tended to be cynical, and they disliked the glitz and phony glamour of most TV variety shows, but they could relate to the way Dave looked at the world. His ability to bring in young viewers made NBC very happy, since the typical talk show usually attracted people over forty-five; advertisers really wanted to support shows that were watched by young people, especially the eighteen- to thirty-four-year-olds, and they became some of Dave's biggest fans.

Even though it seemed Letterman was truly becoming the star that Fred Silverman and others had predicted he would be, reporters who tried to interview him found he was a very private person. In fact, he seemed shy and uncomfortable when asked to talk about himself. Over the years, that attitude did not change. Reporters who tried to get information about his personal life or his past found he preferred to discuss his show. And even his friends have acknowledged that Letterman is frequently insecure; no matter how much other people think of him as a success, he has continued to be a worrier.

While his constant concern about his show may have been unnecessary, he did have several good reasons for worrying. One was that in the late 1980s, he was being stalked by a fan. His stalker was Margaret Ray, a woman with a history of schizophrenia, who broke into his home, trespassed repeatedly on his property, and even stole his car. It was after the stolen car incident in May 1988 that the media first learned about her. For nearly a decade, she would be a recurring presence in Letterman's life, arrested and imprisoned, then set free and once again trying to get near him. Her delusion was that he was her husband and they were meant to be together. The story was frequently written up in the tabloids and was even the subject of jokes, and it could not have been easy for Letterman to constantly wonder what Ray would do next. She ultimately committed suicide in 1998, but before that, it sometimes seemed as if she would never leave him alone.

One other reason for Letterman's worry was his health. Like his father, he, too, would develop heart problems. In mid-January 2000, he needed quintuple bypass surgery after doctors found a serious blockage in one of his arteries. Letterman had long feared that his heart was not in good shape, so he wasn't shocked when he had to have the surgery. He was very grateful to the team of doctors and nurses at New York Presbyterian Hospital who had saved his life. In fact, when he came back to work after being out for nearly two months, the normally reserved late-night host became uncharacteristically emotional when he brought them all out onstage and thanked them.

NEW CHALLENGES, NEW SUCCESSES

After the decision was made to give *The Tonight Show* to Jay Leno and to try to keep Letterman's show right where it was, he decided to leave NBC, and in late August 1993, *The Late Show with David Letterman* made its debut on CBS. While Jay Leno's NBC show frequently defeated him in the ratings, Letterman continued to have a large and devoted audience. As time passed, he had some clashes with CBS executives, especially network president Leslie "Les" Moonves, and there were rumors that he wasn't entirely happy at the network. In early March 2002, when his CBS contract was up for renewal, ABC tried to hire him for the late-night slot on its network. The problem was that the late-night time period on ABC was already occupied by respected journalist Ted Koppel, whose newsmagazine *Nightline* had been on the air for several decades. A controversy ensued, as Koppel took an understandably dim view of being replaced; he wrote a scathing opinion piece for the *New York Times* about why his nightly program mattered, and he criticized ABC executives for wanting to replace a show that focused on investigative reporting with yet another entertainment show. In mid-March, Letterman announced that he would be staying at CBS, and he also publicly praised Koppel, agreeing with him that *Nightline* was important and should be saved. By July, the two had been on each other's programs, joking about the incident.

Although Letterman has repeatedly stated that he is not active in politics, he has had a number of politicians on his show. Nearly every political candidate has stopped by, and on *The Late Show with David Letterman*, the interviews have always included humor. While some critics have found this approach disrespectful, it is a natural part of Letterman's persona. Whether his guest is a celebrity or a presidential candidate, he is going to ask the offbeat and unexpected questions, providing the audience with a different perspective on normally serious politicians. For example, in early 2008, Letterman made fun of Republican presidential candidate Senator John McCain, suggesting that he was a cranky old man. McCain then appeared on the show and did a comic assessment of Letterman, the two trading sarcastic comments. It was obvious to the audience that the jibes were all in good fun and showed that McCain could take a joke. Letterman also invited the 2008 Democratic candidates in the presidential election primary to be guests on his show, and he joked with them as well. Because his sense of humor continues to appeal to the younger demographics, CBS made sure the next time his contract was up for renewal that there was no chance he would go elsewhere. In 2006, CBS executives renewed his show until 2010, at a salary of more than $30 million.

Notoriously private about his personal life, Letterman seemed to mellow after his 2000 battle with heart disease. In mid-September 2003, he shared with his TV audience that his longtime girlfriend, Regina Lasko, was pregnant and he was about to become a father at the age of fifty-six. He also admitted he was nervous. Then, in November 2003, he let everyone know that he and Regina were the proud parents of a baby boy, named Harry Joseph, after Letterman's father. Dave promptly delivered a top-ten list of "Reasons I'm Excited to Be a Father." Of course, viewers knew this was not the first time he had shared something about his family. In February 1994, he had sent his mother, Dorothy, a vibrant eighty-year-old, to cover the Winter Olympics in Norway. The segment was so well received that "Dave's mom" became a recurring character on his show. Gradually, beginning in the mid-1990s, when he left NBC for CBS, it did seem that the moody and intensely self-critical Dave Letterman had become somewhat more content.

Letterman has been able to pursue his ongoing interest in auto racing by joining with Bobby Rahal (who won the Indianapolis 500 in 1986) to become part owner of RLR (Rahal Letterman Racing) in 2004. The RLR team has sponsored a number of drivers, including Buddy Rice, who finished second in the 2005 Indy 500, and Danica Patrick, the first woman to ever finish in the top five (she finished fourth in the 2005 race).

Appreciative of the role that Ball State University played in getting his career started, Letterman has funded several scholarships to the university. In September 2007, the university responded by naming a new building after him, the David Letterman Communication and Media Building, at a dedication ceremony attended by large crowds of cheering students.

With his own production company (Worldwide Pants), a successful late-night show, a new family, and above all, good health, David Letterman has come a long way from the shy and awkward youth who wished he could be a star. And while not every critic has liked his show and not every guest has appreciated being the butt of his jokes, there is no denying that Letterman has carved out his own successful niche in late-night talk.

DAVID LETTERMAN TIMELINE

1947: born in Indianapolis, Indiana

1969: graduates from Ball State University; begins radio and TV career

1982: debut of *Late Night with David Letterman* on NBC

1992: does not get the job hosting *The Tonight Show*; decides to leave NBC

1993: debut of the *Late Show with David Letterman* on CBS

2000: needs quintuple bypass surgery due to heart problems

2003: becomes a father at age fifty-six

2006: show renewed by CBS until 2010 at a salary of more than $30 million.

FURTHER READING:

Barol, Bill. "A Fine Madness at the Midnight Hour." *Newsweek*, 3 February 1986, p. 46.

Carter, Bill. "Behind the Headlines in the Leno-Letterman War." *New York Times*, 30 January 1994, Section 6, p. 28.

Graves, Gary. "Letterman Gets Moment in Hot Seat." *USA Today*, 23 May 2005, p. 1C.

Kart, Larry. "David Letterman and the Great Tonight Show Circus." *Chicago Tribune*, 6 January 1980, p. G12.

Koch, Gail. (Ball State University Daily News) "After Two Decades, Letterman's Wit Shows No Sign of Stopping." *Logansport (IN) Pharos-Tribune*, 1 March 2002, p. A 10.

"Late Night with Letterman on NBC," *Doylestown (PA) Daily Intelligencer*, 8 February 1982, p. 26.

Latham, Caroline. *The David Letterman Story*. New York: Franklin Watts, 1987.

Mermigas, Diane. "Will an Uncertain Today Give Way to Tonight?" *Chicago Daily Herald*, 28 January 1980, Section 2, p. 1.

Rutenberg, Jim. "In a Response, Ted Koppel Writes That Nightline Still Fills a Need." *New York Times*, 5 March 2002, p. C1.

Shales, Tom. "Letterman's Lunacy, The Other Side of Midnight." *Washington Post*, 8 August 1982, p. L1.

Courtesy of Photofest

Rush Limbaugh

There is probably not a more polarizing figure in talk radio than Rush Limbaugh. He has a huge audience that he has maintained for nearly twenty years, and his success in conservative talk radio paved the way for numerous other right-wing talkers to follow. Even his detractors agree that it was he who brought listeners back to AM radio. Those who dislike him believe he is a bigot and a partisan whose first loyalty is to the Republican Party, while those who admire him believe he is the most honest man in talk radio and has put the "liberal media" in their place. Whichever side of the controversy people choose, there can be no doubt that the popularity of political talk radio since the mid-1990s owes a lot to Rush Limbaugh.

WHERE IT ALL BEGAN

Rush Hudson Limbaugh III was born on 12 January 1951 in Cape Girardeau, Missouri. He came from a long line of attorneys—notably his father, his grandfather, and an uncle—and everyone in the Limbaugh family was a conservative Republican. Coming from such a strong legal background, he too was undoubtedly expected to study law. But his mother Millie learned that her son, who was called Rusty, was interested in only one thing: radio. He graduated from Cape Central High School in 1969, and he had left both the high school football and debating teams to work part time at KGMO, the local radio station. His parents were able to persuade him to go to college, but college wasn't where he wanted to be. He dropped out of Southeast Missouri State College after slightly more than two semesters.

Limbaugh then began the life of a typical radio disc jockey, moving from city to city in search of success. By 1971, he was hired to do the morning show at WIXZ, a small station in McKeesport, Pennsylvania, not far from Pittsburgh. He then moved to KQV in Pittsburgh. His first radio name had been Rusty Sharpe, and now he was Jeff Christie. But whatever name he used, he was far from being a star; in fact, he was fired from most of the stations where he worked. While this résumé may seem somewhat negative, firing was actually a common occurrence for inexperienced radio announcers, and Limbaugh was learning as he went along. One thing he learned, after numerous cities and numerous jobs, was that it was time for a change.

In 1979, Limbaugh left radio and went to work in marketing and promotion for the Kansas City Royals baseball team. He stayed for five years, but while he enjoyed the work and made friends with several of the players, his heart was still in radio. However, he had come to the conclusion that if he did go back to radio, he wanted to be a talk show host rather than a disc jockey. In 1983, he persuaded a Kansas City, Missouri news/talk station, KMBZ, to give him a chance doing political commentary, even though he had had little experience in talk radio. What he did have were some very strong political opinions, and the station let him express his views. That was how Rush Limbaugh, political talker, was born.

BECOMING A POLITICAL TALKER

His first attempt at talk did not end in success. He was fired again, and by October 1984, Limbaugh found work in Sacramento, California on station KFBK. He stayed there for four years, boosting the station's ratings and fine-tuning his on-air persona. It was while he was in Sacramento that he also perfected some of the features he would become known for, including song parodies that made fun of Democratic political figures. Fortunately for Limbaugh, radio was on the verge of a major change, thanks in large part to Republican president Ronald Reagan, who had promised that he would deregulate broadcasting. He encouraged the Federal Communications Commission to do away with the Fairness Doctrine, a rule that talkers and newspeople had to give both sides of an issue, and that if they verbally attacked anyone, that person had the right to issue a rebuttal on the air. By 1987, the Fairness Doctrine was gone, and broadcasters were free to be as one-sided as they wanted to be, a blessing for all opinionated talkers. Limbaugh was about to benefit from it. It was a truism among Republicans that the media were dominated by liberals, an assertion that was debatable but fervently believed. However, what was beyond dispute in 1987 was that no high-profile and successful right-wing talkers could be found on radio. There had been a few in the 1960s and 1970s, but radio was ready for the next big thing, and that would turn out to be Rush Limbaugh.

While Limbaugh was in Sacramento, a San Francisco–based radio consultant named Norman Woodruff discovered his show and became a mentor to Rush, even helping him to dress more professionally so that he would make a better impression on media executives. Woodruff's advice proved helpful, because a media executive had indeed become interested. Edward F. McLaughlin was the former president of the ABC Radio Network, and in 1987, he had started his own company, syndicating a medical advice show featuring Dr. Dean Edell. Now McLaughlin was seeking another talent, and Woodruff told him about Limbaugh. At first, it was not a match: McLaughlin felt the talk host sounded too egocentric and arrogant. Limbaugh later explained that these qualities were part of his on-air persona: for example, he had begun using as the introduction to his show, "With talent on loan from God, this is Rush Limbaugh." At the time, McLaughlin wasn't impressed until he had met with Limbaugh and listened to his show a few more times. He came to agree that Limbaugh was in fact a compelling and unique radio personality and could become a star. He and Limbaugh entered into a partnership, and McLaughlin prepared to market his newly acquired talent.

In 1988, when Limbaugh signed with EFM Media Management, McLaughlin's new company, there were few national political talkers. Most such programs were local. But it was an interesting time to be proposing a new idea, because AM radio was in serious trouble. By the mid-1980s, FM had entirely taken over as the place for music, leaving AM owners struggling to find programming that would attract new listeners. In many cities, playing oldies and broadcasting local talk were the only options that attracted any audience at all. While some syndicated national talkers were available to local stations, most were on at night, and they tended to be interviewers like Larry King or advice givers like Sally Jessy Raphael. Today, opinionated national shows that focus on current events are everywhere, but in 1987, McLaughlin was taking quite a risk in proposing one, since the current belief was that politics was best discussed at the local level. Another risk was that he wanted to put Rush Limbaugh on the air from noon to 3 p.m., a time not considered best for talk. McLaughlin took Limbaugh to New York City and then began persuading stations in other cities to replace one of their local shows with Limbaugh's. At first, the concept was greeted with skepticism, but on 1 August 1988, the new Rush Limbaugh talk show made its debut, with 57 stations on board. Limbaugh, supremely confident and driven to succeed, created a construct that he named the EIB (Excellence in Broadcasting) Network, but in reality, it was EFM Media that continued to syndicate the new conservative talk show. The results were spectacular. By 1990, Limbaugh was heard on 177 stations, with more to come.

KING OF CONSERVATIVE TALK RADIO

To even the most casual listener, the Rush Limbaugh program was, as media critic Joe Logan of the *Philadelphia Inquirer* put it, "a daily national conservative caucus, more slickly produced than any Republican convention." But it would be an oversimplification to dismiss Limbaugh as just another partisan. After all, there had been right-wing talk show hosts on the air prior to Limbaugh, but none became as popular or as dominant. It is not an exaggeration to say that Rush Limbaugh put conservative talk radio on the map. How it happened is still the subject of scholarly debate, but the short answer is that as the country was becoming more conservative, Limbaugh reflected that change and gave voice to millions of people who felt he spoke for them and understood their issues. As Limbaugh told David Kupelian, editor of a conservative news magazine, in 1992, his father had raised him with strong conservative principles, and he was firmly convinced that those principles were correct. He believed that there was a liberal bias in the media, and that liberal attitudes had been harmful to America, and he wanted to use his radio show to reach out to likeminded listeners who felt the country was going in the wrong direction.

Unlike earlier conservative talkers like Joe Pyne, Limbaugh didn't curse his callers or call them names, although he certainly was vocal in his disdain for liberals and Democrats. And he did not position himself as the archetypical "angry white male" host. On the air, he was often erudite, humorous, glib, and very well informed on the issues as he saw them. He seemed to genuinely enjoy doing his show. Even his critics agreed he was entertaining and very good at talk radio, and some liberals did in fact listen to him for that reason. He also seemed to thrive on controversy, and he didn't mind generating outrage

Michael Savage

Michael Savage is one of the most controversial of all the conservative radio talkers and is also one of the most listened to. His ratings place him in the top three most listened to talk show hosts nationally, according to *Talkers* magazine, and some estimates say he has a weekly audience of over eight million people. Michael Savage, whose real name is Michael Weiner, wrote best-selling books about nutrition and herbal medicine before he became a talk show host in 1994 at a San Francisco AM radio station, KGO. One of talk radio's most caustic and abrasive personalities, he regularly accuses public figures whose views he dislikes of being communists. In the tradition of Joe Pyne, he has frequently insulted gay people, immigrants, Muslims, feminists, Democrats, and anyone he believes is liberal. (Among his best-selling books is one called *Liberalism Is a Mental Disorder*.) He has also asserted that gays and immigrants spread disease, and he has railed against what he believes is the favoritism shown to minorities. Like Joe Pyne's, Savage's commentaries have struck a chord with his audience. Sometimes, however, he has gone too far. In March 2003, he was given a TV talk show on MSNBC, but it was canceled in July after he hung up on a gay caller, to whom he said, "Oh, you're one of those sodomites. You should only get AIDS and die." The protest that erupted caused the TV network to fire him, but he kept his popular radio show. However, similar protests occurred in July 2008 after incendiary remarks Savage made on the radio. He claimed that autism is usually a fake disease, and children labelled autistic are really ". . . brat[s] who [haven't] been told to cut the act out." Outraged parents and advocates picketed stations that carried his show, but he remained on the air. Savage is syndicated by Talk Radio Network, and by 2007, over four hundred stations were carrying his show. Despite his often-contentious statements, his audience believes he is right, and he continues to inspire loyalty in his fans and outrage in his foes.

in his detractors. He frequently used sarcasm to make his points, calling feminists "femi-nazis," and making fun of the gay rights movement in ways that convinced his critics that he was a bigot. When he did updates on openly gay Massachusetts congressman Barney Frank, he played the top-forty song "My Boy Lollipop." When he made fun of environmentalists and animal rights activists, he used special sound effects to introduce his reports, such as the hit song "Born Free" peppered with the sound of gunshots and animals trying to get away. There had been conservative talk hosts who disliked liberals, feminists, and gay activists, but Limbaugh expressed his disdain in a way that, while cutting, wasn't irate. His audience found his persona appealing; they even accepted the brash and braggart nature of his performance. Fans who agreed with him would say "ditto" when they called in, and the term *ditto-head* became the generic expression for a loyal Rush Limbaugh listener. And lots of fans did agree with him. In 1992, Limbaugh issued a book of opinions, many of which he regularly expressed on his show. *The Way Things Ought to Be* became a best seller and spawned several left-wing responses, including one called *The Way Things Ought to Be but Aren't* by Steve Rendall, Jim Naureckas, and Jeff Cohen. By 1993, college conservatives were setting up listening parties in venues called Rush Rooms, where they gathered to socialize and enjoy the show. Advertisers, who had at first hesitated to support Limbaugh, were now eager to be on the air with him: By some accounts, his show was charging national advertisers as much as $12,000 to $14,000 per commercial minute, and as a result of his show's national success, Limbaugh, the self-described "most dangerous man in America," had become a millionaire by the mid-1990s. He was heard on 660 stations in 1995 and was now syndicated by the Premiere Radio Network. He was without question one of talk radio's most influential personalities, the kind of phenomenon that both he and Ed McLaughlin had believed he would be.

The Republican Party appreciated what an ally Limbaugh was. In fact, he was widely credited with being a major force in the Republican Revolution that brought his party back to the control of Congress in 1994. A number of political pollsters had already noted that the typical talk radio listener is a conservative, and fans of Rush Limbaugh's show did more than just listen to it. They called their members of Congress when he was upset over an issue. They agreed with his assessment of how liberalism had been bad for America, and they voted overwhelmingly for Republicans. In 1995, the congressional freshman class of newly elected Republicans named him an honorary member, and his advocacy was praised by many Republican Party leaders. He was even called on to give motivational talks to the new members of Congress. In his first speech, he warned them not to trust the media. He also said that the election results had proved how morally and fiscally bankrupt liberal policies were, and that he had simply reflected what the public already felt.

Of course, talk radio has always been subjective. What Limbaugh's fans considered political truths sounded like Republican talking points to his critics, but at that time, there were no successful liberal hosts to challenge him. Limbaugh was the first of a new breed of nationally syndicated, opinionated political talk hosts, and from 1988 until about 2004, nearly every one of the hosts followed a conservative ideology and maintained a large audience. Critics felt this conservative dominance presented a very one-sided view of current events, but there was no longer any FCC rule about offering both sides, so the hosts felt no obligation to do so. Furthermore, Democrats had failed to prepare for the new world of opinionated talk shows and had had no strategy to counter the Republican domination of the genre. By some accounts, Limbaugh had as many as twenty million national listeners in the mid-1990s, and there wasn't much that Democrats could do about it. Even President Bill Clinton often remarked to news reporters that he felt at a disadvantage, since

Limbaugh had a three-hour-a-day national platform to deliver the conservative view of current events, and without a similar radio show to present the Democratic interpretation, Limbaugh's claims went unchallenged.

SUCCESS AND CONTROVERSY

Limbaugh's success not only helped individual AM stations to fill the slot from noon to 3 p.m., but it also proved there was a need for more political talk, and soon, hundreds of stations were filling the entire day with this kind of programming, broadcasting a live and local morning show and then offering the audience the high-profile talkers like Limbaugh and other conservatives who were now in syndication. It was a winning formula. Whereas in 1990 no more than two hundred stations were using an all-talk format, by 2000 over one thousand stations were broadcasting all talk all the time—and getting good ratings doing so. As the Internet became a factor, Limbaugh began offering his show in streaming audio, starting in March 1999, to complement his Web site, which announced his show as "the greatest radio show on earth." A master self-promoter, Limbaugh also offered his fans an assortment of memorabilia, such as T-shirts, hats, mugs, and a political magazine called the *Limbaugh Letter*. Year after year, no matter what the issues, Limbaugh has remained America's most listened-to political talk host. *Talkers* magazine has repeatedly had him at the top of the "Heavy Hundred," the annual listing of the industry's biggest and most important talk show hosts. While all the new competition has affected his ratings, in 2006 Limbaugh still far surpassed any of the other hosts, with as many as fifteen million listeners a week. He has also been handsomely rewarded for bringing audiences back to AM radio: In 2001, he had signed an eight-year contract for $31.25 million a year. By 2008, Clear Channel Communications signed him to another eight-year contract, but this time, he was given $38 million a year.

Of course, someone who courts controversy the way Rush Limbaugh does will certainly receive his share of negative publicity. Some has come from Limbaugh's political detractors, who feel that his show distorts the facts and is polemical. But some has resulted from his own actions. In October 2003, a tabloid reported that he was under investigation for illegally obtaining the prescription drug oxycodone, and he had to admit to his listeners that he was addicted to painkillers, an addiction he attributed to his severe back pain. He entered a rehabilitation program and ultimately returned to the air, but his critics found it ironic that someone so vocal about punishing those who abuse drugs would assert that he himself should not be held criminally liable. And he was not. While he was arrested for one count of prescription fraud, the charges were dropped once he had completed a treatment program for his addiction and paid a $30,000 fine. His fans continued to be supportive throughout the ordeal.

Also in the fall of 2003, Limbaugh was hired as a football commentator on ESPN's *Sunday NFL Countdown*, but he made remarks about popular quarterback Donovan McNabb that forced him to resign. He asserted that McNabb's team, the Philadelphia Eagles, had given him preferential treatment because he is black and they wanted a black quarterback to succeed. While this sort of comment might have gone over well on Limbaugh's politically incorrect radio show, many in the sports audience found it inappropriate (as well as untrue), and Limbaugh was accused of racism. He resigned rather than attract ongoing negative attention to ESPN.

Another controversy occurred during the 2006 midterm political campaign. There was a heated political battle over federal funding for stem cell research, which President George W. Bush opposed. Actor Michael J. Fox, who suffers from Parkinson's disease, recorded a pro-stem-cell ad. Limbaugh then went on the air and did a parody of Fox's symptoms, accusing him of faking and exaggerating his condition to win sympathy for his cause. Because Limbaugh's radio show is streamed on the Internet, people saw as well as heard his parody, and while his supporters thought it amusing, fans of Michael J. Fox and Limbaugh detractors were outraged. Fox himself took to the airwaves to condemn Limbaugh, and even some of the newspapers that normally praised him as a clever radio talk host felt that he had gone too far.

There have been other incidents and other controversies, but there is no denying that Rush Limbaugh is still the most influential American talk host, whose comments can still inspire days of media debate. He is no longer as all-powerful because the country has changed again. The Democrats won back a majority in Congress in 2006, and many of the policies Limbaugh has championed are now unpopular. He was opposed to the presidential candidacy of Senator John McCain, but his strong opposition was not enough to keep McCain from getting the 2008 Republican nomination. His influence may have waned since the days in the mid-1990s when Republicans praised him for helping them recapture Congress. But his fans still listen and many follow his advice, such as during the 2008 Democratic primary when he suggested something he called "Operation Chaos." Limbaugh wanted to prolong the battle between Democratic candidates Hillary Clinton and Barack Obama, so they would be busy fighting with each other and unable to concentrate on defeating the Republican candidate. When it seemed that Obama was pulling ahead, Limbaugh told his audience that they should register as Democrats and vote for Hillary, helping her to defeat Obama in certain key states. While there is no way of knowing how many of his listeners in fact did as he asked, some Democratic strategists believes "Operation Chaos" helped Hillary Clinton win the Texas primary.

Whether or not Limbaugh can still influence an election, his own popularity, as measured by the Arbitron ratings, remains constant, and the weekly conservative magazine *Human Events* named him its man of the year in 2007. In explaining why he was chosen, editor Mark Levin wrote, "Try as they might, the Rush-haters cannot silence him, or persuade his massive audience to tune him out. After two decades as the top talk host in the nation, his ratings are stronger than ever. He is more popular and influential than ever." While there will continue to be a debate over the Limbaugh view of current issues, the fact that Limbaugh has changed the face of talk radio is beyond dispute.

ACKNOWLEDGMENT

Special thanks to Gabe Hobbs, Vice President of Talk Programming for Clear Channel Communications, for his help with this essay.

RUSH LIMBAUGH TIMELINE

1951: born in Cape Girardeau, Missouri

1983: has his first talk show on a Kansas City news/talk radio station, KMBZ

1984: has a successful conservative talk show on KFBK, Sacramento, California

1988: debut of his new syndicated talk show, with fifty-seven affiliates

1993: syndication of his show by the Premiere Radio Network; Limbaugh is inducted into the Radio Hall of Fame

1994: is widely credited with helping the Republicans return to the majority in Congress

1995: his show heard on more than 660 stations

2007: named man of the year by *Human Events* magazine

FURTHER READING

Barker, David C. *Rushed to Judgment: Talk Radio, Persuasion and American Political Behavior.* New York: Columbia University Press, 2002.

Killian, Linda. *The Freshmen: What Happened to the Republican Revolution?* Boulder, CO: Westview Press, 1998.

Kupelian, David. "Breaking the Rules." *New Dimensions*, August 1992, pp. 21–23.

Levin, Mark R. "Man of the Year: Rush Limbaugh." *Human Events*, 7 January 2008, pp. 1, 9.

Logan, Joe. "The King of Talk: Remarkable Rise. When Rush Limbaugh Speaks, Politicians Listen." *Philadelphia Inquirer*, 2 June 1995, p. A1.

Montgomery, David. "Rush Limbaugh on the Offensive against Ad with Michael J. Fox." *Washington Post*, 25 October 2006, p. C1.

Seelye, Katherine Q. "Republicans Get a Pep Talk from Rush Limbaugh." *New York Times*, 12 December 1994, p. A16.

Rush Limbaugh's Web site is www.rushlimbaugh.com.

Courtesy of the Delaware County Daily Times

Joe Pyne

The modern talk show format is known for heated debate and angry confrontation, but the father of that style of talk comes from the 1960s, a time when talk radio was usually much more courteous. Joe Pyne didn't believe in being courteous. He said on many occasions that he wasn't a nice guy and didn't want to be a nice guy. In an era when talk shows were just coming to the forefront, and technology had finally made it possible to put callers on the air, Pyne was not the kind of host who sounded happy that people were calling. Critics wondered why anyone would want to call Pyne to be insulted, but his listeners kept on calling. And Joe kept on insulting them. It is not a myth that he once told a caller to go gargle with razor blades. And when he took his ornery and cantankerous style to television, rather than alienating the audience, his nasty on-air persona propelled him to the top of the ratings. Joe Pyne was one of broadcasting's unique figures, detested and criticized by some, admired and emulated by others. But as polarizing as he was, it cannot be denied that he changed the talk show.

HOW PYNE DISCOVERED RADIO

Joe Pyne didn't start out with dreams of being a talk show host. Joseph Edward Pyne was born in Chester, Pennsylvania, on 22 December 1924. His father, Edward, was a bricklayer, and his mother, Catherine, was a homemaker. Joe's family moved to Atlantic City when he was five. His childhood was marred by the loss of his younger brother, who was killed in an auto accident when Joe was eleven. The Pyne family returned to Chester in time for Joe to attend Chester High School, and after graduating in 1942, he joined the U.S. Marines. During intense combat in the South Pacific, he earned three battle stars. In 1943, he also received a purple heart as a result of a serious wound to his knee during a Japanese bombing of his marine base. Years later, in 1955, he would find that he had a rare form of cancer in that leg, requiring an amputation. From then on, he wore a wooden leg, which went along with the image he had developed of being a tough ex-marine. (On the other hand, reporters found him surprisingly reticent to discuss his time in the service; although his critics would later accuse him of being an egomaniac, he didn't like to brag about what he had done during the war.)

When Joe came out of the service in November 1945, he had no idea what career to pursue, but first, he wanted to take care of a speech impediment that had always annoyed him. He had a slight stutter and had difficulty saying words that contained the letter *L*. He decided to take a course at a local drama school, with the hope of not only correcting his speech impediment but becoming a better public speaker. Recalling that period of time for an April 1959 profile in the *Chester Times*, Joe admitted to reporter Don Murdaugh that back then, he hadn't been very confident; in fact, he had had a bit of an inferiority complex. And although the course was helpful, he still didn't know what he wanted to do with his life. He was driving a taxi in Chester to pay the bills, but his newfound ability in public speaking made him think about trying to get a job in broadcasting. In the late 1940s, it seemed that every city and town had at least one local station, and since radio was still done live, there was frequently a need for new on-air talent. Joe sent out many letters of application before he finally found a station willing to give him his first announcing job. It was 1946 and WTSB in Lumberton, North Carolina, had just gone on the air. Management could offer Pyne only twenty-five dollars a week, but he felt he had to start somewhere, so he said yes. When he got to Lumberton, he found that the studio was visible to the street, so that people walking by could stop and watch the announcers through the window. That turned out to be a mixed blessing: If they didn't like a song or disagreed with something the announcer said, they spat tobacco juice at the window. Joe tried to be philosophical since he really did need the experience, but it soon became obvious that he would never advance or make more money in Lumberton, so within a year, he had returned to Chester. He was soon hired by the newest station in the area, WPWA in Brookhaven. However, in what would be a pattern in his life, he got into a dispute with the owner and ended up being fired after working there only six weeks. His next job was at WILM in Wilmington, Delaware, the first of three times he would work at that station, but this time his stay was brief, and then it was on to another new station, WVCH in Chester in March 1948.

PYNE CREATES HIS PERSONA

A typical radio gypsy, Joe Pyne next went to Kenosha, Wisconsin, where he was hired by another new station, WLIP, which had been on the air only since May 1947. But there, too, he got into a dispute with the station owner, William "Bill" Lipman, and was fired; he had lasted about six months. The experience wasn't a total loss, however. It was in Kenosha, according to some sources, that Joe first began to experiment with talk. Instead of just playing records, he started making comments about politics and current events, which was not what he had been hired to do. WLIP was a community-oriented station, and in the postwar era, commentators were still members of the news department. Announcers and disc jockeys played music and read commercials. It is not surprising that Bill Lipman wanted Pyne to confine himself to playing the hits and interviewing local businesspeople.

But by this time, Joe was convinced that being a small-town disc jockey was not what he wanted. He liked being on the air but wished for something far more interesting than attending county fairs or going to the openings of new stores, some of the expected duties of a small-town announcer. At his next job, in Atlantic City, New Jersey, at WFPG, he continued to work on his new idea. Never shy about expressing an opinion, he had decided to turn that trait into a radio show that would allow him to express his opinions about the issues and interact with the listeners. He had seen nightclub comics using sarcasm to comment on current events, and the more he thought about it, the more he decided that the same approach would work for a talk show. So in 1951, he returned to WILM, where he created a show that he called *It's Your Nickel*. The name referred to the five cents it cost to make a call from a pay phone.

Sports Talk Pioneer Pete Franklin

Pete Franklin was as angry and confrontational as Joe Pyne. He had very definite opinions and hung up on callers who disagreed. And yet, in the era before the sports-talk format, Pete Franklin was one of America's most successful sports-talk hosts. There were other sports-talk shows before his, but most had been hosted by former athletes, and most were very civil, neither of which descriptions fits Pete's show. A veteran announcer, he went to Cleveland in 1967 and hosted his *Sportsline* first on WERE; in 1972, he moved the show to WWWE. Passionate about sports, he gave regular callers nicknames like "The Piranha" or "Mr. Know-It-All" and railed about the poor play of Cleveland's professional sports teams. He criticized the managers, the coaches, and even the sportswriters. His predominantly blue-collar male audience seemed to love him because he was outspoken and expressed their own frustration over having so many losing teams. In 1987 Franklin tried to duplicate his success in New York City but failed. Pete Franklin, the father of "in-your-face" sports talk was a Cleveland phenomenon. He died of cancer in 2004, and although he hadn't been a star in nearly twenty years, his death made page one of the local newspapers. Many sports fans in Cleveland still remembered how he changed sports talk.

Over the next six and a half years, Joe Pyne developed a reputation as an abrasive, controversial, and confrontational air personality. That he was able to do so is actually quite surprising. The Federal Communications Commission had mandated the Fairness Doctrine in 1949; it stated that since radio station owners were public trustees, they had a duty to present the contrasting sides of the issues, and to allow responsible spokespeople to defend themselves if they felt their viewpoint had been unjustly attacked. While talk radio was quite new at this point, the FCC was concerned that stations would misuse their power by preventing the discussion of opposing viewpoints. And yet, even in a conservative time, when radio stations were taking very few risks, Joe Pyne took the biggest risk of all in creating a show that was neither polite nor unbiased. Today, the rude and angry talk host is all too common. In the early 1950s, Joe was undoubtedly the first.

Each segment of *It's Your Nickel* began benignly enough. In his nightly introduction, Pyne said, "The mike is open. My name's Joe Pyne. I guess you know yours. This program is dedicated to the free exchange of ideas and to differences of opinion. I don't propose to have all the answers, but I do promise to talk about the things that interest you." From there, the show quickly became a shouting fest, with Joe Pyne definitely in control. No topic was sacred, from sex to religion to politics, and when he felt a caller had gone on for too long or was making no sense, Pyne would make a rude remark like "You're sick!" and hang up. Enduring Joe's abusive rhetoric was the challenge for the callers, many of whom tried to debate him before he hung up on them. His views were quite conservative most of the time, and he seemed to dare his listeners to disagree with him. He was known for being adept with words, and his arsenal of insults and putdowns became the stuff of legend. Among his best-known were "If your brains were dynamite, you couldn't blow your nose"; "Go gargle with razor blades"; and "Take your teeth out, put 'em in backwards and bite your throat." *Time* magazine, in a 1966 profile, quoted some of those notorious putdowns, as it tried to explain the popularity of the abrasive host, who could be as rude to guests as he was to callers. When asked why anyone would bother to argue with him, he explained to *Time*, "It's a masochism syndrome. They look to me for approbation, as a father figure, but sometimes they feel the need to be punished—and they know I'll punish them" (*Time*, 1966). Joe seemed to enjoy making controversial statements to the media. In 1959, he told *Chester Times* reporter Don Murdaugh that radio was geared to the mentality of a thirteen-year-old, and that the average American was both apathetic and easily persuaded. He also insisted that he was making a positive contribution by making people think, a stance he continued to maintain. In a 1965 opinion piece in the *Los Angeles Times*, he wrote that while some people called him "a rabble-rouser and a hate-monger," all he was trying to do was encourage some "stimulating dialogue."

CONTROVERSIAL BUT SUCCESSFUL

The critics weren't so sure. While they found him quotable, they didn't perceive his often angry style as stimulating; rather, it often made them uncomfortable. The longer he remained on the air, the more the critics wondered how he managed to keep his job. It wasn't just the critics who were ill at ease with Joe Pyne. His outspokenness made him enemies in Wilmington, where he not only commented about national issues but also criticized Delaware's attorney general, Wilmington's mayor, and several other local political figures. Perhaps that's why the audience kept listening: They never knew what they'd hear when Joe opened the microphone.

Then, in May 1957, Pyne decided he'd been at WILM long enough. He had made a name for himself, was earning in excess of 42,000 dollars a year (an excellent salary in the 1950s), had inspired plenty of controversy, and had even fended off a number of threats of violence by disgruntled listeners and guests. It was time for a new challenge, and he headed for the West Coast in mid-1957. He found a radio job at a station in Riverside, California, sixty miles from Los Angeles. That job led to an opportunity at a Los Angeles television station, KTLA. Joe had some TV experience; in 1954, he had been on WDEL-TV in Wilmington, but only for a couple of months. Now, he was on the West Coast, in one of America's largest cities, doing a TV talk show. He would later claim that this show had been a big success, yet within a year, he was back in the Chester-Wilmington area again. In the summer of 1958, he began hosting a talk show on WVUE-TV, Channel 12, a Wilmgington station that could also be seen in Philadelphia. At that time, Pyne was not regarded as a bigot: he discussed controversial topics, but some of the local black newspapers praised him for inviting black newsmakers onto his show and addressing issues that mattered to the black community. In addition to his TV show, Pyne hosted a talk show on WILM radio, but he told reporters that he was just biding his time, that he had big plans.

And he certainly did. In late 1959, Joe moved back to Los Angeles, and by 1960, he was hosting his usual angry and abrasive radio talk show at KABC. Once again, he polarized the audience, some listeners and guests complaining he was too caustic and others saying his candor was refreshing. But as in Wilmington, he had people talking about him and his show. From KABC, he went to KLAC in 1965, doing the 9 p.m. to midnight shift. Never one to avoid controversial guests, he put Nazis and members of the Ku Klux Klan on the air, earning the displeasure of the American Jewish Committee and a warning from the FCC. He also had guests who believed in eugenics, guests who were racists, guests with strange theories about past lives or UFOs—and the arguments continued. He was again making a big salary—about $200,000 a year by some estimates—and getting plenty of attention from the critics, as well as many listeners.

And then, Pyne's biggest opportunity yet offered itself: syndication. The NBC Radio Network began syndicating his show nationally in March 1966; it was soon carried by over two hundred stations. Billed as "fist-in-the-mouth" radio, Pyne's show didn't disappoint. His syndicated talk show delivered the same rage, the same controversial guests, the same insults—and the same results. While the critics were disgusted, Pyne's fame spread and he continued to attract large audiences. The one thing that was different was the time slot. Whereas in the past Joe had usually broadcast at night, this time he was on during the mid morning. In an era when women were still homemakers, having an outrageous talk show on the air at that hour was actually a bold move. And to the consternation of those who disliked him, it worked. In 1967, when KNWA in Fayettville, Arkansas was about to become an affiliate of Pyne's syndicated radio show, management placed a large advertisement in the local newspaper, describing the Joe Pyne show, listing some of its famous (and infamous) guests, and concluding with "You may agree or disagree with Joe Pyne. You may scream in rage at some of his remarks. BUT YOU WON'T TURN HIM OFF!" It was true. Even in "housewife time," he continued to win new fans.

Pyne projected a "tough guy" image that critics found especially disturbing. On one episode of his TV show, he got into an argument with black militants, and as the debate grew more heated, he opened a desk drawer to show that he kept a revolver hidden, just in case he needed to defend himself. Another time, he brandished a handgun when discussing his solution to the race riots that occurred in the Watts neighborhood of Los Angeles. And while his radio show continued to get good ratings, it was on his TV show that he pushed the envelope the most. On TV, he had some of the most controversial guests (including followers of cult-leader and convicted murderer Charles Manson, members of the American Nazi Party, and members of the Ku Klux Klan). And when there were complaints about his show, he was unapologetic. As Pyne told reporter Bob Rose in a 1967 interview, "I have been accused of fostering a hate program. [But] my aim is to provoke people into listening and thinking . . . I believe I am doing my country a service by exposing these fanatics to the public eye."

Pyne's TV show also showcased an array of eccentrics, as well as people whom society considered immoral or deviant, such as homosexuals. Pyne regularly made fun of these guests and ridiculed the way they lived or how they looked. Most of the guests seemed to be there so Joe could argue with them and fire up the viewers. He even had a feature in which members of the studio audience came up and stepped into what he called the Beef Box, where they had a chance to air a complaint. That chance included Joe's insulting and disagreeing with them, but still they kept coming. Because Joe Pyne was known for being rude and confrontational with guests, there are stories about the few guests who got the better of him. For example, there is a much-quoted story about his losing a verbal duel with rock star Frank Zappa. Pyne, a supporter of the Vietnam War, had an intense dislike for "hippies," especially men with long hair. He immediately insulted Zappa by saying, "So I guess your long hair makes you a woman." Zappa allegedly responded, "So I guess your wooden leg makes you a table." The difficulty is that although the story has been repeated on the Internet and in magazines, it has never been verified as authentic.

FINAL DAYS

In July 1966, Pyne briefly became a game show host. He was the master of ceremonies for *Showdown*, a summer replacement that lasted only three months. There is no evidence that anyone argued, and no chairs were thrown, but acting as the benign guide of a game show seems uncharacteristic of Pyne;

critics were puzzled at how Pyne could be friendly and effusive on the game show, while being outraged and angry on his talk show. But while Pyne's radio and TV career continued to be a success, his personal life was about to catch up with him. He had been a chain smoker for years, even smoking on the air and being very vocal about his right to continue smoking. He was diagnosed with lung cancer, and after doing his show from a studio in his home for a while, he had to stop the broadcasts in November 1969 to undergo treatment. By that time, he had finally stopped smoking, but it was too late. The king of the provocateurs died in Los Angeles on 23 March 1970. He was forty-five. Remembering his career, someone who worked with him told fellow talker Hilly Rose that throughout his career, Pyne had "wanted to be powerful and feared . . . He never lost control in any situation" (Rosen, 1978).

One of Pyne's few defenders was his daughter, Cathee, who saw a side of him that the public seldom did. At home, she said, he was nothing like the angry talk host. In fact, "he was really a very mellow person who loved peace and quiet and to be with his family" (quoted by Gebhart, 1974). The picture of a kinder, gentler Joe Pyne was one that few in the public would have believed, and yet Cathee insisted that her father had always provided her and her brother, Eddie, with much encouragement and mentoring. But the public persona Joe created, of the intimidating talk show host who shouts down the guests and insults the callers, is the one that lives on, and angry talkers are still compared to him. Among the most successful of those who use the "perpetual outrage" persona is syndicated radio talker Michael Savage, but there are numerous others who use the style that Joe Pyne originated. Yet, even forty years later, some media historians insist that nobody has ever done it quite as well as the original angry talker, Joe Pyne.

JOE PYNE TIMELINE

1924: born in Chester, Pennsylvania

1945: at the end of military service, seeks work in radio

1946: first radio job, at WTSB, Lumberton, North Carolina

1951: creates *It's Your Nickel* on WILM, Wilmington, Delaware

1955: loses a leg to cancer

1957: makes first attempt to become a talker in Los Angeles

1958: does TV talk show on WVUE-TV in Wilmington, Delaware

1960: makes second, more successful, attempt at KABC

1965: moves his show to KLAC radio; begins doing a local TV version on KTTV

1966: show syndicated by NBC radio network

1969: stops broadcasting due to worsening cancer

1970: dies of cancer at age forty-five

FURTHER READING

Gebhart, Ed. "Joe Pyne's Daughter a Lot Like Her Famous Father." *Delaware County (PA) Daily Times*, 9 August 1974, p. 3.

Gould, Jack. "Joe Pyne's Electronic Peep Show." *New York Times*, 5 June 1966, p. D15.

"Killer Joe." *Time*, 29 July 1966, p. 30.

Murdaugh, Don. "Joe Pyne Saw Tobacco Juice Fly." *Chester (PA) Times*, 22 April 1959, p. 19.

———. "Radio Geared to 13 Year Old." *Chester (PA) Times*, 23 April 1959, p. 22.

Page, Don. "Profile of Joe Pyne." *Los Angeles Times*, 9 February 1964, p. C34.

———. "Pyne Answers Final Call on Two-Way Radio." *Los Angeles Times*, 21 February 1969, p. J1.

Pyne, Joe. "Call Joe. He Won't Call You." *Los Angeles Times*, 12 September 1965, p. N39.

Rose, Bob. "Kook-Baiting Pyne Likes Controversy." *Washington Post*, 29 July 1967, p. D15.

Rose, Hilly. *But That's Not What I Called About*. Chicago: Contemporary Books, 1978.

"Tribune Comptroller Scores on TV Show." *Philadelphia Tribune*, 8 July 1958, p. 2.

Courtesy Nova M Radio

Randi Rhodes

Randi Rhodes never expected to become a talk show host, let alone a progressive radio icon. In fact, growing up, she didn't know what she wanted to be. Raised in a home where her parents argued constantly and finally divorced, by her own admission she was in and out of trouble. She loved to read, and briefly thought about becoming a writer, but it was after a stint in the U.S. Air Force that she discovered broadcasting. And without realizing it, she became a trailblazer—one of the few female shock jocks—and later on, one of the equally small number of women with political talk show. Most of these female talkers were conservatives, but Randi's liberal views attracted large numbers of listeners to the fledgling Air America Radio network. She became so popular that she was the subject of a cover story in the radio trade publication *Talkers* magazine and was interviewed by Brian Lamb on his cable-TV show *Q & A* on C-Span. Rhodes has become known for being both colorful and controversial, a polarizing figure that people either love or hate. In only four years, she has become one of progressive talk's best-known personalities, surviving both personal and professional problems to carve out a career that even her political opponents admit is a success.

DIFFICULT EARLY YEARS

Randi Buten was born in Brooklyn, New York, on 28 January 1959, and to this day, she jokes about her accent. Her childhood was difficult; she has told interviewers that she was a "depressed kid from a dysfunctional family." When her father, Norman, and her mother, Loretta, ultimately divorced when she was fifteen, she went to live with her father in Oxnard, California. After completing high school, she couldn't decide on a career. She did office work for several years, but she didn't enjoy it, and in 1977, she enlisted in the military. She was stationed at McGuire Air Force Base in New Jersey, where she attained the rank of airman first class, working as a mechanic; she then served in the reserves. She later said that her military service helped her to acquire self-confidence, and while she was grateful for the structure it provided, she decided not to make it her career. One reason for her decision was that she had become involved with a man who was about to leave the air force; she left too, and went with him to Ohio. It turned out to be an abusive relationship, and when it ended, Randi found herself once again searching for a way to make a living.

While she was growing up, she had fond memories of listening to her favorite late-night radio shows, and she began wondering whether she might be able to get a job as a disc jockey. At the time, the easiest way to get experience was at a small-town radio station. She found her first opportunity in the West Texas town of Seminole, where in 1979 she played country music on the local station, KIKZ-FM. As was typical of small-town stations, the pay was only minimum wage; announcers on the way up often endured the low salary in order to get experience, and Rhodes was no exception. Because she had bills to pay, she also worked as a waitress in a Mexican restaurant. In a pattern that was typical of up-and-coming dj's, she didn't stay at small stations for very long; she had her sights set on the bigger markets, where the money and the opportunity were. She worked next for a rock station in Mobile, Alabama. Very much aware that successful dj's had an on-air persona, she began to use the air-name Randi St. John, the Holy Toilet, and became one of the first, woman shock jocks. It would turn out to be a good career move.

SUCCESS AS A SHOCK JOCK

When the bills piled up again, Rhodes took time away from radio and briefly became a long-distance truck driver, one of the few honest jobs where a woman with only a high school diploma could make good money. For a year, she hauled beer from Milwaukee and paper from Fort Worth. But by this time, she knew she really did want to be in radio, and she was ultimately hired by New York City's WAPP-FM. She was excited by finally being back home in New York City. When she arrived at the station in 1983, the management told her she would have to choose a new last name because the station already had a dj using the name St. John. Randi was a big fan of controversial rock star Ozzy Osbourne, so she decided to use the name of Osbourne's guitar player, Randy Rhoads, who had died in an accident in March 1982 at the age of twenty-five. And so it was that she became Randi Rhodes.

Unfortunately, while the opportunity to be a rock dj at a major New York FM should have led her to considerable success, her dependence on alcohol and cocaine kept her from making the most of the opportunity and led to her being fired from the station. It also led to her dismissal from her next job, at KHYI in Dallas. She was then hired by veteran program manager Kevin Metheny to work at another Dallas station, KTKS-FM. (Metheny was accustomed to working with difficult people. In 1982, he had been the program director at New York City's WNBC and had clashed repeatedly with his controversial dj Howard Stern.) Metheny recognized that Rhodes was a talented announcer, and he was among those who told her to straighten herself out, sooner rather than later. Randi also realized that her addiction might cost her the career she loved and went into a substance abuse treatment program, cut back on drinking, and stopped using drugs in early 1986.

In 1987, Randi relocated to the Miami area because her mother, who lived in Miami, was ill and needed assistance. She was also there to help her sister Ellen, who had been diagnosed with breast cancer. Ellen had a daughter, Jessica, from a failed marriage, and when Ellen died in 1998, Randi took Jessica in and raised her. As for her radio career, Rhodes began working the overnight shift at WSHE-FM in Fort Lauderdale for a while, but she didn't get along with the program director and was fired in 1991. She again took various office jobs and began auditing some liberal arts courses at Broward County Community College. She had no plans to get a degree; she was studying because she felt it would help her to get hired at a radio station whose format interested her. WIOD in Miami was doing something called "hot talk." Unlike traditional talk, which targeted a much older audience, hot talk featured announcers who used the same irreverent style as many rock stations, and who talked about subjects that would interest people in their twenties and thirties. Hot talk was crude and controversial, and nearly all of its announcers were men. Randi believed that to do hot talk the right way, she had to be more knowledgeable about current events and politics, which is why she was auditing courses in political science, popular culture, and law. In the fall of 1992, she got an on-air audition at WIOD and thanks to the station's star talk host Neil Rogers, who recommended her, she was hired to do the evening shift in late September. She soon became known to the Miami audience as "the goddess" and is still remembered there as the woman with the New York accent, the sometimes sexy voice, the brash and outspoken style, and the fearless approach to talk. On her show, very few subjects were off-limits. At this point in her career, Rhodes wasn't yet doing political talk, although current issues did come up. Ordinarily she discussed her current boyfriend, her relationship with her mother, her impressions of South Florida, and whatever else came to mind, in addition to interacting with her callers in a way that was friendly or caustic, depending on the attitude of the caller. It didn't take long for her to become a sensation, and she was surprised when critics labeled her a shock jock. She didn't think of her show as particularly shocking, even though she wasn't afraid to speak her mind. She knew she was going against the traditional radio role for women, who even in the early 1990s still tended to give advice, be the sidekick who laughed at the male host's jokes, or do human interest features on the news. In South Florida, Randi Rhodes changed all that. She became so popular that in late April 1993, she was featured on the tabloid TV show *A Current Affair*, where the story line focused on how she had gone from being a member of the air force and a truck driver to being a controversial shock jock.

BECOMING A POLITICAL TALKER

Unfortunately, Rhodes encountered a truism in the business world: Even a woman who is doing an excellent job does not get equal pay. During her year and a half with WIOD, she had excellent ratings and continued to attract favorable media attention, but no matter how good her ratings were, her pay stayed about the same. As she told Michael Harrison, who interviewed her for a cover story in *Talkers* magazine in late 2005, "Neil [Rogers] was making half a million. Something like that. Rick Riley was making $325,000. I was making $42,000 a year. And I was #1. Men 25–54. At WIOD." Frustrated, she finally decided to leave the station, but she wasn't out of work for long. WJNO in West Palm Beach wanted to hire her and was willing to give her a sizable salary, even though it was in a smaller radio market than Miami. Rhodes found 1994 quite an eventful year. After living with her boyfriend, Jim Robertson, for ten years, she married him, but the marriage was short-lived—only a few months—and it did not end amicably. In September 1994, she started at WJNO, again as the afternoon-drive announcer. Little did she know that this job would change the direction of her career.

Barbara Walters and *The View*

Few women on television have a longer résumé than Barbara Walters. Born into a show business family, she was a writer and researcher on *Today* in the early 1960s and then became the "Today Girl," an attractive female whose job was to look glamorous. But Walters expanded the job, doing interviews with female celebrities. By the early 1970s, she was hosting a TV talk show on NBC called "Not For Women Only," and was well respected for her interviews with newsmakers, from movie stars to heads of state. In 1976, ABC hired her as the first female network news anchor. By all accounts, her coanchor, veteran Harry Reasoner, hated the idea of women anchoring the news, and so did the critics. Walters ultimately left, becoming a cohost of *20/20*, ABC's popular news magazine, where she stayed for twenty-five years. Walters was supposed to retire but decided instead to produce and cohost a new talk show. Called *The View*, it debuted on ABC on 11 August 1997. Critics labeled it a "guilty pleasure" as Walters and her four female cohosts, sat around a table, drinking coffee and chatting. *The View* quickly got excellent ratings, and despite several changes in cohosts, it has continued to be one of the most popular shows on daytime TV.

Like 1960s talker Virginia Graham, who inspired her, Walters is a good conversationalist, but it is her cohosts who often get media attention, clashing with her and with each other as they discuss everything from movies to current events to celebrities behaving badly. The tabloids have eagerly followed the rumors surrounding several of the show's former cohosts—did they leave or were they fired? The interactions between cohosts often resemble a soap opera more than a talk show, but the audience continues to love *The View*.

Two more events in 1994 affected Randi's life. One was the O. J. Simpson trial. The country became preoccupied with the case, which involved former football player and movie actor Simpson, who was accused of murdering his wife, Nicole, and a friend of hers named Ron Goldman. Until the summer of 2004, when Nicole Brown Simpson and Goldman were found dead, Randi's show had only occasionally touched on current news. As the case unfolded and O. J. Simpson was charged with the two murders, Randi could not avoid talking about it. Fortunately, the law courses she had audited at Broward County Community College, along with her own reading on the subject, enabled her to conduct conversations with her callers that earned her considerable praise. She had good insights into the case, and her audience grew as a result of her commentary on the trial. From then on, commenting on the news and current events became part of her show.

The other 1994 event that affected Rhodes was the Republicans' winning back the majority in Congress. She admired Bill and Hillary Clinton, and she hated the partisan attacks she felt were being unfairly directed at them. It looked to her as if the country was going in a much too conservative direction. That subject also became fodder for her radio show. And the more she talked about politics, the more angry and frustrated she became. She was one of the few liberals on the air, and evidently many people either shared her opinions or thought she expressed them in a compelling way, because her ratings kept going up. Interestingly, she was on the air opposite conservative icon Rush Limbaugh, and her show got higher ratings than his. In fact, she was frequently the number-one-rated show in the West Palm Beach market.

Randi was very disappointed in the way the country was changing, and those changes also impacted the broadcasting industry. The Telecommunications Act of 1996 enabled a number of giant conglomerates—like Clear Channel Communications, which had a history of making large donations to the Republican Party—to buy up many of the previously locally owned stations (including WJNO). The Republicans in the House of Representatives attempted to impeach Bill Clinton after it was discovered in 1998 that he had been involved in a sexual affair with a White House intern. Clinton was not convicted by the Senate, but the country grew even more polarized politically, and Rhodes grew more frustrated. And then came the contested 2000 presidential election, in which George W. Bush was given the presidency by a U.S. Supreme Court decision after former Vice President Al Gore had won the popular vote but seemed to be losing the electoral vote; Florida was the state whose electoral votes would decide the presidency. Gore asked for a recount in Florida, and Randi was an eye-witness to history when the Court ordered the recount halted. Years later, many Democrats still believed that the Republicans had stolen the election, as questions persisted about voting irregularities, along with accusations that many minority votes weren't counted. Because talk radio was more than 95 percent conservative, there were few places where liberals and moderates could express their outrage.

Randi became a frequent critic of President George W. Bush, his administration, and his policies. After the tragic events of 11 September 2001, the president ultimately took the country into a military invasion of Iraq, a decision many liberals opposed, since Iraq was not connected with 9/11. In addition to what she felt was an unwarranted war, there were many other presidential decisions with which she vehemently disagreed. Now proficient in political talk, Rhodes felt it was time to take her show to a wider audience because there was a lack of examination and discussion of important issues from a liberal perspective, and being number one in West Palm Beach wasn't enough. She also saw that Clear Channel, being a Republican-dominated company, was doing little to promote her highly rated show, and it had also refused to syndicate her as it did Rush Limbaugh. The company did, however, give her permission to seek out a syndication deal of her own and still keep her job at WJNO. Her resulting search led her to Air America Radio.

PROGRESSIVE TALK RADIO

In 2002–2003, a number of Democrats who were frustrated by the dearth of liberal voices on the radio decided to act. One group, led by Tom Athans, who ranked high in the Michigan Democratic Party, wanted to develop and promote liberal talk show hosts. The group raised money, started a company called Democracy Radio, and then held an audition. The choice came down to two veteran talkers, Ed Schultz of Fargo, North Dakota, and Rhodes. In the end, Democracy Radio chose Ed, and its marketing campaign helped to get him onto more than ninety stations. The other Democratic group determined to break through and get some liberal talk shows on the air was originally started in late 2002 by two Chicago entrepreneurs, Sheldon and Anita Drobny, and was called AnShell Media. AnShell hoped to become a liberal network and a provider of programming for radio stations that wanted to broadcast the liberal point of view. It soon attracted a number of Democratic venture capitalists, political figures, and celebrities who felt the airwaves had become totally unbalanced and wanted to make a change in the media environment. While accounts of the early days of the project are still contested, the Drobnys weren't able to raise enough money to guarantee success and sold AnShell to another group, led by a wealthy businessman named Evan Cohen. His group was able to bring the idea to fruition. Now known as Air America Radio, the new liberal network took to the air on 31 March 2004. The decision was to call the programming "progressive talk," *progressive* seeming more acceptable to the general public than *liberal*, a word that had been demonized by conservative talk hosts for several decades. Among the people Air America Radio hired were the well-known comedian and veteran of *Saturday Night Live* Al Franken and the Florida talk show sensation Randi Rhodes.

Within months, Randi was being heard on twenty-six stations in sixteen states, and the number of affiliates kept growing. Unfortunately for all concerned, Evan Cohen was not as wealthy or financially stable as he had claimed, and the new network found itself in financial trouble almost immediately. Frequent changes of executives and rumors of bouncing checks made conservative talkers gleeful. Nevertheless, Randi and some of the other announcers were carving out a niche for themselves. As in Florida, much of Rhodes's show was extended commentary on current events. She was very thorough in her preparation for her show, and while she did have some guests and take some calls now and then, there was no mistaking that she was the star of the show. It gave her the national platform she needed to express her opposition to the Republican political agenda, and large numbers of listeners agreed with her. However, being on a national network also meant being noticed and scrutinized by many more people, including her political opponents. In late April 2005, she broadcast a comedy routine that appeared to advocate taking a shot at the president. Although Randi insisted that she had been doing a satirical piece that was misunderstood, the right-wing publications and talkers were highly critical, and she was forced to apologize. On the other hand, her outspoken and frequently enraged assessments of the Bush administration struck a chord with many people. When *Talkers* magazine's "Heavy Hundred," an annual list of the hundred most influential radio talk hosts, came out in 2006, Rush Limbaugh was number one, as he had been for years, but Randi Rhodes was in the top ten. It was the first time an Air America host had reached that status. And when Rhodes made the cover of *Talkers* in December 2005/January 2006, it was further proof of her success, since *Talkers* seldom wrote about liberal hosts. Since 2006, Rhodes's national ratings have declined, perhaps due partly to the turmoil of Air America Radio's continuing financial problems. In mid-October 2006, the network filed for bankruptcy, although it was able to reorganize and stay on the air. Still, this sort of instability resulted in the loss of some key affiliates; nevertheless, Randi's show was being heard by about two million listeners a week. Having survived the many ups and downs of working for Air America, she could not have suspected that by 2008, the network where her national career as a progressive talker had begun would want to get rid of her.

CHANGES IN RHODES'S LIFE

Much had changed for Randi Rhodes since 1994, the year when she suddenly found herself doing political talk. While her afternoon-drive talk show (which also aired on the Air America network) continued to be broadcast by WJNO, by 2007 she was the only progressive on that station, and her liberal views were surrounded entirely by those of conservative hosts, including Rush Limbaugh. On the other hand, four years on Air America Radio had made her sufficiently well known nationally to be asked to give keynote speeches at progressive political events, and she appeared as a guest pundit on such talk shows as CNN's *Larry King Live*. Randi has remained a very polarizing figure. She is sometimes profane and scatalogical. She has never been shy about calling President Bush a liar or lashing out at political figures in both parties who she believes are hypocrites. In fact, while many listeners agree with her, others say they find that her style has become far too angry. Because she is one of the few women doing the angry style of talk, Randi may be affected by the fact that listeners still don't seem comfortable with an enraged woman, whereas some of the most popular male talk hosts are regularly enraged and listeners don't seem to mind. Nevertheless, she had a dedicated and loyal following, a popular Web site and blog, and a stable career that had survived the chaotic management changes at Air America. In early 2008, Randi Rhodes had no plans to leave the network, nor did Air America executives seem to have plans to sever the relationship.

The situation suddenly changed in early April 2008. Randi had done a speaking engagement for one of Air America Radio's affiliates, KKGN in San Francisco, and part of her appearance was what she called a stand-up comedy routine, never intended for broadcast. It was a profane discussion of several political figures, including presidential candidate Hillary Clinton, whom Randi called vulgar names several times. Segments of the routine, privately filmed, were soon seen on the Internet video site YouTube, and controversy ensued. Upper management at Air America announced to the media that Randi was being suspended for comments that were deemed offensive and inappropriate, given that she was representing her network at the event. Randi, of course, found this statement disingenuous: She had been hired to do a stand-up routine, the audience seemed to like it, and it had never been intended for public dissemination. As a comedian who had done political stand-up comedy in nightclubs, Randi saw nothing wrong with using profanity or vulgarity in her act, and felt she was being punished for expressing herself honestly.

What happened next depends on whose version of the story one believes: Randi's friends said she was fired, but Air America said she quit. Randi made a brief appearance on *Larry King Live*, during which she accused Air America of looking for an excuse to restructure her contract, and of trying to get rid of her. Fortunately for her many fans, she wasn't unemployed for very long. She was hired by Nova M Broadcasting, a progressive talk syndication service that was started by Sheldon and Anita Drobny in 2006. Suddenly Randi had to prepare for a new chapter in her career. She made the transition with ease. The *Randi Rhodes Show* was back on the air on Nova M's affiliated stations on 14 April 2008. And with the presidential race heating up, Randi went back to doing what she does best: being an outspoken and unpredictable progressive talk show host.

RANDI RHODES TIMELINE

1959: born in Brooklyn, New York

1977: joins the U.S. Air Force

1979: gets her first radio job in Seminole, Texas

1983: on air at WAPP-FM in New York City

1992: is hired as a shock jock at Miami's WIOD

1994: begins doing political talk on WJNO in West Palm Beach, Florida

2004: debuts on the new Air America Radio network

2008: fired for controversial remarks at a speaking engagement; hired by Nova M

FURTHER READING

Brecher, Elinor J. "Mistress of Flip." *Miami Herald*, 5 September 2004, p. 1M.
———. "Talk Radio's Brassy Goddess of Gab." *Miami Herald*, 31 January 1993, p. 1J.
Harrison, Michael. "Interview with Randi Rhodes." *Talkers*, December 2005–January 2006, pp. 16, 34, 40, 44.
Kovacs, Joe. "Air America Host: Punish Me If I Broke the Law." 28 April 2005, online at http://www.worldnetdaily.com/news/article.asp?ARTICLE_ID=44014.
Lamb, Brian. "Interview with Talk Show Host Randi Rhodes." 18 December 2005, online at www.q-and-a.org/Transcript/?ProgramID=1054.
Passy, Charles. "Talk Radio: The Big Business of Big Mouths." *Palm Beach Post*, 10 May 2008, p. 1A.
Span, Laura. "Radio Waves: Talk show Host Randi Rhodes Joined a New Liberal Network." *Washington Post*, 12 September 2004, p. W11.
The Web site of Nova M Radio is http://www.novamradio.com/live/
Randi has her own web site at http://www.therandirhodesshow.com/

AP Photo/Henny Ray Abrams, File

Cristina Saralegui

In the Spanish-speaking world, Cristina Saralegui has often been compared to Oprah Winfrey. Some media critics even refer to her as "Oprah with salsa." There is good reason for this comparison, and it's not just that the two women share the same birthday. What Oprah has done for African American women in media, Cristina has done for Latinas. During a television career that has lasted more than thirty years, she has expanded the traditional role of women in Spanish-language broadcasting, while serving as a role model of what an immigrant can achieve in the United States. Before becoming a TV talk show host, she rose to the top of her profession in print, first as a reporter and ultimately as a magazine editor. Since 1989, the much-loved talk show host has led *El Show de Cristina* for Univision; she is not only the host but the executive producer. When she first hosted the show, it was quite a departure from the typical talk shows aimed at Hispanic women. The common wisdom was that women wanted only scandal and celebrity gossip, but Cristina decided that her talk show would be different.

To this day, Saralegui gives viewers a blend of the serious and the sensational. Sometimes the show focuses on tabloid subjects, such as guests who are cross-dressers or who believe they have talked to aliens. But some segments of *El Show de Cristina* have offered frank and informative discussions of teenage pregnancy, drug addiction, child abuse, and gangs. Saralegui has interviewed the most well-known celebrities and political leaders, but she has also continued to provide a forum for counselors and health advocates to speak about the dangers of smoking or about AIDS prevention. While some viewers are uncomfortable with certain subjects or find Cristina too outspoken (she isn't shy about expressing her opinions), her consistently high ratings make her one of the most popular hosts in Spanish-language television. In the process, she has earned the respect and trust of her audience, who think of her as much more than just a talk show host. To them, she is like a best friend.

COMING TO AMERICA

Cristina Maria Saralegui was born in Havana, Cuba, on 29 January 1948, the daughter of Cristina Santamarina de Saralegui and Francisco Saralegui. Theirs was a successful and prosperous family with longstanding ties to the media. Her father, uncle, and grandfather were involved in publishing, and in fact, it was her grandfather, Francisco Saralegui y Arrizubieta, who founded three of the most popular Spanish-language magazines: *Bohemia, Carteles*, and *Vanidades*. Her grandfather also provided her with an introduction to journalism as a profession. Cristina's mother was a homemaker, as was the tradition when Cristina was growing up, but she was also adventuresome and not afraid to create her own identity. Cristina recalls that her mother loved to go fishing with her father and his fishing companions; fishing was something most women of that era would not have done, but Cristina's mother was good at it and saw no reason why she shouldn't pursue it. Undoubtedly, Cristina took this lesson with her: Don't listen when the culture says that a woman shouldn't try something.

Unfortunately for the Saraleguis, the revolution that brought Fidel Castro to power in 1959 meant the end of the family's business. When the Castro regime also seized their property, the family fled to Miami. When they arrived in the United States Cristina was twelve, just another of the many Spanish-speaking immigrants who had come here. She was immediately encouraged to study hard and to learn English, without which, she was told, she would not be successful, advice that turned out to be useful. she attended the University of Miami, and she was able to study entirely in English, majoring in mass communications and creative writing. Years later, when she became a well-known personality on Spanish-speaking television, she was a strong advocate for bilingualism, encouraging Spanish-speaking immigrants to become fluent in English.

While Saralegui was at the University of Miami and doing well, her father began to have serious business problems, which caused him to reevaluate the money he had set aside for her education. Her brother was in boarding school and planned to attend college. Forced to make a choice, her father believed it was more important for a son to go to college, even if it meant the daughter wouldn't graduate. Suddenly, there was no money for her tuition, and Cristina had to drop out of college, only nine credits shy of her degree. In those days, very few people questioned the machismo of the Hispanic culture, and Saralegui was no exception. But having to leave college became a blessing in disguise. Saralegui needed to find work, and she was determined to have a career in media. Her first job was as an intern working for one of her grandfather's magazines, *Vanidades*, which had been brought back to life once the Saralegui family settled in Miami. The job was more about filing than about journalism, and it paid only forty dollars a week, but it was a start. Ultimately, in 1973, she got a job as a staff writer at the Spanish-language edition of the women's magazine *Cosmopolitan (Cosmopolitan en Español)*. She wasn't happy there, and soon left to work for the *Miami Herald*'s Spanish-language edition and once again found it wasn't a good fit. She tried to go back to *Cosmopolitan*, but the editor turned her down. Fortunately, *Vanidades* didn't, and this time, she was hired for something more than a low-wage internship. The magazine was about to launch a new publication, called *Intimades*, and Saralegui she was asked to run it. She had acquired a very important skill during her time in college and at the two previous magazines: She had learned to write a conversational Spanish that would be understandable all over Latin America and the United States. Many Spanish-speaking countries have their own slang, and words that are neutral in one country may be offensive in another. (This would continue to be a problem when she had her TV show. Depending on where the guests came from, they might say something that was completely neutral in their country but insulting in another country. Fortunately, Cristina's work in print journalism prepared her and enabled her to explain to her viewers what the guest had been trying to say.)

Thanks to her experience in the magazine field, Cristina not only developed a familiarity with all the different kinds of Spanish but, just as important, was also able to understand the cultural differences of her readers and create a magazine that anyone could read and enjoy. She also wanted to expand the scope of the typical women's magazine. She continued to focus on core subjects like food and fashion and relationships, while adding articles that encouraged women to do more than be housewives or sex objects. Cristina wanted Spanish-speaking women to be stylish and have a nice home (and buy the products of the magazine's advertisers), but she believed it equally important to encourage women to think for themselves, and to formulate goals that went beyond getting married and making their husbands happy. The more she worked in Spanish-language journalism, the more determined she became to challenge the macho culture and change some of the traditional attitudes about what women could and could not achieve.

EL SHOW DE CRISTINA

Under Saralegui's guidance, *Intimades* soon became a successful magazine, and by 1979, she was ready for her next challenge. She was named editor in chief of *Cosmopolitan en Españo*. and became especially impressed by her colleague Helen Gurley Brown, editor in chief of *Cosmopolitan*'s English-language edition. Brown had taken over in 1965 and transformed the magazine from one that not many people read into one that no young woman wanted to be without. The new version was splashy; it was sensual; it was cutting-edge. Not only did Cristina admire Brown for what she had achieved, but she also regarded Brown as a mentor. Cristina worked at the Spanish-language *Cosmo* for ten years, and when she left, it was for a very good reason: the opportunity to have her own television show.

In the late 1980s, changes were on the horizon for Spanish-language television in the United States. What had formerly been known as the Spanish International Network (SIN) had new owners and a new name: Univision. It was also seeking new ideas for programs. Chilean TV star Don Francisco had brought his program *Sábado Gigante* to Univision and was doing well. Cristina was still with the Spanish-language *Cosmo*, which had become very successful under her leadership. She was asked to be a guest on *Sábado Gigante* to discuss a couple of the stories in the magazine, and she made a very good impression. Univision executives liked her and wanted her to do a women's show, but their concept was traditional and, in her view, very sexist, so she turned them down. In return, they gave her a chance to devise a women's show as she thought it ought to be. The result was *El Show de Cristina* (The Cristina Show), which debuted in April 1989. Cristina was not only the host but the executive producer, so she had control over the show's content.

One of the network's first questions was whether the Latina audience would accept Saralegui, since she didn't "look" Latina: she was blond and very light-skinned, coloring typical of her Basque ethnicity. Within six months, she had won the viewers over with her empathy for their problems and her ability to find topics that would interest them. Cristina was on her way to becoming the biggest Latina star on television. In the next few years, her show was seen not only in the United States but in seventeen other countries, including Spain, Argentina, and Mexico. At her highest point, she had a worldwide audience of 100 million viewers. In 1991, she started her own magazine, *Cristina La Revista*, which was published until December 2005. And as more people were going online, she started a bilingual Web site in 1998. That same year, she also issued her autobiography, entitled in English *My Life as a Blonde* and in Spanish, *Confidencias de una Rubia*. Critics called it shallow and superficial, but fans were delighted to learn more about their hero.

From its inception, *El Show de Cristina* has been unlike anything seen before on Hispanic television. In a macho culture, the idea of a confident and assertive woman was new. So were a number of the topics that Cristina discussed and the way she discussed them. When discussing the macho nature of Hispanic culture, for example, she uses her own egalitarian marriage as an example of how a husband and a wife can help each other and work together as partners. And if a male guest says something she finds sexist, she lets him know, although usually with a smile or a joke. In some respects, she has always done the typical women's show, with celebrities who drop by, and guest experts who talk about the latest fashions, or exciting places to travel, or how to have a better relationship. But unlike the typical show, Cristina's show has become known for introducing issues that were not usually mentioned on programs aimed at the Latin-American audience, an audience that is over-whelmingly Catholic and often very traditional. Her show has tackled spousal rape; birth control, and family planning; whether gay marriage should be permitted; and the importance of condom use to prevent AIDS. She admits that she sometimes gets irate letters from viewers who are offended. But when asked by an advertiser or an offended viewer not to talk about sensitive issues, she replies that they need to be discussed, and she continues making the time to discuss them.

One thing that Saralegui does not do, however, is take stands on political issues. Although she has sat and talked with newsmakers of every political persuasion, she does not want her show to be perceived as partisan in any way. She also says that she tries to keep her show friendly, even if she is some-times irreverent and outspoken, and if sometimes the topics border on the vulgar or the bizarre. While she likes to discuss important issues, she under-stands that on TV, entertainment must come first or people won't continue to watch. So viewers get to find out about the latest celebrity sex scandals or watch people who believe in vampires. On the other hand, while gossip and double entendre are acceptable, Cristina says she avoids any subjects that

Tyra Banks and Ellen DeGeneres

At the beginning of the new century, several new talk shows with women hosts became popular. One featured Tyra Banks. Banks earned fame in the 1990s as one of the few African American supermodels, and became the producer of "America's Next Top Model," and then she answered the question of whether she could also be a talk show host. Since the *Tyra Banks Show* debuted on 12 September 2005, it has attracted a predominantly young female audience, and earned Banks a Daytime Emmy award in early 2008. Banks interviews the usual celebrities, but she also addresses health and fitness issues that matter to her young audience, and has talked with newsmakers like 2008 presidential candidates Barack Obama and Mike Huckabee. Another successful host is Ellen DeGeneres, who was once considered controversial, but not for anything she said. One of the few popular female stand-up comics in an occupation dominated by men, she even performed on Johnny Carson's *The Tonight Show*, and from 1994 to 1998, had her own successful TV situation comedy, *Ellen.* But controversy arose in early 1997, when she revealed on Oprah Winfrey's show that she is a lesbian. That revelation made the cover of *Time* magazine, and it became a plot line in an episode of Ellen's sit-com when her character admits to her therapist (played, interestingly, by Oprah) that she is gay. DeGeneres was criticized by religious conservatives, notably Rev. Jerry Falwell, and *Ellen* was ultimately canceled. But the vast majority of the public continued to enjoy her work, so it was no surprise when she reemerged in September 2003, this time with an afternoon talk show, *The Ellen DeGeneres Show.* With her sly humor that reminds critics of stand-up comic (and former sit-com star) Jerry Seinfeld, Ellen's talk show became a ratings success almost immediately and has won a number of Daytime Emmy awards.

An exuberant host, Ellen opens her show by dancing, sometimes getting her guests, or even members of the studio audience, to dance with her. Whether interviewing celebrities or newsmakers, the interviews are lighthearted, like friends chatting. Critics praise Ellen for her humorous observations, which like Steve Allen's many years before her, are neither crude nor unkind. In a late 2007 Harris Poll of America's favorite TV personalities, Ellen DeGeneres ranked number one.

glorify violence, and she doesn't allow her guests to get overly irate. In fact, whenever a discussion becomes too heated or contentious, Cristina does what many daytime talk hosts do: She acts as a mediator, or perhaps even a judge. For example, when a couple is on the show to discuss their relationship problems, she will tell whoever has done wrong that it's time to stop making excuses and instead find a solution.

A LATINA SUCCESS STORY

In mid-December 2001, after twelve busy years, Saralegui decided to stop doing a daily show, cutting back to a once-a-week program. In addition to many guest appearances, she has a syndicated radio show called *Cristina Opina* (Cristina's Opinions). And proving that she was still a major player in Hispanic media, in August 2005 Cristina was named one of the "25 Most Influential Hispanics in America" by *Time* magazine. That same year, she became the first Latina inducted into the Broadcasting and Cable Hall of Fame. She has earned many awards over her long career: twelve Emmys, the 2006 National Academy of Television Arts and Sciences award as a Leader of Spanish-Language Television, and in 2007 the award for Outstanding Lifetime of Achievement in Hispanic Television, presented by two influential television trade publications, *Multichannel News* and *Broadcasting and Cable.* In 2007, as she celebrated her eighteenth year on the air, Saralegui became one of the new members of the American Red Cross's National Celebrity Cabinet, comprising some of the best-known of entertainers; members donate time and money to promoting the services of the Red Cross in times of need, whether taping public service announcements about the need to give blood or performing at celebrity events that raise money for disaster victims.

Reporters who interview Saralegui find that as she approaches age sixty, she seems still to have unlimited energy, whether doing charitable work or fund-raising for causes she cares about, or going wherever she has to go to publicize her show or her newest venture. In all of her business dealings, she is assisted by her husband, Marcos Avila, who is president of Cristina Saralegui Enterprises. (They have three children, who are now grown.) The "Cristina" name has become so identifiable in Spanish-language media that getting her endorsement or having her do a commercial can make a product more successful. A 2004 poll by Synovate, a worldwide market research company, found 80 percent of the respondents twenty-five to fifty-four years old regarded Saralegui as trustworthy, and 70 percent of women of all ages saw her as a role model.

Saralegui can also change popular buying habits. In 2004, she created the Casa Cristina™ collection with the intention of showing her audience that Hispanic homes be stylish and elegant. (She has told reporters that she is frustrated when Hispanics are stereotyped as people who can't afford anything nice.) Casa Cristina is a line of home furnishings that includes attractive living-room furniture, accessories for the bed and bath, rugs, lamps, and more. When the collection came out, Saralegui explained that she had always been fascinated by interior decorating, and this was her chance to implement some of her concepts. The launch was so successful that by November 2006, she had been chosen one of the "50 Most Influential People in Home Furnishings Style and Design" by *Home Furnishings News* (HFN), a respected retailing and marketing magazine. As further proof of her impact, in June 2007 she appeared at Kohl's Department Store in Buena Park, California, to introduce the Casa Cristina line; according to *PR Newswire*, which covered the event, over eight thousand people showed up. As might be expected because of her high profile, Cristina has her critics. She has been accused of doing a talk show that can be suggestive and crude. She insists that she tries to handle hot-button issues tastefully, but her critics say her show panders to the viewers who want scandal and discussions of sex. Cristina disagrees with that assessment, pointing out that over the years, she has discussed many serious topics, and she reminds her critics that as a TV talk show host, she has to take ratings into account. Like it or not, viewers are interested in celebrity scandals, and they like to watch people with relationship problems confess their sins. Another area of criticism is the accusation that her show encourages materialism and consumerism in an audience that, for the most part, is working-class. She replies that she regards herself as a motivator and wants her viewers to aspire to something better. Given how women have historically had subordinate status in macho cultures, she believes are empowered by having nice things.

Saralegui is just as passionate about wanting women to have a healthy lifestyle, and she advocates for many organizations that promote good health. She is quick to point out that she frequently uses her show to provide the audience with accurate information about ways to prevent the diseases common to Hispanics. One such disease is hepatitis C, which can cause permanent liver damage if left untreated. It is a leading cause of death in the Hispanic community, so she joined forces with Latino Organization for Liver Awareness (LOLA). Cristina has long been an activist in the fight against AIDS. In 1996, she started a foundation called Arriba la Vida (Up with Life), whose purpose is dispensing information and support to people with the disease, as well as promoting awareness about prevention. She has also made a series of public service announcements to promote breast cancer awareness.

Cristina likes to remind her detractors that her show has always maintained a balance between celebrity gossip and serious subjects. For example, she points out that she has frequently discussed immigration on her show, giving her audience a chance to talk about their experience in their new country and their problems with assimilation. Ever since she first went on the air in 1989, she has demanded and got control over how her show is run. When she signed her contract with Univision, she was very specific about not wanting to be considered "talent"; that is, she wasn't willing to be told what to say and then smile sweetly for the camera. She sees herself as a journalist, somebody with opinions of her own, and she made sure her network understood her need for creative freedom.

One issue now of personal importance to Saralegui is aging. She understands that in the media, it's often the young women who are the stars, and she is determined to show that an older woman can be attractive and interesting.

She has been open with her audience about why some women, herself among them, have opted for cosmetic surgery. She has even discussed the attitudes of older women about sex. And proving no subject is taboo on Cristina's show, she has discussed her experiences in going through menopause. Because she has proven time and time again that an older woman can be successful in the competitive TV world, AARP (formerly known as the American Association of Retired Persons), an organization that serves people over fifty and advocates for government policies that benefit them, chose her as one of its official spokespeople in 2006 and began to use her image in its promotional materials.

Saralegui is justifiably proud of having earned so many distinctions, and she remains one of the best-known Latina talk hosts in the world. She was given a Lifetime Achievement Award at the Fifth Annual Hispanic Television Summit in October 2007, further proof that her popularity has not diminished over the years. She can be outspoken, she can be charming, she can be controversial, but she has turned out to be exactly what she planned: a strong and successful woman who is in charge of her own life.

CRISTINA SARALEGUI TIMELINE

1948: born in Havana, Cuba

1960: arrives in Miami with her family

1973: hired by the Spanish-language edition of *Cosmopolitan*

1979: named editor in chief of *Cosmopolitan en Español*

1989: debut of her TV talk show, *El Show de Cristina*

1998: launches a bilingual Web site

2004: creates the Casa Cristina line of home furnishings

2005: named one of the twenty-five most influential Hispanics by *Time* magazine

FURTHER READING

De Quine, Jeanne. "The Queen of the Airwaves." *Time*, 22 August 2005, p. 49.

Downey, Kevin. "The Power of Cristina." *Broadcasting and Cable*, 1 October 2007, p. 8A.

"Q & A: A Latina Icon with Multimedia Presence." *Television Week*, 16 October 2006, p. 26.

Rifkin, Janey M. "International Talk show Host Exists in a Variety of Worlds." *Hispanic Times Magazine*, March–April 2001, pp. 44–46.

Rohter, Larry. "Aqui Se Habla English." *New York Times*, 26 July 1992, p. 60.

Valdes, Alisa, "Talk TV's Numero Uno: 100 Million Listen as Cristina Saralegui Tackles Latino Taboos." *Boston Globe*, 10 February 1998, p. E1.

Von Dare, Gregory. "A Woman Involved: Cristina Saralegui." *Road and Travel*, February 1999, online at www.roadandtravel.com/celebrities/christinasaralegui.html.

Waldman, Alison J. "Six Who Shine in Whatever Language." *Television Week*, 16 October 2006, pp. 25–32.

Wiltz, Teresa. "Spanglish Star: Can Univision's Cristina Translate into Prime Time? Stay Tuned." *Washington Post*, 31 January 2004, p. C1.

Cristina Saralegui's Web site is http: www.cristinaonline.com.

AP Photo/Susan Sterner

Laura Schlessinger

Laura Schlessinger is the nation's fourth most influential talk show host, according to the 2008 rankings in *Talkers* magazine, and she has a larger national audience than any other female host in the United States. To her critics, she's a moralistic scold who condemns gay people and working mothers; to her fans, she's taking a stand for traditional family values in a permissive society. Her advice is given in a tough-love style, and while her critics find her harsh, millions of people depend on her guidance. She says she isn't interested in trying to make her listeners feel good; she just wants them to stop doing foolish things. As she told reporter Robert DeFranco who asked about her style, "This isn't self-help. . . . I preach, teach and nag." But the woman known for morality and family values was not always such a traditionalist, nor was she a practitioner of what she preaches today.

HOW SCHLESSINGER BECAME "DR. LAURA"

Laura Catherine Schlessinger was born in Brooklyn, New York, on 16 January 1947. Her mother, Yolanda (often called Lundy), and her father, Monroe (Monty), had met in Italy during World War II, and Yolanda had come to America as a war bride after she and Monroe married in 1946. After Laura was born, she remained an only child for eleven years, until the birth of her sister, Cindy. By Schlessinger's account, growing up in the Schlessinger home was difficult; in fact, she has used words like *dysfunctional* to describe her family. Her mother was distant and unloving, her father constantly criticized her, and neither parent had any religious values to share with her. Schlessinger's mother was a nonpracticing Catholic, and her father had little connection to Judaism.

Growing up amid so much negativity, Laura retreated into her studies. She was fascinated by science and recalls that when the other children in her neighborhood were playing outside, she preferred her make-believe laboratory in the basement of her home, where she would put on a lab coat and pretend she was doing experiments. Eventually, she was able to make her dreams of a career in science come true. In 1968, she earned a bachelor of science degree in biology with honors, from the State University of New York at Stony Brook, and then continued her studies, receiving a PhD in physiology from Columbia in 1974. By the mid-1970s, she had moved to the West Coast, where she was hired by the University of Southern California to teach physiology and human sexuality.

And then she discovered radio. One day in 1975, she was listening to the controversial talk show host Bill Ballance on KABC in Los Angeles. He was famous (or notorious) for having created "topless radio," where he invited women to call in and confess intimate details about their sex life. On one show, he asked whether it was better to be a divorcée or a widow. Schlessinger, who had had a brief and unhappy marriage while in college, called the show to chat, saying she'd rather be a widow. Ballance was impressed by how articulate she was, and they talked on the air for about twenty minutes. Many talk hosts like to use certain regular callers to get discussions started, and Ballance decided Laura Schlessinger was perfect for that role. She soon became Ballance's resident expert on sex, dispensing advice to callers.

Ballance believed Schlessinger had talent, and he became her mentor. He encouraged her to pursue her own radio career, something she had not previously thought of doing. By July 1976, she had her own Sunday night program on a station in Santa Ana, California, KWIZ, simulcast on KWIZ's AM and FM stations. Using the name Dr. Laura, she dispensed advice and encouragement. Her detractors later criticized the name Dr. Laura, since it implied that she had a medical degree, and she did not. But she never hid what her degree was in, and she told reporters that she was not a therapist, nor was she trying to provide therapy on her show. She also told them that she was studying for her license in marriage and family counseling.

Unlike the Bill Balance *Feminine Forum*, which was often suggestive, Schlessinger's show made use of her background as an educator and counselor. She impressed her audience almost immediately with her confidence and forceful personality. At this time in her radio career, she had a kinder, gentler on-air style. In fact, when the media critics from newspapers like the *Los Angeles Times* profiled her, they described how caring and compassionate she was and praised her for offering practical solutions to her callers' problems.

What the listeners didn't know was that her personal life was more complicated than what appeared in the newspaper profiles. For one thing, she had begun a sexual relationship with Bill Ballance that would come back to haunt her in the late 1990s when some nude photographs he had taken of her in the mid-1970s surfaced on the Internet. Additionally, Marshall Berges's laudatory 1979 article about her in the *Los Angeles Times* described how she loved to keep physically fit, jogging or bike riding with a man identified as her "companion. He was Dr. Lewis Bishop, a professor of neurophysiology at the University of Southern California, and he was married when she began to date him. Bishop ultimately got a divorce, and he and Schlessinger were married in October 1984. They had a son, Deryk, and while he was little, Schlessinger stayed home with him, although she still did some fill-in radio work and continued to work as a counselor part time.

By March 1990, Schlessinger was back on the radio, at talk station KFI in Los Angeles. Bishop became her business manager, and he was determined to get her show into national syndication. In June 1994, he and Schlessinger created a syndication company called Synergy Broadcasting, and in 1997, the rights to syndicate her show were purchased by the Premiere Radio Network, which still syndicates her.

GROWTH IN SCHLESSINGER'S POPULARITY

Schlessinger's 1990s incarnation was somewhat different from her empathetic persona of the late 1970s. As the society became more conservative, her show and the advice she gave to callers also became more conservative. In fact, the talk host who had once said she wanted to be a friend to her audience now seemed to want to be their judge. She became more blunt and more outspoken, stressing morality and traditional family values. She was now opposed to women's working when their children were small, opposed to day care, opposed to couples' living together before marriage, and opposed to abortion except to save the life of the mother. She also increasingly expressed her opposition to the women's movement, speaking of herself as a "recovering feminist" and accusing feminism of promoting a lifestyle of immorality in which women were encouraged to have sex whenever they wanted to, with no strings attached. She told women not to whine about their lives and scolded callers for not making better decisions. She spoke out against permissive parenting and the importance of parents setting a good example for their children. In fact, morality became the central issue of her show. In one area she was still a moderate: In the early to mid-1990s, she seemed tolerant of gay men and lesbians, although she believed children should be raised in a home with a male and a female parent.

The more militantly conservative Schlessinger became, the more her ratings increased. Once she was syndicated nationally, her no-nonsense style and emphasis on ethical behavior immediately began to win large numbers of listeners. As she attracted more national attention, reporters commented on how driven she seemed, no matter what was happening in her life. When in September 1992 an electrical fire burned her home to the ground, she still showed up the next day to take a karate exam for her black belt, which she passed. When in 1993 her husband had a heart attack and needed bypass surgery, she continued to do her show, as if keeping busy gave her some comfort. Critics were also surprised to find that although she gave daily advice about family, she had no relationship with her own mother and little with her sister, and lack of any closeness with them did not appear to bother her. But trying to figure her out was not easy; by her own admission, she didn't trust the mainstream media and was far more comfortable giving advice to others than talking about her personal life.

In the mid-1990s, she began to write self-help advice books for her many fans. One of her first was 1994's *Ten Stupid Things Women Do to Mess Up Their Lives*, and like many of her books, it became a best seller.

Something else changed for Schlessinger in the mid-1990s: She rediscovered her Jewish roots. Granted, her father had not been especially religious, but she had wanted to have a faith, and Judaism appealed to her. At first, she studied to become a Conservative Jew (Reform Judaism is the least traditional, Orthodox Judaism is the most traditional, and Conservative Judaism falls in between), but she ultimately decided to become an Orthodox Jew and underwent a formal conversion. Her son also converted to Judaism, but while newspaper stories said her husband had also converted, it was later revealed that he had never formally gone through the ceremony. Schlessinger incorporated her new Orthodox Jewish beliefs and ethics into her talk show, frequently referring listeners to the moral code in the Mosaic law. In fact, in 1998, she wrote *The Ten Commandments: Do They Still Count?* Although the majority of her listeners were not Jewish, the rhetoric on her show remained very much aligned with what a listener might hear on an Evangelical Christian talk show, except the references were to God rather than to Jesus.

Schlessinger's politics also became more identified with right-wing Republican causes: She was opposed to vulgarity in the popular culture, and she lobbied Congress for mandatory filtering software on public library computers so that children would not be exposed to crude or obscene material.

MORALITY AND CONTROVERSY

As Schlessinger grew even more conservative and focused on traditional morality, her attitude toward homosexuals changed. She began asserting on her show that being gay is what she called a "biological error" that prevents homosexuals from having a normal relationship with the opposite sex. She called homosexual practices deviant and associated being gay with promiscuity and even pedophilia.

Because she was a great success on radio, heard on over four hundred stations and with ratings that placed her in the top three most-listened-to talk show hosts nationally, Paramount Television decided to put her show on television in September 2000. Although some radio talkers had been able to make the transition to TV, for the most part radio hosts tended to do best when they stuck to radio. Schlessinger turned out to be no exception. What also complicated her effort to move to TV was a very organized movement, led by gay rights advocates, labeling a bigot and a homophobe who didn't deserve her own show. Plagued by threats of sponsor boycotts by these groups, she spent considerable time defending herself, but to no avail. She apologized, although not for her beliefs but for expressing them hurtfully. She even appeared on daytime talk shows like ABC's *The View* to explain why she felt she had been misunderstood; but the more she tried to explain she wasn't a bigot, the more defensive she seemed. When the new syndicated talk show finally went on the air, critics noticed that she didn't seem comfortable. The tough talk that worked on radio seemed shrewish on TV. The show was canceled in May 2001, after only six months, and Schlessinger went back to radio exclusively.

Schlessinger had to overcome two other major crises in her life. As mentioned earlier, in 1998, her former mentor, Bill Ballance, allegedly disgruntled because Schlessinger had never acknowledged the important role he had played in her career success, published some nude photos he had taken of her when they were romantically involved in the mid-1970s. The photos immediately made their way to the Internet, although Schlessinger tried unsuccessfully to get a court order to prevent their display. She told the media it was immoral of Ballance to release the photos after all these years, and her devoted listeners accepted her explanation that they were from a time in her life before she had found her moral compass.

Then, in mid-December 2002, it was revealed that Schlessinger's mother had been found dead in her apartment. Yolanda Schlessinger had not been heard from in weeks, and when her body was found, Schlessinger's official statement was that her mother had shut everyone out of her life, and that she prayed for her mother's soul. Several people who knew Schlessinger's mother disputed that version of events, saying there had been an altercation between the two of them years ago and Schlessinger had cut off contact with her mother. Schlessinger disputed that charge, but whatever the truth, her mother had died alone. One neighbor recounted that Mrs. Schlessinger had listened to her daughter on the radio even though they were estranged.

In August 2003, Schlessinger issued an announcement that stunned a number of her colleagues and friends. She said she no longer wanted to practice Judaism. As she had done in her strained relationship with her mother, she seemed to place the blame outside herself. In this case, she said she had renounced Judaism partly because the organized Jewish community had never been warm toward her, a statement that mystified several rabbis who thought they knew her fairly well. Whatever her religious faith, she did not speak publicly about Judaism after that. However, she continued to do the same faith-based radio show, dispensing the same no-nonsense advice, which often included references to faith in God and the power of prayer, and advocating for traditional Judeo-Christian values just as she had before.

In 2005, Schlessinger's show attained an even wider reach, as the satellite radio network XM added her to its roster.

Over her long career in broadcasting, Schlessinger has won a number of awards, including a 1997 Marconi award from the National Association of Broadcasters as Syndicated Personality of the Year and a 1998 Genii Award from the Southern California chapter of American Women in Radio and Television; according to the organization's Web site, the Genii Award is given to women who have made significant contributions to promoting progress and creating change in broadcasting. Schlessinger has been nominated several times (most recently in 2005 and 2007) for induction into the Radio Hall of Fame, a tribute to the strong fan base she maintains.

Schlessinger is a polarizing figure, and her critics regard her as a hypocrite who dispenses advice that she herself does not follow. She also arouses controversy with her opinions on current issues. In early 2008, New York's governor Eliot Spitzer resigned after the discovery that he was having sexual relations with prostitutes, and his wife, Silda, seemed to stand by him.

Her loyalty became a topic of discussion on many talk shows. During an appearance on the daytime talk show *The View*, Schlessinger seemed to blame Silda for her husband's aberrance, saying, "I hold women accountable for tossing out perfectly good men by not treating them with the love and kindness and respect and attention they need" (quoted in Stanley, 2008), reiterating a belief expressed on her show and in books like her 2004 best seller *The Proper Care and Feeding of Husbands:* All too often today, "the wife does not focus in on the needs and the feelings, sexually, personally, to make him feel like a man, to make him feel like a success, to make him feel like our hero" (quoted in Haas, 2008). Schlessinger remains adamant about her disdain for feminism, which she associates with "man-bashing." She criticizes the women's movement for denying that the man is the head of the house and for encouraging women to work outside the home rather than make their marriage the top priority.

In spite of comments that her critics regard as controversial, Schlessinger's fans find her both inspirational and courageous. They believe she is misunderstood, and that her advice makes sense common sense. Further, they believe she has been persecuted by the media for having conservative beliefs. While Schlessinger is no longer on as many radio stations as she was in the mid to late 1990s, she still has millions of listeners who love her.

Schlessinger has continued to write about love, marriage, and having successful relationships. In 2006, she published a book undoubtedly inspired by her own experiences, *Bad Childhood—Good Life: How to Blossom and Thrive in Spite of an Unhappy Childhood*. In January 2007, she released *The Proper Care and Feeding of Marriage*, and in early 2008, this prolific author issued her newest book, *Stop Whining, Start Living*, which debuted at number two on the *New York Times* best-seller list. She has also written several books for children about morals and ethics, including the 2001 *Growing Up Is Hard*.

The woman who has proudly referred to herself as "my kid's mom," to show that what matters most in her life is motherhood, has remained a force in conservative talk radio. She continues to do her show as she has always done it, without interviewing celebrities or spending time on what she regards as tabloid talk. Rather, her show remains about her callers and the advice she gives them, a formula that works. She is still the most listened-to female radio talk show host in America.

LAURA SCHLESSINGER TIMELINE

1947: born in Brooklyn, New York

1974: gets her PhD in physiology from Columbia University

1975: becomes a regular guest expert on Bill Ballance's radio show

1976: gets her own advice show on KWIZ in Santa Ana, California, using the name Dr. Laura

Female Advice Givers

While roles for women in radio were limited for many years, the female advice giver has been in evidence since the 1930s, usually as a guest on a "women's show." By the 1950s, women with degrees in psychology were beginning to have shows of their own, among them the following.

Joyce Brothers had first appeared on a 1955 TV quiz show, the *64,000 Question*, as an expert on boxing and then got her own radio show. With her PhD in psychology and her empathetic manner, Brothers became popular on both TV and radio and was on the air giving advice for more than thirty years.

In the early 1960s, Abigail Van Buren began doing a daily version of her well-known syndicated newspaper column, "Dear Abby," on radio. The show lasted for twelve years.

In 1975, Toni Grant began giving therapy by radio on KABC in Los Angeles. She was ultimately syndicated nationally and remained on the air in Los Angeles for two decades.

While female advice giver shows proliferated in early 1980s, so did some controversy, as the American Psychological Association questioned whether such programs were helpful or whether they exploited people with problems. But the shows continued to be popular with listeners, who seemed to like the ability to get advice while remaining anonymous and not having to pay for a therapist. The kinds of advice shows also branched out. Where they had mainly been about family and relationship issues, by the early 1980s, Dr. Ruth Westheimer was offering a unique radio program during which she gave non-judgmental advice about human sexuality, discussing even the most personal topics without being crude or sensational. In late August 1984, a cable TV version of her show, titled "Good Sex! with Dr. Ruth Westheimer" made its debut on Lifetime, and became one of that cable network's most popular programs.

Another popular radio therapist of that time was Dr. Joy Browne, who, like Dr. Toni Grant, is a licensed clinical psychologist. She was heard on WITS in Boston in the late 1970s before before moving to WOR in New York City. Since the early 1980s, she has remained one of WOR's most popular hosts. Her show also went into syndication in the early 1990s.

1984: marries Lew Bishop, who becomes her manager

1990: gets a show on KFI in Los Angeles

1994: publishes her first best seller, *Ten Stupid Things Women Do to Mess Up Their Lives*

1997: show picked up for national syndication by the Premiere Radio Network; also wins a Marconi Award as Best Syndicated Broadcaster

2000: tries unsuccessfully to do a TV version of her talk show

2005: radio show added to the roster of satellite network XM

FURTHER READING

Ayres, Chris. "Just Ditch Those Difficult Parents," *The Times* (London), 6 April 2006, p. 8.

Berges, Marshall. "Laura Schlessinger: She's a Sensitive, Sympathetic Counselor Who Believes in the Therapy of Humor." *Los Angeles Times*, 15 July 1979, p. R26.

Boteach Shmuley. "Self Hating Spitzer." *Jerusalem Post,* 17 March 2008, p. 14.

Deutsch, Stephanie. "Women Must Make Time for Marriage, Dr. Laura Avers." *Washington Times*, 4 April 2004, p. B8.

Duke, Sherlean. "She Sends Care over the Air." *Los Angeles Times*, 25 May 1978, p. C1.

Flanagan, Caitlin. "Do As I Say: Dr Laura's Counsel Is Caustic and Oftentimes Hypocritical, but It Is Also Persuasive." *Atlantic Monthly*, January–February 2004, pp. 182–185.

Gottlieb, Walter J. "Dr. Laura's Dose of Reality." *Washington Post*, 26 July 1995, p. D1.

Keys, Lisa. "Dr. Laura Loses Her Religion." *The Forward*, 15 August 2003, online at www.forward.com/articles/dr-laura-loses-her-religion.

La Franco, Robert. "Morality Pays." *Forbes*, 17 June 1996, p. 47.

Stanley, Alessandra. "Mars and Venus Dissect the Spitzer Scandal on the TV Talk Shows." *New York Times*, 12 March 2008, p. E1.

Tresniowski, Alex, Maureen Harrington, and Vickie Bane. "Alone at the End: Long Estranged from Her Daughter, Dr. Laura's Mother Dies Mysteriously." *People Weekly*, 13 January 2003, p. 64.

Laura Schlessinger's Web site is www.drlaura.com.

Courtesy of the Jones Radio Network

Ed Schultz

Ed Schultz is the most successful liberal talk-radio host of the past fifty years. Since the 1960s, the majority of talk radio's most popular hosts have been conservative, and while an occasional liberal has done well, the annual rankings year after year have shown few, if any, liberal (or progressive) talkers in the top fifteen most-listened-to talk show hosts But Ed Schultz has demonstrated that liberal talk can be successful. His ratings consistently put him in the top ten nationally, and his show's profitability belies the claims of skeptics that liberal talk shows cannot succeed. In 2007, *Talkers* magazine named Schultz one of talk radio's five most influential personalities, and he has become so well known that in addition to doing his own nationally syndicated radio show, he is frequently called on by television talk shows like *Larry King Live* or MSNBC's *Hardball* to offer the liberal spin on the day's news.

When Ed was growing up, he never planned a radio career; all he wanted was to become a professional athlete. And as for being a liberal talk host, for most of his radio career he was a conservative.

EARLY YEARS

Edward Andrew Schultz was born in Norfolk, Virginia, on 27 January 1954, the youngest of five children. His father, George, worked for the government as an aeronautical engineer. His mother, Mary, was an English teacher. In his 2004 book *Straight Talk from the Heartland*, he recalls the turbulent times growing up, with frequent kitchen-table discussions about Vietnam. He also grew up during the era of school desegregation and was bused to a school that was predominantly black: Maury High School. He loved sports, and with hard work, he made the football team (the Commodores) as the quarterback job. In 1971, he was named the team captain.

After he graduated from high school in 1972, Schultz got a football scholarship to what was then called Moorhead State University (today Minnesota State University at Moorhead). Moorhead was not very far from Fargo, North Dakota, where he later settled. In college, his goal was to become a professional athlete and play in the National Football League. His plan seemed plausible. He was an excellent quarterback, in 1977 the Division II passing champion of the National Collegiate Athletic Association. Division II schools were smaller and often not noticed like Division I schools, but Schultz still hoped he would be drafted for professional football because the Green Bay Packers of the NFL had sent scouts to watch him, and they seemed to be interested. Unfortunately, the Packers didn't draft him, nor did any other professional team, much to his shock. But his coach made some calls and persuaded the Oakland Raiders to give him a chance. Unfortunately, he was cut from the team without ever playing a game. Determined to stay in football, he signed with the Winnipeg Blue Bombers of the Canadian Football League, but the rules in the CFL were substantially different and he couldn't adjust to how the game was played. Coming back to the United States, he had one more opportunity, signing as a free agent with the New York Jets. Again, he was cut from the team. At that point, he had to face the reality that he was not good enough to play pro football.

Ed had done some sports announcing while he was in the Fargo/Moorhead area, working briefly at KXJB-TV in the summer of 1978, but he hadn't given announcing much thought as a career option. Now, it seemed like a good idea: If he couldn't play sports, at least he could announce them. One of his first broadcasting jobs was sports reporting at KTHI-TV in Fargo, in the spring of 1981. By 1983, he had moved to Fargo radio station WDAY, where he became known for his play-by-play announcing of North Dakota State University football and basketball. During this time, he was also on the sister station, WDAY-TV, as sports director. In addition to announcing college sports on the station, he began a popular show about fishing and hunting, two of his favorite leisure activities.

BROADCASTING IN FARGO

Schultz's enthusiasm and his knowledge of sports won him many fans, but he also had a lot of detractors. By his own admission, he was outspoken and wasn't shy about expressing his opinions. He also had a volatile temper. During an incident in September 1988, a fan threw a bottle at the WDAY broadcast team, and after uttering what the newspapers called "a string of pro-fanities," Ed went into the stands in search of whoever had thrown the bottle. His reaction resulted in a brief suspension, but it kept people talking about him. As time passed, it became obvious that Ed was a very polarizing personality. Letters to the editors of local newspapers demonstrated that people either liked him or hated him; there seemed to be no middle ground. However, his ratings continued to grow, proving that people were paying attention.

By 1992, Ed Schultz was talking about more than just sports; he had begun doing a current-events-oriented talk show called *Viewpoint*. His views were solidly conservative, and his knowledge of local politics led him to take very strong stands on issues and to criticize certain politicians. Like his sports shows, this show caused debate, and his listenership increased. But problems in his personal life suddenly became public when in 1993 he and his wife, Maureen Zimmerman, got divorced. A popular newswoman in the Fargo market, Zimmerman had been his coanchor on the WDAY-TV evening news since 1983, so their divorce was the subject of more scrutiny than either of them would have preferred. Then, in March 1996, Schultz was hired by radio station KFGO, one of the stations of the new Mid-States Broadcasting Company; he was asked to be the company's executive vice president. There was also talk of the company's acquiring a TV station. It was on KFGO that he began his *News and Views with Ed Schultz* morning show.

At this point in his life, he was what he described as a "typical conservative," who agreed with the Republicans on most issues and had voted for both
Ronald Reagan and George H.W. Bush. In fact, in 1994, he had briefly considered running for Congress but decided he didn't have enough money to
mount an adequate campaign. So he continued to use his radio show to rail
against the people he believed were causing America's problems: illegal immigrants, the homeless, even farmers (who, as he saw it, were addicted to government subsidies). It was angry radio, and most of his callers were men who
shared his worldview. He was still also known for his play-by-play announcing skills. In 1998, he went from announcing the North Dakota State Bisons
games to announcing the games of their arch rivals, the University of North
Dakota Sioux. And in 2001, he was a finalist in the competition to become a
broadcaster for the NFL's Minnesota Vikings, but he finished second. Still, life
was good for Ed Schultz. He was popular, he was controversial, and he was
well paid. But in the background, several things were happening that would
profoundly change him, more than his listeners could have imagined.

SCHULTZ'S LIFE CHANGES

In the late 1990s, Schultz's mother developed Alzheimer's disease and began a
long, slow decline. Schultz observed firsthand the inadequacies in the health
care system as he tried to get services for her. Also in the late 1990s, he met a
woman named Wendy, a nurse who ran a homeless shelter in Fargo. In his
book, Schultz attributes much of his attitude change to her, and she eventually
became his wife. At her shelter, he met homeless men, the people he had accused on his show of being lazy.

When he began to talk to them, he found that many of the men were Vietnam
and Gulf War veterans, who needed job training and medical help more than
they needed contempt. He also began taking trips to rural parts of South Dakota,
where he saw people who were struggling, unable to find work or afford basic
necessities. As he tells it, what he saw during these trips challenged his belief
that the economy was fine and anyone who wanted a job could get one. His
politics did not change overnight, but as he later explained to reporters, one day
he realized that his views had shifted, and that on many issues, he was now
closer to the Democratic position.

Ed's new attitude was puzzling to his listeners. He had been a passionate
North Dakota State Bison supporter, and then one day he was a North Dakota
Sioux fan. He had been a vehement conservative, and then one day he was a
liberal. As often happened in Fargo, whatever Schultz did or said was news,
and his political transformation lit up the phone lines and was the subject of
many letters to newspaper editors. Schultz himself tried to explain that his
political evolution had been gradual, and that he was actually what he called
a progressive, liberal on some issues but still quite conservative on others.

Still, it was very obvious that he no longer toed the Republican Party line, and his audience wasn't quite sure what to make of the "new" Ed Schultz.

The cynics said the change in Schultz was a career move. Most talk show hosts in North Dakota, and everywhere else, were conservative. Surveys showed repeatedly that more than 95 percent of talk shows were done by right-wing Republicans, and Democrats were eager to change that percentage. A good liberal talk host would certainly be noticed quickly. North Dakota's two Democratic senators, Byron Dorgan and Kent Conrad, had long expressed an interest in finding someone to do talk radio from a more liberal perspective, and when Ed made his shift, they both became friendly with the man who, as an angry right-wing host, had criticized both senators frequently. Now, Schultz was taking the side of the Democrats on many, but not all, issues. He referred to himself on the air as a "meat-eating, gun-toting liberal," alluding to the stereotype that Democrats don't like to hunt and want to take away people's guns. In fact, Schultz's views were rather nuanced. Like many conservatives, he was antiabortion and a strong supporter of the military. But like many liberals, he was pro-worker, pro-union, pro-women's rights, and pro-education. He had always prided himself on calling the issues as he saw them, but now his perspective was closer to that of a moderate Democrat. The slogan for his show became "straight talk from the Heartland," as he pointed out the areas where he felt Republican policies were hurting people in his part of the country.

The more Schultz got into doing his new talk show, the more interested in him the Democratic Party became, to the point where he was asked to run for governor. He had been very critical of Republican governor John Hoeven, and local Democrats suggested that Ed Schultz was well known enough to defeat him.

In the end, there was something more important for Schultz to do. He was told about an organization called Democracy Radio, which was seeking a liberal host it could market nationwide. Liberal talk hosts had tried and failed many times in the past, but when Ed went for his audition, the people who heard him were convinced they had found the liberal talker who could finally succeed. They put up several million dollars to launch a national version of the *Ed Schultz Show*. Schultz insisted that he have a signed agreement that allowed him to be totally independent, even if that meant criticizing other Democrats, but again, skeptics wondered if he hadn't been bought and paid for by the Democratic Party. He would have to refute those charges repeatedly.

SUCCESSFUL SYNDICATED TALKER

On 5 January 2004, Schultz's show debuted, on only two small stations. A year later, he was being heard on seventy stations, many of which were in large cities like Portland, Oregon, and Miami, Florida. Syndicated by the Jones Radio Network, and on the air from 3 to 6 p.m., Eastern Standard Time, he was suddenly a rising star in a new format called *progressive talk*. (*Progressive* was a substitute for *liberal*, a term demonized by the right wing for a number of years.) Schultz chose a new slogan for his show—"Where America comes to talk"— explaining that he believed his views were actually quite mainstream; further, unlike most talk hosts, he did not screen his calls, so anyone could call in and talk about the issues. While most of his callers were liberals who were thrilled to finally have a kindred spirit on the air, a number of the callers were conservatives. Some called to argue with him, and he didn't hang up on them. And while Ed was still capable of being opinionated and sure of himself, he seemed to genuinely believe in progressive talk. He also seemed very sincere about his newfound concern for the working person; he did a number of fund-raisers and speaking engagements for unions, and he worked tirelessly to get Democrats elected to Congress. He also began spending time in Washington, DC, where he met the movers and shakers in politics. But he insisted he didn't want to move his show to a bigger city. He loved the lifestyle in Fargo and intended to continue broadcasting from what the recorded introduction to his show called "the heart of America." And always a hard worker, despite the growth of his national show he continued to do his local show, *News and Views*.

National Public Radio

In 1970, National Public Radio went on the air. Its critics have accused it of being snobbish, and several U.S. presidents have considered it too liberal. Yet, year after year, its in-depth news coverage and wide variety of talk shows earn NPR's programs many awards. In 2006, NPR achieved some of the highest ratings in its history, as 26.5 million listeners a week tuned in. More than eight hundred stations nationwide broadcast some NPR programming. Among its most popular talk shows is *Car Talk*, hosted by Tom and Ray Magliozzi, often referred to as Click and Clack, the Tappet Brothers. Their once-a-week show originated on NPR's Boston affiliate, WBUR, in 1977. NPR picked it up for national distribution in 1987, and by early 2007, nearly four hundred stations were broadcasting it. The premise of the show is simple: Listeners who have problems with their car, truck, or van call in and describe the problem to Tom and Ray, who can often diagnose or solve it over the air. Also popular is *Talk of the Nation*, currently hosted by Neil Conan, a former NPR anchor and reporter. This show focuses on current issues, and listeners can question the guests by phone or e-mail. Close to three million people a week listen. Another show that has shown ratings growth is *Wait Wait Don't Tell Me*, a combination of news quiz and comedy that originates from Chicago Public Radio. The audience and listeners at home compete with the celebrity panel to answer tricky questions about what's in the news. By the end of 2006, the show had more than 2.3 million weekly listeners.

By mid-2006, the number of stations that carried Schultz's show had grown from seventy to nearly one hundred. Schultz was especially proud that his show was turning a profit: Unlike previous attempts at progressive or liberal talk, his show had national sponsors. And in many markets, he was getting good ratings. Unfortunately, some of the affiliates that carried his show were small stations with weak signals that made it more difficult for him to be heard, but by the end of 2006, he had more than 2 million weekly listeners. In 2007, that figure rose even further, to 3.25 million, according to *Talkers* magazine, which named him one of the five most influential hosts in talk radio; Ed was the first liberal talker ever to win such recognition.

From his days in sports, Schultz had always been very competitive, and while he knew that right-wing talkers like Rush Limbaugh were on hundreds more stations than he, it was important to him to occupy a time period in which he could compete directly with them. On 30 November 2006, Schultz moved the hours of his national show to noon to 3 p.m., the same hours as Limbaugh's show. Schultz was also able to purchase a satellite uplink, enabling him to be telecast from Fargo to any network that wanted him to appear as a pundit. And gradually, CNN, MSNBC, and even the right-wing network Fox began to call on him for the progressive perspective on current issues. Among the TV shows on which he appeared from 2006 through early 2008 were *Hardball* and the *Tucker Carlson Show* on MSNBC, *Larry King Live* on CNN, and the *O'Reilly Factor* on Fox News. He has been asked to comment on current events, including the presidential elections, and has also been asked to debate with conservative talk hosts. He is now able to get the well-known guests on his show (he has interviewed John Kerry, Hillary Rodham Clinton, Barack Obama, Ted Kennedy, and a few conservative politicians, too). Even his detractors have to agree that Ed is an entertaining and informative talk show host, whose progressive views are expressed forcefully but not angrily. While the *Ed Schultz Show* has not yet reached the number of affiliates that he would like, Schultz has proved that an interesting progressive or liberal talk show attracts an audience.

It also attracts controversy. In early April 2008, Schultz was asked to warm up the crowd before a Democratic Party fund-raiser for presidential candidate Barack Obama. In the course of his remarks, Schultz referred to Republican candidate John McCain as a "war monger." When local Republicans heard about this remark, they immediately demanded an apology and even insisted that Senator Obama, who had not been present when Schultz was speaking, apologize. Obama did so, saying he would not have used that terminology to describe his opponent, but Schultz refused to apologize for his comments. In fact, the more he stood by them, the more media attention he received. Soon, he was being asked to explain his comments on MSNBC's *Road to the White House* and CNN's *American Morning*. He even appeared on the conservative TV network, Fox News, to speak with Bill Hemmer on *America's Election Headquarters*. In every case, he insisted that what he had said wasn't particularly unusual; he had said it on his radio show numerous times. He asserted that because Senator McCain supported the war in Iraq and wanted to go to war with Iran, he could indeed be described as a warmonger. The controversy may have been typical of the petty politics that occur during campaigns, but Schultz was right in the middle, getting his show, and himself, more national attention.

These days, he and Wendy spend time visiting the cities where the show has a new affiliate, and they continue to make appearances to raise money for causes that they believe in. They also keep an eye on the career of their son, David, who is a professional golfer.

In April 2008, the *Ed Schultz Show* was finally heard on a New York City affiliate, WWRL Radio, but as for the markets where he still is not heard, Schultz says that he never expected his show to become a success overnight, especially given how few stations broadcast any progressive talk at all. He knows that winning over the radio listeners will take time. Ed Schultz has always loved a challenge, and he says that he intends to continue sending the progressive message out to as many listeners as possible. When he first went on the air as a progressive talk show host, his detractors predicted he wouldn't last a year, but in 2008, having celebrated his fourth anniversary, he continued to be one of America's best-known progressive talkers.

ED SCHULTZ TIMELINE

1954: born in Norfolk, Virginia

1981: becomes a sports reporter at KTHI-TV in Fargo, North Dakota

1983: is hired by WDAY radio for play-by-play announcing of North Dakota State University football and basketball; is also sports director at WDAY-TV

1992: begins doing a current-events radio talk show on WDAY

1996: debuts popular local talk show *News and Views with Ed Schultz* on KFGO

2004: debuts his progressive talk show to a national audience

2006: moves his live broadcast to the noon to 3 p.m. time slot (he had previously been on from 3 to 6 p.m.)

2007: named one of the top five most influential talk show hosts by *Talkers* magazine

FURTHER READING

Haga, Chuck. "Going against the Grain: Ed Schultz, Once a Staunch Conservative, Is a Rarity: A Liberal Talk-Radio Host." *Minneapolis Star-Tribune*, 19 February 2004, p. 1B.

"Jab at McCain Rejected." *Chicago Sun-Times*, 6 April 2008, p. A2.

Klosterman, Chuck. "Q&A with the Man with the Microphone." *The Forum* (Fargo, ND), 10 August 1995, p. D1.

Kolpack, Dave. "Republican-Turned-Democrat Broadcasts from the Heartland; is he really a liberal?" Associated Press release, 23 February 2004.

Kurson, Robert. "Ed Schultz: Man of the Month." *Esquire*, 1 February 2004, n.p.

Kurtz, Howard. "A Voice from Above, and to the Left; North Dakota Talker Ed Schultz Is Set to Blanket Washington." *Washington Post*, 10 January 2005, p. C1.

Roepke, Dave. "Inside Ed's Head: Schultz Ponders Moving His Syndicated Radio Show from Fargo after Being Replaced on KFGO." *The Forum* (Fargo, ND), 19 February 2006, p. B1.

Schultz, Ed. *Straight Talk From the Heartland*. New York: Regan Books, 2004.

Vowell, Roberta T. "And from the Left . . . Norfolk's Ed Schultz Is Liberal Challenger to Conservatives on the Radio." *Virginian Pilot* (Norfolk, VA), 13 March 2004, p. E1.

The *Ed Schultz Show* Web site is www.wegoted.com.

Paul Drinkwater/NBCU Photo Bank via AP Images

Tavis Smiley

Despite the many gains that African Americans have made, they have historically been seen in the mainstream media as either entertainers or athletes. Tavis Smiley falls into neither of these categories. He is a well-respected journalist, a commentator on both radio and TV, an interviewer, and a motivational speaker. He is also an outspoken opponent of racism who doesn't hesitate to challenge persistent media stereotypes of minorities. He sponsors an annual symposium, "State of the Black Union," that brings together some of the most important African American leaders in education, science, politics, and the arts to discuss problems in the black community and to strategize about possible solutions. This symposium is typical of the events that Smiley sponsors, events that follow his philosophy of "Enlightenment, Encouragement, and Empowerment." The story of how he transcended an impoverished childhood to become an influential broadcaster is both inspiring and instructive.

OVERCOMING POVERTY

Tavis Smiley was born on 13 September 1964 in Gulfport, Mississippi, to Joyce Marie Roberts and a young man with whom she had a brief sexual relationship when she was eighteen. Joyce married Emory Garnell Smiley in 1966, and he became the only father Tavis knew. His new stepfather, who preferred to be called Garnell, was in the U.S. Air Force, training to be an airplane mechanic. Wherever he was sent, the family had to follow, and by 1967 they had moved from Mississippi to Indiana, the location of Grissom Air Force Base.

Joyce was deeply religious and made sure that attending church was part of Tavis's young life. Eventually, she also won over her husband, and they all became devoted members of the Holiness Church in Kokomo, Indiana. The churches were still segregated then, and being part of a black congregation gave the family a sense of acceptance and belonging. The Smiley family didn't have much money—Garnell's military pay wasn't high—so they rented a trailer. Tavis recalled that even living in a trailer park, going to the Pentecostal church, with its exuberant style of worship, brought the family closer together and gave them great joy.

But then, there was a tragedy. Joyce received a phone call saying that her sister in Gulfport had been murdered, leaving behind five children, the Smiley family made a decision. Although their own financial situation was difficult, they believed it was the right thing to take those children in and give them a stable home. In the summer of 1974, the children arrived from Mississippi to live with Tavis and his family.

The Smiley family was not finished growing: Joyce and Garnell wanted to have a large family, and soon Tavis had more sisters and brothers, eventually thirteen children in all. The family moved into a bigger trailer, and Garnell took extra jobs to support them all. He also encouraged his children to help out.

He set up a little cleaning business, and after school, Tavis and some of his siblings cleaned offices at the air force base. While it was undoubtedly sometimes a very difficult life, Tavis was relatively content. He loved his family, and he wanted to be helpful.

Smiley's parents provided a lot of structure. The children weren't allowed to watch much television, and only when their chores were done were they allowed to play sports; Tavis especially liked baseball. There wasn't much money, and sleeping so many in one trailer was uncomfortable, but the children were taught to accept things and make the best of them. And the church remained the center of their life.

Of course, Smiley noticed the de facto segregation that existed in Indiana. He had seen it in the local churches, but it also occurred on the air force base. White families got bigger and nicer trailers than the black families. On the other hand, he received a good education. Even though he was one of the few black students in his elementary school, his teachers saw that he was bright, and they encouraged him to achieve, showing him how to make effective use of his writing and public speaking skills. Although he didn't realize it at the time, the mentoring he received in school would be helpful to him later, when he chose a profession.

While his childhood was stable, there were some problems. Smiley's stepfather was a hardworking and very moral man, but he was sometimes short-tempered and verbally abusive. His mother, too, was very strict, and the children got a whipping if she felt they had misbehaved. Under most circumstances, the whippings were mild, but one particular incident would change Smiley's life forever. He and his sister Phyllis were accused of being disruptive in church. They both claimed they were innocent, but their stepfather didn't want to hear their side. Instead, he became enraged and beat them with an electrical cord, and in Tavis's eyes, his mother defended his father's right to discipline his children. This beating was so severe that Child Protective Services became involved with the family, and the two children were temporarily placed in foster care. Tavis was sent to live with a pastor and his wife. Even though his foster parents were devout Christians, they seemed more tolerant of certain aspects of the secular world. When he was living at home, Tavis had been exposed to only one way of looking at the world, and any deviation from it was punished. Now, he was seeing that there were different approaches to living a Christian life.

CHOOSING HIS OWN PATH

In the Pentecostal church to which the Smiley family belonged, the rules were very clear, and Smiley had accepted them without much question. He knew, for example, that the church frowned on spending too much time with people who were not religious Christians. Even attending a public school sporting event was forbidden, as was going to a party with classmates who were not church members. In addition to opposing all forms of popular culture, such as rock music and movies, the church did not encourage going to college. Young people were expected to attend high school and be good students, but the main emphasis was on religious education; too much secular learning was considered contrary to a life of faith. Smiley's mother had become a preacher, and working in the church was strongly preferred to going away to a secular university.

But gradually, Tavis was beginning to have mixed feelings about how much the church dominated the life of the Smiley family. His Pentacostal faith had given him a strong sense of right and wrong and had taught him the importance of caring about the less fortunate, core values that he carried with him into adulthood, but his innate curiosity about literature and sports and current events had begun to put him at odds with his parents. By the time he got to high school, he had made friends with several white students, had entered some public speaking contests, and had even run for student government. He was also influenced by the work of Martin Luther King Jr. and committed several of King's speeches to memory. While Tavis still loved his religion, devoting seven days a week to attending church and studying Scripture no longer appealed to him. People like King had died while trying to end racism, and Tavis, too, wanted to find a way to make a positive impact. To his parents' surprise, he soon decided he wanted to go to college.

After the beating and some time in foster care, Smiley was returned to his family, as the authorities were convinced that the beating had been a serious overreaction and a one-time occurrence. They believed that the Smileys were good parents who had snapped under difficult circumstances. But Tavis couldn't forgive them for what they had done to him and his sister. He was even more determined to get away from a life he now saw as excessively rigid. His teachers often praised him for his skill in oratory, and he had even won a contest in high school by delivering King's famous "I Have a Dream" speech. But while he knew his family might have liked him to become a preacher, he was certain he would be more useful in other fields.

Smiley became interested in politics when, by chance, he met Councilman Douglas Hogan of Kokomo, Indiana. They became friends and Tavis began working in the councilman's office. He was impressed by what Hogan was trying to do for his constituents. In addition to mentoring Tavis, Hogan had him invited to attend a Democratic Party fund-raiser. He had never before met political figures (or gone to a hotel). At the event, he was introduced to Indiana senator Birch Bayh. Councilman Hogan even told the senator that Tavis was a young man who was interested in politics. Senator Bayh took the time to chat with Tavis; they discussed current issues, the importance of King's message, and using government to stand up for "the little guy." That evening was transformative: Tavis was amazed that he could hold his own in a conversation with an influential member of Congress and now understood that he had the ability to talk intelligently with anyone. How could he use that talent to make society better in some way?

In his senior year at Maconaquah High School, Smiley was voted "Most Likely To Succeed," but he still wasn't certain what path to take. He was sure college had the answer, however, so over his parents' objections, he applied and was accepted to Indiana University. In 1982, he prepared to go to Bloomington, Indiana, ready to begin his new life. The problem was that as a result of living in such a sheltered, religious environment for so many years, he had little understanding of how to adapt to the secular world. He arrived at Indiana University with only forty dollars, his letter of admission, and the contents of his suitcase. He had no idea how to get a room in a dormitory, or how to apply for financial aid so that he could pay tuition and buy books. But his communication skills and his self-confidence helped him to find mentors, and he basically talked his way into obtaining the assistance he needed. He was given a debating scholarship and was soon able to begin learning about college life.

For the first time, Smiley heard black pop music and jazz, read newsmagazines, and studied African American history. He met black students from all over the country, some religious and some not. He found a church to attend, but since he had a debating scholarship, he spent much of his time with the debating club. He joined Kappa Alpha Psi fraternity, and he began dating. He found that he much preferred good conversation and listening to music over going to parties. Because of all the new things to try, he was never attracted to drugs or drinking. He studied political science and became involved in student government, having remained interested in politics and wanting to build on what he had learned while working for Councilman Hogan. He was now thinking of attending graduate school at Harvard and possibly becoming a lawyer.

FROM POLITICS TO MEDIA

While Smiley loved his college experience, two incidents affected him deeply. One involved a tragic occurrence. He had a friend named Denver Smith who played football for Indiana University. They worked out together and often talked about their lives. Denver was a big man, but easygoing and likable, a family man with a wife and a baby daughter. He hoped one day to be drafted by the National Football League. Instead, in mid-September 1983, Smith was shot to death, under very questionable circumstances, by two local police officers. The news story said Smith had been violent and was acting in a deranged manner, and the implication was that he had been on drugs at the time. The two police officers said they had shot him in self-defense, since he was attacking a third officer. But Tavis and everyone who knew Smith found that version of events difficult to believe, given Smith's devotion to health and his desire to make it into the NFL. Black students on the IU campus grew increasingly angry as the charges against Smith came out in the press. The Bloomington police force was all white except for one officer, and the students felt Smith was being unfairly accused. They wondered if racism had anything to do with his death: Smith was unarmed, and the police had shot him in the back. An autopsy revealed he had not been high on drugs; the police officers' explanation was even more puzzling. Smiley could not remain silent. He and the other black students wanted an objective investigation into what had really happened. He organized vigils and protests and became the person who spoke to the local media. He and several other student activists even went to city hall to demand that the mayor look into the tragedy. In the end, the students' efforts were unsuccessful. An internal investigation exonerated the officers, and what had really happened to Denver Smith would never be known. But Tavis and other black students had seen firsthand that they could work together, state their case, get media attention, and try to bring about positive change when they saw injustice. He would later say that the Smith incident had motivated him to be an advocate and informed his work in politics and media.

The other occurrence that made an impact on Smiley took place in his junior year, when he went out to the West Coast to attend a conference of student leaders. While there, he made arrangements to meet Los Angeles mayor Tom Bradley, one of the country's most influential black politicians. Tavis decided the best way to learn about politics was from someone like the mayor, and when he was at the mayor's office, he inquired about internships. Application for internships was very competitive, but Tavis was determined to persuade the mayor that he should get one of the positions. For months, he called, faxed, and sent eloquent letters making his case, and finally, he got one of those prized internships. He took a semester off from Indiana University to work in Los Angeles, living at the Kappa Alpha Psi fraternity house at the University of Southern California, and putting his efforts into making a good impression on the mayor. He was so successful that the mayor promised him a job once he graduated from IU.

Smiley had been scheduled to get his bachelor's degree in law and public policy in 1986, but he left school a few credits shy of the degree to go back to Los Angeles and work as an aide to Mayor Bradley. (He finally finished his coursework and got the degree in 2003.)

Being an aide to the mayor was often exciting, and Smiley met many interesting people. But after some staff changes in the mayor's office, he felt the new deputy mayor wasn't including him, and there weren't as many projects for him to work on. It became obvious that he had no more future working for Mayor Bradley, so Tavis decided to run for office himself. In 1991, he ran for a seat on the city council, and when he lost, the defeat was demoralizing. A confident person who was accustomed to talking his way into new opportunities, he had not expected to lose the election. After a period of reevaluation, he decided to try his hand at the media. There were issues he wanted to discuss, so he created a daily radio commentary program called the *Smiley Report* and began trying to persuade stations to carry it. None did at first, but eventually, he got a sponsor and renamed the show *Just a Thought*. It was first carried by one small station, KGFJ, then by others that were bigger, such as a station that popular vocalist Stevie Wonder owned, KJLH. As the show was carried on more stations, Smiley attracted the attention of local TV as well and was hired as a commentator by KABC-TV. He spoke about issues that affected the black community and offered a liberal perspective at a time when most commentators were conservative. One example of how important his perspective was occurred in 1992, after the beating of an African American named Rodney King by four police officers. When they were acquitted and riots followed, journalists wanted to know more about the feelings and attitudes in the black community, and Tavis was a valuable resource, as well as somebody quotable. Having lived through the exoneration of the police in the mysterious 1983 death of Denver Smith, he was very much aware that many African Americans believed the justice system did not treat them fairly.

As he became more experienced on the air, Tavis began using his media commentaries to articulate that black perspective, speaking up about the injustices he felt the mainstream media ignored. His ability as a communicator was noticed by *Time* magazine, and when it published "50 for the Future," profiles of America's most promising leaders under the age of forty, in December 1994, among them was Tavis Smiley, who was referred to as "a young black man unafraid to take on the white Establishment."

In May 1996, Tavis Smiley published his first book, a compilation of some of his commentaries entitled *Hard Left*. By this time, he was known for his liberal views, and during the mid 1990s, he guested on several TV talk shows, usually debating a black conservative talker named Larry Elder. It was also in 1996 when his radio commentaries went national, as the *Tom Joyner Show*, syndicated by ABC radio, began to use his work regularly. Tavis had always wanted a way to create conversations about race in America, and that desire led to his doing his own talk show on BET (Black Entertainment Television). That talk show, originally called *BET Talks*, was one of the first to feature celebrities discussing issues of importance to African Americans. Tavis tried to do his interviews civilly, rather than in the shouting confrontational style of many talk shows. Of course, things didn't always turn out that way. In one notable appearance by hiphop producer Russell Simmons, Simmons directed a crude slur at Smiley when he disagreed with a point Tavis had made. But the talk show enabled Tavis to cover current issues, such as racial profiling as well as music and film news. It also attracted very high-profile guests, from political figures like President Bill Clinton and Fidel Castro and religious icons like Pope John Paul II to nearly every major black music star. The show stayed on the air until its sudden cancellation in 2001, which caused an irate reaction from not only his viewers but also a number of black celebrities.

Reaching the Black Audience

African Americans were on radio from the earliest days, but usually as entertainers. By the late 1920s, a few black educators were giving educational talks during what was then called Negro History Week. Throughout the 1930s, America's first black announcer, Chicago's Jack L. Cooper, did a popular show with mostly music and comedy, but he broadcast some news and commentary, too. In 1930, a black newspaper owner from Kansas City, Missouri, William J. Thompkins, tried to buy a station to provide black programming, but the Federal Radio Commission wouldn't approve the sale. Not until the mid-1940s were more black-themed news and public affairs shows heard on the air.

In mid-February 1944, *America's Town Meeting of the Air* devoted a program to discussing racism. Also in 1944, journalist Roi Ottley produced a series of programs about black contributions to America, *New World A-Coming*. By the 1950s, as more small AM stations adopted black programming, local talk shows aimed at the black audience were becoming popular. During times of racial strife, they provided encouragement and useful information. In the late 60s, there was an interesting experiment with a national talk show for the black audience. "Night Call," hosted by Del Shields, put black newsmakers on the air and let the audience question them. The program was heard weeknights from 11:30 p.m. to 12:30 a.m., and at the height of its popularity, it was heard on 75 stations. Throughout the 1960s, there were also more black pundits on TV, usually discussing civil rights. One of them was Louis Lomax, an author and educator, who was a guest with such talk hosts as Jack Paar and Joe Pyne; in 1964, he got his own show on KTTV in Los Angeles. Perhaps the longest-running black talk show, *Tony Brown's Journal*, began on PBS in 1970; it was still on the air in early 2008.

Smiley next hosted a radio show for National Public Radio, *The Tavis Smiley Show*, beginning in January 2002. It was one of the few non-music shows aimed at the black audience. Tavis continued to write and do guest appearances, giving motivational speeches to African American civic groups. He stayed with NPR until December 2004. His departure was not amicable, as he accused NPR of not having a sufficient commitment to reaching the black audience, a viewpoint with which NPR management strongly disagreed.

RECENT ACCOMPLISHMENTS

Smiley was not out of the public eye for long. During 2004, he began doing work as a correspondent for cable TV's CNN and for ABC's *Good Morning*

America, and in early 2004, he was doing a late-night television talk show on PBS. By April 2005, he began hosting a radio talk show syndicated by Public Radio International, which meant his work was back on NPR, which carries a number of PRI programs.

As the presidential campaign began heating up in September 2007, Tavis was asked to moderate one of the Republican debates, a nationally televised event aimed at informing the black community. The debate made headlines not for what was said but for which candidates refused to participate: The four top contenders, Rudy Giuliani, Mitt Romney, John McCain, and Fred Thompson, all said they had scheduling conflicts and were not able to appear. Tavis and PBS held the debate anyway, since it gave the lower-tier candidates a chance to make their views on the issues known.

As the race for the White House continued, he was also able to do interviews with the top Democratic candidates, including Senator Hillary Clinton and Senator Barack Obama. He aroused some controversy in the black community by being critical of Senator Obama, the first African American to be a serious presidential candidate. Tavis was disappointed when Obama chose not to attend the 2008 State of the Black Union symposium, and he expressed that disappointment to the media, saying that while he understood the senator's need to be out campaigning, this was an important event and he should have been there. For these comments, Smiley was harshly criticized by supporters of Obama, who seemed to feel that an African American talk host should not be critical of the popular African American candidate. As the presidential campaign continued, Tavis used one of his radio commentaries on the *Tom Joyner Show* to explain his views, but a segment of the black community continued to be upset with him. It may have been for this reason that Tavis announced he would no longer be doing his commentaries on Joyner's show after June 2008.

Meanwhile, Smiley has continued doing what he loves to do. A prolific writer, by the end of 2007, he had written or edited eleven books, including his 2006 memoir *What I Know for Sure*. Several of his books have been on the best-seller list.

In January 2008, Smiley celebrated the fifth anniversary of his PBS talk show. In addition to the State of the Black Union symposium, he had begun planning an event called "Living the Dream" to be held at New York's Apollo Theater in January 2009, honoring the legacy of Martin Luther King Jr. And not forgetting his days in poverty, he remained actively involved in a foundation he had established to mentor black youth. The man who says that his slogan is to "Enlighten, Encourage, Empower" certainly has done that through his writings, his Web site, his broadcasts, and his speaking engagements. From growing up in a trailer park to attaining media stardom, Tavis Smiley is a role model for many young African American men, and a popular liberal commentator who has achieved success on both radio and TV.

TAVIS SMILEY TIMELINE

1964: born in Gulfport, Mississippi

1982: persuades Indiana University to admit him

1986: leaves college in his senior year to work for Los Angeles mayor Tom Bradley

1991: runs unsuccessfully for Los Angeles City Council; begins doing political commentary on local radio

1996: begins doing commentary on the nationally syndicated *Tom Joyner Show*

2002: *The Tavis Smiley Show* broadcast on National Public Radio

2004. begins doing a late-night television talk show on PBS

2005: debuts a new talk show, syndicated by Public Radio International

2006: publishes his memoir, *What I Know for Sure*

2007: moderates one of the Republican presidential debates

2008: celebrates the five-year anniversary of his PBS TV talk show

FURTHER READING

Dennie, Sheila P. "The Tavis Factor." *Tennessee Tribune*, 9 July 1998, p. 29.

Dolliole, Deona. "National TV Talk Show Host, Tavis Smiley Is a Star on the Rise." *Black Collegian*, February 1999, p. 34.

Farhi, Paul. "Tavis Smiley Will Cut Ties with Joyner Radio Show." *Washington Post*, 12 April 2008, p. C1.

LaRue, William. "NPR Host Brings Late-Night Talk to PBS." *Syracuse (NY) Post-Standard*, 1 February 2004, n.p.

Meisler, Andy. "A Different Voice Comes to Public Radio." *New York Times*, 21 April 2002, n.p.

Smiley, Tavis, with David Ritz. *What I Know for Sure*. New York: Doubleday, 2006.

Tavis Smiley's Web site is www.tavistalks.com.

Courtesy of Photofest

Tom Snyder

Tom Snyder always loved radio from the time he was a boy, but his college plan was to study medicine. Instead, he discovered that the local radio station had some openings, and while the health profession lost a potential doctor, broadcasting gained an outstanding news anchor. But radio was just a stepping-stone to where Snyder would gain his fame, first anchoring television newscasts in major markets like Philadelphia, Los Angeles, and New York City, and then as a late-late-night TV talk show host on NBC. He was brash, he was confident, and he had mannerisms that comedians delighted in imitating, particularly his overly loud, staccato way of laughing, a "ha-ha-ha" sound that, once one had heard it, was difficult to forget.

Tom genuinely enjoyed being on the air, and he never lost that enthusiasm. His late-late-night show was simple: just Tom and his guest, sitting opposite each other chatting, TV the way it had been done in its early years. Few people were as good at this format as Tom Snyder. When he died in 2007, even critics who had been harsh on him for his sometimes quirky mannerisms acknowledged that his passing was the end of an era.

EARLY YEARS

Thomas James Snyder was born in Milwaukee, Wisconsin, on 12 May 1936. His parents, Frank and Marie, wanted him to have a solid Catholic education, and after attending St. Agnes Elementary School, he went to the Jesuit-run Marquette High School. In 1953, he entered Marquette University, where he planned to take premed courses. Somewhere along the way, he decided he really wanted to be in journalism and changed his major. He also began seeking part-time jobs in local broadcasting. He had always been a big fan of radio, and when a new station, WRIT, went on the air in 1955, he heard that the management might have some openings. It turned out the station wanted to expand its news coverage, and Snyder got a job helping with the morning police reports. Soon, he was spending much of his free time at the station, to the detriment of his studies. He covered local news, and he learned how to ad-lib, a valuable skill for any broadcaster, who must often think quickly and report without notes. In 1957, the year he was scheduled to graduate from college, he dropped out—only a few credits shy of getting a journalism degree—and began pursuing full-time work in broadcasting. That pursuit led him to jobs in a number of cities, and by now he wasn't confining his career path to radio.

One of Snyder's earliest jobs was in Savannah, Georgia, at WSAV-TV. He also worked briefly in Atlanta at WAII-TV before making his way to the West Coast and finding work at KTLA-TV in Los Angeles. Typically, he did not hold onto this job for long and was soon out of money and desperate for his next opportunity. Fortunately for him, there was an interesting opening in Philadelphia at KYW-TV, where he began working in 1965. He did the noon newscast, which he coanchored with Marciarose Shestack, the station's first woman anchor. He was also asked to debut a morning talk show called *Contact*. It turned out that he had a natural talent for doing talk, a talent that would be beneficial to him later in his career.

Snyder got good ratings at KYW-TV, and he remained in Philadelphia until 1970. At that point, he had the opportunity to return to Los Angeles, and with more experience now, he was much more successful. He became a news anchor at KNBC, and his ratings were excellent. The critics took notice of his unique way of delivering the news. His style was very enthusiastic, and he was not afraid to sometimes insert his opinion or express emotion about a story. He also had an unusual laugh, and as time went on, it was described as "boisterous" and a "deep-throated guffaw." It was also imitated by comedian Dan Aykroyd on *Saturday Night Live*.

Despite his idiosyncratic laugh, most critics were impressed by Snyder's ability to be both articulate and personable. In a world where TV anchors were usually serious and robotic, Snyder was praised for being so human.

FROM NEWS ANCHOR TO TV TALKER

Snyder's success attracted the attention of the executives at NBC. There was a plan to put a new late-late-night TV talk show on the network, and they thought he would make a good host. Television, like radio before it, had been slow to accept the fact that there was enough of a late-night audience to keep stations on the air after midnight. In the early 1970s, the idea of a late-late show, broadcast from 1 to 2 a.m., was seen as a gamble. But it became obvious to NBC that things were changing when in February 1973, the network began to broadcast a Friday night music program called the *Midnight Special*. It featured taped performances from the hottest rock and pop stars, and was broadcast from 1 to 2:30 a.m. It got such good ratings with young adults that NBC decided to put more late-night programming on the air. The concept for the new late-late show was that should be "provocative, controversial and sometimes newsmaking," as NBC executives told the *Wall Street Journal* in May 1973. The new show would be called *Tomorrow*, and it would focus on interesting talk, rather than musical performances or comedy. Tom Snyder had the skills the network sought in their effort to win over the younger audience: He was known for his incisive interviewing skills, wry sense of humor, and willingness to speak his mind.

The first *Tomorrow* show aired on 15 October 1973. Snyder taped it in Los Angeles, where he continued to be a news anchor for KNBC. If the aim of the show was to be provocative, the network evidently found the first one a little too much so: Snyder first launched into a critique of former vice president Spiro Agnew, who had recently resigned amid charges of corruption, but the comments were censored by NBC, and the opening had to be reshot. The first few episodes seemed to focus on the sensational, with discussions of group sex and rock groupies. Snyder, who chain-smoked throughout the show, asked questions so insistently that sometimes the guests didn't have a chance to respond to one before he came at them with another.

Gradually, the show smoothed out its rough edges. Snyder grew more relaxed and made more use of his ability as a storyteller, a skill he had developed during his radio days in the mid-1950s. Snyder loved to talk, and in his long career in news, he had collected many stories of places he had been and people he had met. Some critics found him egocentric and said he talked too much, but others found him a fascinating raconteur. His show was praised for its simplicity. Unlike most shows on television, *Tomorrow* wasn't fake or glitzy. The set was very basic: just some comfortable chairs, an end table, and Snyder, sitting across from his guests, chatting with them. It was as if the viewer had been invited into Snyder's living room.

While outgoing and personable, Snyder was neither handsome nor photogenic. In fact, Andy Friendly, his former producer, who was also Snyder's longtime friend, described what viewers saw when they first tuned in to Snyder's new show: "Wild hair, super-wide tie, cigarette smoke wafting above his head when he came back from commercial. A sparkle in his eye and a voice so strong that he almost came through the lens of the camera" (Friendly, 2007). And yet, he soon won over the audience, due in large part to his ability to ask interesting questions of his guests.

It didn't take long for the TV audience to warm to Snyder's quirky style. After all, this was an era when late-late-night television was mostly old movies. Snyder offered something fresh and different. Critics tried to describe his on-air persona. One later wrote that Snyder was "goofy, serious, provocative . . . occasionally edgy [and] compelling" (Garofoli, 2007). Slowly, viewership increased, and soon the show was reaching about three million viewers a night, far more than network executives had expected of a late-late-night show.

What kept fans coming back was not just Snyder's larger-than-life personality. It was also exclusive interviews. Among the people Snyder interviewed over the years were author and philosopher Ayn Rand, science fiction writer Harlan Ellison, rock music legend John Lennon in his last televised interview, broadcasting executive Gordon McLendon, mass murderer Charles Manson, and movie director Alfred Hitchcock. Although some of his guests had appeared on other programs, it was Snyder's off-beat interviewing style that fascinated viewers. He was also known for his unpredictable choice of guests: viewers never knew who might show up on Snyder's show. He talked with a mafia hitman. He talked with members of a nudist colony. He talked with presidents, star athletes, and rock musicians. The current musicians were sometimes difficult for him to interview, because he was in his forties and, by his own admission, knew very little about the music that appealed to young people. And yet, he seemed to want to learn. He asked rock star guests like the Clash about the message in their music, and he admitted to being puzzled by how some of the punk rockers dressed. At times, he was sarcastic, but more often than not, he was just curious.

In December 1974, *Tomorrow* moved from Los Angeles to New York, and so did Snyder. Now, instead of anchoring on KNBC, he became a news anchor for WNBC's local *Newscenter 4* and continued to do *Tomorrow* as he had while on the West Coast.

Snyder was never reticent about asking tough questions as a news reporter, and he was similarly inquisitive as a talk show host. He asked Elton John about his homosexuality at a time when it was still a subject most broadcasters considered too controversial to discuss. Speaking to a very young director named Steven Spielberg, Snyder wondered if Spielberg believed in UFOs. Sometimes he argued with a guest, as in a heated exchange with opinionated sportscaster Howard Cosell, but Snyder was seldom the angry or confrontational host. He was also seldom flustered, no matter what a guest might say to him.

While *Tomorrow* was not known for music, sometimes well-known rock stars performed on the show. Snyder also interviewed a number of pop culture icons, such as sports stars like Muhammad Ali, members of the Irish rock band U2, and punk rocker Johnny Rotten. Snyder's catch phrase was "Fire up a colortini, sit back, relax, and watch the pictures, now, as they fly through the air." People debated what a "colortini" was, with the general assumption that it must be some kind of drink that was a perfect accompaniment to watching a color TV show (in 1973, many homes still did not have a color TV, and many people considered it special).

LATER YEARS

In 1977, Snyder moved back to the West Coast when a number of New York City–based shows abandoned the East to broadcast from Los Angeles. Snyder also wanted to be closer to his thirteen-year-old daughter, who lived with his ex-wife in Los Angeles. In addition to hosting *Tomorrow*, he was seeking a new challenge, having boosted WNBC's ratings and feeling that he had done as much as he could for the New York City station. His next project was to be a magazine-style show called *People*, and he planned to work on several NBC documentaries as well.

His stay on the West Coast turned out to be temporary: NBC needed him back in New York City to anchor a new weekend newsmagazine, *Prime Time Sunday*, so in the summer of 1979, he was back in Manhattan again. This show opened to great fanfare, but despite an excellent staff and some hard-hitting investigative pieces, it never attracted an audience. Rumors began flying that Snyder was a prima donna who was hard to get along with, but the truth was that the entire NBC news division was showing some ratings declines, and a number of newsmagazine shows were on the air already. The failure of

Prime Time Sunday, which was canceled in July 1980, could not be attributed entirely to Snyder.

NBC made further changes as it tried to shore up its ratings, and some of the changes affected Snyder. The good news was that *Tomorrow* was given thirty additional minutes, partly as a result of a contract dispute between NBC and Johnny Carson, whose show came on before Snyder's. The bad news was that Snyder was given a partner, an arrangement he disliked. Gossip columnist Rona Barrett was now his cohost, she on the West Coast and he on the East Coast. A live studio audience was also added in New York, something else that displeased him. The show was renamed *Tomorrow Coast to Coast* in the fall of 1980. Snyder, who had always been vocal in his criticism of NBC in the past, let everyone know he didn't want Rona Barrett (or anyone else, for that matter) as his partner, but the executives had decided, and no matter how Snyder complained, he and Barrett were stuck with each other. The partnership didn't last for long though. It became very obvious to both the viewers and the critics that this was a match with no chemistry whatsoever. The two bickered, the show's ratings declined, and ultimately, Barrett left the show. But the ratings never recovered, and in November 1981, NBC announced that *Tomorrow* would be canceled. In February 1982, Snyder's show was replaced by a show hosted by an up-and-coming comic named David Letterman.

Snyder was bitter about how NBC had treated him. He felt he had got the network some excellent ratings over the years, yet when major openings in news came up, they now went to somebody else. He thought he was going to get a chance to anchor NBC's network nightly news, but that never came to pass. The rumor was that people identified him with entertainment rather than news, an assessment he believed to be inaccurate. He was also angry at Fred Silverman, the president of NBC, for having changed the *Tomorrow* show so drastically.

Being a survivor, Snyder didn't stay angry long; he found another job, working for two years as an anchor for ABC news in New York City before once again returning to the West Coast to be a news correspondent on KABC-TV in Los Angeles. Occasionally he did some fill-in work as a talk show host. For example, when Larry King of CNN had a heart attack, it was Snyder who did Larry's show. He also went back to radio, doing a three-hour call-in show on ABC's radio network for five years, beginning in November 1987. His interviewing style and ability to charm an audience translated well to talk radio, and within a year, he was heard on 155 stations.

Snyder's television career was not over. He got a job at cable channel CNBC doing his own show in 1993–1994, and though the show was short-lived, David Letterman and others saw it and were convinced that Snyder hadn't lost his touch. Letterman had always been a fan of Snyder, and now he had a chance to do something to help get Snyder back on network TV. Letterman persuaded CBS to hire Snyder for a new late-late-night show, which went on the air in January 1995. It was called the *Late Late Show with Tom Snyder* and aired

Controversial TV Talk Shows

When radio went "topless" in the late 1960s and early 1970s, television was pushing the envelope, too. The Joe Pyne style of insult and outrage worked for some hosts, but increasingly, a new kind of daytime talk show emerged on TV. It was still aimed at housewives, but it had a friendly and conversational host who tackled controversial subjects without screaming or shouting. Among the founders of this type of program was Phil Donahue, who had done a call-in talk show called *Conversation Piece* on a Dayton, Ohio, radio station, WHIO, in the early 1960s. That show led him to WHIO-TV, where in early November 1967, he introduced his new concept for a talk show. It was just him and a guest; there was no orchestra, no jokes, just conversation and a studio audience that could ask questions. The first *Phil Donahue Show* featured militant atheist Madalyn Murray O'Hair discussing her opposition to school prayer. Subsequent shows offered frank discussions about abortion, homosexuality, and interracial relationships.

In addition to Phil Donahue, the late 1960s saw the debut of a talk show featuring *Cosmopolitan*'s editor, Helen Gurley Brown. Called *Outrageous Opinions*, the show ran in the mid-afternoon on New York's WOR-TV and featured Brown chatting with celebrity guests about their sex life, as well as their views on everything from lesbianism to jealousy to what made somebody sexy. A skillful interviewer, Brown was able to elicit all sorts of surprising admissions and confessions.

By the late 1960s, even topics previously taboo, like birth control, divorce, and infertility, were often discussed on daytime talk shows. One program, NBC's *For Women Only*, moderated by former newswoman Aline Saarinen, won critical praise for its thoughtful and informational discussions of these "mature subjects."

from 12:35 to 1:35 a.m. It was also simulcast over CBS radio. Snyder did the show until late March 1999, with his usual blend of interesting guests, probing questions, and skill in talking to the audience as if he were sitting in their homes. By all accounts, he had mellowed somewhat and was nowhere near as brash or abrasive as he had sometimes been in his early years, but he hadn't lost his talent as an interviewer, and he still didn't like to use a script or a teleprompter.

MEMORIES OF TOM SNYDER

Snyder didn't want to retire from broadcasting, but the entire industry had changed, he was older, and he now had some health problems, perhaps exacerbated by the years of heavy smoking. He found that he couldn't find a job on TV any longer. He became increasingly frustrated by what was happening to the profession he loved: He felt that network news had become too intertwined with celebrity gossip, and he saw cable news becoming more aligned with entertainment. He told a critic friend of his that he was glad he had got out of TV when he did. He moved to Marin County, outside San Francisco, and he tried to enjoy retirement. He maintained his own Web site (colortini.com), and on it, he chatted with fans and discussed his theories about contemporary media. And then, in 2005, he announced on his Web site that he had leukemia. He seemed upbeat and determined to triumph over adversity, but in late July 2007, Tom Snyder died at the age of seventy-one.

Today, most young viewers don't know who Snyder was, except perhaps when they see the caricature of him on a *Saturday Night Live* rerun or watch a snippet from one of his shows that somebody has posted on YouTube. But those who recall the advent of late-late-night talk shows associate Tom Snyder with creating a genre that is still popular today. He was one of the last of that generation of talkers who believed that good conversation was more important than having a flashy set or using other gimmicks to attract the public's attention. Tom attracted viewers with his larger-than-life personality, but it was his ability to make an interview interesting that kept them watching. And those who knew him or had worked with him believed his contributions to the late-late-night talk show ought to be remembered. As his former executive producer wrote in a tribute piece, Tom Snyder "was fearless and often politically incorrect. He asked the tough questions we all wanted answered, and he spoke truth to power. He never tried to make himself 'commercial' or 'sellable.' He cared about getting at the truth and cutting through the layers of pre-packaged, canned responses that personify most interviews" (Friendly, 2007). A former media critic who knew him from his days in Milwaukee added, Tom Snyder "called what he did 'picture radio'—chatting with his guest, offering personal asides, cracking inside jokes to an unseen studio crew, letting the smoke from his omnipresent cigarette fill the studio" (Cuprisin, 2007). And longtime media critic Marvin Kitman referred to Snyder as "a giant in the land of pygmies that is broadcasting," remembering that Snyder was an interviewer, not just a talker (Kitman, 2007). Snyder was from a simpler time, and perhaps today's audiences wouldn't appreciate what he did. But it's because of how well he did it that late-late-night talk prospers today.

TOM SNYDER TIMELINE

1936: born in Milwaukee, Wisconsin

1955: while still in college, gets his first radio job at a new AM station, WRIT

1965: hired as news anchor by KYW-TV in Philadelphia

1970: leaves Philadelphia TV for a job a news anchor at KNBC in Los Angeles

1973: debut of *Tomorrow* show on NBC-TV

1982: cancellation of *Tomorrow* and replacement by new David Letterman show

1987: does a syndicated radio show for ABC

1995: does a late-late-night show on CBS, following Letterman

2007: dies of leukemia at age seventy-one

FURTHER READING

Brooks, Tim, and Earle Marsh. *Complete Directory to Prime Time Network and Cable TV Shows*, 8th ed. New York: Ballantine Books, 2003.

Cuprisin, Tim. "Milwaukee Native Was Late-Late-Night TV Pioneer." *Milwaukee Journal Sentinel*, 30 July 2007, p. B1.

Cyclops. "No Sense Losing Any Sleep over It." *New York Times*, 4 November 1973, p. 19.

Edelstein, Andrew J., and Kevin McDonough. *The Seventies: From Hot Pants to Hot Tubs*. New York: Dutton, 1990.

Friendly, Andy. "Recalling Snyder, a Fearless, Peerless Friend." *Television Week*, 6 August 2007, p. 10.

Garofoli, Joe. "Tom Snyder, King of Very Late-Night TV, Dies at 71." *San Francisco Chronicle*, 31 July 2007, p. E2.

Kitman, Marvin. "Tom Terrific." 31 July 2007, online at www.huffintonpost.com/marvin-kitman/tom-terrific_b_58555.html.

Rosenberg, Howard. "Regrouping Time? NBC News Future Assessed." *Los Angeles Times*, 11 September 1979, p. C6.

Zoglin, Richard. "Tom Snyder Has Gone West but Still Hankers for the Big Apple." *New York Times*, 17 July 1977, p. 77.

AP Photo/Max Nash

Jerry Springer

Of all the syndicated talk shows, none has been more outrageous and controversial than the *Jerry Springer Show*. Often referred to as the "ringmaster," Springer manages, with varying degrees of success, a motley crew of pugnacious guests discussing often raunchy subjects. Sometimes, the guests become so enraged that they try to attack each other, as the audience roars its approval and Steve Wilkos, Springer's head of security, leaps into action. It's a soap opera. It's professional wrestling. It's the *Jerry Springer Show*. But Jerry wasn't always an outrageous talk host. In years past, he was a politician who even became the mayor of Cincinnati, Ohio, and then a respected TV news anchor and reporter in that city. People who remember him from that period of time are probably stunned by Jerry's change in careers, but like it or not, being the ringmaster of a show critics have called trashy and sleazy has made him a very wealthy man.

HOW IT BEGAN

Gerald Norman Springer was born in London, England, on 13 February 1944. His parents, Richard and Margot, had escaped from Germany to England during World War II, and in 1949, seeking a better life for the family, they emigrated to America. They settled in Kew Gardens, Queens, New York, where Jerry and his sister, Evelyn, grew up in a small four-room apartment. Mr. Springer sold stuffed animals, and Mrs. Springer worked in a bank. Jerry's parents liked to talk about politics, and even at a young age, Jerry, too, became interested. One of his early political memories is watching the 1960 Democratic National Convention on television; although he was still in his teens, not an age when young people were interested in politics, he was immediately impressed by John F. Kennedy. After he graduated from high school, Jerry enrolled at Tulane University in New Orleans, Louisiana, where he became involved in the civil rights movement and marched with supporters of school integration. He was also involved in the college radio station, WTUL. Jerry earned a bachelor of arts degree in political science from Tulane in 1965 and then went on to get a law degree from Northwestern University in 1968. He was hired as a campaign aide to Democratic presidential candidate Robert F. Kennedy, but after RFK was assassinated in June 1968, Springer went to work for a Cincinnati, Ohio, law firm, Frost & Jacobs.

A liberal Democrat, Springer decided he wanted to get into politics, so in 1970, he ran for the House of Representatives in Ohio's Second Congressional District. While his anti-Vietnam war views and his eagerness to have the voting age lowered to eighteen were popular with a certain segment of the electorate in Cincinnati, he failed to defeat the incumbent, conservative representative Donald D. Clancy. However, in 1971, he won a councilor-at-large seat on the Cincinnati City Council. And there he remained until a scandal broke in 1974. The vice squad raided a massage parlor and found one interesting canceled check to a prostitute for services rendered: It had been written by Councilman Springer. After the story broke, Springer resigned, but even though Cincinnati was known as a very conservative city, his political career was far from over. A year later, he won back his seat, having first gone to the public, admitting what he had done and asking for forgiveness. To the surprise of his political enemies, the public gave him a second chance, and he won his seat back. And even more surprising to those who followed Cincinnati politics, despite his being liberal and having admitted to a sexual indiscretion he was elected mayor in 1977. Conservative Cincinnati gave Springer the largest plurality in the city's history: He won by more than ten thousand votes over his closest challenger. In his acceptance speech, he praised the city for being "open, progressive and compassionate."

FROM POLITICS TO BROADCASTING

As the "boy mayor" (he was only thirty-three), Springer worked hard to help ordinary citizens and was known for being very approachable: He even had a mobile van that he took all around the city, listening to people and trying to solve problems. He was especially popular with young voters, probably as a result of his antiwar days and his efforts to lower the voting age. Then, in 1982, he tried to get his party's nomination for the governorship of Ohio. In his campaign advertisements, he mentioned the scandal of 1974, talked about turning his life around and working hard as mayor. He said he was unafraid of telling the truth, and if elected governor, he would be just as honest about the difficult decisions needed to turn Ohio's economy around. Despite how popular he had been as mayor, he was unsuccessful in his bid for the Democratic gubernatorial nomination, losing to former lieutenant governor Richard Celeste. He briefly became one of Celeste's advisers, but after Celeste became the governor of Ohio, Springer left politics for television. At this point in his career, he was not doing talk shows. Rather, he was still involved in politics, as a news reporter and commentator. He had already worked part time for Cincinnati's News 5, WLWT-TV, but by 1983, he was employed there full time. It was a good career move. Within several years, he had brought a low-rated station to the top, and along with Norma Rashid, his coanchor, he anchored the news throughout the rest of the 1980s and into the early 1990s, winning several local Emmy awards for his news commentaries. He also earned the award for best anchor from *Cincinnati Magazine*. In addition to reporting on every major event in the local area, he also went on location to distant places like Sudan and Ethiopia, where he earned critical praise for his reports on the famine there and what local residents were doing to help. There was no evidence at that time that he might one day become a purveyor of trash TV.

In 1991, the owners of WLWT-TV were trying to develop a new talk show, similar to the *Phil Donahue Show*, which it also broadcast. Looking back on the early years of his talk show, Springer would tell *TV Week*'s Allison Waldman in 2006 that he never expected the show to be on for a long time, and he certainly didn't expect to become the ringmaster of a video circus. Actually, he said, he was perfectly happy being the managing editor of his TV station's newscasts, and he began to do a talk show because his bosses wanted him to try it. That talk show debuted on 20 September 1991, and at first, it seemed like just one more of the many talk shows on TV, with famous guests and friendly chat. In fact, when promoting Springer's new show, the syndicator stressed Springer's background as a former lawyer, politician, and news anchor—Springer even remained coanchor on WLWT-TV news until January 1993.

The new talk show featured a number of well-known guests, including the Reverend Jesse Jackson, exercise guru Richard Simmons, actress Ali MacGraw, and talk show host Sally Jessy Raphael. To be closer to a major city with more available guests, the show's base of operation was moved from Cincinnati to Chicago, but no matter what topics were discussed and no matter how good the experts, the ratings never increased. Frustrated and on the verge of the show's being canceled, Springer and his staff made some serious changes. Springer and the show's new executive producer, Richard Dominick, decided to take the show in a much younger and much more controversial direction, and in May 1994, the tabloid Jerry Springer show made its debut.

CONTROVERSIAL TALK SHOW HOST

The critics were appalled by the new incarnation of Springer's show. The topics, said one critic, were some of the most tacky and tawdry he had ever seen. It was like watching a peep show. The new Jerry Springer shows included one entitled "My Boyfriend Turned Out to Be a Girl," and there were shows about girls who wanted to be porn stars and of whether large-breasted or small-breasted women are sexier. The studio audience was now made up of younger people, and their role was to chant, "Jerr-EE! Jerr-EE!" or boo or shout insults. With each successive show, it seemed, the subject matter got more crude, and fights erupted onstage, accompanied by a barrage of bad language (the worst of which the producers beeped), as the audience cheered the guests on. As another critic noted, just when viewers thought they had seen it all, Springer came up with something even more tasteless. Several stations that had begun to carry his show when it went into syndication soon regretted their decision and canceled, but most stayed with it for one very important reason: As lowbrow and trashy as the show was, people had started watching it. The ratings began to rise, especially among young adults. But the trashiness was a bit too much for the syndicator and owner, Multimedia Entertainment, which syndicated such talk shows as Sally Jessy Raphael's and Phil

Donahue's. Executives of Multimedia, which had been involved with Springer's show since 1991 and had begun syndicating it sometime in 1992, now advised the producers to tone the show down a little. The company was getting complaints from clergy and educators that the show was much too coarse and could be detrimental to children who might watch it. Thus began an ongoing power struggle between the owners and the producers over how trashy the show could be and still avoid problems with the FCC. Complicating matters was the sale of the show to another company, which also wanted the producers to be more careful about what they aired. Finally, in 1997, Universal Television bought the show and basically gave the producers permission to do what they thought would work. By 1998, more than seven million viewers were watching the *Jerry Springer Show*.

Despite the show's popularity, its excessive trashiness made it a magnet for criticism, including scrutiny by Congress. In April 1998, Senator Joseph Lieberman, a conservative Democrat from Connecticut, gave a speech to the National Association of Broadcasters in which he accused the show of "perversity and violence" and encouraged stations to restrict it to late-night viewing, rather than having it on in the daytime when children could see it. This was not the first time the senator had been critical of Springer's show. He had already spoken out about Springer and other similar trash TV shows in a 1996 feature article in the journal *Policy Review*, in which he warned that if the airwaves continued to be trashy and vulgar, Congress would have to look into taking some of the more disgusting material off the air.

Whether or not Congress really could do anything about Springer in this era of deregulation, all the bad publicity was not helpful, and it made sponsors uncomfortable. Universal agreed to place limits on the violence and tone down the Springer show. But Springer planned to first make a statement about how much he disliked government meddling in what he believed was his freedom of speech. In mid-May 1998, he decided to do an episode of the show that he called a simple love story—except the lovers were humans and animals. One guest described sex with a horse; another described sex with a dog. We may never know if the segment about bestiality was really intended for the airwaves, or if it was just meant to make a point and cause a stir; however, the outrage and intense criticism of the topic resulted in the show's never being broadcast. As for less violence, for a while the show did tone down the chair throwing and people trying to beat each other up, but in typical Springer fashion, what was substituted was more topics about sex and lustful behavior, including an increase in passionate lesbian kisses.

While the show alternated between guests fighting and guests kissing, several media critics raised the question of whether the guests on the show were fake. There were rumors that some of them were paid actors, a charge Springer vehemently denied. In fact, to prove that the guests were real, he introduced "SpringerCam" in 2000, allowing viewers to see some of the tapes that people who wanted to be on the show had sent in. Meanwhile, for all of the complaints, people continued to watch. In some cities, Jerry Springer had even bigger ratings than Oprah Winfrey.

Being such a controversial figure was also lucrative: Springer was reputed to be making more than $4 million a year.

Whether he was in fact the king of sleaze or just a normal guy doing an outrageous talk show, Jerry Springer was now so thoroughly identified with trash TV that when he tried to return to serious news, he found himself unwanted. In early May 1997, WMAQ-TV in Chicago tried to hire him during the ratings period (called *sweeps week*) to deliver political commentary, a task he had won awards for during the 1980s. But when the word got out that he was coming to WMAQ, one of the TV station's anchors resigned rather than work with him, and so many viewers wrote irate letters to the station's management that Springer delivered only two commentaries before he decided to resign.

Springer tried serious media again in January 2005, when he began a daily call-in talk-radio show on the liberal Air America Radio network, but as sincere as Springer may have been about wanting to do political talk, the show never caught on with the audience. Perhaps people expected the rude and raucous Springer and were not comfortable with the erudite Democrat who wanted to discuss the war in Iraq. By December 2006, Springer's radio show had been canceled.

SPRINGER AND HIS CRITICS

Springer was frequently interviewed on radio and TV talk shows, and he defended his show on First Amendment constitutional grounds, saying that the critics who wanted to censor him were doing a disservice to the millions of people who wanted to watch his show. He also told reporters that the Jerry Springer show was all in good fun, and he used adjectives like "silly" to describe it, insisting it was just part of the popular culture and not to be taken too seriously. In fact, he said it wasn't really a talk show per se; rather, it could be compared to a circus.

Because the majority of his guests came from the lower classes, critics had said he was exploiting them to get ratings. Springer disagreed with the accusation, claiming that nobody was on the show who didn't want to be there, and in fact, he said, his show had broken new ground by providing something other than the white upper-class view of life that was so dominant on TV. Of course, those rationalizations never impressed the critics. In fact, in 2002, the editors of *TV Guide* named Springer's show the "Worst TV Show of All Time," although they also admitted that it was a guilty pleasure (Waldman, 2006, p. 37). On the other hand, *USA Today* named the show one of the "Ten Turning Points for Television," explaining that Springer had not only "provided a platform for people who had been shut out of TV" but had also created the style of reality TV show that thrives on exposing the excesses and problems of people who seem eager to confess them (Bianco, 2004).

However, Springer was not as eager to confess his own secrets. He had married in 1973, and by his own admission, the incident that cost him his seat on the Cincinnati City Council in 1974 had nearly cost him his marriage. After he and his wife, Micki, reconciled, the gossip columns accused him of infidelity on other occasions over the years. Reporters who interviewed him were given a list of subjects they were not allowed to ask about, and one of them was the status of his marriage. More than one reporter found it ironic that someone who made his living spilling the secret lives of other people would be so reticent to discuss his own. While he did publish a memoir, with Laura Morton, in 1998 called *Ringmaster*, it was mainly about the show and about his childhood. His more recent personal scandals were not included.

Angry Talk Host Morton Downey Jr.

Joe Pyne was the first of the angry male talk hosts, but there was one 1980s talker who reminded critics of Pyne: Morton Downey Jr. Like Pyne, Downey was a chain smoker, and his on-air persona was to insult his guests and bully anyone who dared to disagree with him.

Morton Downey Jr. (real name: Sean Morton Downey Jr.) was the son of Morton Downey, a popular Irish tenor who had often performed on the radio. Mort tried a number of career paths before finding his own home in radio in the early 1980s, but it was on TV that he finally achieved success, doing a Joe Pyne-style talk show. Originally a liberal, Downey had become an ultraconservative by the time his TV show debuted in New York in October 1987. He seemed to reserve his most vehement verbal attacks for people he perceived as left wing. His logo (the symbol with which he was identified) was called the Loud Mouth, and his catch phrase was "Zip it!" when a guest offended him or talked too long. His studio audience, mostly working-class men, loudly chanted, "Mort! Mort! Mort!" when he screamed at a guest. In fact, the guests were booked with the intention of provoking a confrontation: The more inflammatory or outrageous the guest, the better. Occasionally, Mort and his guests got into shoving matches, and his security force would intervene.

In May 1988, the show went into nationwide syndication. Like Pyne's before him, Downey's rage and his battles with guests fascinated viewers but horrified critics. The term *shock jock* was not yet in use, but it would have applied to Downey. However, the viewers' fascination with Downey's show quickly burned itself out, and his syndication deal ended after only fourteen months. He is remembered for taking the persona of the angry male host to a whole new level.

In addition to having a persistent number of critics who despised his show, Springer found that he had another problem common to the most outrageous talk shows: the unforeseen consequences that sometimes occurred on the air. In May 2000, a woman named Nancy Campbell-Panitz was murdered by her ex-husband, Rolf Panitz, after a Springer episode about love triangles. She had thought that on the show, she was going to reconcile with her ex-husband, who had been seeing a woman named Eleanor, but it turned out that he had secretly married Eleanor, and the two of them, along with the audience, mocked and insulted Campbell-Panitz as she left the stage. Rolf Panitz hadn't wanted the two women to know that he was trying to maintain relationships with both of them, even after divorcing Campbell-Panitz. Several months after the show was taped, while in a drunken rage, he murdered Campbell-Panitz, who had finally thrown him out of the home they had shared. He was found guilty and received a life sentence. Then, Campbell-Panitz's son, Jeffrey Campbell, sued the Springer show for inflaming the tensions between Rolf Panitz and his former wife and thus creating what the legal charges called "a mood that led to murder." Springer and the producers denied all responsibility, saying there was no way to predict what guests who had been on the show might do later. The suit was ultimately dropped in early 2006.

The year 2006 turned out to be a busy one for Springer. His controversial and still outrageous talk show had outlasted all of its critics, and in May, it celebrated its three thousandth episode. Springer also made several appearances in September and October on an ABC-TV program *Dancing with the Stars*, a show on which celebrities with little experience in ballroom dancing were paired off with professional dancers to learn the steps and then perform competitively. Springer learned the tango and the waltz, and while his performances were awkward at best, his enthusiasm and his ability not to take himself too seriously won the praise of the audience. The judges were another matter, and he was soon eliminated from the competition.

In the summer of 2007, Springer received the good news that his show had been renewed through 2010, giving his detractors plenty of time to find new reasons to criticize the *Jerry Springer Show*.

By 2008, Springer was off on another speaking tour of college campuses (he had done several such tours in past years). Fans turned out in large numbers to hear him, as critics once again lamented what Jerry was doing to corrupt the youth of America. While Springer sometimes injected his own still-liberal political views into his lectures, encouraging the students to vote for candidates who would provide universal health care or end the Iraqi war, he remained somewhat a victim of his own success: The students applauded and chanted, "Jerr-EE! Jerr-EE!" loudly and enthusiastically when he talked about some of his weirdest guests. They hadn't come to hear Jerry the political talk show host; they were there to hear the Jerry they knew and loved reminisce about some of his most outrageous shows. It was further evidence that since the debut of the trashier and sleazier *Jerry Springer Show*, American popular culture has never been quite the same.

JERRY SPRINGER TIMELINE

1944: born in London, England

1965: graduates from Tulane University

1971: wins seat on Cincinnati City Council

1977: elected mayor of Cincinnati

1983: hired as news anchor at WLTW-TV in Cincinnati

1991: debut of first TV talk show

1994: decides to make the show more tabloid and trashy; debut of new version of show

1998: publishes a memoir about his life called *Ringmaster*

2005: does political talk radio on the Air America Radio network

2006: the three thousandth episode of the *Jerry Springer Show*

2007: his TV talk show renewed through 2010; becomes host of *Americas' Got Talent* on NBC

FURTHER READING

"Cincy's New Mayor Makes His Comeback." *Elyria (OH) Chronicle Telegram*, 2 December 1977, p. 3.

Hiltbrand, David. "Jerry Springer Takes His 'Mindless Show' to College Campuses." *Philadelphia Inquirer*, 28 February 2008, n.p.

Johnson, Rebecca, and Kathleen Powers. "Jerry Springer under Siege." *Good Housekeeping*, September 1998, pp. 114–119.

Waldman, Allison J. "American Pie: The In-Your-Face Success of 'The Jerry Springer Show,'" *Television Week*, 8 May 2006, pp. 26, 31, 34, 37.

Waxman, Sharon. "King of the Trash Heap: Jerry Springer Digs the Dirt On Television." *Washington Post*, 20 January 1998, p. D1.

Williams, Scott. "Springer Foes Talk Trash: Dump It or Clean It, Execs Told." *New York Daily News*, 8 April 1998, p. 5.

Courtesy of Photofest

Howard Stern

What Rush Limbaugh is to political talk, Howard Stern is to "guy talk." Stern sometimes discusses politics and serious subjects like race relations, but mostly, his show is about sex, and not the kind of sex that you'd hear about from Ruth Westheimer. The millions of young males who make up his audience love to listen as he interviews porn stars, discusses his sexual fantasies, jokes about bodily functions, and chats with guests about subjects seen only in the tabloids. He refers to himself as the "King of All Media," and he certainly is the king of all shock jocks. Since the late 1980s, he has been among the ratings leaders and has commanded one of the biggest salaries of any radio announcer. According to some sources, he earned more than $300 million in 2006, and in 2007, Sirius, the satellite network that broadcast his show, gave him an $83 million bonus for boosting the number of their subscribers so dramatically. (Stern's compensation includes his book sales, stock options, and other bonuses for good ratings.)

Howard Stern is also the poster child for what his detractors believe is too much vulgarity and crudity on the air, and throughout his career, he has been the subject of numerous complaints to the FCC. Of course, his fans don't see him that way: To them, he is a fearless truth teller and a defender of freedom of speech on the air.

DISCOVERING BROADCASTING

Howard Allan Stern was born in Jackson Heights, New York, on 12 January 1954 to Ben and Rae Stern. His early years were spent in Roosevelt, Queens, New York, in a neighborhood that was predominantly black. Howard later asserted in his 1993 book *Private Parts* that he felt like a pawn in his parents' experiment in integration, being frequently teased and even beaten up by neighborhood bullies. In that book, he also related that his childhood was unhappy because his mother, a homemaker, was overprotective, and his father, a radio engineer, was judgmental and critical: His father frequently called him "stupid" and a "moron." On the other hand, he credits his father's "incredible sense of humor" with influencing his own interest in comedy. And while Howard may have felt that his father shouted at him too much, his work as the co-owner of a Manhattan recording studio inspired young Howard, who was impressed by watching the celebrities who came to record; he also recalls being attracted to broadcasting from a very young age.

Howard's parents finally left Roosevelt and moved to Rockville Center, Long Island, New York, where he graduated from South Side High School in 1972. He then attended Boston University's College of Communication, from which he graduated in 1976. His first foray into radio was working as a volunteer at the campus station, WTBU, and his first professional job was at WNTN in Newton, a city not far from Boston. In 1977, he was hired by a station in upstate New York, WRNW in Briarcliff Manor, where he worked as the afternoon disc jockey; the management wanted him just to play the hits. His starting pay was ninety-six dollars a week, and he stayed in that job for two years. At that early stage in his career, he was not yet a shock jock, but he felt stifled by what was expected of him, even when he took over the duties of station program director.

In 1978, Stern learned of an opening at station WCCC AM and FM in Hartford, Connecticut, and was hired by owner Sy Dresner to do the morning show. The station was not doing very well in the ratings, so Stern had more freedom to experiment and begin to shape his radio persona. In addition to playing music and taking calls from his listeners, he did political commentary at the time of a fuel crisis, with long lines and high prices at gas stations. Howard decided to organize a boycott of one of the major companies. He called his movement "The Hell with Shell," and it attracted so much attention that lawyers from Shell threatened a lawsuit. Howard also got a large amount of publicity, telling his story to the national media. He recalls that this was the first time he saw how powerful a radio announcer could be.

HOWARD'S CONTROVERSIAL PERSONA

As successful as Stern was at WCCC, the pay remained low, and when he got an offer at WWWW (known as W4) in Detroit in the spring of 1980, he went to work there. He was being paid well and was even beginning to attract some positive attention as a morning-show host, but unfortunately, as often happens in radio, W4 changed formats from rock to country music, and through no fault of his own, Stern was suddenly out of work.

Stern didn't stay unemployed for very long, finding his next job in Washington, DC, at WWDC-FM in March 1981. It was here that he assembled the team he would continue to work with, notably comic impressionist Fred Norris, whom he knew from his days in Hartford at WCCC. Another important addition was his sidekick, Robin Quivers, a former U.S. Air Force nurse and news reporter who at first served mainly as an object of Stern's jokes. As time went on, Quivers assumed more of a cohost role, although Howard was always the star.

During his tenure at WWDC, Stern attracted many new listeners with his often scatological humor. He frequently mentioned that he had a small penis, and discussions of breasts, penises, masturbation, and orgasms were staples of his show. He would ask callers to tell him the strangest places they had made love, or he would do his feature "Dial-a-Date," which was frequently "Lesbian Dial-a-Date" or even "Dwarf Dial-a-Date." He had a comedy routine about the "Cleavages," a parody of the wholesome 1950s TV family comedy *Leave it To Beaver*, which had revolved around Ward and June Cleaver and their children. In Howard's version, Ward was having a sex change, and when Howard mentioned "the Beaver," he wasn't referring to Ward and June's TV son but using a slang expression for the female genitalia. In the early 1980s, sexual humor was not commonly heard on radio, which had already endured FCC scrutiny in the early 1970s over "topless radio." But Howard Stern brought it back, and with great success. Interestingly, although some of his material was crude, it seems not to have attracted the FCC's attention.

Howard also managed to be controversial. He often spoke about his personal life on the air, making it fodder for some of his show's humor. One day, he made fun of his wife Alison's recent miscarriage. When he turned such a personal tragedy into a comedy skit it was very painful for her, but she had married Howard in 1978 and had long since become accustomed to the content of his radio shows. Using the miscarriage as a skit on his show was seen as insensitive, and it attracted a firestorm of public criticism.

An Air Florida flight crashed in a snowstorm in early 1982, striking the Fourteenth Street Bridge in Washington and killing seventy-eight people. On the air, Howard called the airline the next day to ask about the price of a one-way fare from the airport to the Fourteenth Street Bridge. While this sort of black humor was to become his trademark and a part of his persona, critics immediately called it tasteless and insensitive. Howard felt that the incident reflected his commitment to say whatever he wanted to, and to ask the questions he felt the average announcer lacked the courage to ask.

Stern tripled the ratings at WWDC, and in 1981, he was named *Billboard* magazine's "Album Oriented Rock (AOR) Air Personality of the Year." But he wasn't making the salary he felt he deserved, and when he took his salary dispute public by calling his bosses "scumbags" on the air, his contract was not renewed (contrary to the bland explanation given to the media, it was later acknowledged that he had in fact been fired).

By this point, Howard had little trouble finding another place to work, and it was somewhere he had always wanted to be: New York City. He had grown up listening to the great radio personalities on New York radio, and he dreamed of becoming one of them. Now he was back home. He was hired in September 1982 by an AM station, WNBC, where he and sidekick Robin Quivers continued the same irreverent and outrageous skits that had got such good ratings in Washington, DC. Howard also attracted the same controversy, offending advertisers by making fun of their commercials on the air. He had ongoing feuds with the station's management, especially with then program director Kevin Metheny, about how far he could push the envelope. He was even suspended for a skit that made fun of the Catholic Church. Howard parodied various ethnic groups and continued to do outrageous skits about all sorts of sexual practices. Although his show took a while to get the kind of ratings he had had in Washington, he began to build a fan base. He also got celebrities to visit his show, including comedians Eddie Murphy and Joan Rivers. David Letterman was a fan and had Howard as a guest on *Late Night with David Letterman* in June 1984. Howard was making a reported $200,000 a year and was being promoted as "radio's bad boy." Meanwhile, the critics remained divided on whether Howard Stern was a brilliant social satirist in the style of Lenny Bruce or whether he was just vulgar for the sake of being vulgar.

BECOMING THE KING OF ALL MEDIA

By late September 1985, the constant feuding with WNBC's management over what he could and could not say resulted in Stern's being fired, but he soon found another job. In November, he joined New York City's WXRK (K-Rock) to do the afternoon shift; K-Rock's executives promised him they would not put any restrictions on his show. By February 1986, he was back to doing the morning show, with his expanding cast of characters and his regular sidekick, Robin Quivers. One ongoing aspect of his show was talking about his personal life, including his marriage. He insisted he was faithful to his wife, Alison, but he also discussed his every sexual fantasy on the air. Once Howard had been promoted to the morning shift, his immediate goal was to beat his competitor and rival, another controversial morning show host named Don Imus, who was still at WNBC. In May 1986, Stern did in fact defeat Imus in the ratings and needled his rival by holding a mock funeral in front of the NBC studios at 30 Rockefeller Plaza. By August, Infinity Broadcasting, which owned K-Rock, had begun offering Howard's show to affiliated stations, the first one of which, WYSP-FM in Philadelphia, began broadcasting it in 1986. When in late September 1988 Infinity's WJFK in Washington, DC, began airing Howard's show, bringing him back to Washington again, there was little doubt that Howard was becoming America's best-known shock jock.

In the late 1980s, what would become a recurring theme, the Federal Communications Commission took notice of Howard Stern's show, because the FCC had been receiving complaints. While Howard had never used the "seven dirty words," he regularly talked about bodily functions and sexual acts, using euphemisms some people evidently found excessively crude. It would later turn out that many of the complaints had come from a handful of conservative groups, especially one led by Rev. Donald Wildmon, whose American Family Association regularly complained about on-air vulgarity. The FCC was duty-bound to take complaints seriously, no matter who was making them. In December 1988, Infinity was fined $6,000 for something said on one of Howard's shows. This was one of the smaller fines. More were to come. In late July 1991, a non-Infinity station, KLSX in Los Angeles, picked up Howard's show, but his entrance into the Los Angeles market proved to be a mixed blessing. He had new opportunities to gain a wider audience, but he also gained a new enemy, a musician named Al Wescott, who objected to the broadcasting of such an offensive radio show at a time when children could listen. Westcott began sending complaints about the show to the FCC, meticulously transcribing the skits he felt were indecent. By December 1992, the FCC had fined Infinity $600,000 for a series of 1991 broadcasts.

The fines didn't stop Stern nor even slow him down. The more his critics pointed out his vulgarity, the more he invited porn stars on the show or did skits about lesbians or even skits that made fun of his detractors. His notoriety with the FCC didn't harm his popularity, and by January 1993, Arbitron estimates were that he had more than 3.5 million listeners, the majority of whom were men twenty-five to thirty-four years old. By 2004, when his show was syndicated by forty-five stations, that audience had grown to eight million, putting him on *Talkers* magazine's list of the most listened-to talk show hosts. When he published his memoir, *Private Parts*, in 1993, it took only seventeen days for the book to reach the top of the *New York Times* best-seller list. However, because of its often racy content, including intimate details of his sex life and his marriage, as well as insights into how he had thought up some of his most popular on-air skits, he admitted to a reporter that he wouldn't let his children read it. In 1997, that book was made into a movie, and it, too, did remarkably well: According to *Billboard* magazine, the movie, also called *Private Parts*, set a box-office record with ticket sales of $15.1 million, outperforming theatrical rereleases of *Star Wars* and *The Empire Strikes Back*. On the other hand, critics wondered how Howard's former program director at WNBC, Kevin Metheny, felt about being the model for a character known as Pig Vomit.

Howard had also developed a skill in subverting what his competitors were doing, and he especially enjoyed getting his listeners to prank TV news shows. One of his biggest fans, "Captain Janks" persuaded call screeners for the news anchors on CNN that he was really on the scene of an event, or that he was just a caller wanting to talk to the guest on *Larry King Live*. Once he got on the air, he started off sounding very sincere, and then he made a rude remark related to Stern's show. The CNN anchors were very unamused, but Howard would play the sound clips over and over, and fans seemed to find them hilarious. Howard was also able to exert an influence on *People* magazine, when in 1998, Hank the Angry, Drunken Dwarf (a character, but also a real person on Howard's show) received a large number of votes in the annual online poll the magazine did for the "50 Most Beautiful People."

By now, in a joking tribute to Michael Jackson, who called himself the "king of pop," Stern was calling himself the "king of all media," and his many fans agreed. In fact, in 1994, he decided to run for governor of New York on the Libertarian Party ticket, and many of his New York fans immediately called into his show to offer their support. Whether he was really serious about running, his "campaign" attracted much media attention, and even some high-profile political figures offered him their support. Other politicians, especially those serious about running for governor, said he was making a circus out of the process of being nominated. In the end, they needn't have worried. Stern called off the campaign when he found that he had to make his tax returns and other financial records public.

HOWARD'S CONTINUED SUCCESS

In June 1994, the cable channel E! (Entertainment Television) began broadcasting half-hour episodes of Howard's radio show, enabling viewers to see for themselves the assortment of porn stars, dominatrixes, odd and unusual personalities, and characters in his skits. The TV version lasted until July 2005.

Howard was often critical of the FCC on his show, but in 2004, he finally had a chance to deliver the message personally. In late October, FCC chair Michael Powell was a guest of San Francisco's KGO radio. Howard called in and took Powell to task for having a vendetta against him, and he accused Powell of being a water carrier for conservative President George W. Bush, as well as an enemy of free speech. One reason for Howard's ire was that earlier in the year, the FCC had fined Clear Channel Communications, which now carried his show, $495,000. Clear Channel had also pulled his show from six of their stations.

When Don Imus Went Too Far

Since the early 1980s, controversial talkers like Howard Stern have used language perceived by some to be racist or sexist, but they haven't been fired. That changed in early April 2007, when veteran talker Don Imus lost his job due to remarks he made during his morning show. Simulcast on both WFAN radio in New York and cable TV's MSNBC, the outspoken Imus is beloved by his predominantly white middle-aged male audience. After the Rutgers University women's basketball team lost a hard-fought National Collegiate Athletic Association championship game, he ridiculed several team members for having tattoos, and he called the players "nappy-headed hos," *ho* being a slang pronunciation of *whore*. These comments about a Cinderella team which was made up mostly of young minority women who were good students, and who had taken Rutgers all the way to the final four in the tournament, seemed unfair even for Imus. The media reports about the comments began to generate outrage, first from spokespeople in the African American community but then joined by ordinary listeners, and even some of Imus's advertisers, who removed their commercials from his show. Imus offered his apologies repeatedly, but he was soon fired from his show. Afterward, he met with the team and its coach and tried to make amends. Then, as he had so many times during his long career, he was able to persuade a major radio station, this time WABC in New York, to give him another chance. In early December 2007, he was back on the air again, to the delight of his fans and the frustration of his detractors.

Howard kept getting good ratings, many sponsors continued to support him, and his influence continued to increase. He had also gone back to speaking out about politics: He was especially angry about the efforts of conservative groups to restrict what he could say, and during the 2004 presidential election, he spoke out against President Bush and advocated for his opponent, Senator John Kerry. The president was reelected, the FCC continued to keep an eye on Howard, and life went on.

Then, Howard did something that stunned many of his fans. In October 2004, he announced that he was leaving so-called terrestrial radio and moving his show to satellite transmission. His reason was simple: The FCC had no jurisdiction in space, and nobody would be telling him what to do. He signed a multimillion-dollar agreement to broadcast his show on the Sirius Satellite network, beginning in early 2006. It was a major risk. Would his fan base abandon terrestrial radio and follow him? After all, doing so required buying the receivers, costing between $50 and $300, and paying the $12.95 monthly subscription fee to get Sirius. The equipment would have to be plugged into a car or home stereo. Stores reported that they definitely were seeing an upsurge in demand for the receivers, but only time would tell. Meanwhile, ever outrageous, Howard used the time during which he was still under contract to his terrestrial affiliates to rail against the corporations that had gone along with the FCC and against censorship. He also told his listeners to stop listening to terrestrial radio and follow him to satellite. Such comments did not please the stations that still employed him, and he was suspended on at least one occasion during 2005 for those remarks. The suspension only reinforced his certainty that it was time to move to satellite.

On 9 January 2006, Howard and his team first appeared on Sirius. He would no longer have the millions of listeners he had had before, but he was definitely attracting new listeners to satellite: When he announced that he was moving to Sirius, the company had about 600,000 subscribers, and by 2007, that number had grown to nearly 8 million total. Sirius executives attributed much of this growth to the publicity Stern's impending arrival had brought the network. At the end of 2007, Sirius broadcast a radio retrospective of Howard's career, "The History of Howard Stern," featuring sound clips from his early shows, commentary by people who had worked with him, and rare material not heard before. The ratings data, released in early 2008, showed that while Stern's Sirius audience was not as big as when he had been on terrestrial radio, he was by far the most popular personality on the network, with over 1.2 million listeners willing to pay the monthly subscription fee to hear his shows.

In addition to changes in Stern's professional life, there have been changes in his personal life. He and Alison divorced in 2001, and he soon had a new girlfriend, a model named Beth Ostrosky. As Howard Stern continues to seek new challenges and chart his own course, it is impossible to predict what he will achieve next. He has proved to even his detractors that he is still the king of all media.

HOWARD STERN TIMELINE

1954: born in Jackson Heights, New York

1976: graduates from Boston University; gets his first radio job, at WNTN in Newton, Massachusetts

1978: hired by WCCC AM and FM in Hartford, Connecticut

1980: hired by WWWW-FM in Detroit, Michigan

1981: hired by WWDC-FM in Washington, DC

1982: hired by WNBC in New York City

1985: hired by New York City's WXRK-FM (K-Rock)

1986: show syndicated to Philadelphia's WYSP-FM

1988: show syndicated to Washington, DC's WJFK-FM

1992: FCC fines of more than $600,000 against Howard's parent company

1993: publishes his memoir, *Private Parts*

1994: begins doing a late-night cable TV version of his show for E! (Entertainment Network)

2004: announces he will depart terrestrial radio for satellite

2006: does his first show on the Sirius Satellite network

2008: marries his long-time girlfriend Beth Ostrosky

FURTHER READING

Cobb, Nathan. "Howard Stern between the Covers." *Boston Globe*, 26 October 1993, p. 53.

Gross, Jane. "For Radio's Bad Boy, This Isn't Prime Time." *New York Times*, 5 October 1985, p. 26.

Harrington, Richard. "Howard Stern: All Id, No Lid." *Washington Post*, 28 October 1993, p. D1.

———. "Wild Man of the Airwaves." *Washington Post*, 31 July 1981, pp. B1, B4.

James, Caryn. "Now a Nice Guy and an Oprah Antidote." *New York Times*, 10 March 1997, p. C1.

Reed, Keith. "Fans Following Stern to His New Sirius Home." *Boston Globe*, 21 December 2005, p. C11.

Stern, Howard. *Private Parts*. New York: Simon & Schuster, 1993.

Span, Paula. "The Irreverent Voice." *Washington Post*, 26 December 1983, pp. D1, D12.

AP Photo/Steven Senne

Jerry Williams

In his heyday, Jerry Williams was known as the dean of talk radio. His radio career began during a time when two-way talk was still new, and in several cities, he was credited with making the format a success. Nowhere was that more true than in Boston, where he was the first talk show host to get big ratings with two-way talk. There had been a few attempts at call-in shows in the late 1940s, but when Jerry put two-way talk on the air at Boston's WMEX in 1957, his name became synonymous with the format.

Jerry knew how to get a reaction. His critics said he sometimes acted like a demagogue (an act that many successful talkers have used), but usually, he discussed the issues in a way that was passionate but not necessarily angry. Some things did outrage him, however, especially corrupt politicians and waste of the taxpayers' money. It was not just in Boston that he proved he knew how to make the talk radio format his own; wherever he went, he motivated his listeners to take action or gave them a new way to look at the issues. He didn't have the stereotypically deep announcer voice; in fact, he just sounded like a regular guy, and that persona served him well. A liberal whose political views gradually turned conservative on certain issues and libertarian on others, Jerry genuinely believed that talk show hosts should be advocates, and for more than forty-five years, that is what he often was.

FINDING A CAREER PATH

Gerald Jacoby was born in Brooklyn, New York, on 24 September 1923. His parents, Samuel and Frieda, ran a small clothing shop. Like many kids growing up in the 1920s and 1930s, Gerald (his parents never called him by any nickname) loved radio. He and his brother, Herbert, especially enjoyed listening to the Brooklyn Dodgers baseball games. But while Gerald would have been quite happy to spend his after-school time listening to his favorite shows, his father wanted him to learn to be more responsible and pressed him into service working part-time in the family clothing store. His brother was the good student in the family, and it seemed likely that he would go to college. Gerald, on the other hand, liked to read, but by his own admission, he was indifferent to school. He couldn't wait to get a job somewhere and make his own way in the world, preferably in some aspect of the entertainment business.

Williams didn't finish high school, much to his parents' disappointment, and what he preferred to spend time doing, rather than looking for a job, was going to the movies, rooting for the Dodgers, and listening to his favorite radio shows. As his father saw it, his son was just wasting time and needed to grow up and find a career, so once again, he worked part-time in the family's store. That was not where Gerald wanted to be, but then current events intervened. When World War II broke out, he received his draft notice. It was 1942, and he was in the U.S. Army.

Even as a high school dropout, Gerald Jacoby was always articulate. He also had some business and office skills (he had been taught to type), and after assessment, the army decided to place him in the U.S. Army Air Corps, where he received flight training. He was sent to India, where his unit transported supplies to the Allied troops. He did this often dangerous work for two years, until he began to have unexplained fainting spells. After one incident in which he fell and hit his head, he was allowed to leave military service. Unlike so many others, he had survived, and now he was a veteran of the war. It was 1945, he was back home in New York, and he still had no idea what he would do with his life.

Williams continued to think about becoming an entertainer, but he could neither sing nor dance. Meanwhile, although new technologies like television would soon gain popularity, radio still dominated, and radio remained largely dependent on live talent; there was always a need for people to perform in dramas and comedies as well as for announcers and newsreaders. He thought that training for work in broadcasting might be worth trying, so he enrolled in a course. It turned out to be exactly the right decision. While he only got some work at New York's city-owned educational station, WNYC, and didn't get paid for it, he was convinced that radio was where he should be. His instructor told him to read the industry trade publications, which listed jobs, and suggested he start applying in small towns, where inexperienced announcers were hired. At some point in filling out applications, he decided he needed a name that wasn't so ethnic. At that time, most announcers used a pseudonym on the air, and by 1946, he was applying for jobs as Jerry Williams.

Williams's early radio jobs were in some very low-paying and unglamorous cities, where there wasn't much to do other than work. His first job, in December 1946, took him to Bristol, Virginia, where he worked as a newsreader and announcer, as well as hosting a live music show, at a new country music station, WYCB. After he had some much-needed experience, his next jobs were in Pennsylvania, first at McKeesport's WEDO and then Braddock's WLOA. Neither job was much fun for him: long hours, low pay, bosses with unrealistic expectations. He was fired from both stations and was somewhat relieved to leave that area of the state, which he found lacking in culture, and with few opportunities for entertainment. It was late 1947, and he had learned only that he had no talent for doing the news. He did show some promise as a disc jockey in an era when the "personality dj" was becoming more important.

In 1948, Jerry found his next job at another new station, WKAP in Allentown, Pennsylvania. He named his afternoon dj show *A Date with Jerry*, and in addition to playing the hits, he did man-on-the-street interviews and read live commercials. But this was another job that didn't last, and ultimately, he went back to New York to take an acting course, hoping to find work in the new medium of television. After getting only a few bit parts, he returned to looking for radio work. In 1951, he became a dj and program director at WKDN in Camden, New Jersey. The pay was better than in his previous radio jobs, and the station was near Philadelphia. Things seemed to be looking up.

In the late 1940s and early 1950s, an increasing number of late-night and overnight announcers had begun involving their listeners by doing talk shows. Nobody used that terminology yet, and what they did wasn't exactly two-way talk. Most announcers hesitated to put callers on the air live, since a tape delay wasn't yet in common use, and management feared that a caller might say something vulgar. So announcers paraphrased the callers or put celebrity callers, but not the listeners, on the air.

Jerry became convinced that call-in talk should not just be relegated to late nights, and he was eager to try talking with the audience during the daytime hours. He believed this would get WKDN more listeners, so in 1951, he created a show called *What's on Your Mind*, and encouraged listeners to call with their opinions on a variety of topics. They did. Management insisted that he paraphrase, but at least he was hearing from the audience and discussing what they were thinking. It was a start. The topics quickly grew more controversial: local politics, religion, the exploits of Senator Joe McCarthy. But Jerry's on air persona was conversational; he didn't insult the callers. Of course, if they insulted him, he paraphrased their words and then refuted what they had said. The public loved the show, and it became the talk of the area.

BRINGING TALK RADIO TO BOSTON

A Philadelphia man named Maxwell Richmond who owned an advertising agency liked what he had heard of Jerry's work and decided to place some commercials on Jerry's show. Richmond was eccentric and very intense, but their relationship was profitable, and as Jerry later told a reporter, for all of Richmond's quirks, "He knew what radio was all about." This relationship would become important later in Williams's career.

Jerry now wanted to work in a bigger city, and he had his eye on Philadelphia. He and a WKDN colleague, newsman Bud Smith, had developed a comedy routine for Jerry's show, and their comic sketches became so popular that another listener, Ben Gimbel, of the department store by that name, asked Jerry and Ben if they wanted to do a show in Philadelphia. So, in 1952 they moved to Philadelphia's WIP, using the name "The Gagbusters." The show did well, and advertisers liked it, but the grind of doing a comedy show and also entertaining in nightclubs, something Jerry had done periodically during his radio career, began to wear on him, and he decided to return to talk. By late 1955, he was no longer part of a comedy duo and was on the air at WIBG in Philadelphia from 11 p.m. to 2 a.m. with the *Jerry Williams Show*. He never looked back.

By the mid-1950s, putting callers on the air was becoming more common, as rudimentary tape delays were being created, but at this point, the only two-way talk was when Jerry interviewed a guest. He loved to talk politics, and he loved to discuss serious social issues. But he wasn't happy with paraphrasing.

Then he heard about what Long John Nebel was doing in New York City on WOR. He had a tape delay, which, despite a beep every fifteen seconds, made it sound as if the caller was live in real time, when in fact the announcer had seven seconds to censor anything vulgar. Williams had a tape delay installed, and another piece of the puzzle was finally in place. Now he could hold spontaneous conversations with the listeners rather than with himself.

The baby boomers were in their preteen years and wanted to hear the newest music: rock-and-roll. Top-forty stations were springing up everywhere, along with fast-talking top-forty dj's. WIBG decided to woo that young audience, and in 1957, Jerry's talk show days in Philadelphia were over. Fortunately, his earlier good business dealings with Mac Richmond were about to rescue him from unemployment. Mac and his brother, Richard, had bought a radio station in Boston, WMEX, and they were programming top-forty on it during the day and early evening. But late at night when the kids had gone to bed, the station needed an interesting show. Mac thought Jerry would be perfect. And so it was that Jerry was hired to do a talk show in Boston There had been other talk shows in Boston before Jerry's—Steve Allison did one on WVOM, the Voice of Massachusetts, in the late 1940s, just to give one example. But Jerry would reinvent the talk show and reach a much larger audience.

Jerry started on the air at WMEX in September 1957. Mac Richmond was famous for being stingy, and some of what he had promised Jerry didn't materialize, including the salary they had supposedly agreed on. But Jerry saw a chance to make something happen. There were no other shows like the one he wanted to do, and his approach to what was then called the "comment and controversy" style of radio was unique. Other shows had guests, but they were mostly celebrities. Williams envisioned a talk show only about the issues of the day, and he wasn't afraid to talk about the subjects that were on everyone's mind, whether civil rights, or poverty, or local politics. He saw the show as a town meeting on the air, and he asked only that his callers observe the ABC's (to be accurate, brief and concise) and keep their calls in good taste. In addition to knowing what topics were likely to motivate people to call, Williams knew what events in daily life irritated or upset the average person, so he talked about incidents in his own life that the listeners could relate to, like his car being towed for no apparent reason. He also took on the political establishment and asked why the system seemed to favor a privileged elite. The listeners were impressed. He understood how they felt.

Within a year, WMEX's ratings had grown dramatically, thanks to the combination of the top-forty format and the *Jerry Williams Show*. Gradually, Jerry Williams became Boston's dominant talker, and he was soon able to get the biggest newsmakers as guests: authors, politicians, athletes. Even Richard Cardinal Cushing made an appearance. While Williams's personal politics tended to be liberal, he invited to his show the guests with the most interesting points of view, whether they were right, the left, or the center.

By 1965, Williams had not only established himself as a success but also proved that talk radio could get impressive ratings. More stations were now doing talk shows, but the competition didn't bother him. What Jerry found annoying was that Mac Richmond persisted in not giving him the salary and the publicity he felt he had earned. When a new opportunity presented itself, he took it, even though it meant leaving Boston.

In the summer of 1965, Jerry Williams agreed to go to Chicago to work at the CBS-affiliated station WBBM. Unlike Richmond, who had made Jerry fight for every small improvement, WBBM gave him an excellent salary, a professionally produced ad campaign, a beautiful studio, and plenty of publicity. What the station's managers wanted in return was ratings because they were consistently behind their competitors and believed Jerry could change that. He did his first show in Chicago in early September 1965, and what management expected, he delivered. Williams knew how to get the right guests, whether a priest with a controversial viewpoint about the humanity of Jesus or a white supremacist with controversial views about Jews and blacks. As he had in Boston, he addressed poverty and civil rights, but he also gave time now and then to a psychic who said he could tell you about yourself just from hearing the sound of your voice. He used the slogan "America's Largest Town Meeting of the Air," perhaps referring back to the popular radio talk show of the 1930s and 40s, but also reminding the audience that talk radio allowed people have their say, just by placing a phone call. Williams also became the subject of controversy on several occasions during his time in Chicago. On one occasion, in November 1965, Richard B. Cotton, editor of an ultra-conservative West Coast publication, launched into an anti-Semitic tirade. Another guest, author Meyer Levin, who was Jewish, disputed what Cotton was saying, and ultimately became so frustrated that he walked out of the studio. Rather than cutting Cotton off, Williams let him continue. Some critics felt that Williams should not have permitted Cotton's bigotry to get so much airtime, but Williams explained that such speakers were on many radio stations, and the public ought to know their beliefs.

TAKING ON THE POLITICIANS

The 1960s were a turbulent era, and a number of talkers benefited from being able to talk about the major events, from the escalating war in Vietnam to the assassination of such important figures as President John F. Kennedy and Dr. Martin Luther King Jr. WBBM briefly shifted Williams from nights to mornings, and the ratings were all right, but by early 1968, there were rumors that change was in the air for WBBM. CBS decided to switch some of its stations to all news, a format that was doing well for the network in New York City, where WCBS had changed to all news in June 1967. WBBM made the change in mid-1968, and Jerry Williams was out of a job. When he had a chance to return to Boston, a city he had grown accustomed to, he was eager to make the move.

Williams's new Boston job was with WBZ, an AM station with a massive signal, and he picked up where he had left off, except now he could be heard in more than thirty states. The war in Vietnam generated many of the calls, and on 4 September 1972, he received one that would become famous. The anonymous caller said he was a recently returned Vietnam veteran. In impassioned and often emotional remarks, the man described the atrocities, the bombs, the use of napalm, the horrors he had seen. People who were listening were stunned, whether they supported the war or not. The veteran's eye-witness testimony was one of the most effective antiwar calls Williams had ever aired. He later gave a transcript to George McGovern, the Democratic candidate for president, who was campaigning on an antiwar platform. Appearing on talk shows didn't get McGovern more votes, and Nixon won in a landslide. Nevertheless, the call was another flashpoint in the discussion, as people on both sides debated whether the veteran was a hero or a traitor. Years later, many of Williams's fans still remembered that call. At some point in the 1990s, questions arose about whether the veteran was who he had claimed to be, but the question of his identity didn't diminish the power of that moment in 1972.

Williams enjoyed great success at WBZ, talking about everything from Watergate to the busing crisis (a controversial issue in Boston, where schools had long been de facto segregated and a judge ordered black students bused to white schools). But when his contract came up for renewal, WBZ chose not to renew it. Williams believed the reason was that he was a liberal and the management was extremely conservative, but his show was also very expensive to produce, since it required not just the host but a separate producer to find and book the guests. Or perhaps WBZ may have decided it was simply time for some new blood. His time with WBZ was over in early October 1976.

LAST YEARS OF WILLIAMS'S CAREER

Williams had little trouble finding another station to take his show, although he was getting older and was accustomed to doing talk radio in his own way. He briefly went back to WMEX (Mac had died, but brother Dick was still there), then to WMCA in New York City, then back to WMEX again in the summer of 1977, then to WRC in Washington, DC, in October 1978, to WWDB-FM in Philadelphia in March 1979. WWDB was one of the few FM stations doing talk at that time and Williams was briefly the station's program director. But again, he didn't stay long, and by November 1980, he was working at Miami's WNWS. Williams seemed never able to find a place where he could stay and re-create his old magic. But then, he got one more opportunity, and it took him back to Boston again. WRKO, which had programmed top-forty very successfully in the late 1960s and through the mid-1970s, was now changing to an all-talk format, and Williams was hired for the afternoon drive time. In the fall of 1981, Jerry Williams was back on the air in Boston. He would stay there for the rest of his career.

Doing what he did best, he took on Boston's mayor, Kevin White. There had been a crackdown on parking and other traffic violations, and Williams was convinced it was a scheme to generate more revenue at the expense of ordinary people. He asked listeners to send him copies of all the tickets they had received (which they did, in large numbers), and he then organized a protest, complete with T-shirts and a march to protest the unfairness of the parking crackdown. Nothing was accomplished, but this campaign got Jerry and the station some good publicity.

Kings of Civility

While the angry and confrontational talkers often get much of the attention, there have always been talk hosts who are well informed and have strong opinions, yet who conduct their show civilly, never raising their voices to the callers or insulting the guests. One of the best examples of this style is Michael Jackson; with his British accent and erudite manner, he was a fixture at KABC in Los Angeles for over thirty years. In 1966, when he started at KABC, the station had several liberals and several conservatives, including the volatile Joe Pyne. When the liberal Jackson beat the conservative Pyne in the ratings, he told reporters that this success proved a talk host didn't need to be rude to be successful. No one ever accused Jackson of being rude. In fact, critics repeatedly praised him for enlightening and informing the audience on topics as wide-ranging as international politics and economics, as well as lighter subjects like celebrity news.

In Boston, David Brudnoy was an equally respected talk show host with a long career. A libertarian conservative, the popular "Bruds" actually read the books his guests wrote and, whether or not he agreed with them, always asked insightful questions. One of the last of the talk hosts who preferred intelligent conversation to shouting matches, Brudnoy had an evening show on WBZ that consistently received top ratings. His fans included members of both political parties, who respected his ability to conduct a civil conversation even about contentious issues.

Another event that got Williams publicity of a different sort occurred in May 1985, when he was even a guest on "AM Chicago," a TV show hosted by then up and coming host Oprah Winfrey. Williams was part of a panel discussion which brought together a number of the nation's controversial radio talkers, all discussing how they appealed to their particular audience.

At some point in the discussion, one of the hosts, a conservative talker named Warren Freiberg of WLNR-FM in Lansing Michigan, who had been making incendiary and racially-charged statements throughout the broadcast, got into a verbal altercation with Williams, who represented the liberal point of view. At some point in their heated exchange, Freiberg sprayed a chemical substance in Williams's face (it later turned out to be liquid soap), at which point, Williams knocked Freiberg off of his chair. By all accounts, Oprah was stunned by the exchange. So were Freiberg's employers, who fired him not long afterward.

But while the incident on Oprah's show got him some national coverage, Williams continued to be best known in Boston, where his influence on political discourse had not waned. This was especially true after the new governor of Massachusetts, Michael Dukakis, took office. By 1986, Williams was sounding a lot more conservative, and he seemed to genuinely dislike most of the governor's policies, especially his support for a mandatory seat-belt law. It wasn't that Jerry disliked traffic safety. He disliked the government's mandating what people could and could not do in their own cars. In 1986, Williams continually expressed his outrage over being forced to wear a seat belt, and he was able to persuade the audience that whether or not to buckle up should be an individual decision. He generated so much opposition to the seat belt law that a ballot referendum repealing it won, and the media credited Williams with generating the outrage that led to the law's defeat. It wasn't until the mid-1990s that a bill reinstating mandatory seat-belt use passed.

The 1980s version of Jerry Williams raised ire about other issues, too. When Congress tried to vote itself a large pay raise in late 1988, Williams organized a protest. His listeners sent tea bags to members of Congress, to remind them of the Boston Tea Party. Listener phone calls persisted as well, and in the end, the pay raise bill was killed. Again, many in the media attributed the results to the way Williams had mobilized his listeners. Although Williams's politics seemed more conservative in the 1980s and 1990s, he never entirely abandoned some of his liberal beliefs. In June 1992, he attended a talk by Republican Vice President Dan Quayle, who was speaking to the National Association of Radio Talk Show Hosts, a group that Williams had been instrumental in founding. Williams grew dismayed when the assembled talkers, most of whom were conservative, didn't ask any hard questions of Quayle. Finally, Williams felt he had to speak up, criticizing Quayle's blaming the media for declining moral standards. He told the vice president that such claims were nonsense, and that the phony outrage at the media was just intended to distract the public from the real issues, including rising unemployment and other economic problems.

Despite his many years on the air, Williams's influence had been declining, and in the mid-1990s, WRKO gradually cut back his hours. Although his many achievements as a talker earned him a place on the *Talkers* magazine "Top 25 Radio Talk Show Hosts of All Time" in 1995, and in 1996, he was inducted into the Radio Hall of Fame, other Boston talkers were surpassing him. As the style of talk radio grew increasingly angrier and more confrontational, his ratings continued to dip. He represented the style of another era, and even some of his fans thought he sounded old. WRKO finally fired him in 1998. Williams tried to get back on the air on other Boston stations, but by now, his health was failing. On 29 April 2003, Jerry Williams, who had put talk radio on the map in Boston, died at age seventy-nine.

In 2008, Steve Elman (Jerry's former producer at WBZ) and Alan Tolz (his former producer at WRKO), two men who knew and respected Williams's work, published a biography of his career. The format he popularized continues to live on in the many talk hosts who have picked up where the dean of talk radio left off.

JERRY WILLIAMS TIMELINE

1923: born in Brooklyn, New York

1942: drafted into the U.S. Army

1946: first radio job, at WYCB in Bristol, Virginia

1951: becomes announcer and program director at WKDN in Camden, New Jersey; begins doing talk shows

1952: part of a comedy duo ("The Gagbusters") on WIP in Philadelphia

1955: talk show host at WIBG in Philadelphia

1957: begins doing his talk radio show on WMEX in Boston

1965: moves to WBBM in Chicago

1968: returns to Boston, on WBZ radio

1978: on the air at WRC in Washington, DC

1979: program director of Philadelphia talker WWDB-FM

1981: hired by WRKO radio in Boston

1985: gets into an altercation with another talk show host on Oprah Winfrey's "AM Chicago" program

1995: named by *Talkers* magazine one of the twenty-five most influential talk hosts of all time

1996: inducted into the Radio Hall of Fame

2003: dies after a long illness at age seventy-nine

FURTHER READING

Elman, Steve, and Alan Tolz. *Burning Up the Airwaves: Jerry Williams, Talk Radio, and the Life in Between.* Beverly, MA: Commonwealth Editions, 2008.

Holland, Bill. "Talk-Show Host Williams Has Harsh Words for Quayle." *Billboard*, 4 July 1992, p. 73.

Kennedy, Dan. "In Memoriam: Jerry Williams." *Boston Phoenix*, 2–8 May 2003.

Pothier, Mark. "Jerry Williams, Boston's Irrepressible Dean of Issue-Oriented Talk Radio, Never Got to Say Goodbye." *Boston Globe Sunday Magazine*, 16 June 2002, pp. 11, 29–33.

Rose, Hilly. *But That's Not What I Called About.* Chicago: Contemporary Books, 1978.

Zoglin, Richard. "Bugle Boys of the Airwaves." *Time*, 15 May 1989, pp. 88–89.

AP Photo/Dima Gavrysh, File

Oprah Winfrey

If Howard Stern jokingly calls himself the king of all media, it is not a joke to say that Oprah Winfrey is the queen. *Time* magazine has named her one of the one hundred most influential people in the world. *Forbes* magazine has listed her as one of the wealthiest. *Business Week* says she is one of America's top philanthropists: Passionate about causes that further social justice, she established the Angel Network, an organization that donates to charities worldwide that are involved in literacy and education. Her awards include a number of Emmys, both for Outstanding Talk Show Host and Outstanding Talk Show. Her typical daily audience is about thirty-three million viewers. She is also one of the rare American media stars whose first name is sufficient to identify her. Even her critics admit that there is probably no one in the media today with more influence: When she likes a book and says so on the air, people go out and buy it. When she lists something among her "favorite things," that item gets a major boost. In late 2007, for the first time, she publicly supported a presidential candidate, Senator Barack Obama; political pundits wondered if her support would make a positive impact on his campaign.

When she was growing up poor in the South, Winfrey probably never expected to become one of the world's most well-known celebrities.

POVERTY AND OPPORTUNITY

Oprah Gail Winfrey was born on 29 January 1954 in Kosciusko, Mississippi, a town that was still segregated. Her father, Vernon Winfrey, was in the military, and her mother, Vernita Lee, was a maid. The two unmarried teenagers had a brief relationship and then split up, neither of them ready to care for their baby daughter. Her name wasn't supposed to be Oprah: She was named after Orpah, Ruth's sister-in-law in the Old Testament's Book of Ruth, but somehow the name was transcribed incorrectly—*Oprah*—on her birth certificate.

Young Oprah's childhood was difficult. She spent her first six years living on a farm with her maternal grandmother, Hattie Mae Lee. Her grandmother knew that her little granddaughter was bright, but because she was extremely poor, Hattie Mae could not afford toys or new clothes for the child. In fact, the little girl sometimes had to wear dresses made from potato sacks. As a result, other children mocked her, and the memory stayed with Oprah.

In 1960, when she was six years old, Winfrey moved to Milwaukee, Wisconsin, to live with her mother. Vernita lived in Milwaukee's ghetto and worked as a housekeeper. She made little money, but that was the least of Oprah's problems. As she would later tell reporters (and then her TV audience), she was raped by a nineteen-year-old cousin when she was only nine, and a few years later, she was sexually assaulted again, this time by her mother's boyfriend. At the time, she didn't talk about these incidents; she just decided to run away when she was thirteen. Her mother, who thought she was merely being stubborn and rebellious, threatened to send her to a juvenile detention facility. Instead, she was sent to live with her father in Nashville. When she was eight, she had stayed briefly with him and his wife, Zelma, who had welcomed her. The reasons for her then going to live with Vernita in Milwaukee are not entirely clear. Now, she had the chance to go back to Nashville, and she did.

Vernon was strict. He wouldn't let his daughter wear makeup or revealing dresses, but he was interested in seeing Oprah become successful. By now, Vernon had a skilled profession: He was a barber and would soon have his own shop. He was also deeply religious, a deacon in the Missionary Baptist Church. He and Zelma involved Oprah in their religion and also taught her the importance of studying and working hard. They expected her to read several books a week, and if she got a C in school, she was told that it was not acceptable, that she could do better. Whereas nobody seemed very interested in her potential when she lived with her mother, suddenly she was surrounded by people who believed she had intelligence and wanted her to use it wisely. It is doubtful that her father and stepmother knew all that Oprah had gone through in Milwaukee, but they believed love, along with discipline and faith, were what she needed. They were right.

Of course, at that time, Oprah saw all the rules and regulations as excessive. She would take a while to appreciate the mentoring she was receiving. Meanwhile, whether she liked it or not, she was expected to study hard, and when she finally began to apply herself, she quickly got results, becoming an honor student at East Nashville High School, which she helped to integrate. She did so well that she was one of only two students in Tennessee to win the right to attend a conference on youth at the White House in Washington, DC.

Winfrey also became active in the high school drama club, and she applied some of her newfound confidence to beauty pageants. One event that influenced her was seeing Diana Ross, the lead vocalist of the popular black singing group the Supremes, on television. There were few blacks on TV then, and she was impressed by how glamorous and confident Ross looked. She decided she wanted to be a performer of some kind, and beauty pageants were one way to start. By the time Oprah was seventeen, she had won the title of Miss Fire Prevention, being the first black woman ever to win it. She won other pageants as well, including Miss Black Nashville, but it was the Miss Fire Prevention award in 1971 that turned out to be the most important to her future. She had attracted the attention of a local black radio station, Nashville's WVOL, which found her not only attractive but articulate. In 1971, she was asked to read some news for the station, and the manager liked her voice. WVOL hired her, and she worked there part time during her senior year in high school, reporting the news from 3 p.m. to 8 p.m. By this time, she knew she wanted to be a broadcast journalist.

WINFREY'S MEDIA CAREER BEGINS

After graduating from East Nashville High School in 1971, Winfrey attended Tennessee State University in Nashville on an academic scholarship. While there, she was able to continue working in news at WVOL, gaining valuable experience. And the time was opportune: In the early 1970s, the Federal Communications Commission, encouraged by the federal Equal Employment Opportunities Commission (EEOC), was telling broadcasters to increase the number of women and minorities they hired; until that time, radio had been a predominantly white male medium. Women had been consigned to off-air clerical work, and African Americans had been able to find jobs only at all-black radio stations. Winfrey was among those who benefited from the changes. While she was still in college, a local television station—Nashville's CBS affiliate, WTVF-TV—hired her as a reporter. At first, she tried to model herself on Barbara Walters, one of the few newswomen of that era, but gradually she developed her own style.

In June 1976, Winfrey applied to work in a larger city and was hired as a reporter and coanchor by Baltimore's WJZ-TV. Her first foray into a large market news operation was not an instant success. While she showed promise, her youth and inexperience sometimes made her seem awkward. She also had a problem controlling her emotions. The accepted style for a news anchor or reporter was to be dispassionate, but some of the tragic stories Oprah had to report moved her to tears. Subjected to intense scrutiny and criticism, she began to overeat because eating made her feel better. The management at WJZ-TV removed her from anchoring the 6 p.m. news, a role she clearly wasn't suited for, but they wanted to find another vehicle for her talent. In 1977, they installed her as cohost of their popular feature *People are Talking*, along with Richard Sher. The two of them interviewed local newsmakers and discussed a variety of social issues. As it turned out, Oprah was a natural for the talk show. She enjoyed chatting with the guests and was much more relaxed than she had been doing news. The show's ratings began to take off, and soon Oprah was out and about, making appearances at local events, giving talks to civic organizations, and becoming a popular TV personality. By 1983, she felt she was ready for another step up.

Debbie DiMaio, one of Winfrey's producers at WJZ-TV, had been looking for a better job and had applied to Chicago's WLS-TV, which had a low-rated morning show called *AM Chicago*. When DiMaio showed her reel of accomplishments, Oprah's program was on the tape. Not only did WLS-TV's management hire DiMaio, but they became interested in hiring Oprah, too. They brought her in for an audition and decided she was just the one to improve *AM Chicago*.

In early January 1984, Oprah was on the air at WLS-TV and getting accustomed to her new home. Fortunately, she fell in love with Chicago and became one of its biggest boosters, praising the city repeatedly on *AM Chicago*. At first, the station's management tried to script her, but it quickly became apparent that she was at her best when she was free to be spontaneous, so the management decided to let her do the show her way. It turned out to be a wise decision. Critics, especially those who were female, soon began to comment about what a natural communicator she was and how she made even everyday experiences interesting. They also remarked that her enthusiasm was contagious. She was very much like a best friend: She could be frank, and she wasn't afraid to speak her mind, but she could also be warm and empathetic. Audiences liked her almost immediately. She became so popular that the name of the show was changed to the *Oprah Winfrey Show*.

One promotional stunt from January 1985 stood out for many of her viewers because it had such a positive impact. Oprah's struggle with her weight had been no secret, and she had mentioned it to her audience a number of times. When she decided to try another diet, this time she involved her audience, asking them to provide her with moral support. She also got some encouragement from an unlikely source: comedian Joan Rivers. As a fast-rising talk show host, in late January 1985 Oprah had, for the first time, been invited onto the *Tonight Show*, where she and Rivers made a bet. Oprah promised to lose fifteen pounds if the normally slender Rivers would lose five. Rivers agreed. Oprah said that her ultimate goal was to lose fifty pounds, and her TV station's doctor designed a special diet for her. She also began an exercise regimen. Some overweight viewers began to diet along with Oprah, and the *Chicago Tribune* printed regular updates, as well as some of the recipes that the doctor had suggested for her. There were features about Oprah at home, features about her being tempted to have some fast food—Oprah's diet became the talk of Chicago. She received about twenty thousand letters asking for more information about the diet, as well as additional fan letters offering encouragement By early March, Oprah had lost eleven of the fifteen pounds she had promised, and she returned to *The Tonight Show* to give a progress report.

Oprah's diet spread her name nationally. Millions saw her appearances on *The Tonight Show*, articles were written in a number of newspapers, and several book publishers asked her to write a diet book. Her effort to lose weight struck a chord in many viewers, and even those who didn't need to diet empathized and cheered her on.

Winfrey's rationale for using her show to go on a diet was that her struggles, as a public person, might be an example to others. She frequently had guests who stressed having a positive attitude, overcoming obstacles, and never giving up. And even though the *Oprah Winfrey Show* was not overtly religious, many of her fans felt it was inspirational.

BECOMING FAMOUS

In 1985, another event put her name before a wider audience: She was chosen for a role in Steven Spielberg's movie *The Color Purple*. That big break came about when a well-known composer and record producer, Quincy Jones, was in Chicago on business and, as he relaxed in his hotel room, saw Oprah's show on TV. Jones was coproducing the movie with Spielberg, and he suggested that Oprah audition for the character of Sophia. Although she had never acted before, Oprah's performance earned her a Best Supporting Actress Academy Award nomination. In addition to being personable, Oprah Winfrey was versatile.

During the mid-1980s, Chicago was host to another popular daytime talk show, Phil Donahue's show. Donahue was a legendary talk host and dominated daytime talk until Oprah arrived on the scene. Their two shows were in direct competition at 9 a.m., but almost immediately, Oprah began to get substantially higher ratings than Phil. Once she had proved that she could win ratings higher than someone of Donahue's stature, it wasn't long before there was discussion of syndicating her show nationally. She had shown great poise on *The Tonight Show*, had become adept at handling the national media, and seemed to genuinely enjoy being in the spotlight.

In early September 1986, the *Oprah Winfrey Show* went into national syndication, thanks in large part to a television executive named Roger M. King, co-owner of King World, a major syndication company. It was King who persuaded skeptical station managers to take a chance on a new talk show that featured an African American woman who had a weight problem. King believed Oprah had star power, and when she launched her syndicated show, more than 120 stations had agreed to give the show a chance. Within a few months, it became obvious that King was right about Oprah Winfrey. As she had in Chicago, Oprah won over viewers nationwide. There had been a belief that white audiences would not watch a black talk show host, but Oprah proved conclusively that people of all races and ethnicities would watch her show, and not in just a few cities. Within six months, hers was the highest-rated talk show in syndication. By 1989, she had either surpassed or tied Phil Donahue, her main competitor, in the majority of the markets that carried her show. She did the show live in the morning in her home city of Chicago, even allowing viewers to call in and comment.

Just as in 1985 in Chicago, she went on the air in mid-November 1988 to discuss her successes and failures with dieting. She had lost sixty-seven pounds by spending four months on a liquid diet. Unfortunately, the results were so temporary that she soon put much of the weight back on. Conversations about Oprah's battles with obesity became staples of tabloids, magazines, and newspapers. It seemed that whatever she did was of great interest to large numbers of Americans, especially the women who made up the majority of her audience.

Her battle with her weight was not the only personal topic she shared with her viewers. Her very first syndicated show was about how to find Mr. or Ms. Right, but what her fans really wanted to know was if she would ever marry her longtime boyfriend, Stedman Graham. (In 2008, she still had not.) Oprah was willing to reveal things about her life that helped her to establish empathy with her guests: When she did her first show about sexual abuse, she comforted a guest by admitting that she, too, had been abused as a child. In one much-reported episode from early 1995, her guests were four women who had struggled with giving up drugs, and Oprah admitted that while in her twenties, she had used cocaine and had felt guilty about it for years. Celebrities found her easy to talk to. She had the rare ability to encourage them to reveal their own joys and struggles, in ways that did not seem scripted or artificial. Oprah became known for creating a rapport with her guests and making them feel that she cared about them. She made her audience feel the same way.

What many of her viewers didn't know was that by now, she had become wealthy. Her syndication deal with King World was a lucrative one, and in its first year alone, she made $10 million. Thanks to her ratings successes, that figure grew to $25 million in 1988. The young girl who had worn potato sacks to school had certainly come a long way, but she wasn't finished achieving. In 1986, she had started her own company, Harpo Productions (*Harpo* is *Oprah* spelled backward), and when she became its CEO, she was the first black woman to own a television and film production house. Harpo would soon go on to produce a television miniseries *(The Women of Brewster Place)* and a feature film *(Beloved)*. But the first thing it accomplished was establishing Oprah's control over her own TV show. She successfully bargained with WLS-TV and ABC (the network that carried her show locally) for a better contractual arrangement. Such negotiations had previously been carried on only by stars with the stature of Johnny Carson. But Oprah was now at that level, and neither WLS-TV nor ABC wanted to lose her. When she let them know she planned to let her current contract come to an end so she could pursue a more lucrative deal elsewhere, there was no question about giving her the control she sought. She was given ownership rights to her show, becoming one of the most powerful women in the media.

From that point on, Oprah proved herself a shrewd and resourceful businesswoman as well as a popular talk show host. By 2005, the twentieth anniversary of the *Oprah Winfrey Show*, the show was seen in 121 countries, had an average weekly viewership of forty-nine million people, and had remained the number one daytime television talk show for nineteen consecutive years. Winfrey had also founded her own magazine, *O*, in 2000, and by 2003, it had nearly three million readers. Harpo Productions also continued to generate critically acclaimed programming. In addition to producing the 1998 film adaptation of Toni Morrison's novel *Beloved*, in which Oprah costarred, Harpo produced a syndicated advice show that featured psychologist Phil McGraw, beginning in 2002, as well as a 2005 made-for-television movie based on a novel by Zora Neale Hurston, *Their Eyes Were Watching God*. But there was even further expansion: In 2006, Oprah signed a contract with XM to have her own satellite radio channel, and in 2008, she made arrangements to have a cable TV channel, purchasing the Discovery Health Network and renaming it OWN, the Oprah Winfrey Network.

THE LEGEND GROWS

By the early 1990s, Oprah's daily talk show was an essential part of American popular culture. She was attracting not just guests who discuss the typical "women's show" subjects like love and marriage, but also newsmakers and pop culture icons. In February 1993, she obtained a rare interview with controversial and reclusive superstar Michael Jackson; the show was watched by more than ninety-six million viewers. Presidential candidates have also felt that her show provides much-needed exposure to female voters: George W. Bush and Al Gore both appeared on the show during the 2000 presidential election. In fact, political figures in high-profile races often feel that her show gives them a boost: When California's candidate for governor (and former movie star) Arnold Schwarzenegger was under fire in 2003, amid accusations he had sexually harassed women and made sexist remarks, an appearance on Oprah's show softened his image and gave him a chance to tell his side of the story. Some critics saw the appearance in negative terms, however. For example, the *New York Times* said Oprah had given Schwarzenegger free publicity and that she hadn't asked him any tough questions. Still, the fact that public opinion of Schwarzenegger improved after he appeared on Oprah's show demonstrated once again her importance in the public discourse. When in 2007 she endorsed Senator Barack Obama in the primary race for the Democratic presidential nomination, critics again wondered if she was using her influence excessively, but while she held an event for him and praised him when she introduced him, she continued to have other political figures from both parties on her show.

Oprah continues to have a great influence on public perception, and media critics gave it a name: the "Oprah effect." When Oprah expresses her approval of a certain product, sales often go up dramatically. For example, in mid-November 2005, she did a segment of her show about how women too often wore the wrong-sized bra. She also invited some professional bra fitters from Nordstrom's Department Store to give fittings to members of her studio audience. After that show, sales of bras at Nordstrom's increased nearly 200 percent, and other stores saw dramatic increases in bra sales as well. In the late 1990s, she began doing an annual show called "My Favorite Things," which focuses on items she has selected because they are unique, very useful, or special in some way. They have ranged from cosmetics to clothing to small electronic devices. When it was still rather new, Oprah added the Apple iPod to her 2003 list, and sales soared. Many of her "favorite things" come from small businesses, and she stresses what good gifts these items make. She also gives the items out to members of her studio audience, creating even further buzz. Appearing on Oprah's annual list frequently puts manufacturers on the map and dramatically increases sales. It is not surprising that in 2005, *Time* magazine named Winfrey one of the "100 Most Influential People in the World."

Before There Was Oprah: Mary Margaret McBride

In the era before feminism, the only acceptable role for a female host was on a "women's show," a mid-morning program where the guests chatted about recipes, gave homemaking tips, and discussed how to be a successful wife and mother. These shows were punctuated by numerous live commercials. The queen of this genre was Mary Margaret McBride, who first broadcast from WOR in New York City in 1934 before getting into network radio, first on CBS in 1937 and then NBC in 1941. McBride had great rapport with her listeners: When she praised her sponsors' products, the listeners trusted her advice, and when she asked her audience to help with the war effort during World War II, they responded immediately. What made her show unique was her understanding that women wanted to hear about current events and the arts in addition to how to bake a pie. Because she had come to radio from a successful career writing for magazines, she knew how to do an interesting interview. Among her many guests were authors like Fanny Hurst and Langston Hughes, First Lady Eleanor Roosevelt, legendary blues composer W. C. Handy, comedian Jimmy Durante, and movie star Gary Cooper. She became so popular that her tenth-anniversary show was held at New York City's Madison Square Garden, and her fifteenth at New York City's Yankee Stadium. While her show was not able to make the leap to television, she remained a beloved radio talker until the early 1950s.

There is a down side to all this fame and influence as well. In one widely covered case, Oprah was sued because of something she said. In April 1996, during a show about dangerous foods and food-borne diseases, she made an offhanded remark about not wanting to eat hamburgers anymore because they might carry mad cow disease. Sales of hamburgers temporarily plummeted, and a group of cattlemen from Texas brought a lawsuit against her, saying she had libeled their product and caused them to lose business. The verdict went in Oprah's favor, but the case was another example of how profound Oprah's influence is perceived to be.

And it isn't just in regard to products or candidates or what to eat for dinner that Oprah's opinion makes a difference. Take Oprah's Book Club. Critics and educators had long lamented that people weren't reading as much as they used to, so in 1996, Winfrey created a book club that would introduce her audience to books she felt they ought to read. Some are well-known but underappreciated by modern audiences, such as John Steinbeck's *East of Eden*, but others are by new or unfamiliar authors, such as Wally Lamb, whose *She's Come Undone* became a best seller thanks to his exposure on Winfrey's show. Unfortunately, one of the books she chose got her some unwanted bad publicity: In 2005, she selected what was supposed to be a work of non-fiction about addiction and recovery by James Frey, *A Million Little Pieces*. It was soon revealed that the author was dishonest and that many events in the book were fictional. Oprah had to defend herself and the integrity of her club on *Larry King Live*, and she then did a show during which she confronted Frey and demanded the truth. Still, the book club does in fact encourage more people to read and to buy books they might not have otherwise considered.

Oprah has also become well known for her generosity. In addition to sharing her "favorite things" with her audience, in September 2004 she gave every member of her audience a new Pontiac sedan. But far beyond working with various sponsors to get gifts to give to her viewers, she has become known as one of the world's biggest philanthropists. Among her gifts has been $5 million in scholarships for the historically black Morehouse College in Atlanta. She also set up the Angel Network, a charitable foundation that awards grants to fund projects that help the poor, especially projects related to literacy and education. In 2007, funds from the Angel Network were instrumental in making a project of her own come to fruition: She founded the Oprah Winfrey Leadership Academy for Girls, a new school located near Johannesburg, South Africa. She told the media that her future plans include opening another school in South Africa, this one coeducational.

Even after more than twenty years as a talk show host, she remains one of the true iconic figures in the mass media, who has used her celebrity stature to bring about positive change and who still uses her talk show to focus on issues she thinks will matter to her audience. It is doubtful that anyone in the media, male or female, is more influential than Oprah Winfrey.

OPRAH WINFREY TIMELINE

1954: born in Kosciusko, Mississippi

1971: wins beauty contest that leads to an audition at a Nashville radio station, WVOL

1973: begins working as a reporter for WTVF-TV in Nashville

1976: hired by WJZ-TV in Baltimore as a reporter and coanchor of the evening news

1984: hired by WLS-TV in Chicago as host of "AM Chicago"

1985: chosen for a movie role in *The Color Purple*

1986: national syndication of the *Oprah Winfrey Show* by King World; founds Harpo Productions

1996: establishes Oprah's Book Club

2005: twenty-fifth anniversary of her syndicated show; named by *Time* magazine as one of the world's one hundred most influential people

FURTHER READING

Anderson, Jon. "Wingin' It with Channel 7's Oprah Winfrey." *Chicago Tribune Tempo*, 13 March 1984, pp. 1, 4.

Colander, Pat. "Oprah Winfrey's Odyssey: Talk Show Host to Mogul." *New York Times*, 12 March 1989, p. H31.

Harris, Paul. "The Observer Profile: Oprah Winfrey." *The Observer* (London), 20 November 2005, p. 27.

Morgan, Thomas. "Troubled Girl's Evolution into an Oscar Nominee." *New York Times*, 4 March 1986, p. C17.

Moss, Clarisse Ritter. "Oprah: There's So Much Kid in Me, I Don't Even Feel like an Adult Yet." *Chicago Daily Herald*, 25 October 1984, Section 3, pp. 1, 3.

Nelson, Jill. "The Man Who Saved Oprah Winfrey." *Washington Post*, 14 December 1986, p. W30.

Novit, Mel. "Oprah: Talk Show Dynamo Treats the Audience like a Friend." *Syracuse (NY) Post-Standard*, 4 September 1986, p. A9.

Ouchi, Monica Soto. "Oprah Support Starts Run on Nordstrom Bras." *Seattle Times*, 18 November 2005, pp.

Tracy, Kathy. "Marathon Woman." *Variety*, 21 November 2005, p. B1.

Winfrey, Lee. "Praise from All Corners for New Talk Show Host." *Syracuse (NY) Herald Journal*, 9 September 1986, p. 44.

Appendix A: What People Were Talking About

1920

(16 January) The Eighteenth Amendment to the U.S. Constitution is enacted, bringing prohibition to the United States. Whether alcoholic beverages should or should not be sold becomes a topic for numerous radio speakers.

(20 August) Radio station 8MK (later known as WWJ) in Detroit does its first broadcast. By the end of the month, the station has aired local election results and news reports. It is the first radio station owned by a newspaper—the *Detroit News*—and some historians believe it is the first commercial radio station in the United States.

(26 August) Women are granted the right to vote, as the Nineteenth Amendment to the U.S. Constitution is enacted. The League of Women Voters is founded, and speakers from this group are heard on the air throughout the 1920s.

(2 November) Republican Warren G. Harding is elected president, and the results are broadcast on KDKA in Pittsburgh. Owned by Westinghouse, this station is regarded by many as the first commercial station in North America, while others believe Montreal's XWA, Detroit's 8MK, or Boston's 1XE were all on the air before the better-known KDKA. What cannot be debated is that 1920 is the first year in which radio stations begin providing the public with access to the news as it is happening. Harding is a strong supporter of radio and is heard on the air several times.

1921

(23 May) *Shuffle Along*, a musical produced, written, and performed by African Americans, opens on Broadway in New York. Featuring the songs of

Eubie Blake and Noble Sissle, it runs for more than five hundred performances, and a road version achieves just as much success. Meanwhile, several songs from the show become big hits that are heard on the radio. (Detractors will soon say radio plays "too much dance music.")

(5 August) Major league baseball is broadcast on the radio, as the Phillies and Pirates game is carried by KDKA in Pittsburgh, as well as by the two other Westinghouse-owned stations, WJZ in Newark, New Jersey, and WBZ in Springfield, Massachusetts.

(2 November) Concert pianist Dai Buell performs from the studios of 1XE in Medford Hillside, Massachusetts, and is heard by thousands of listeners all over the United States. People are amazed that they can hear a live concert without leaving home.

1922

(early March) Long-distance telephone calling is the newest sensation, even though a minute costs five dollars during the day and people must wait their turn to be put through by the operator.

(14 June) President Harding becomes the first president heard on the air when he dedicates the Francis Scott Key Memorial in Baltimore and the event is broadcast.

(16 June) Inventor Guglielmo Marconi arrives in the United States to work with engineers on the reception problems that plague radio listeners.

(21 July) When WIAE receives its license, Marie (Mrs. Robert) Zimmerman of Vinton, Iowa, becomes the first woman to own a radio station.

(4 October) Fans hear play-by-play descriptions of baseball's World Series between the New York Yankees and the New York Giants, broadcast from the Polo Grounds in New York City. Renowned sportswriter Grantland Rice is the sportscaster.

1923

(4 January) French psychologist and self-help guru Emil Coué arrives in the United States to demonstrate his self-help theories, becoming big news on radio and in print. Coué claims that diseases can be cured by autosuggestion, and he starts a health fad in America as he did in France. He recommends chanting, "Every day, in every way, I'm getting better and better." (He will die suddenly of overwork in July 1926.)

(2 August) His administration plagued by scandals, which have caused him considerable stress, President Harding takes ill. He dies suddenly in a hotel in San Francisco, having recently completed a trip to Alaska. Out of respect, many radio stations are silent for a day, except for broadcasts of the president's funeral. Vice President Calvin Coolidge is sworn in as president.

(10 December) President Coolidge pays tribute to the late President Harding in a radio address that is heard all across the country.

1924

(12 February) Innovative composer George Gershwin performs "Rhapsody in Blue" in public for the first time. Gershwin's modern jazz composition is soon recorded by bandleader Paul Whiteman and it becomes a hit. Meanwhile, jazz and dance music continue to be very popular on radio, as both black and white orchestras are heard on the air.

(12 June and 9 July) Ready to choose their presidential candidates, the Republicans meet in Cleveland in June, and the Democrats meet in New York in July. Radio covers both conventions.

(4 November) Republican Calvin Coolidge is elected president by a wide margin over John W. Davis. Two women are also elected governor: Nellie T. Ross of Wyoming and Miriam "Ma" Ferguson of Texas.

1925

(4 March) A nationwide radio audience is listening when Calvin Coolidge is inaugurated for his first full term as president.

(5 May) High school biology teacher John T. Scopes is arrested for teaching the theory of evolution, contrary to Tennessee law. His trial will become a major media event, covered by print and by radio. In late July, he will be convicted and fined one hundred dollars.

(8 August) The Ku Klux Klan, which experienced a dramatic rise in membership throughout the early 1920s, holds a march in Washington, DC, and over forty thousand Klansmen take part.

1926

(9 May) As exploration by air captures the national imagination, Lieutenant Commander Richard E. Byrd successfully flies to the North Pole.

(18 May) California evangelist and radio star Aimee Semple McPherson vanishes, and there is much speculation about what has happened to her. She later reappears, claiming she was kidnapped. In reality, she had run off with Kenneth G. Ormiston, a former colleague at her Los Angeles radio station.

(15 November) The first national radio network, NBC (National Broadcasting Company), takes to the air. It will feature major name performers, who are paid by advertising revenues. Among those who perform at the debut of the network are comedian Will Rogers, opera star Mary Garden, the New York Symphony Orchestra, and vaudevillians Weber and Fields.

1927

(23 February) Congress creates the first government agency to oversee and regulate American broadcasting: the Federal Radio Commission (FRC).

(21 May) Charles A. Lindbergh becomes the first aviator to fly across the Atlantic, from New York to Paris, in his plane the *Spirit of St. Louis*. Radio covers his journey and he becomes a national hero.

(2 August) To the surprise of many, President Coolidge announces he will not run for reelection.

(30 September) New York Yankees Slugger Babe Ruth hits his sixtieth home run in one season, a record that will endure for more than three decades.

(6 October) The first successful talking picture, *The Jazz Singer*, starring Al Jolson, opens in New York City. Although there had been earlier experiments with talking pictures, this one does so well that it signals the end of the silent film era.

1928

(12 January) Ruth Snyder is executed in the electric chair for the murder of her husband. A photographer with a hidden camera captures the image, and it appears on the front page of the *New York Daily News*. It also revives the debate over capital punishment, and over whether women should be executed.

(19 March) A local Chicago program originally called *Sam 'n' Henry* appears on the air at WMAQ as *Amos 'n' Andy*. It will find a home on the NBC radio network in August 1929 and become one of America's most popular radio comedies. It will also generate some controversy among black community leaders because it features two white men playing the roles of stereotypical black characters.

(17 June) Amelia Earhart becomes the first woman to successfully complete a flight across the Atlantic.

(29 June) The Democrats nominate Alfred E. "Al" Smith, a Catholic, for president. Unfortunately, prejudice against Catholics is still a factor, and Smith will ultimately lose the election in November to Republican Herbert Hoover.

(1 December) The American Academy of Arts and Letters decides to give an annual gold medal to the radio announcer with the best diction.

1929

(18 January) Entrepreneur William S. Paley purchases a struggling radio network, the Columbia Phonograph Broadcasting Company, and renames it the Columbia Broadcasting System (CBS). It will soon become known for its news broadcasts.

(14 February) Gang violence makes the news, as six gangsters are shot dead in Chicago by a rival gang. The event becomes known as the St. Valentine's Day Massacre.

(23 April) The first annual award for good radio diction is awarded to NBC announcer Milton J. Cross. Also receiving a gold medal for good diction on the stage is actress Julia Marlowe.

(18 August) The first air races for women, jokingly called the Powder Puff Derby, attracts some of the country's best women aviators, including Amelia Earhart, Bobbi Trout, and Gladys O'Donnell. The race, won by Louise Thaden, receives extensive press coverage.

(24 October) Known as Black Thursday. Prices on the stock market collapse. It is followed on 29 October by an even worse day, Black Tuesday, as the Great Depression is about to begin.

1930

(7 February) Researcher Archibald Crossley puts the finishing touches on what will become the first radio ratings service, so that advertisers will know which programs have the most listeners. The Cooperative Analysis of Broadcasting (CAB) will be the only ratings service until 1935, when a competitor, the Hooper ratings, comes along.

(21 April) A terrible tragedy occurs at the Ohio State Penitentiary, as 318 prisoners are killed in a fire. Local radio station WAIU in Columbus not only reports on the event but is instrumental in calling for more help to fight the blaze. However, when one station (WEAO) finds a way to interview some of the prisoners, it angers the warden and raises questions about whether radio is making a bad situation worse.

(23 July) In Detroit, Gerald W. "Jerry" Buckley, a popular radio announcer who has been a vocal critic of organized crime, is shot dead. Thousands attend his funeral, as speculation about who ordered his murder continues for weeks.

(4 November) The Democrats gain control of the House of Representatives in mid-term elections, but the Republicans are still in control of the Senate.

1931

(7 January) According to U.S. government statistics, between four and five million people are unemployed. As the Depression continues, radio provides the public with a welcome means of escape.

(11 February) The great inventor Thomas Edison dies, and tributes to him are heard on nearly every radio station.

(6 March) A unique radio newsmagazine takes to the air. Broadcast on Friday night on the CBS radio network, in conjunction with *Time* magazine, the *March of Time* makes the news interesting by acting out each week's stories as dramatic skits. Actors and actresses are chosen to sound as much like the actual newsmakers as possible.

(17 October) Gangster Al Capone is sentenced to eleven years in prison for tax evasion.

1932

(15 February) The Federal Radio Commission relaxes the rules about playing phonograph records; previously, before a record could be played, on-air personnel had to inform the listeners that they were about to hear something recorded rather than live. Now, such announcements become optional.

(1 March) One of the year's biggest news stories takes place when the infant son of aviator Charles A. Lindbergh is kidnapped. The baby's body will be found on 12 May. The hunt for the murderer and the subsequent trial will consume the nation.

(2 July) People begin talking about the New Deal because the Democratic presidential candidate, Franklin Delano Roosevelt, starts to use that term.

(8 November) As the Depression drags on, Franklin Delano Roosevelt wins the presidential election in a landslide.

(9 December) First Lady Eleanor Roosevelt begins a series of regular broadcasts, sometimes about life in the White House, sometimes about current events.

1933

(5 January) Former president Calvin Coolidge dies of a sudden heart attack. A longtime friend of radio, he is memorialized on a number of stations.

(4 March) Newly elected president Roosevelt is inaugurated. (From now on, inauguration ceremonies will be moved to 20 January, as a result of the recently passed Twentieth Amendment.) Roosevelt appoints Frances Perkins as his new Secretary of Labor she is the first woman to serve in any president's cabinet.

(12 March) President Roosevelt delivers his first Fireside Chat on radio, to a nationwide audience.

(23 June) Without much fanfare, a new morning show goes on the air on NBC Blue. *The Breakfast Club*, with host Don McNeill, will become a very successful and long-running program, paving the way for numerous imitators.

(5 December) Prohibition finally ends as the Twenty-first Amendment to the Constitution is adopted.

1934

(28 May) In Ontario, Canada, the Dionne quintuplets are born. The five little girls will become a media obsession.

(19 June) The Federal Communications Commission (FCC) is created to replace the Federal Radio Commission.

(21 June) Meeting in Cincinnati, Catholic bishops who are active in the recently formed Legion of Decency announce the creation of a national council to review movies and decide which films are immoral or indecent. They organize boycotts and also encourage Catholics to abstain from attending such films.

(22 July) The notorious gangster John Dillinger, declared Public Enemy Number One by the FBI, is shot dead by federal agents. Crime shows on radio become a topic of debate, as some critics believe they glorify criminal behavior.

(29 September) A new radio network, the Mutual Broadcasting System, is on the air. It will soon be known for popular programs like *The Lone Ranger* and *The Shadow*.

1935

(2 January) The trial of Bruno Hauptmann begins. He is accused of the kidnapping and murder of aviator Charles Lindbergh's son. The trial receives

intensive media coverage. Hauptmann is found guilty on 13 February and sentenced to death.

(3 February) *Make-Believe Ballroom* makes its debut on New York City's WNEW, featuring announcer and news reporter Martin Block. Block plays phonograph records and asks his listeners to imagine the most famous bands performing onstage in a beautiful ballroom. The show proves popular, and Block goes on to become a legendary and influential disc jockey.

(24 March) *Major Bowes' Original Amateur Hour* debuts on the NBC radio network, after first being a local hit show in New York City. Much like later TV shows where contestants compete in hopes of being discovered, the radio version takes America by storm, becoming so popular that it often receives as many as ten thousand applications a week. Some hopefuls sell everything they own to get to New York City to audition.

(24 May) Night baseball is played for the first time in the major leagues, at Crossley Field in Cincinnati, Ohio. The hometown Reds defeat the Philadelphia Phillies two to one.

(30 May) *America's Town Meeting of the Air*, one of the first current events shows to actively involve both the studio audience and the listeners at home, goes on the air. On the show, guest pundits debate the major issues of the day. Not only are audience members allowed to ask questions, but they can also heckle speakers with whom they disagree.

(15 August) Americans are stunned to learn that popular radio humorist Will Rogers and aviator Wiley Post have died in a plane crash in Alaska.

1936

(3 April) Bruno Hauptmann, the man convicted of the murder of the Lindbergh baby, is executed in the electric chair at the New Jersey state prison.

(5–16 August) At the Summer Olympics in Berlin, the star is black athlete Jesse Owens. Hitler's philosophy of white supremacy is seriously challenged when Owens wins four gold medals.

(31 October) Using faulty polling techniques, the respected news and commentary magazine *Literary Digest* predicts that the Republican presidential candidate, Alfred "Alf" Landon will defeat President Roosevelt.

(3 November) President Roosevelt is easily reelected. His policies have inspired considerable debate, but he and his wife, Eleanor, remain enormously popular.

(23 November) The first issue of *Life* magazine appears. Published by Henry Luce, who also publishes *Time*, *Life* specializes in photojournalism and illustrates current news in some of the era's best photography.

(11 December) King Edward VIII of England abdicates his throne to marry an American divorcée, Wallis Simpson.

1937

(20 January) For the first time since the Twentieth Amendment went into effect, the inauguration of the new president occurs on this day. President Roosevelt begins his second term.

(6 May) The German dirigible *Hindenberg* explodes while trying to land in Lakehurst, New Jersey, killing thirty-six people. Radio announcer Herb Morrison, in Lakehurst for another event, provides live reporting of the tragedy.

(2 July) While on a round-the-world flight, the famous woman aviator Amelia Earhart vanishes over the Pacific Ocean. Neither she nor her plane are ever found.

1938

(12 March) With conditions in Europe becoming more dire, CBS sends Edward R. Murrow to report from the scene. His first report is from Austria, and he will soon cover the news from England, with his famous introduction "This . . . is London." As conditions in Europe worsen, radio networks expand their news coverage.

(22 June) In a rematch and another blow at Hitler's belief in white supremacy, heavyweight champion Joe Louis of the United States defeats German boxer Max Schmeling in only two minutes and four seconds. More than seventy thousand see the match live at New York City's Yankee Stadium; interest in the fight is so high that it is broadcast worldwide, in four languages.

(18 July) Major Edwin Howard Armstrong, inventor of a new technology called *frequency modulation* (FM), promises a solution to one of AM radio's biggest problems: static and interference from the atmosphere. He puts his first "staticless" FM station, W2XMN, on the air in Alpine, New Jersey. A few days later, on 24 July, Boston radio executive John Shepard III opens his first FM station, W1XOJ, in the central Massachusetts town of Paxton.

(30 October) Orson Welles is on the CBS radio network with a presentation of H. G. Wells's science-fiction drama *War of the Worlds*, about an alien invasion from Mars. Unfortunately, in a number of cities, people are convinced that the invasion is real, and a panic ensues. The event proves how influential radio can be in persuading the public, and how seriously people take what they hear. Many sociologists and researchers, worried about whether radio can be used for propaganda, begin studying the effect that radio is believed to have.

(1 November) In Baltimore, Maryland, the popular racehorse Seabiscuit competes against War Admiral, a former winner of racing's Triple Crown, in what is billed as the match of the century. Seabiscuit wins and is named Horse of the Year.

(20 and 27 November) Father Charles Coughlin, the popular radio priest whose weekly talks have been enjoyed by millions, has become increasingly more hateful in his speeches, lashing out at President Roosevelt and "the international bankers." Now he gives two anti-Semitic talks and appears to be defending the Nazis. A few radio stations decide to drop his show. He will be forced off the air in 1940, thanks to new standards issued by the National Association of Broadcasters.

1939

(30 April) The New York World's Fair officially opens, featuring exhibitions of the "world of tomorrow": new technology, new inventions, and a demonstration of television. The newsreels and radio try to predict what life will be like fifty to a hundred years from now.

(2 May) Iron man Lou Gehrig of baseball's New York Yankees ends his amazing string of consecutive games, at 2,130.

(4 July) Suffering from the symptoms of Amyotrophic lateral sclerosis (ALS), Gehrig is forced to retire. More than 62,000 fans crowd Yankee Stadium for Lou Gehrig Appreciation Day. Gehrig gives a speech in which he says that despite the illness, ". . . today I consider myself the luckiest man on the face of the earth."

1940

(9 February) Popular boxing champion Joe Louis defends his world championship, defeating Arturo Godoy; Louis will also defeat Godoy in a rematch on 20 June. (Many other sporting events, including the Olympics, are being canceled due to the war in Europe.)

(23 March) One of radio's more unusual shows, *Truth or Consequences* debuts. It is part quiz show, part comedy. Created and hosted by Ralph Edwards, it offers participants prizes if they get the right answer; if they are wrong, they must do something humorous or embarrassing. The show is wildly popular and will ultimately transfer to TV.

(30 April) First Lady Eleanor Roosevelt begins a series of programs on the NBC Red network, sponsored by Sweetheart Soap. She doesn't talk politics, but she does have guests and chats about causes that matter to her. She donates

her $3,000 salary to the American Friends Service Committee, a Quaker group committed to peace.

(16 September) President Roosevelt signs the Selective Training and Service Act, which requires all men between the ages of twenty and thirty-six to register for military training. It is the first law in U.S. history to require a peacetime draft.

(5 November) For the first time in history, a U.S. president is elected to a third term, as President Roosevelt wins decisively over Wendell L. Willkie.

1941

(1 May) The controversial movie *Citizen Kane*, produced and directed by Orson Welles, finally opens. It is believed to be about the life of publisher William Randolph Hearst, who has not wanted it released.

(1 July) WNBT (formerly experimental station W2XBS), NBC's first television station, goes on the air, as does CBS's WCBW. Not many people are aware of this event, since very few people own television sets.

(2 July) Baseball legend Lou Gehrig dies at age thirty-seven. The illness that first paralyzed him and then caused his death will come to be known as "Lou Gehrig's Disease."

(16 July) "Joltin' Joe" DiMaggio of the New York Yankees sets a new baseball record when he gets a hit in his fifty-sixth consecutive game. (That same year, Boston's Ted Williams sets a batting record, hitting .406, but DiMaggio wins baseball's annual Most Valuable Player Award.)

(7 December) The Japanese attack the U.S. military base at Pearl Harbor, Hawaii. This momentous event results in a massive print and broadcasting response. The following day, President Roosevelt's speech asking Congress for a declaration of war has the highest ratings in broadcasting history.

1942

(9 February) Clocks are moved ahead by one hour to save electricity; the president says the change should be called "war time," rather than "daylight savings time," so that becomes the accepted terminology.

(9 May) Graham McNamee, one of radio's first and most popular network announcers, dies suddenly of a brain embolism at fifty-three. His cheery "How do you do, ladies and gentlemen of the radio audience" became a catch phrase in early broadcasting. McNamee had done it all—news, sports, and commentary—and he was the MC of many popular NBC programs.

(14 May) Through the efforts of Massachusetts congresswoman Edith Nourse Rogers, the Women's Army Auxiliary Corps (WAAC) is created. Oveta Culp Hobby, wife of Texas governor William P. Hobby, is its first director. Debates continue over whether women should serve in the military.

(6 October) People are impressed by popular vocalist Kate Smith's amazing twenty-hour radio marathon, during which she raises nearly $2 million for war bonds.

(28 November) The Cocoanut Grove nightclub fire in Boston kills over 490 people and raises serious questions about fire safety in overcrowded clubs.

1943

(31 March) Entertainment keeps people from thinking about the war; the new musical *Oklahoma,* written by Richard Rodgers and Oscar Hammerstein II opens on Broadway.

(16 June) In the latest celebrity scandal, fifty-four-year-old actor Charlie Chaplin marries eighteen-year-old Oona O'Neill, daughter of playwright Eugene O'Neill.

(4 July) The American Forces Radio Service (AFRS) officially takes to the air; it is a network created by the U.S. War Department to broadcast to the troops overseas and boost their morale. Among its most popular shows is *Command Performance*, which features the biggest stars from stage, screen, and radio.

(24 December) General Dwight D. Eisenhower is named Supreme Commander of the Allied Forces in Europe.

1944

(6 June) War news continues to dominate every conversation. Today is D-Day, which becomes the most decisive battle of the war. The Allied forces, under General Eisenhower's command, mount a massive (and successful) invasion in Normandy, France; it will lead to the liberation of France from Nazi control.

(26 June) At the Republican convention, New York Governor Thomas E. Dewey is nominated for president.

(19 July) President Roosevelt is nominated for an unprecedented fourth term. He chooses Missouri Senator Harry S. Truman as his running mate. Roosevelt wins his fourth term in November.

(15 December) Popular bandleader and now U.S. Army Major Glenn Miller is missing. His plane disappears on a flight over the English Channel and is never found.

1945

(15 January) A new talk and variety show, *House Party*, debuts on CBS radio, starring Art Linkletter. In addition to contests, music, and fashion tips, it features a segment where five or six young children are interviewed, with often-amusing results.

(12 April) Due to President Roosevelt's sudden death, Vice President Harry Truman becomes president. The nation goes into mourning, as radio stations remove all commercials and programs deemed inappropriate; stations play only tributes, commemorations, and classical and religious music until his funeral.

(8 May) V-E Day. President Truman officially announces the German surrender and the Allied victory; the Hooper ratings service estimates that more than thirty-six million listeners hear his speech on radio, an all-time high.

(8 May) One of radio's most inspirational and widely praised programs, Norman Corwin's *On a Note of Triumph*, is broadcast for the first time (it will ultimately be recorded and released as a set of 78-rpm records). Corwin, an award-winning writer and producer, says he created the program to celebrate and reflect on the Allied victory in Europe.

(6 August) A new television network, DuMont, makes its debut with New York City's WABD and Washington, DC's WTTG. It is owned by inventor and scientist Allen B. DuMont, rather than by a radio network like NBC or CBS.

(8 September) Bess Myerson of New York is named Miss America. She is the first Jew ever to win the crown, and her reign will at times be marred by anti-Semitism.

(5 October) *Meet the Press* makes its debut. It is a radio press conference, in which a newsmaker is questioned by a panel of journalists. Its cocreator is Martha Rountree, who for a time serves as its host. The show will eventually move to television, and more than sixty years later, *Meet the Press* will still be on the air.

(6 October) A panel discussion show for women, *Leave it to the Girls*, debuts on Mutual. Another show created by Martha Rountree, it is a battle of the sexes, 1940s-style, with a panel of celebrity women and a token male answering questions about love, relationships, and other topics. In the late 1940s, it will be seen briefly in a TV version.

1946

(14 June) Major Edward Bowes dies. In his heyday during the 1930s, his *Original Amateur Hour* was one of the most listened-to programs on the radio and inspired thousands of would-be stars to audition in the hope of achieving fame and fortune. Few ever succeeded, but the show did give a small number of performers a start, including opera star Beverly Sills, pop singer Teresa Brewer, and Frank Sinatra, who is at that time a young vocalist with the Hoboken Four.

(20 December) Today, a movie still regarded as a classic Christmas film, *It's a Wonderful Life*, directed by Frank Capra, opens to mixed reviews, as many reviewers find it overly sentimental. With the war over and people trying to get on with their lives, the hopeful message resonates.

(24 December) Showing what TV is capable of, New York City's DuMont station, WABD, televises a church service, from Grace Episcopal Church, in one of the earliest examples of televised worship.

1947

(23 January) After not being heard on radio since her husband died, popular former First Lady Eleanor Roosevelt returns to the air to raise money for the March of Dimes.

(15 April) Jackie Robinson of the Brooklyn Dodgers becomes the first black player in major league baseball.

(4 October) Bing Crosby's popular program, *Philco Radio Time*, returns to the air, with far better sound quality than in his previous season, thanks to improvements in audiotape. In subsequent weeks, his engineer Jack Mullin will create an applause track and a laugh track to enhance Crosby's show.

(18 November) Proving that radio is still important, over nine million people listen to President Truman's address to a special session of Congress, according to the Hooper ratings service.

1948

(15 August) CBS radio news anchor Douglas Edwards does his first TV newscast. Soon, many of the best-known radio newscasters will also be on television, and news will gradually become more visual. (In the early years of TV news, the stories are written as if they are for radio only.)

(30 June) The transistor is demonstrated for the first time by the Bell Telephone Laboratories. Not many people are impressed, but this invention will

be the savior of radio, making the small, portable transistor radio available for rock-and-roll-loving teens to carry anywhere.

(30 September) The FCC announces a freeze on new television licenses. The freeze is supposed to be temporary, so that the FCC can resolve some technical matters, but it lasts until April 1952.

(2 November) In an upset, Harry S. Truman wins the presidency after polls and pundits (and the early edition of the *Chicago Tribune*) predicted a win by his opponent Governor Dewey.

1949

(17 January) One of radio's most popular comedies, *The Goldbergs*, moves to television.

(25 January) Television's first annual Emmy awards are handed out by the Academy of Television Arts and Sciences. Only programs seen on TV in Los Angeles are eligible for the first awards. One of the first shows to win is *Pantomime Quiz*, a program similar to charades. After winning the local award, *Pantomime Quiz* is picked up by CBS for national broadcast.

(1 June) Forty thousand fans of Mary Margaret McBride pack Yankee Stadium to express their appreciation on the fifteenth anniversary of her radio show.

(3 October) The first radio station owned by African Americans, WERD, goes on the air in Atlanta. (Another station, WDIA in Memphis, was broadcasting programming for blacks in 1948, but the station was owned by whites.) Owner Jesse B. Blayton Sr.'s WERD will program not only music but news and talk shows of interest to the black community and will be emulated by other black radio stations in the 1950s.

1950

(16 February) The popular quiz show *What's My Line?* debuts on CBS-TV. Celebrities on the panel try to guess the occupation of the contestant, with often hilarious results. Among the celebrities who will be on the show during its long run are Steve Allen, Arlene Francis, and columnist Dorothy Kilgallen. The host is John Daly, who is also a news reporter.

(19 March) In golf, one of America's most popular female athletes, Mildred "Babe" Didrikson Zaharias wins the U.S. Women's Open.

(22 June) *Red Channels: The Report of Communist Influence in Radio and Television* is first issued. It will be used by Senator Joseph McCarthy to accuse numerous people of communist subversion.

(25 June) The Korean War begins. Two days later, President Truman orders U.S. Armed Forces to aid South Korea, since North Korea is being aided by the Chinese communists. Whether the United States should be in Korea will become the subject of considerable debate.

1951

(25 June) Color television is introduced to the public—sort of. CBS broadcasts a popular one-hour variety program, the *Ed Sullivan Show*, in color, using its own system and its own compatible TV sets. Unfortunately, there are only two dozen sets able to receive the CBS color broadcast. (Later, a competitive system by RCA wins out, and all color TVs will be compatible with RCA's system.)

(28 June) *Amos 'n' Andy* comes to TV, after years on radio. It is the first TV show with an all-black cast (replacing radio's white cast), and it is immediately criticized for stereotyping African Americans.

(18 November) Edward R. Murrow's *See It Now* debuts on TV. (It was called *Hear It Now* on radio.)

(6 December) The first Code of Practices for television is introduced by a committee of television executives. It is similar in many ways to the Hays Code that has regulated movies (no profanity or vulgarity, no ridicule of the clergy, no glorification of crime), and those TV stations that agree to its standards are allowed to display the Seal of Good Practice.

1952

(14 January) NBC's first morning news and variety show, *Today*, debuts, with host Dave Garroway.

(2 March) As the red scare expands, the U.S. Supreme Court rules that people who are considered subversives can be barred from teaching in the public schools.

(26 July) At the Democratic National Convention, Governor Adlai Stevenson becomes the presidential nominee.

(1 September) The popular CBS radio show *House Party* makes its television debut. It still stars Art Linkletter and still has the popular segment featuring the children who give adorable replies to the questions Linkletter asks them.

(19 September) *Superman* debuts on TV. Based on the well-known comic book, it stars George Reeves. In an insecure time, with the red scare and the

Korean War going on, this children's program features a clear-cut view of good and evil and a hero who always triumphs.

(4 November) Dwight D. Eisenhower, the popular World War II general, is elected U.S. president, with Richard M. Nixon as his vice president.

1953

(19 January) In a major media event, millions of Americans watch *I Love Lucy* on the night Lucille Ball has her baby. (Ball was actually having a baby in real life, not just on TV; the newspapers covered the birth like a news story because of her celebrity at the time.)

(25 May) KUHT in Houston goes on the air. It is the first educational television station, a project that Frieda Hennock of the FCC has championed, and it is part of the newly created National Educational Television network (NET), which will later be replaced by the Public Broadcasting System (PBS).

(19 June) In the midst of the cold war, Julius and Ethel Rosenberg are put to death for espionage. Their execution will spark heated debate over the death penalty, and questions will persist about whether they were really guilty.

1954

(20 January) The National Negro Network makes its debut. Created by Chicago-based advertising executive W. Leonard Evans, it provides syndicated programs for black radio stations.

(9 March) Edward R. Murrow begins his series of exposés about Senator Joseph McCarthy.

(17 May) The U.S. Supreme Court rules in *Brown v. the Board of Education of Topeka* that racial segregation in U.S. public schools is unconstitutional.

(14 June) Still caught up in the red scare, Congress changes the words of the Pledge of Allegiance, adding "under God." Acknowledging devotion to God is meant to differentiate Americans from the communists, who practice atheism.

(1 September) Hurricane Carol strikes the East Coast, killing sixty-eight. Among the news photographs of the damage is one of the WBZ-TV tower in Boston, which falls, hitting several cars in the station parking lot. Fortunately, no one is injured.

(27 September) *Tonight*, a late-night variety show, makes its debut on NBC. Steve Allen is the first host.

(7 November) *Face the Nation* makes its debut. It is a Sunday morning talk show on which major newsmakers are interviewed.

1955

(9 July) The first top-forty record to reach number one is "Rock Around the Clock" by Bill Haley and the Comets. Musical tastes now begin to change, thanks in large part to the baby boomers, and top-forty hits will start to dominate AM radio.

(1 September) Unable to find work because he has been blacklisted as a communist, television actor Philip Loeb, formerly of *The Goldbergs,* commits suicide.

(8 September) Everyone is wondering if there's life on Mars when the National Geographic Society announces the presence of blue green areas on the planet, which some speculate might be signs of vegetation.

1956

(28 January) Elvis Presley makes his first TV appearance on the *Dorsey Brothers Stage Show.* (The Dorsey Brothers' success originated in the big-band era, and they are probably quite puzzled by this rock-and-roll sensation and his suggestive dance moves.) Presley sings "Shake, Rattle and Roll" and "I Got a Woman."

(29 October) Videotape is used for the first time on a newscast when Douglas Edwards's East Coast evening news show is recorded for play later on the West Coast.

(6 November) President Eisenhower is reelected; he is the first Republican to be reelected since 1900.

1957

(22 January) The popular game show *Truth or Consequences* is the first network show to be videotaped.

(2 May) His reign of terror at an end, Senator Joseph McCarthy dies at the age of forty-eight.

(12 July) A scientific link between smoking and lung cancer is established, according to the U.S. Surgeon General. Radio and TV face a dilemma: How much of the story should they report, since most of the news shows are sponsored by cigarette companies?

(5 August) *American Bandstand* with Dick Clark debuts. It has been a local hit in Philadelphia, but now it is on ABC, where young baby boomers will watch faithfully to learn the newest dances; boomers also become fans of the show's photogenic teenaged couples who dance to the hit songs.

(24 September) President Eisenhower has to send a thousand U.S. Army troops to restore the peace when racial unrest occurs in Little Rock, Arkansas, caused by resistance to the desegregation of Central High School.

(4 October) The Soviet Union launches the first satellite, Sputnik I; American scientists are stunned by the USSR's preceding the United States into space, and a major initiative is introduced to regain U.S. superiority.

1958

(28 January) The popular African American catcher of baseball's Brooklyn Dodgers, Roy Campanella, is in a car accident and is left permanently paralyzed.

(4 April) In the latest celebrity scandal, Lana Turner's fourteen-year-old daughter stabs and kills Turner's gangster boyfriend, ostensibly because the boyfriend was abusive to Turner.

(15 October) The first indication that popular big-money quiz shows may have been rigged surfaces when a notebook with answers to the questions turns up, causing the show *Dotto* to be canceled. On 16 October, the most popular quiz show of all, *Twenty-One*, is also canceled, with no explanation. A year later, congressional hearings will reveal that even the most beloved contestant, Charles Van Doren, was given all the answers ahead of time. Quiz shows will vanish from the air for years.

(17 October) Videotape is now available in color. The first show to use it is a special on NBC, *An Evening with Fred Astaire.*

1959

(3 February) Three rock stars—Buddy Holly, Richie Valens, and J. P. Richardson (The Big Bopper)—die in a plane crash, a traumatic event for young baby boomers. This date is later referred to as "the day the music died."

(9 April) Determined to get back in the space race, the National Aeronautic and Space Administration (NASA) selects the first seven men to prepare to be astronauts. All are military test pilots, and one will be selected to go up in the Project Mercury space capsule, scheduled for 1961.

(4 May) The first Grammy awards are presented by the National Academy of Recording Arts and Sciences. Although rock-and-roll has come to dominate record sales, the winners are all from the older adult genre.

(15 September) Soviet premier Nikita Khrushchev comes to America for talks with President Eisenhower. The talks are reported as cordial.

1960

(29 February) In St. Louis, one of the first full-service radio formats, makes its debut. A format that features no music, and relies on a combination of news, sports, and call-in talk, is inaugurated at KMOX, where it is called *At Your Service*. The full-service format will be emulated by a number of AM radio stations seeking to target the thirty-five- to fifty-four-year-old audience.

(13 September) The FCC bans payola in broadcasting, with heavy fines for those who violate the ruling. It is the culmination of the Payola Scandal of 1959, in which a handful of powerful disc jockeys were accused of taking bribes from record companies in exchange for giving their records extra play. One, Alan Freed, is driven out of radio entirely.

(26 September) The first in a series of presidential debates is shown on TV, between presidential candidates John F. Kennedy and Richard M. Nixon. An estimated seventy-five million people watch. Kennedy makes an excellent impression on TV; Nixon does not.

(17 October) Charles Van Doren, former quiz show champion, has now been discredited, and he is indicted for perjury. He has lied to a grand jury investigating whether the TV quiz shows were in fact rigged.

(8 November) John F. Kennedy wins the presidential election. Scholars will later say his appearances on TV contributed to his victory.

(25 November) CBS, which has resisted to the end, finally cancels the last of its radio soap operas. The other networks have already moved their daytime radio dramas to television, and CBS now joins them, a disappointment to older listeners who have listened to these radio shows for many years.

1961

(25 January) President Kennedy holds a press conference, and it is broadcast by both radio and television. Televised coverage of news continues to expand.

(9 May) In a speech to the National Association of Broadcasters, FCC chairman Newton N. Minow first praises some of what is on television and then

says stations aren't doing enough to serve the public interest, calling American TV a "vast wasteland."

(1 October) New York Yankees slugger Roger Maris hits his sixty-first home run, breaking Babe Ruth's record. Sports fans continue to debate whether it's a "real" record, since Maris has done in 162 games what Ruth accomplished in a season of only 154 games.

(1 October) WYAH-TV begins broadcasting. It is the first station in what will become the Christian Broadcasting Network, led by televangelist Marion G. "Pat" Robertson.

1962

(14 February) People are fascinated when television permits them to see inside the White House, as First Lady Jacqueline Kennedy conducts *A Tour of the White House,* broadcast on CBS and, ratings companies say, watched by more than 46 million Americans.

(20 February) Lieutenant Colonel John Glenn is the first American to orbit the earth, in the *Friendship 7* space capsule.

(2 March) For the first time in basketball history, a player scores one hundred points. Wilt Chamberlain of the Philadelphia Warriors accomplishes this feat in a game against the New York Knicks.

(16 April) Walter Cronkite becomes the anchor of the CBS evening news, replacing Douglas Edwards.

(25 June) The U.S. Supreme Court rules that the reading of prayers in the New York public schools is unconstitutional. Decades later, the ultimate ban on school prayer, which is the result of another case from June 1963, continues to be a hot-button issue.

(8 August) In Chile, a variety show called *Sábados Gigantes* makes its debut. Hosted by Don Francisco (whose real name is Mario Kreutzberger), it will become one of Latin America's most popular shows. More than twenty years later, it will debut in the United States as *Sábado Gigante* and become an even bigger success.

(2 October) Johnny Carson debuts as host of NBC's late-night *The Tonight Show.*

(7 November) One of America's most visible First Ladies, Eleanor Roosevelt, dies at age seventy-eight. Since leaving the White House, she has spent her time advocating for civil rights and serving as head of the United Nations Human Rights Commission.

1963

(11 February) *The French Chef*, a cooking show starring Julia Child, debuts on PBS. She will become one of the best-known cooks on television.

(28 August) Martin Luther King Jr.'s powerful "I Have a Dream" speech is telecast from the steps of the Lincoln Memorial in Washington, DC. Over 200,000 are in attendance.

(2 September) As surveys say Americans want longer TV newscasts, CBS expands its evening news from fifteen minutes to a half hour. Other networks follow.

(22 November) President Kennedy is assassinated in Dallas, Texas. Vice President Lyndon B. Johnson becomes president. Television covers unfolding events nonstop for four days, allowing the nation to witness the state funeral and the burial of the president. Cameras are also rolling on 24 November, during the shocking moment when the president's accused killer, Lee Harvey Oswald, is himself gunned down.

1964

(9 February) In pop music, the British invasion begins when the Beatles arrive for their first U.S. tour and make an appearance on the *Ed Sullivan Show*. More than seventy-three million viewers, this author included, watch. Numerous groups from England will soon dominate the pop music charts.

(25 February) In Miami, Muhammad Ali defeats Sonny Liston for the world's heavyweight boxing championship.

(19 August) Satellite transmission begins to be a factor for television when a new communications satellite, Syncom 3, has a successful launch from Cape Kennedy, Florida. It will transmit images from the 1964 Olympic games in Tokyo and will enable American TV stations to cover news overseas more quickly.

(28 August) Comedian Gracie Allen dies of a heart attack. As half of the comic duo Burns and Allen, she and her husband, George Burns, have performed on radio, in the movies, and then on TV since the 1930s.

1965

(21 February) In New York City, controversial Black Muslim leader Malcolm X is shot dead by members of a rival Black Muslim sect. With his separatist rhetoric, he had been a subject of debate as well as a guest on several talk

shows, notably Bob Kennedy's *Contact* on WBZ in Boston and on WMCA in New York's *Barry Gray Show.*

(8–9 March) Thirty-five hundred U.S. Marines land in South Vietnam. It is the first time combat troops have been sent. (There were other troops there, but up to this point, they have been serving only as advisers.)

(27 April) Edward R. Murrow dies at the age of fifty-seven. A heavy smoker, he succumbs to lung cancer.

(11–16 August) Rioting erupts in a black section of Los Angeles called Watts, and when it is over, thirty-five are dead and hundreds are injured. Racial unrest will continue in other cities over the next several years.

(12 September) The Beatles perform on the *Ed Sullivan Show* for the final time.

(9 November) A massive electrical failure shuts down electricity all over the East Coast. Some cities are without power for hours, others for more than a day.

1966

(4 March) In a comment he insists has been misinterpreted, John Lennon says the Beatles are more popular than Jesus. Outrage results, on talk shows and in opinion columns; church groups organize the burning of Beatles records, and some radio stations ban their music completely. (In England, where the remark was made, none of those reactions occurred.)

(8 September) What will become a cult classic, *Star Trek*, makes its TV debut with little fanfare.

(14 September) Gertrude Berg, creator and star of *The Goldbergs*, dies. The first series to feature an identifiably Jewish family, the show was very popular on both radio and TV before running into the blacklisting of one of the cast members (Philip Loeb) for alleged communist leanings and being temporarily canceled.

1967

(15 January) In football, the first Super Bowl is played in Los Angeles. The Green Bay Packers defeat the Kansas City Chiefs thirty-five to ten.

(5 February) The *Smothers Brothers Comedy Hour* debuts. At first, it's just another comedy show, but soon, Tommy and Dick Smothers will be pushing

the envelope, using satire to address controversial issues like racism and the war in Vietnam, and making network executives nervous.

(7 April) In San Francisco, announcer Tom Donahue begins to play rock album tracks, rather than just top-forty hit singles. His innovation mixes songs from other musical genres, including Indian raga, folk music, and jazz. He puts the new format on an FM station, KMPX. At the time, FM is still not much of a factor, but the baby boomers, tired of listening to top-forty hits over and over, are seeking a greater selection of music. Donahue is one of the first to create what will be called album-oriented rock (AOR).

(15 April) A large antiwar demonstration takes place in New York City, and several hundred thousand people protest the war in Vietnam.

(17 September) More rock-and-roll controversy arises, as The Doors appear on the *Ed Sullivan Show*. They are asked by the network censors to change a line in their song "Light My Fire" because the network thinks it is about drugs. The Doors agree but then, when they perform the song that night, they use the original lyrics. Sullivan bans the group from his show.

1968

(4 April) Martin Luther King Jr. is assassinated in Memphis at the age of thirty-nine. Rioting breaks out in a number of urban ghettos.

(5 June) Robert F. Kennedy, brother of the late president, is gunned down in Los Angeles. He dies the next day. Kennedy has been running for the presidency and has just won the California Democratic primary.

(29 August) The Democratic National Convention takes place in Chicago, and Hubert Humphrey receives the presidential nomination. However, the convention will be remembered more for violent clashes between antiwar protestors and the police. Television cameras see journalists (including CBS's Dan Rather) being manhandled, and as protesters are being beaten, they chant, "The whole world is watching."

(19 October) In celebrity news, the widow of President Kennedy, Jacqueline "Jackie" Kennedy marries a wealthy Greek tycoon named Aristotle Onassis.

(5 November) A close presidential race is won by the Republicans, Richard Nixon being elected president.

1969

(9 June) The "Red Lion" case is decided by the FCC (the name refers to a radio station owned by Red Lion Broadcasting). The ruling is related to the

Fairness Doctrine and states that if a radio program broadcasts a personal attack on someone, that person has the right to respond and should be given free airtime to do so.

(18 July) Senator Edward "Ted" Kennedy is involved in a mysterious late-night car accident on the island of Chappaquiddick in Massachusetts, and his female passenger, Mary Jo Kopechne, is drowned. Questions emerge about why he waited a full day to report the accident, and on 25 July he apologizes and tries to explain on television.

(20 July) The United States puts a man on the moon. Neil Armstrong, mission commander of the *Apollo 11* spacecraft, takes his famous televised walk on the lunar surface, having touched down with fellow astronaut Buzz Aldrin (also on the mission was Michael Collins).

(15–18 August) The Woodstock Music and Art Festival takes place on the grounds of Max Yasgur's farm in Bethel, New York. Billed as "Three Days of Peace and Music," it features performances by some of rock's best known stars. It also features plenty of drugs, plenty of mud (ongoing rainstorms turn the field into a muddy morass), and massive numbers of young people who clog the roads for miles. For the most part, the festival is entirely peaceful, but critics are horrified by all the drug use.

1970

(10 April) Paul McCartney announces that he is leaving the Beatles; the breakup becomes official on 31 December, after Paul has filed a lawsuit to disband the group.

(22 April) The First Earth Day is held, and millions of Americans nationwide celebrate and commemorate the importance of preserving the environment.

(22 June) President Nixon signs the Twenty-sixth Amendment to the Constitution, lowering the voting age from twenty-one to eighteen.

(21 September) Sports fans are delighted when the NFL's *Monday Night Football* makes its debut on ABC-TV. Outspoken sportscaster Howard Cosell is hired as a commentator on the broadcasts.

1971

(12 January) A new situation comedy, *All in the Family*, debuts, with its controversial portrayal of a bigot named Archie Bunker and his long-suffering family. Critics wonder if the public will accept jokes about prejudice, but they do. The show will win an Emmy later this year.

(24 April) As the war in Vietnam drags on, the war protests continue. Vietnam Veterans against the War has organized a week of demonstrations, and as a part of it, more than 200,000 protesters gather in Washington, DC, to demand that the United States withdraw its troops.

(3 May) On the newly created National Public Radio, a two-hour afternoon news show called *All Things Considered* debuts, giving in-depth (and its critics say, liberal) coverage of current events.

(6 June) One of the most popular variety shows from TV's early days finally does its last episode when the *Ed Sullivan Show* is canceled.

1972

(25 January) New York representative Shirley Chisholm, the first African American woman ever elected to the U.S. House, announces her plans to run for president. She doesn't win the nomination but continues to have a distinguished career in Congress.

(21 February) President Nixon arrives in Shanghai, China, as the first president to visit the communist country in an attempt to normalize U.S. and Chinese relations. He will meet with Chairman Mao Tse-tung and other Communist Party leaders in a visit that many Americans find extremely controversial.

(1 April) Baseball fans are puzzled when ballplayers strike. There hasn't been a strike before, and many people are calling sports talk shows to talk about it. The strike lasts until 13 April.

(10 July) At the Democratic National Convention in Miami Beach, antiwar candidate Senator George McGovern is the presidential nominee.

(21 August) Also in Miami Beach, President Nixon and Vice President Spiro Agnew are renominated at the Republican National Convention.

(11 September) In a shocking event at the Summer Olympics in Munich, Germany, eleven Israeli athletes are murdered by Palestinian terrorists. ABC-TV sportscaster Jim McKay suddenly finds himself doing news reporting as events unfold. Amazingly, the Olympics are neither postponed nor canceled, much to the surprise of many Americans.

(7 November) President Nixon wins reelection with 60 percent of the popular vote.

1973

(11 January) Baseball fans are divided about a new ruling that allows American League teams to use a "designated hitter" (DH) so that pitchers, notorious for

weak hitting, no longer have to bat. Traditionalists hate the new rule, but many fans think it will bring about more exciting games.

(22 January) The U.S. Supreme Court legalizes abortion in its *Roe v. Wade* decision, which will be debated on talk shows for many years to come.

(29 March) The last U.S. troops are finally withdrawn from Vietnam, but the debate over whether the United States should ever have been involved in the war continues.

(22 May) In a scandal that has been slowly building for months, President Nixon finally admits that he was complicit in illegally spying on his political enemies, a story known as Watergate because much of the spying occurred at Democratic Party headquarters in the Watergate hotel-apartment-office complex in Washington, DC.

(20 September) Before what is billed as the "Battle of the Sexes"—a tennis match between a man and a woman—tennis pro Bobby Riggs brags that women athletes are inferior and that no woman can beat him. Women's pro tennis star Billie Jean King wins the nationally televised match convincingly.

(10 October) Controversial vice president Spiro Agnew, accused of taking bribes, resigns. President Nixon replaces him with Gerald R. Ford.

(30 October) WBAI-FM broadcasts the George Carlin monologue titled "Filthy Words," about the seven words banned by network censors. A father with a young son hears the show and complains to the FCC, which fines the station. WBAI appeals, citing freedom of speech.

1974

(13 January) The big sports story is the 1973 Miami Dolphins, who, by winning the Superbowl over the Minnesota Vikings, complete the first undefeated season in National Football League history.

(15 January) Baby boomer nostalgia for the 1950s manifests itself as the TV show *Happy Days* debuts, featuring Henry Winkler as The Fonz.

(27 February) A new celebrity magazine, *People*, makes its debut. Interest in celebrities continues to grow, thanks in large part to TV talk and variety shows.

(8 April) A national television audience is watching as Hammerin' Hank Aaron of the Atlanta Braves breaks Babe Ruth's all-time home run record by hitting number 715.

(9 May) As it becomes obvious that President Nixon tried to cover up his role in the Watergate scandal, both houses of Congress investigate. Two of the president's aides will soon be convicted of conspiracy and perjury.

(8 August) Before he can be impeached, as mandated by the House Judiciary Committee, President Nixon announces in a televised speech that he will resign the presidency. Vice President Gerald Ford takes over as president.

(8 September) In a decision that stuns millions of Americans, President Ford issues former President Nixon a pardon saying that Nixon can never be prosecuted for anything that may have happened during his presidency.

1975

(19 April) A dance song by Van McCoy, "The Hustle," debuts on the *Billboard* magazine pop charts. It will go on to reach number one and sell over ten million copies, as the disco craze begins. Critics hate the music, but disco clubs proliferate and so do more hit disco songs.

(30 July) The powerful president of the Teamsters' Union, James R. "Jimmy" Hoffa is missing, and even the FBI is unable to locate him or find out what has happened to him.

(10 August) Television talk host David Frost announces that he has obtained an exclusive interview with former president Richard Nixon.

(5 September) Lynette "Squeaky" Fromme tries to assassinate President Ford; it turns out her gun has no bullets in it. On 22 September, another woman, Sara Jane Moore, will also try unsuccessfully to shoot the president. Her gun is loaded, but she misses.

(11 October) *Saturday Night Live* (called *NBC's Saturday Night* when it is first broadcast) makes its debut. The show's political satire and pop culture parodies will be emulated by other shows, and comics like Steve Martin become stars after appearing on *SNL*.

(4 November) Herb Jepko's *Nitecaps* becomes the first nationally syndicated call-in talk show when the Mutual Broadcasting System broadcasts it coast to coast.

1976

(22 April) Barbara Walters becomes television's first female anchor, on ABC's *Nightly News*. Her coanchor is Harry Reasoner, who is not happy about having a female coanchor. The television critics subject Walters to intense scrutiny.

(25 May) In the latest chapter of "politicians behaving badly," Ohio Representative Wayne Hays admits that he hired his mistress, Elizabeth Ray, as his secretary, the taxpayers footing the bill for her salary. She tells reporters she has no office skills at all; she doesn't even know how to type.

(4 July) It's the bicentennial, and the two hundredth birthday of the United States is observed nationwide with parades, concerts, and fireworks.

(2 November) Southerner James Earl "Jimmy" Carter defeats Gerald Ford to become the new president.

1977

(21 January) President Carter gives pardons to all Vietnam War draft evaders who have not committed any violent acts.

(23 January) The miniseries *Roots* begins its eight-night run. Based on the novel by Alex Haley, it will earn ABC some of its highest ratings and win nine Emmy awards.

(2 March) Up-and-coming comedian Jay Leno appears on Johnny Carson's *The Tonight Show* for the first time.

(26 March) With little notice at first, Christian conservative James Dobson debuts his radio talk show, *Focus on the Family* on thirty-six stations. After eighteen months, it is being heard on over a hundred affiliate stations.

(16 August) The king of rock-and-roll, Elvis Presley, is found dead at the age of forty-two. Although there are rumors that prescription drug abuse led to his death, he is still beloved. Millions of baby boomers who grew up with his music have never forgotten him.

1978

(12 May) Proving that egalitarianism is here to stay, the National Weather Service announces that instead of giving all hurricanes women's names, it will alternate male and female names.

(15 June) In a love story that gets much media attention, Lisa Halaby, member of a prominent Arab-American family, marries King Hussein of Jordan and becomes Queen Noor.

(3 July) In its case appealing the FCC fine for broadcasting George Carlin's monologue "Filthy Words" in 1973, WBAI-FM loses before the U.S. Supreme Court; the Court rules that the FCC does have the authority to ban the airing of indecent and vulgar language at a time when children might be listening.

(9 July) Over a hundred thousand members of the National Organization for Women and other feminist groups march in Washington in support of the proposed Equal Rights Amendment. The amendment is later defeated, as liberal and conservative groups debate the role of women in a changing society.

(18 November) In Guyana, the shocking story of Jim Jones and the People's Temple is unfolding, as the world learns that he and more than nine hundred of his followers have committed suicide. Just before the mass suicide, an American congressman, Leo Ryan, sent to investigate the cult, was shot dead, along with four of the people who accompanied him on his fact-finding mission.

1979

(16 January) The shah of Iran is overthrown. He is replaced by a theocratic regime led by Ayatollah Ruhollah Khomeini.

(28 March) There is a serious nuclear accident, involving a partial meltdown of a reactor at the Three Mile Island nuclear power plant, not far from Harrisburg, Pennsylvania. It is later determined that both equipment malfunctions and human error contributed to what was nearly a catastrophe. Over three hundred members of the media descend on the area to report on what caused the meltdown and what is being done to ensure public safety.

(7 May) More than 125,000 people hold a rally in Washington, DC, to express their opposition to nuclear power.

(7 September) An all-sports cable network, ESPN (Entertainment and Sports Programming Network), makes its debut. Its first major program is *Sports-Center*, which recaps the day's top sports news and video highlights.

(4 November) A hostage crisis begins in Iran as the U.S. embassy is taken over by militant anti-American students who are followers of Ayatollah Khomeini. The students will hold fifty-two Americans hostage for 444 days.

(8 November) The ABC news organization begins a late-night feature, *Crisis in Iran: America Held Hostage*, to update viewers on the day's events. That program will evolve into *Nightline* in late March 1980, with Ted Koppel as the anchor. When the hostage crisis ends, *Nightline* remains on the air as a popular newsmagazine.

1980

(22 February) The "miracle on ice" occurs at the Winter Olympics at Lake Placid, New York. Led by team captain Mike Eruzione, the U.S. Olympic ice hockey team, who are mostly college students, upsets the veteran team from the Soviet Union by a score of four to three. The U.S. team goes on to win the gold medal.

(21 March) President Carter announces that the United States will boycott the Summer Olympics in Moscow to protest the Soviet Union's invasion of

Afghanistan. Many national opinion polls say that Americans feel the athletes are the ones being penalized, and the decision not to compete is very unpopular.

(1 June) Atlanta media executive Robert Edward "Ted" Turner inaugurates the first twenty-four-hour cable news network, CNN.

(4 November) Former movie actor and California governor Ronald Reagan wins decisively over Jimmy Carter in the U.S. presidential election.

(8 December) Former Beatle John Lennon is murdered in front of his apartment building by an obsessed fan, Mark David Chapman. Baby boomers and Beatles fans worldwide mourn Lennon's death.

1981

(14 January) As part of President Reagan's pledge to deregulate broadcasting, the FCC removes the limitations on how many commercials per hour stations can play.

(6 March) Once called "the most trusted man in America," CBS-TV news anchor Walter Cronkite signs off for the last time as anchor of the evening news. Dan Rather replaces him.

(30 March) A young man suffering from mental illness, John Hinckley Jr., tries to assassinate the president. President Reagan's wounds are not serious, but his press secretary, James Brady, is permanently disabled. Hinckley is found not guilty of attempted murder by reason of insanity and is sent to a psychiatric hospital. An intense debate over gun control breaks out on talk radio, on TV, and in newspaper opinion columns.

(5 June) The first manifestations of a mysterious new disease emerge. It is a severe pneumonia, often fatal, and it seems to attack only gay men. Once more is known about it, the disease comes to be known as acquired immunodeficiency syndrome (AIDS).

(29 July) In a ceremony watched worldwide by more than 750 million people, Great Britain's Prince Charles marries Lady Diana Spencer.

(1 August) A cable network dedicated to pop music, and especially music videos, makes its debut: Music Television (MTV). The first video it plays is "Video Killed the Radio Star."

(21 September) Sandra Day O'Connor is unanimously confirmed by the U.S. Senate, and becomes the first woman justice on the U.S. Supreme Court.

(31 December) CNN launches *Headline News*, a cable channel for people who wanted the big stories quickly and concisely.

1982

(20 January) Outrageous pop culture stories always attract attention: Rocker Ozzy Osbourne bites the head off a live bat onstage. He later explains he thought somebody had thrown him a toy, as fans often throw objects onto the stage when bands perform.

(15 September) *USA Today*, the first national newspaper, makes its debut. It features such innovations as color graphics and will eventually be distributed via satellite to remote locations across the United States. Using this technology, *USA Today* is better able to include breaking news before the paper goes to press.

(13 November) In an emotional ceremony, the Vietnam Veterans Memorial Wall is dedicated in Washington, DC. The memorial contains the names of the more than fifty-eight thousand service members killed or missing in action as a result of the Vietnam War.

1983

(26 February) In music news, Michael Jackson's new album, *Thriller*, is setting records for sales and will be number one on the *Billboard* album charts for an amazing thirty-seven weeks.

(2 March) Sony and Phillips introduce the compact disc, and while its arrival in stores is delayed until the late summer, it raises a discussion among critics about whether the long-playing album will soon be obsolete.

(5 March) Because MTV is a success for the pop and rock audience, Country Music Television makes its debut, first as CMTV and later as CMT.

(2 November) President Reagan signs legislation designating the third Monday in January as a national holiday to honor slain civil rights leader Martin Luther King Jr.

1984

(12 July) Walter Mondale, the Democratic candidate for president, names Representative Geraldine Ferraro as his running mate, the first time a woman has ever been on a major political party's national ticket.

(23 July) Vanessa Williams becomes the first reigning Miss America ever to have to resign, when *Penthouse* magazine publishes nude photos that were taken of her several years earlier.

(20 September) The *Cosby Show* makes its debut. Starring Bill Cosby as Cliff Huxtable, a successful doctor, and Phylicia Ayers-Allen (later Phylicia Rashad) as his attorney wife Claire, the *Cosby Show* is considered the first TV show about a successful, upscale black family.

(6 November) President Reagan wins reelection in a landslide.

(22 December) A white electrical engineer named Bernhard Goetz shoots four black teenagers who are attempting to rob him on a New York subway train. Some New Yorkers, frustrated by high crime rates, applaud Goetz as a hero.

1985

(1 January) VH1, or Video Hits 1, a music video channel aimed at baby boomers, debuts. It offers music and programs for viewers who love pop culture but find MTV too youth-oriented.

(28 January) An all-star lineup of rock, pop, rap, and jazz stars assembles at the A & M Recording Studio in Hollywood, California, and records a song to benefit famine relief in Africa. "We Are the World" is produced by Quincy Jones, written by Michael Jackson and Lionel Richie, and it will bring in millions of dollars for the people in Ethiopia, Sudan, and other African countries.

(23 April) A marketing fiasco occurs when Coca Cola changes the formula of its popular soft drink, offering a sweeter version. "New Coke" is received so negatively that by mid-July, the company is forced to return to the original formula, renamed Classic Coke.

(1 July) The Home Shopping Club (later called the Home Shopping Network) is launched nationwide. Shopping at home will become a favorite activity for many viewers.

(13 July) Continuing the trend of performers trying to help the poor in Africa is "Live Aid," a seventeen-hour concert telecast by international hookup from London, Philadelphia, and several other cities. Organized by Irish rocker Bob Geldof, it features many stars, including Bob Dylan, Tina Turner, and Phil Collins. ABC and MTV carry it live.

(25 July) In celebrity news that shocks many people, it is revealed that actor Rock Hudson is dying of AIDS. In an era when sexual orientation was hidden, few fans knew Hudson was gay.

(26 August) AIDS continues to be in the news: Thirteen-year-old Ryan White, a hemophiliac who has contracted the disease from a blood transfusion, is allowed to continue attending school only by a telephone hookup; he is barred from actually setting foot at his Kokomo, Indiana, middle school. Fear and misinformation about the disease proliferate.

(19 November) President Reagan meets with Soviet leader Mikhail Gorbachev in Geneva, Switzerland. They sign no agreements, but they plan to meet again in 1986 to continue discussions.

1986

(20 January) The first Martin Luther King holiday is observed. Only seventeen states choose to honor the holiday.

(28 January) In a major tragedy, the spacecraft *Challenger* explodes seventy-three seconds after launching, killing instantly all those aboard. Children have been watching in schools all over the country because the first "teacher in space," Christa McAuliffe, was on board the space shuttle.

(26 April) Nuclear energy is again in the news, as the worst nuclear accident in history occurs: A reactor at the Chernobyl power plant in the northern part of Ukraine explodes. Hundreds of thousands of people in Ukraine, Belarus, and parts of Russia are exposed to high levels of radiation. Subsequently, an elevated number of cases of cancer, birth defects, and thyroid disease will affect many of those who were exposed and the debate over the safety of nuclear power breaks out again worldwide.

(8 September) The *Oprah Winfrey Show* debuts in syndication. It will soon become the number one talk show on daytime television.

(10 October) As promised, Reagan and Gorbachev meet again, this time in Reykjavik, Iceland. The subject is arms control, but again, no agreements are signed.

(25 October) The Boston Red Sox, who haven't won a World Series since 1918, seem on the verge this time, but a costly error by normally reliable first baseman Bill Buckner gives the New York Mets the win in the sixth game of the World Series. The Mets go on to win the seventh and deciding game, and once again, the Red Sox go home disappointed.

1987

(16 January) A TV station in San Francisco, KRON, is one of the first to accept advertisements for condoms. A few weeks later, the U.S. Surgeon General, C. Everett Koop, will encourage more stations to do so, since the use of condoms can slow the spread of AIDS. Fearing a backlash from religious viewers, not many stations take his advice.

(19 March) In one of the first of the televangelist scandals in the news, popular TV preacher Jim Bakker is forced to resign from his ministry and his role

as cohost (along with his wife, Tammy Faye) of their syndicated Christian television show, the *PTL Club*, after it is revealed that he has had illicit sex and then paid the woman a large sum of money to cover it up.

(8 May) Having been caught with a woman who is not his wife, amid rumors that he is a womanizer, Democratic presidential candidate Gary Hart drops out of the race.

(1 July) WFAN in New York is considered the first American station to have an all sports/talk format.

(16 October) In a story that has captivated the entire nation, "Baby Jessica" McClure is rescued. The eighteen-month-old fell into a well shaft near her Midland, Texas, home, and the exciting story of her rescue is followed by millions.

1988

(16 January) CBS football commentator Jimmy "The Greek" Snyder is fired from that job after he makes racist remarks about why blacks are good athletes.

(21 February) In more news of televangelists behaving badly, Jimmy Swaggart admits to his congregation that he has committed a grave sin; it is soon revealed that he has been visiting a prostitute, and he is forced to resign from his ministry.

(7 June) Massachusetts governor Michael Dukakis wins the Democratic nomination for president.

(8 August) Another sports tradition ends, as Chicago's Wrigley Field finally has lighting installed for night baseball. Until now, only day baseball games were played at Wrigley, the only major league park without lights for night games.

(3 November) During a talk show, Geraldo Rivera's neo-Nazi, skinhead, white supremacist, black, and Jewish guests begin to brawl. Punches fly, chairs are thrown, and Geraldo's nose is broken.

(8 November) Republican George Herbert Walker Bush easily defeats Governor Dukakis for the U.S. presidency. Critics believe negative ads by Bush's campaign organization and a poor debate performance by Dukakis contributed to the outcome.

1989

(7 February) As a result of public outrage, fueled in large part by radio talk hosts, Congress agrees to cancel the large pay raise it has voted itself.

(24 March) In Alaska, an ecological disaster occurs when the Exxon *Valdez* oil tanker strikes a reef in Prince William Sound, causing a massive oil spill, which will soon extend over 10,000 square miles. It is the worst oil spill in U.S. history and does serious damage to the fish, birds, and plants along Alaska's shoreline, as well as to the livelihood of Alaskans who depend on the Sound for their living.

(3 July) The U.S. Supreme Court votes to place some restrictions on abortion, although it does not overturn *Roe v. Wade* as conservatives have hoped.

(9 November) In a historic event seen on TV worldwide, the Berlin Wall, which has separated communist-run East Germany from democratic West Germany for nearly three decades, is finally dismantled.

1990

(8 April) Ryan White dies at age eighteen. In the mid-1980s, he has been the spokesperson for AIDS on talk shows and educational programs.

(22 April) The twentieth anniversary of Earth Day is celebrated by millions all over the world; many Americans believe their elected officials are not doing enough to protect the environment and save endangered species.

(11 June) Some pitchers never achieve even one no-hitter, but veteran Nolan Ryan of the Texas Rangers pitches his sixth no-hitter, at the age of forty-three.

(26 July) President Bush signs the Americans with Disabilities Act, which gives disabled people more protection against discrimination and greater access to public buildings and public transportation. More cities build wheelchair ramps on main streets; other types of accommodation for the blind and the deaf are also implemented.

(2 August) Iraq invades neighboring Kuwait.

1991

(17 January) The First Gulf War officially begins as U.S. forces start an aerial bombardment of Baghdad. A coalition of thirty-four countries will participate in defeating Saddam Hussein and driving the Iraqi army out of Kuwait in what is called Operation Desert Storm. CNN offers in-depth reporting in a way that few other networks do. The operation ends on 27 February, with the mission declared a success.

(3 March) Rodney King, an African American, is brutally beaten by Los Angeles police officers, who say he was resisting arrest. A bystander videotapes the

event, which seems to show that King was the victim of excessive force, and gives the tape to the media, which show it repeatedly. It is one of the first examples of how "citizen journalism" affects public perception.

(15 October) The Senate votes 52-48 to confirm the nomination of Clarence Thomas, an African American conservative, to the U.S. Supreme Court. The hearings became controversial because a former co-worker of his, attorney Anita Hill, had accused Thomas of sexually harassing her while he was her boss at the Department of Education and the Equal Opportunity Commission. Thomas denied it, and the all-male Senate Judiciary Committee finally sent the nomination to the full Senate, which voted to confirm him. National Public Radio's Nina Totenberg is one of the few reporters who, throughout the hearings, thoroughly addresses the issue of sexual harassment in the workplace.

(4 November) National Public Radio, known mainly for its newscasts, launches a national talk show, *Talk of the Nation*. Its first host is John Hockenberry, who soon leaves for a job at ABC. The show's new host is Ray Suarez.

(25 December) The breakup of the Soviet Union occurs, as Mikhail Gorbachev resigns as premier and the Communist Party is no longer in charge.

1992

(4 January) ESPN makes its debut on radio, giving sports-talk fans the chance to listen to the sports-talk hosts they have come to enjoy watching on ESPN-TV.

(10 March) Arkansas governor William Jefferson "Bill" Clinton is emerging as the Democratic Party's front-runner in the upcoming presidential election.

(29 April) After the four officers who beat Rodney King are acquitted by an all-white jury, rioting breaks out in the ghettos of South Central Los Angeles. When it is finished, fifty-one people are dead and nearly eighteen hundred are injured.

(25 May) Comedian Jay Leno takes over as host of *The Tonight Show*.

(3 November) Bill Clinton is elected president, defeating President George H.W. Bush.

(17 December) The FCC decides to fine Infinity Broadcasting, the company that employs Howard Stern, $600,000 for a number of indecent broadcasts. Infinity promises to appeal.

1993

(8 January) Elvis Presley is the first rock star ever honored with a U.S. postage stamp.

(19 April) In Waco, Texas, there has been a fifty-one-day standoff between a cult known as the Branch Davidians and members of the U.S. Bureau of Alcohol, Tobacco, and Firearms (ATF). Suddenly, the Branch Davidian compound bursts into flames, and about seventy-five of the cult members, including their leader, David Koresh, and a number of children, die in the fire. The government says it was a mass suicide, but critics accuse the ATF of using excessive force.

(30 June) With the issue of TV violence on the minds of Congress and the FCC, the major networks agree to place a special warning at the beginning of programs that might be considered excessively violent.

(30 August) David Letterman, having been denied the opportunity to become host of *The Tonight Show*, leaves NBC and starts his own show on CBS, the *Late Show with David Letterman*.

(13 September) There is renewed hope for peace in the Middle East, as Chairman Yasir Arafat, leader of the Palestinian Authority and Israel's Prime Minister Yitzhak Rabin make a historic agreement, brokered by President Clinton. Video of the two former enemies shaking hands is widely played.

(1 October) ESPN2 (called by some "the deuce") makes its debut, covering sports that there isn't sufficient time on ESPN to broadcast, including soccer and women's basketball.

(23 November) The Food Network makes its debut on cable, as the popularity of celebrity chefs and gourmet-style home cooking continues to grow.

(8 December) As Congress threatens to regulate sexually explicit and violent video games, manufacturers promise to devise a rating system similar to the one used by the movie industry.

1994

(6 January) Star figure skater Nancy Kerrigan is mysteriously assaulted. It soon turns out that one of her skating rivals, Tonya Harding, is one of those behind the assault.

(12 June) Nicole Brown Simpson, ex-wife of former football star O. J. Simpson, is found murdered, along with her friend Ron Goldman. There is evidence that Simpson was involved in the crime, and he will be charged with the two murders.

(12 August) Major league baseball players go out on strike, and with no end in sight by September, there will be no World Series this year.

(8 November) In the midterm elections, the Republicans take the majority in Congress, winning both the House and the Senate for the first time since 1952.

1995

(31 March) One of the most popular Hispanic vocalists, Selena (Selena Quintanilla Perez), is murdered in Corpus Christi, Texas, at age twenty-three. Her killer turns out to be the former president of her fan club.

(19 April) A truck bomb destroys the Murrah Federal Building in Oklahoma City, Oklahoma, killing nearly 170 people, many of them children. At first, suspicion falls on Arab terrorists, but the murderer is then identified as a white supremacist named Timothy McVeigh.

(11 July) Trying to put an end to an unpleasant chapter of our history, President Clinton grants full diplomatic recognition to Vietnam. The decision is controversial among conservatives and veterans' groups.

(31 July) As deregulation continues, another media merger takes place: The Walt Disney Company acquires Capital Cities/ABC.

(24 August) Microsoft introduces its new operating system, Windows 95, as new technology is making it easier for more people to use the Internet.

(22 September) Yet another media merger occurs, as Turner Broadcasting (owner of CNN) merges with Time Warner Inc.

(3 October) O. J. Simpson is found not guilty of the murders of his ex-wife and Ron Goldman. As many as 150 million viewers watch as the verdict is read, and popular reaction breaks down along racial lines: according to public opinion polls, a majority of whites are convinced that he got away with murder, while a majority of blacks believe he deserved to be acquitted.

(16 November) Shareholders of CBS Inc. vote to allow Westinghouse Broadcasting to acquire the struggling network. The FCC votes to approve the acquisition six days later. (Westinghouse Broadcasting is a company that put some of radio's first stations on the air in 1920–1921.)

1996

(8 February) The Telecommunications Act of 1996 is signed into law by President Clinton. It removes many of the ownership restrictions of the past and frees corporations to buy up large numbers of stations.

(7 October) The first conservative news network, Fox News, makes its debut on cable. Owned by Rupert Murdoch, it will soon overtake CNN and become the number one most watched news network in the ratings.

(5 November) President Clinton is reelected, defeating Senator Robert Dole convincingly.

(12 November) The mergers keep on coming. Westinghouse Electric merges with Infinity Broadcasting and becomes the largest radio group to date, with seventy-seven stations in thirteen cities.

(26 December) A child beauty queen, Jon Benet Ramsey, is found dead in the basement of her parents' home. Suspicion initially falls on the parents, John and Patricia Ramsey, as the media obsess about the case.

1997

(26 March) In Rancho Santa Fe, California, thirty-eight believers in a UFO-based cult, along with their leader, Marshall Applewhite, commit suicide together, convinced they are about to be transported by spaceship to the "next level" of existence. They attached great significance to the appearance of the Hale-Bopp comet, which they believed was the sign for them to leave Earth.

(26 June) The first Harry Potter book appears. Written by British author J. K. Rowling, the series will be a sensation, interesting millions of young people in reading.

(5 September) Mother Teresa, the Nobel Prize–winning nun known for her tireless work with the poor in India, dies at age eighty-seven. Her death is overshadowed by the death of Princess Diana of Great Britain.

(6 September) Millions of people worldwide watch the funeral of Diana, Princess of Wales, at Westminster Abbey. She was killed in a car crash in Paris, France, on 31 August.

(December) Westinghouse changes its corporate name to CBS, ending the use of "Westinghouse Broadcasting," a name synonymous with radio (and stations like KDKA in Pittsburgh and WBZ in Boston) since 1920.

1998

(26 January) Amid rumors of a sexual scandal, President Clinton appears on television to issue his famous denial, "I did not have sexual relations with that woman, Miss Lewinsky." Within a few days, it becomes obvious that an affair between the president and Monica Lewinsky, a White House intern, did take place. Throughout the next few months, their relationship and the resulting scandal is the dominant story on radio and TV and in print.

(23 March) The movie *Titanic* ties a record by winning eleven Oscars. It also sets a box office record for consecutive weeks at number one, with fifteen.

(24 September) With Republicans in control of the proceedings, the House Judiciary Committee announces it plans to consider a resolution to impeach

President Clinton, claiming he committed perjury in his grand jury testimony on 17 August.

(27 September) In one distraction from the Lewinsky-Clinton scandal, St. Louis Cardinals slugger Mark McGwire has been striving to be the first to hit seventy home runs in a season. (The single season record had been Roger Maris's sixty-one, but once McGwire and another slugger, Chicago Cubs star Sammy Sosa, had passed that mark, the battle was on to see who could hit the most home runs. Sosa ended up with sixty-six, while McGwire hit an amazing 70.) Today, with millions of fans in the park and on national TV watching, he succeeds.

(29 October) As part of studies of the effect of space travel on the elderly, veteran astronaut John Glenn lifts off on the shuttle *Discovery*. He is seventy-seven, the oldest person to go into space, as well as having been the first to orbit the earth in 1962.

(19 December) The House of Representatives votes to impeach President Clinton.

1999

(12 February) The U.S. Senate refuses to find the president guilty, and he is not removed from office.

(20 April) Two students go on a shooting rampage at Columbine High School in Littleton, Colorado, leaving twelve students and a teacher dead and wounding twenty-three others before killing themselves. A national debate about gun control immediately follows.

(25 November) In a case that will cause great controversy, a little Cuban boy, Elian Gonzalez, is found at sea near Fort Lauderdale, Florida, clinging to an inner tube. His mother and the eleven others who fled Cuba with her have drowned, and only Elian has survived. The battle over whether to let this five-year-old boy stay with relatives in the United States or return him to his father in Cuba will be long and bitter.

(31 December) Computer users are expecting the worst as a computer virus called the Y2K bug is supposed to render computers inoperable when the new century begins. The majority of people's computers continue to function perfectly on New Year's Day.

2000

(31 May) The TV show *Survivor* makes its debut. A prize contest involving sixteen people who are placed on a remote island, divided into two tribes, and given various tests of skill, it quickly becomes a pop culture phenomenon.

(28 June) After months of heated debate, Elian Gonzalez is returned to Cuba to be raised there by his father.

(2 August) At the Republican National Convention in Philadelphia, Texas Governor George W. Bush and former chief executive officer of the Halliburton Company Dick Cheney are nominated for president and vice president.

(14 August) At the Democratic National Convention in Los Angeles, Vice President Al Gore and Senator Joe Lieberman are nominated for president and vice president.

(11 September) Outspoken radio talk host Laura Schlessinger debuts with a syndicated TV show, but within six months, it will be canceled.

(7 November) The outcome of the presidential election is contested and is eventually decided by the intervention of the U.S. Supreme Court on 12 December, when George W. Bush is declared president. The bitterly fought election will inspire debate and discussion for years to come.

(7 November) Former First Lady Hillary Rodham Clinton is elected a senator from New York, the first time a former First Lady is elected to public office.

2001

(15 January) The online encyclopedia Wikipedia makes its debut. Controversial (anyone can edit it, so it may or may not be accurate), it becomes a useful tool for researchers and newsrooms.

(20 January) President George W. Bush is inaugurated as thousands of demonstrators continue to protest his designation as president.

(11 June) Unrepentant until the end, Oklahoma City bomber Timothy McVeigh is executed.

(1 September) In a scandal in Little League baseball, it is revealed that star pitcher Danny Almonte, who has pitched his Bronx, New York, team to the Little League championship, is fourteen, not twelve, and therefore ineligible for Little League; his father and the team's president used fake documents so that Danny could play.

(11 September) Terrorists fly hijacked planes into the twin towers of the World Trade Center in New York City and the Pentagon in Washington, DC, killing an estimated three thousand people. A fourth plane crashes in a field in Shanksville, Pennsylvania. While there are no survivors, reports reveal that just before the plane went down, some of the passengers and crew on the hijacked plane wrested control of it from the terrorists, preventing it from reaching its intended target, the White House. Radio and TV give nonstop coverage, helping the nation to cope with the disaster.

(23 October) Apple debuts the iPod, a digital audio player that is portable. Soon, radio stations will be able to "podcast," offering downloadable audio segments that can be listened to anytime.

(29 November) Former Beatle George Harrison dies of cancer at age fifty-eight.

2002

(29 January) President Bush gives his State of the Union address, during which he calls Iran, Iraq, and North Korea the "axis of evil."

(14 March) During an interview with Diane Sawyer on ABC's *Primetime Thursday*, talk show host Rosie O'Donnell goes public with the fact that she is a lesbian.

(25 March) TV talk host David Letterman turns down an offer from ABC and decides to stay at CBS.

(28 July) Nine miners who have been trapped in the Quecreek mine in Pennsylvania for seventy-seven hours are found alive and are rescued; the rescue effort and the happy ending are broadcast worldwide.

(24 October) A series of deadly sniper attacks, which have terrified Washington, DC, and the surrounding area throughout October and left ten people dead, ends with the arrest of two men, John Allen Muhammad and John Lee Malvo.

(13 December) Boston's Cardinal Bernard Law is forced to resign due to an ongoing scandal in the Catholic Church. Since January, the *Boston Globe* has revealed that not only have priests who abused children gone unpunished, but the church has covered up their crimes. The scandal will soon spread to other cities as well.

2003

(1 February) The space shuttle *Columbia* explodes over Texas, just as the craft is descending into the earth's atmosphere after sixteen days in orbit; all seven astronauts aboard die.

(21 February) In Rhode Island, the Station nightclub goes up in flames during a performance by classic rock band Great White. The fire, which kills a hundred people, was caused by sparks from pyrotechnics the band used.

(March) The online social network MySpace makes its debut.

(12 March) Teenager Elizabeth Smart, who was abducted from her Utah home, is found alive, still held captive by her abductors.

(19 March) President Bush orders the invasion of Iraq.

(1 May) President Bush stages a dramatic event onboard an aircraft career, as he announces the end of major combat in Iraq beneath a sign that reads "Mission Accomplished." It turns out that the war is far from over, and Iraq will become a contentious topic on radio and TV talk shows.

(4 June) Celebrity TV homemaker Martha Stewart is indicted in a stock scandal; she pleads not guilty.

(8 September) Ellen DeGeneres debuts her new talk show. The fact that she is open about being a lesbian has no impact on the success of her show.

(10 October) Popular conservative talk host Rush Limbaugh admits to his radio audience that he has an addiction to prescription pain medication and is about to check into a drug rehabilitation facility.

(13 December) Deposed Iraqi dictator Saddam Hussein is found and captured.

2004

(16 January) Pop star Michael Jackson is in court pleading not guilty to nine felony counts, having been accused of molesting a boy at his Neverland Ranch.

(February) The online social network Facebook, founded by Harvard student Mark Zuckerberg, makes its debut.

(4 February) Massachusetts sees a major victory for the gay rights movement, as the state Supreme Judicial Court rules it unconstitutional to deny gay people the right to marry.

(31 March) Air America Radio, the first liberal/progressive radio network, debuts. Among its key personalities are comedian Al Franken and veteran talk host Randi Rhodes.

(5 June) President Ronald Reagan dies at age ninety-three. His funeral is covered like a news event.

(26 July) At the Democratic National Convention in Boston, Senator John Kerry and Senator John Edwards are the nominees for president and vice president.

(8 September) A scandal erupts at CBS, as news anchor Dan Rather, in a segment of *60 Minutes II*, attempts to prove that President Bush shirked his military obligation when he was supposed to serve in the National Guard during the Vietnam era. But the documents Rather uses to make the case turn out

to be fake, and Rather is charged with bias. His producer is fired and Rather ultimately resigns from CBS.

(27 October) For the first time since 1918, the Boston Red Sox win baseball's World Series, defeating the St. Louis Cardinals after completing a dramatic come-from-behind league playoff series in which they defeated their arch rivals, the New York Yankees.

(2 November) Despite growing dissatisfaction with the war in Iraq, President Bush is reelected, and Republicans also hold onto control of the House and Senate.

2005

(15 February) Three entrepreneurs begin developing a video-file-sharing site called YouTube. It will soon become a factor in the news, capturing video of politicians and celebrities and allowing viewers to watch their favorite video clips as often as they wish.

(31 March) After years of contentious legal battles, Terri Schiavo dies. The Florida woman suffered irreversible brain damage and had been in a persistent vegetative state since 1990, as her husband and her parents fought in the courts over whether to disconnect her feeding tube and let her die.

(2 April) Pope John Paul II dies; his funeral receives intensive worldwide media coverage.

(29 August) Hurricane Katrina reaches land. The destruction and havoc wrought by Katrina is especially severe in Louisiana and Mississippi. Days pass, and government inaction causes rage in the victims, and also in reporters such as CNN's Anderson Cooper, who confronts politicians to ask why nothing is being done.

(26 October) Talk shows continue to debate whether in fact the war in Iraq is worth the cost, as the two thousandth American death is announced.

2006

(5 January) In West Virginia, at the Sago Mine, what seemed at first to be a story with a happy ending turns into a tragedy. Initial reports that thirteen trapped miners have been found alive turn out to be false. Twelve of the miners are found dead, and only one survives.

(9 January) Howard Stern does his first show for the Sirius satellite network.

(5 April) TV morning-show host Katie Couric announces she will be leaving NBC's *Today Show* to become the first woman to anchor CBS's evening news in early September.

(10 April) Hundreds of thousands of immigrants nationwide take to the streets to demonstrate in favor of allowing amnesty for immigrants who have lived here peacefully, worked hard, and paid taxes. Opponents believe people who broke the law by coming here illegally do not deserve amnesty, and the topic continues to be debated.

(27 June) In dissension on the set of TV talk show *The View*, the contract of cohost Star Jones is not renewed, reportedly due to friction between her and the show's creator, Barbara Walters.

(4 September) Popular TV star Steve Irwin, host of the Discovery Channel's *Crocodile Hunter*, is killed by a stingray while on location in Australia shooting a documentary.

(7 November) Dissatisfaction with the war and the economy, as well as scandals involving Republican members of Congress, result in the Democrats' regaining control of Congress by winning narrow margins in both the House and Senate in the midterm elections. Nancy Pelosi will become the first woman in U.S. history to serve as Speaker of the House.

2007

(9 February) Model Anna Nicole Smith dies of an accidental drug overdose. Smith, a former Playboy Bunny, was the widow of billionaire J. Howard Marshall, who was more than sixty years older than she when they married. She left a young daughter, who will eventually inherit the fortune; the custody battle will fascinate TV talk shows over the next few months. TV gossip shows are also fascinated by the increasingly bizarre behavior of pop star Britney Spears.

(15 April) Larry King is marking fifty years in broadcasting this week, and a video celebration with many celebrity guests is planned.

(16 April) In a tragedy on the campus of Virginia Tech University, a lone gunman, a student with serious emotional problems, kills thirty-two students and then himself. The debate about gun control is revived, but again, not resolved.

(late May) Two of the cohosts of *The View*, liberal Rosie O'Donnell and conservative Elizabeth Hasselbeck, debate the Iraqi war and the policies of the Bush administration, and the debate grows heated; clips of the name-calling and insults exchanged are repeatedly watched on YouTube.

(7 August) San Francisco Giants slugger Barry Bonds hits his 756th home run, breaking Hank Aaron's all-time home-run record. Bonds is under suspicion of having used performance-enhancing drugs, but his achievement is greeted with great enthusiasm by fans in San Francisco.

(12 October) Former vice president Al Gore is awarded a Nobel Peace Prize for his work in informing the public about global climate change. He has already won two Oscars this year for his documentary about global warming, *An Inconvenient Truth*.

(5 November) In Hollywood, members of the Writers Guild of America, the men and women who write the scripts for TV dramas and movies and help the big-name comedians come up with new jokes, go on strike. Many popular shows are forced into reruns.

2008

(3 January) The presidential primary season begins, and there are two unexpected winners in the Iowa caucuses: Democratic senator Barack Obama and former Republican governor of Arkansas Mike Huckabee. Obama, an African American, will soon be locked in a fierce contest with the former First Lady, Senator Hillary Rodham Clinton, over who will get the Democratic presidential nomination.

(3 March) Lou Dobbs, long known as an opinionated commentator and host of the *Lou Dobbs Show* on CNN, begins doing a syndicated radio talk show.

(4 March) Senator John McCain becomes the presumptive Republican presidential nominee

(11 May) Tornadoes sweep through the Midwest, causing more than twenty deaths and destroying entire towns in Missouri and Oklahoma; the number of 2008 deaths from tornadoes is already nearly one hundred.

(15 May) The California Supreme Court votes to permit gay marriage.

(20 May) Veteran Democratic Senator Edward "Ted" Kennedy is diagnosed with a brain tumor.

(3 June) A bitter primary fight culminates in Senator Barack Obama becoming the presumptive Democratic presidential nominee, the first African American to reach this position.

(8 August) The summer Olympic games open in Beijing, People's Republic of China.

(15 August) Chris Russo leaves WFAN-AM, breaking up the sports-talk giant's "Mike and Mad Dog" two weeks before the show's nineteenth anniversary.

(1–3 October) Responding to a growing crisis in the economy and the failure of a number of financial institutions, Congress passes a controversial $700 billion aid package that is called a "bail-out" by detractors and a "rescue plan" by supporters. Its intent is to stabilize banks and investment companies, many of which had made a high number of risky mortgage loans.

Appendix B: Sixteen Talk Show Hosts Who Shouldn't Be Forgotten

Some people are going to be left out of any reference work. As much as I wish every person who ever did a talk show could be mentioned in this book, that is impossible. Because I don't want to leave the impression that some people's achievements are unimportant, I'm adding a brief mention of a few more talk show hosts, with my apologies for those others I'm not able to include.

Steve Allison (1915–1969). Some media historians regard Allison as one of two-way talk radio's forgotten founders. A night club comic and stage actor prior to his radio career, he became an announcer in Boston in the late 1940s, gradually turning his show into what was then called a "comment and controversy" program. During the 1950s and 1960s, he enjoyed success in Philadelphia, Washington, DC, and Los Angeles. Because he did a late-night shift, often from a local nightclub, he called himself "The Man Who Owns Midnight." Among the announcers he mentored was the young Joe Pyne.

Art Bell (1945–). A former political talker, Bell changed his focus in the late 1980s, devoting his show to discussions of UFOs, the paranormal, and conspiracy theories. He gained a large following on his syndicated overnight show *Coast to Coast AM*, which he hosted throughout the 1990s and into the next century.

Neal Boortz (1945–). A libertarian conservative with a degree in law, Boortz went on the air in Atlanta, Georgia, in the late 1960s and remained a local talk host there for several decades before becoming nationally syndicated. Throughout the first decade of the twenty-first century, *Talkers* magazine has consistently listed him among the ten most listened-to talk show hosts.

Joyce Brothers (1928–). Brothers first became known for her expertise on boxing history, which made her a winner on the *$64,000 Question* quiz show in late 1955. With her PhD in psychology, she got her first TV talk show in August 1958, discussing relationships and answering audience questions. Since then, she has continued to host advice shows on radio, while writing a number of books and a column for *Good Housekeeping*.

Joy Browne (1944–). A graduate of Northeastern University in Boston, Browne is a licensed clinical psychologist who did her first radio advice show in Boston in the late 1970s. Known for her expertise in relationship counseling as well as her empathy for her callers, she has had a syndicated radio show originating from WOR in New York since the early 1990s. A frequent guest on TV shows like *Larry King Live* and *The Oprah Winfrey Show*, she is the author of several best-selling books.

Dick Cavett (1936–). A former joke-writer for Jack Paar and Johnny Carson, Cavett was regarded as one of TV's most literate and witty talk show hosts from 1968 through 1975 when he did a talk show for ABC, and then on PBS until 1982. While he never got the big ratings that Carson did, critics repeatedly praised him for being well informed and doing interesting interviews; his work, which won three Emmy awards, was considered some of the best on commercial TV.

Dr. Dean Edell (1941–). A former ophthalmologist, Edell did his first call-in medical show on KGO radio in San Francisco in 1978. The program became so popular that it went into national syndication, and by 2008, he was heard on over 400 stations. Edell gives listeners no-nonsense advice on a wide range of topics. He has also written several self-help books based on questions listeners have asked him.

Larry Elder (1952–). A former attorney, Elder is an African American conservative who has been compared to Rush Limbaugh. His views have generated controversy among liberal and moderate members of the black community, with whom he frequently debates. Calling himself the "Sage of South Central," the Los Angeles–based talker is the author of several books and since early 1994 has been on the air at KABC as well as syndicated nationally.

Joe Franklin (1926–). The self-proclaimed "king of nostalgia," Franklin became a radio host in New York City beginning in the late 1940s and became known for his *Joe Franklin's Memory Lane* show. He also hosted a long-running late-night TV show that began in 1951 and lasted into the early 1990s. Critics said he fawned over his guests, but fans found him down-to-earth and personable. His specialty was music from as far back as the vaudeville and big-band eras, and there weren't many celebrities he hadn't met at one time or another. He also published a nostalgia magazine and published compact discs filled with songs from that bygone era.

Bob Grant (1929–). A veteran conservative talker currently on WABC radio in New York City, Grant does a show in the style of Joe Pyne, with whom he competed when both were on the air in Los Angeles during the mid 1960s.

Grant is known for being outspoken as well as controversial: He has been in trouble on a number of occasions for making remarks his detractors felt were racist or anti-immigrant. Like Pyne, he uses clever putdowns when he thinks a caller has said something stupid.

Louis Lomax (1922–1970). A former print journalist who spoke out against racism, Lomax was one of the few African Americans to have his own TV talk show, which ran from 1964 to 1968 on KTTV in Los Angeles. Lomax, whose political views were often liberal, once debated Joe Pyne (most critics said he won). He also did guest appearances on such TV talk shows as Jack Paar's *The Tonight Show* and the *Merv Griffin Show*.

Rachel Maddow (1973–). A Rhodes scholar with a PhD in political science, Maddow became a talk show host in 2004 on the new liberal network Air America Radio and gained respect for her erudition as well as her knowledge of politics. By 2006, she was being asked to appear on television occasionally as a liberal pundit, and by early 2008, she had become a regular political analyst on MSNBC, as well as continuing her radio talk show. MSNBC gave Maddow her own network TV show beginning in September of 2008.

Wally Phillips (1925–2008). From 1965 to 1986, Phillips was the king of morning radio on WGN in Chicago. He was a personable host who liked to crack corny jokes but was never vulgar. He was sometimes serious, reassuring his listeners when there was a crisis in the news, he was sometimes amusing, cheering his audience up and getting the day off to a good start. Whether talking to a celebrity or chatting with a listener, Phillips loved his work, and his audience loved him in return, during a radio career that spanned more than forty years.

Maury Povich (1939–). Son of longtime *Washington Post* sportswriter Shirley Povich, Maury Povich cohosted a television talk show called *Panorama* on WTTG in Washington, DC, beginning in 1967. After broadcasting news in such cities as Los Angeles, Chicago, and Philadelphia, he became the host of a tabloid newsmagazine show called *A Current Affair* before returning to talk, hosting the syndicated *Maury Povich Show* (later renamed just *Maury*) beginning in 1991. Like Jerry Springer, Povich often veered into what critics called trash TV.

Sally Jessy Raphael (1935–). Known for her trademark oversized red-framed glasses, Raphael grew up in Puerto Rico and New York City and worked for a number of radio stations before finally becoming a syndicated advice-giver beginning in 1981. She then began hosting a syndicated TV talk show; this show was not as much about advice as about human interest stories, and it featured guests who were unusual in some way, whether morbidly obese or conjoined twins or women who were over forty when they gave birth. Her critics accused her of doing trash TV, but her fans said she didn't exploit the guests and tried to help them solve their problems. Her TV talk show ran for nearly twenty years.

Montel Williams (1956–). A former U.S. Marine and a motivational speaker, Williams began doing a syndicated TV talk show in 1991 becoming one of the few African Americans hosting on late-night TV. His show lasted for seventeen years and covered a wide range of topics typical of the genre. Williams also became known for featuring health-related issues on his show, such as raising awareness about multiple sclerosis, a disease that he was diagnosed with in 1999.

Selected Bibliography

BOOKS

Alba, Ben. *Inventing Late Night: Steve Allen and the Original Tonight Show.* Amherst, NY: Prometheus Books, 2005.

Allen, Steve. *Hi Ho Steverino! My Adventures in the Wonderful Wacky World of Television.* Fort Lee, NJ: Barricade, 1992.

Altschuler, Glenn C., and David I. Grossvogel. *Changing Channels: America in TV Guide.* Urbana: University of Illinois Press, 1992.

Anderson, Benedict. *Imagined Communities: Reflections on the Origins and Spread of Nationalism.* New York: Verso, 1991.

Apostolidis, Paul. *Stations of the Cross: Adorno and Christian Right Radio.* Durham, NC: Duke University Press, 2000.

Barker, David C. *Rushed to Judgement: Talk Radio, Persuasion and American Political Behavior.* New York: Columbia University Press, 2002.

Barlow, William. *Voice Over: The Making of Black Radio.* Philadelphia: Temple University Press, 1999.

Barnouw, Erik. *A Tower in Babel: A History of Broadcasting in the United States to 1933.* New York: Oxford University Press, 1966.

———. *The Golden Web: A History of Broadcasting in the United States 1933–1953.* New York: Oxford University Press, 1968.

———. *The Image Empire: A History of Broadcasting in the United States from 1953.* New York: Oxford University Press, 1970.

Barrett, Don. *Los Angeles Radio People. Volume 2, 1957–1997.* Los Angeles: DB Marketing, 1997.

Beal, William G., Alice Sapienza-Donnelly, and Richard J. Harris. *When Radio Was Young: Questions and Answers About Early Pittsburgh Radio.* Pittsburgh: Wilkinsburg Commission Inc., 1995.

Brindze, Ruth. *Not to Be Broadcast: The Truth about the Radio.* New York: Vanguard, 1937.

Brock, David. *The Republican Noise Machine: Right-Wing Media and How It Corrupts Democracy.* New York: Crown, 2004.

Brooks, Tim, and Earle Marsh. *The Complete Directory to Prime Time Network and Cable TV Shows*, 9th ed. New York: Ballantine Books, 2007.

Brudnoy, David. *Life Is Not a Rehearsal: A Memoir.* New York: Doubleday, 1997.

Carruth, Gorton. *The Encyclopedia of American Facts and Dates*, 10th ed. New York: HarperCollins, 1997.

Carter, Bill. *The Late Shift: Letterman, Leno, and the Network Battle for the Night.* New York: Hyperion, 1994.

Cogley, John. *Report on Blacklisting. Volume II (Radio-Television).* New York: Fund for the Republic, 1956.

Dempsey, John M., ed. *Sports-Talk Radio in America.* New York: Haworth Press, 2006.

Dobson, James C. *The New Dare to Discipline.* Carol Stream, IL: Tyndale House, 1996.

Don Francisco (Mario Kreutzberger). *Life, Camera, Action.* Miguel Hidalgo, Mexico: Grijalbo, 2002.

Duncan, Jacci, ed. *Making Waves: The 50 Greatest Women in Radio and Television.* Kansas City, MO: Andrews McMeel, 2001.

Dunning, John. *On the Air: The Encyclopedia of Old Time Radio.* New York: Oxford University Press, 1998.

Edelstein, Andrew J., and Kevin McDonough. *The Seventies: From Hot Pants to Hot Tubs.* New York: Dutton, 1990.

Elman, Steve, and Alan Tolz. *Burning Up the Airwaves: Jerry Williams, Talk Radio, and the Life in Between.* Beverly, MA: Commonwealth Editions, 2008.

Fang, Irving E. *Those Radio Commentators!* Ames: Iowa State University Press, 1977.

Firth, Major Ivan, and Gladys Shaw Erskine. *Gateway to Radio.* New York: Macaulay Company, 1934.

Fisher, Marc. *Something in the Air.* New York: Random House, 2007.

Gilgoff, Dan. *The Jesus Machine: How James Dobson, Focus on the Family, and Evangelical America are Winning the Culture War.* New York: St. Martin's Press, 2007.

Gwinn, Alison, ed. *Entertainment Weekly: The 100 Greatest TV Shows of All Time.* New York: Time-Life Books, 1998.

Halper, Donna L. *Invisible Stars: A Social History of Women in American Broadcasting.* Stoneham, MA: Focal Press, 2001.

Hilliard, Robert L., and Michael C. Keith. *The Broadcast Century and Beyond*, 4th ed. Burlington, MA: Focal Press, 2005.

———. *Dirty Discourse: Sex and Indecency in Broadcasting*, 2nd ed. Malden, MA: Blackwell, 2007.

Hilmes, Michele, ed. *NBC: America's Network.* Berkeley: University of California Press, 2007.

———. *Only Connect: A Cultural History of Broadcasting in the United States.* Belmont, CA: Wadsworth, 2002.

———. *Radio Voices.* Minneapolis: University of Minnesota Press, 1997.

Hilton, Jack. *The TV Inquisitors.* New York: Chamberlain, 1981.

Jaker, Bill, Frank Sulek, and Peter Kanze. *The Airwaves of New York.* Jefferson, NC: McFarland, 1998.

Keith, Michael C. *The Radio Station*, 7th ed. Burlington, MA: Focal Press, 2007.

————. *Sounds in the Night: All Night Radio in American Life.* Ames: Iowa State University Press, 2001.

King, Larry, with Bill Gilbert. *How to Talk to Anyone, Anytime, Anywhere.* New York: Gramercy Press, 2004.

————, with Marty Appel. *When You're from Brooklyn, the Rest of the World Is Tokyo.* Boston: Little, Brown, 1992.

Kisseloff, Jeff. *The Box: An Oral History of Television, 1929–1961.* New York: Viking, 1995.

Klinenberg, Eric. *Fighting for Air: The Battle to Control America's Media.* New York: Metropolitan Books, 2007.

Landry, Robert J. *Who, What, Why Is Radio?* New York: George W. Stewart, 1942.

Laufer, Peter. *Inside Talk Radio: America's Voice or Just Hot Air?* Secaucus, NJ: Carol, 1995.

Levin, Murray B. *Talk Radio and the American Dream.* Lexington, MA: D. C. Heath, 1987.

Limbaugh, Rush. *The Way Things Ought to Be.* New York: Pocket Books, 1992.

MacDonald, J. Fred. *Don't Touch That Dial: Radio Programming in American Life, 1920–60.* Chicago: Nelson-Hall, 1979.

McMahon, Ed. *Here's Johnny.* New York: Berkley, 2005.

McNeil, Alex. *Total Television,* 4th ed. New York: Penguin, 1996.

————, and David Fisher. *When Television Was Young.* New York: Thomas Nelson, 2007.

Munson, Wayne. *All Talk: The Talkshow in Media Culture.* Philadelphia: Temple University Press, 1993.

O'Dell, Cary. *Women Pioneers in Television.* Jefferson, NC: McFarland, 1997.

Overstreet, Harry A., and Bonaro W. Overstreet. *Town Meeting Comes to Town.* New York: Harper, 1938.

Ozersky, Josh. *Archie Bunker's America: TV in an Era of Change.* Carbondale: Southern Illinois University Press, 2003.

Phillips, Lisa A. *Public Radio: Behind the Voices.* New York: CDS Books, 2006.

Postman, Neil. *Amusing Ourselves to Death: Public Discourse in the Age of Show Business.* 20th anniversary ed. New York: Penguin, 2005.

Powers, Ron. *The Newscasters.* New York: St. Martin's Press, 1977.

Raphael, Sally Jessy, with Pam Proctor. *Sally: Unconventional Success.* New York: St. Martin's Press, 1991.

Rendall, Steve, Jim Naureckas, and Jeff Cohen. *The Way Things Aren't: Rush Limbaugh's Reign of Error.* New York: New Press, 1995.

Rose, Hilly. *But That's Not What I Called About.* Chicago: Contemporary Books, 1978.

Saralegui, Cristina. *My Life as a Blonde.* New York: Grand Central, 1998.

Schiffer, Michael Brian. *The Portable Radio in American Life.* Tucson: University of Arizona Press, 1991.

Schlessinger, Dr. Laura. *The Proper Care and Feeding of Husbands.* New York: HarperCollins, 2004.

————. *Ten Stupid Things Women Do to Mess Up Their Lives.* New York: HarperCollins, 1995.

Schultz, Ed. *Straight Talk from the Heartland.* New York: Regan, 2004.

Schultze, Quentin, ed. *American Evangelicals and the Mass Media*. Grand Rapids: Academie Books, 1990.

Shattuc, Jane. *The Talking Cure: TV Talk Shows and Women*. New York: Routledge, 1997.

Slide, Anthony. *Great Radio Personalities in Historic Photographs*. New York: Vestal Press, 1982.

Smiley, Tavis, and David Ritz. *What I Know for Sure*. New York: Doubleday, 2006.

Springer, Jerry, and Laura Morton. *Ringmaster*. New York: St. Martin's Press, 1998.

Sterling, Christopher H., and John Michael Kittross. *Stay Tuned: A History of American Broadcasting*, 3rd ed. Mahwah, NJ: Erlbaum, 2002.

Stern, Howard. *Private Parts*. New York: Random House, 1995.

Timberg, Bernard M., and Robert J. Earler. *Television Talk: A History of the TV Talk Show*. Austin: University of Texas Press, 2002.

Walters, Barbara. *Audition: A Memoir*. New York: Knopf, 2008.

Ware, Susan. *It's One O'Clock and Here Is Mary Margaret McBride*. New York: New York University Press, 2005.

Weinstein, David. *The Forgotten Network: DuMont and the Birth of American Television*. Philadelphia: Temple University Press, 2004.

Whitfield, Stephen J. *The Culture of the Cold War*, 2nd ed. Baltimore: Johns Hopkins University Press, 1996.

Wicker, Tom. *Shooting Star: The Brief Arc of Joe McCarthy*. Orlando: Harcourt, 2006.

Wright, John L., ed. *Possible Dreams: Enthusiasm for Technology in America*. Dearborn: Henry Ford Museum, 1992.

JOURNALS, MAGAZINES, AND NEWSPAPERS

Abcarian, Robin, and Meg James. "The Imus Scandal: Firing By CBS." *Los Angeles Times*, 13 April 2007, p. A1.

Adams, Val. "Man and Wife Team" (Mike Wallace and Buff Cobb). *New York Times*, 2 December 1951, p. X25.

Adelson, Andrea. "After Midnight, A Radio Talk Show Is Growing Coast to Coast" (Art Bell). *New York Times*, 18 May 1998, p. D7.

"Air Commercials to Resume Today." *New York Times*, 16 April 1945, p. 9.

Allen, Henry. "The Mother of Media Psychology" (Joyce Brothers). *Washington Post*, 14 December 1989, pp. B1–2.

Alter, Jonathan. "Next: The Revolt of the Revolted." *Newsweek*, 6 November 1995, pp. 46–47.

Andrews, Edmund L. "Howard Stern Employer Faces $600,000 Fine." *New York Times*, 18 December 1992, pp. A1, D17.

Asay, Paul. "Nearly 70, James Dobson Still Focused." *Colorado Springs Gazette*, 9 April 2006, p. 56.

"Attila the Tongue: Michael Savage Invades America." *Radio Ink*, 14 May 2001, pp. 11–17.

Bapis, James. "Utah Radio Program Rekindles Human Values, Listeners Say" (Herb Jepko). *Ogden (UT) Standard-Examiner*, 25 July 1965, p. 16.

Barker, David C. "Rushed Decisions: Political Talk Radio and Vote Choice, 1994–1996." *Journal of Politics*, vol. 61, no. 2, May 1999, pp. 527–539.

————, and Kathleen Knight. "Political Talk Radio and Public Opinion." *Public Opinion Quarterly,* vol. 64, no. 2, Summer 2000, pp. 149–170.

Bartlett, Kenneth B. "Social Impact of the Radio." *Annals of the American Academy of Political and Social Science,* vol. 250, March 1947, pp. 89–97.

Berges, Marshall. "Home Q&A: Alanna and Michael Jackson." *Los Angeles Times,* 13 July 1975, pp. R26–27, 38.

Bernstein, Adam. "Merv Griffin: TV Host, Game-Show Creator." *Washington Post,* 13 August 2007, p. B4.

————. "Tonight Show Host Jack Paar Dies." *Washington Post,* 28 January 2004, p. B6.

Binelli, Mark. "The Most Honest Man in News" (Keith Olbermann). *Rolling Stone,* 8 March 2007, pp. 63–65.

Blake, Mariah. "Stations of the Cross." *Columbia Journalism Review,* May–June 2005, pp. 32–37.

Blomberg, Marcia. "Bible of Talk Radio Published in Springfield" (Talkers magazine). *Springfield (MA) Republican,* 27 May 2007, p. D1.

Blustain, Sarah. "The Stealth Politics of Laura Schlessinger." *Lilith,* Summer 2000, pp. 10–13, 30–31.

Bolce, Louis, Gerald DeMaio, and Douglas Muzzio. "Dial-In Democracy: Talk Radio and the 1994 Election." *Political Science Quarterly,* vol. 111, no. 3, Autumn 1996, pp. 457–481.

Brecher, Elinor J. "Mistress of Flip" (Randi Rhodes). *Miami Herald,* 5 September 2004, p. 1M.

————. "Talk Radio's Brassy Goddess of Gab" (Randi Rhodes). *Miami Herald,* 31 January 1993, p. 1J.

Broder, Mitch. "Small-Talk Show Is Big Draw in Wee Hours" (Herb Jepko). *New York Times,* 23 February 1975, p. D29.

Brown, James. "Herb Jepko: Main Street Mainstay." *Los Angeles Times,* 25 May 1975, pp. Q32, 74.

————. "Relating to People in a Caring Way" (Dr. Toni Grant). *Los Angeles Times,* 27 November 1977, p. P124.

————. "Talk of the Town: Open-Mike Radio Shows That Encourage You to Talk Back." *Los Angeles Times,* 4 December 1979, pp. H1, 8–9.

Browning, Norma Lee. "Johnny Carson: Look Out World, Here I Come." *Chicago Tribune,* 3 March 1967, p. 8.

Bunce, Alan. "Shock Talk: No-Holds-Barred TV Shows Winning New Fans." *Christian Science Monitor,* 5 October 1988, p. 1.

Butman, Carl H. "Nine Months of Broadcasting." *Radio World,* vol. 1, no. 16, July 1922, p. 7.

"Cackleclatsch" (Virginia Graham). *Time,* 7 June 1968, p. 68.

"Cancer Claims Radio Figure Steve Allison." *Los Angeles Times,* 7 March 1969, p. F20.

Carlin, Peter Ames. "Radio Host's Nation Built on Fear" (Michael Savage). *The Oregonian* (Portland, Oregon), 15 March 2003, p. B1.

Carlson, Margaret. "My Dinner with Rush" (Rush Limbaugh). *Time,* 23 January 1995, p. 26.

Carmody, John. "Dave Garroway Dies: First Today Show Host." *Washington Post,* 22 July 1982, p. C5.

———. "FCC To Probe Broadcast Obscenity." *Washington Post*, 28 March 1973, pp. A1, 6.

Carter, Betsy, Lucy Howard, and John Yang. "Radio's Gabfest." *Newsweek*, 29 October 1979, p. 87.

Carter, Bill. "Behind the Headlines in the Leno-Letterman War." *New York Times*, 30 January 1994, pp. SM28, 30, 32.

"Caution Urged in Radio War Broadcasts." *Washington Post*, 9 September 1939, p. 14.

Chambers, Veronica, and Deborah Gregory. "Arsenio Gets Serious" (Arsenio Hall). *Essence*, November 1993, pp. 72–77.

Chandler, Russell. "Airwave Preachers Reach More at Once Than Christ in Lifetime." *Los Angeles Times*, 25 February 1980, pp. B3, 15.

Christy, Marian. "Steve Allen Unveils His Secrets of Success." *Boston Globe*, 9 July 1989, p. A12.

Cilizza, Chris, and Shailagh Murray. "Radio Host Denies Broadcasting His Support for Obama" (Ed Schultz). *Washington Post*, 3 February 2008, p. A2.

Codel, Martin. "Radio Personalities of the Presidential Prospects." *Broadcasting*, 1 March 1936, p. 28.

Cohen, Rich. "The King and I" (Larry King). *Rolling Stone*, 14 November 1996, pp. 74–83.

Colander, Pat. "Oprah Winfrey's Odyssey: Talk Show Host to Mogul." *New York Times*, 12 March 1989, p. H31.

Cook, Fred J. "Hate Clubs of the Air." *The Nation*, pp. 523–527.

Corliss, Richard. "Late Night with David Letterman." *Time*, 22 March 1982, p. 69.

———. "Look Who's Talking." *Time*, 23 January 1995, pp. 22–25.

Crewdson, John M. "An Angry Nation of Insomniacs" (Herb Jepko). *New York Times*, 18 July 1977, p. L14.

Crosby, John. "Cigarettes and Newscasts, Sponsors and Sensitivities." *Hartford Courant*, 4 July 1954, p. SM12.

———. "Expert on Humility Reveals its Dangers" (Arthur Godfrey). *Hartford Courant*, 28 October 1953, p. 18.

Cuprisin, Tim. "Founder Predicts Profits in Liberal Radio." *Milwaukee Journal-Sentinel*, 22 December 2004, p. B10.

Darling, Lynn. "King of the Night Airwaves" (Larry King). *Washington Post*, 19 June 1979, pp. B1, 5.

Denny, George V. "Radio Builds Democracy." *Journal of Educational Sociology*, vol. 14, no. 6, February 1941, pp. 370–377.

DeQuine, Jeanne. "The Queen of the Airwaves" (Cristina Saralegui). *Time*, 22 August 2005, pp. 48–49.

Dominguez, Robert. "Mr. Sabado Night" (Don Francisco). *New York Daily News*, 20 May 2006, p. 75.

Donovan, Doug, and Peter Kafka. "Hosts With the Most." *Forbes*, 19 March 2001, pp. 164–66.

"Dr. Laura Celebrates 10 Years of Syndication." *Radio and Records*, 23 July 2004, pp. 14, 16.

Duke, Sherlean. "She Sends Care over the Air" (Laura Schlessinger). *Los Angeles Times*, 25 May 1978, pp. OC1, 14.

Dutton, Walt. "Controversy Is Lomax Forte." *Los Angeles Times*, 23 April 1965, p. C18.

"Ellen and 'Ellen' Come Out" (Ellen DeGeneres). *New York Times*, 1 May 1997, p. A26.

Ellington, Barbara. "The Circus Master Comes to Jamaica" (Jerry Springer). *The Gleaner* (Kingston, Jamaica), 30 April 2001, pp. 10–11.

Epstein, Debbie, and Deborah Lynn Steinberg. "Life in the Bleep-Cycle: Inventing Id-TV on the Jerry Springer Show." *Discourse*, vol. 25, no. 3, Fall 2003, pp. 90–114.

Eviatar, Daphne. "Murdoch's Fox News: They Distort, They Decide." *The Nation*, 12 March 2001, pp. 11–15.

Farah, Joseph. "Talking Back: How Radio is Empowering People and Democratizing the Media." *New Dimensions*, vol. 6, no. 2, August 1992, pp. 18–19.

Farhi, Paul. "Don Imus Gingerly Steps Back on Air." *Washington Post*, 4 December 2007, p. C1.

"Filthy Words, the FCC, and the First Amendment: Regulating Broadcast Obscenity." *Virginia Law Review*, vol. 61, no. 3, April 1975, pp. 579–642.

Fisher, Marc. "Air America, in the Throes of Victory?" *Washington Post*, 10 December 2006, p. N2.

———. "The Outer Limits; A Lone Voice in the Desert Lures 10 Million Listeners" (Art Bell). *Washington Post*, 29 March 1998, p. F1.

———. "Soul of a News Machine" (National Public Radio). *Washington Post*, 22 October 1989, pp. P16–23, 37–38.

———. "Talk Radio's Founding Father: Barry Gray Understood the Medium's Power." *Washington Post*, 31 December 1996, p. D7.

Fishman, Steve. "Howard Stern in Space." *New York Magazine*, 12 December 2005, pp. 32–377, 153–155.

Flatow, Sheryl. "For Many, His Show Is Home" (Don Francisco). *Parade Magazine*, 9 November 2003, pp. 16–17.

Fleming, Louis B. "Tuning in to Talk Show Therapists." *Los Angeles Times*, 2 July 1982, pp. B1, B3.

Friendly, Andy. "Recalling Snyder, a Fearless, Peerless Friend." *Television Week*, 6 August 2007, p. 10.

Frum, Linda. "Dr. Laura Schlessinger Talks to Linda Frum." *Maclean's*, 27 February 2006, pp. 12–13.

Funt, Peter, "Phil Donahue: TV Underestimates Women." *New York Times*, 20 May 1979, p. D40.

Fussman, Cal. "Howard Goes Berserk" (Howard Stern). *Esquire*, January 2006, pp. 76–81.

"Galleries Barred to Radio Reporters." *New York Times*, 8 November 1933, p.11.

Gardella, Kay. "What Makes Mike Wallace Tick?" *A&E Monthly*, January 1995, pp. 19–22.

Garofoli, Joe. "Tom Snyder, King of Very Late-Night TV, Dies at 71." *San Francisco Chronicle*, 31 July 2007, p. E2.

"George V. Denny, Radio Host, Dead: Founder and Moderator of Town Meeting of the Air." *New York Times*, 12 November 1959, p. 35.

Gersch, Beate. "Class in Daytime Talk Television." *Peace Review*, vol. 11, no. 2, June 1999, pp. 275–282.

Gerston, Jill. "Here's Everybody! After Carson, a Host of Late Night Wannabes." *New York Times*, 16 August 1992, pp. H1, 21.

Gildea, William. "Povich: Off to Chicago." *Washington Post*, 8 December 1976, pp. B1, 6.

Gillis, Charlie. "Is Canada Ready for Loudmouth TV?" *Macleans*, 4 October 2004, pp. 23–27.

Golden, Daniel. "Oprah, Phil, Geraldo, Sally Jessy: Why Do People Tell Their Most Intimate Secrets on National Television?" *Boston Globe Sunday Magazine*, 10 July 1988, p. 16.

Goldman, Kevin L. "Radio's Latest Boom: Late-Night Talk Shows." *New York Times*, 2 May 1982, p. D33.

Goodman, Mark, and John Griffiths. "Don't Blame Your Flame: Controversial Talk Host Dr. Laura Schlessinger Tells Women to Cork That Whine." *People*, 11 July 1994, p. 93.

Goodman, Walter. "Insult as Entertainment: Cultural Evil or Fad?" *New York Times*, 20 May 1984, pp. H1, 19.

Gould, Jack. "Home, Daytime Television Show for Women on NBC, Starts Ambitiously." *New York Times*, 5 March 1954, p. 26.

———. "TV: Literate and Witty" (David Susskind). *New York Times*, 23 October 1958, p. 62.

Graustark, Barbara. "On-Air Psychologists—Healers or Exploiters?" *New York Times*, 9 October 1981, p. D23.

Greene, Bob. "Fame: The Product of a Fickle Audience" (Jack Eigen). *Chicago Tribune*, 30 January 1983, p. J1.

Grossberger, Lewis. "Late Night with David Letterman." *Rolling Stone*, 10 June 1982, p. 25.

———. "The Rush Hours" (Rush Limbaugh). *New York Times*, 16 December 1990, pp. SM58, 62–64, 98–99.

Haga, Chuck. "Going against the Grain: Ed Schultz, Once a Staunch Conservative, Is a Rarity." *Minneapolis Star-Tribune*, 19 February 2004, p. 1B.

Hale, Mike. "When Talk Show Hosts Worked Without a Net." *New York Times*, 9 January 2008, p. 7.

Harrington, Richard. "Howard Stern Fired in New York." *Washington Post*, 2 October 1985, pp. D1, 13.

Harrison, Michael. "Air America's Breakout Star Randi Rhodes." *Talkers*, December 2005–January 2006, pp. 16, 34, 40, 44.

Hass, Nancy. "A Talk Show for an Indelicate Age" (The View). *New York Times*, 8 November 1998, pp. ST1, 7.

Heath, Rebecca Piirto. "Tuning In to Talk." *American Demographics*, vol. 20, no. 2, February 1998, pp. 48–54.

Heffernan, Virginia. "The Un-Rosie: Ellen DeGeneres, the Least Angry Woman on Television." *New York Times*, 29 August 2004, p. AR18.

"Herb Jepko Has Millions of Listeners." *Idaho Falls (ID) Post-Register*, 11 May 1975, p. 11.

Herbert, Bob. "For Tavis Smiley, Promises to Keep." *New York Times*, 15 February 2007, p. A29.

Hertzberg, Hendrik. "Radio Daze: The Talk of the Town." *New Yorker*, 11 August 2003, p. 23.

Hinckley, David. "Barry Gray: Knight of the Night." *New York Daily News*, 23 December 1996, p. 67.

———. "Franklin Steps Off Memory-Go-Round" (Joe Franklin). *New York Daily News*, 2 June 2004, p. 71.

———. "Stern Has Lost His Number 1 Spot." *New York Daily News*, 23 February 2007, p. 122.

———. "Talk Radio Giant Barry Gray Dies in Sleep at 80." *New York Daily News*, 22 December 1996, p. 13.

Hoekstra, Dave. "He was Chicago Radio: Known for Cornball Humor and Giveaways" (Wally Phillips). *Chicago Sun-Times*, 28 March 2008, p.16.

"Hoover Proposes Radio Cooperation." *New York Times*, 7 October 1924, p. 25.

Hull, Anne V. "Talkin' Trash: Something Has Happened to Talk Shows in the Last Couple of Years." *St. Petersburg (FL) Times*, 7 December 1988, p. 1D.

"Interview: Mutual's Larry King Says Goodnight." *Radio Ink*, 15 February 1993, pp. 42–47.

"Interview: Rush Limbaugh." *Pulse of Radio*, 12 August 1991, pp. 18–23.

"Interview: Sally Jessy Raphael." *Pulse of Radio*, 13 May 1991, pp. 22–27.

"In This Corner: The Challenger!" (Steve Allen). *TV Guide*, 23 June 1956, pp. 17–19.

"It's an Unhappy Day for Radio Quiz Fans." *Washington Post*, 17 January 1942, p. 1.

Ivins, Molly. "Lyin' Bully" (Rush Limbaugh). *Mother Jones*, May–June 1995, pp. 37–39.

"Jack Eigen Returns to TV Interviewing." *Chicago Defender*, 22 May 1971, p. 24.

"Joe Pyne, 44, Dies; Talk Show Host." *Washington Post*, 25 March 1970, p. C6.

"Johnny Carson: He's Done It without Tantrums or Accusations." *Chicago Tribune*, 31 March 1963, pp. G34, 36.

Johnson, Dean. "Appreciation: Jerry Williams Was Pioneer in Radio Talk." *Boston Herald*, 30 April 2003, p. 52.

Johnson, Rebecca, and Kathleen Powers. "Jerry Springer under Siege." *Good Housekeeping*, September 1998, pp. 114–119.

Jones, Jack. "Radio and TV Giant Arthur Godfrey Dies." *Los Angeles Times*, 17 March 1983, pp. B3, B22.

Jurkowitz, Mark. "All The Rage—Talk Radio Host Michael Savage." *Boston Globe*, 5 March 2003, p. C1.

———. "Jerry Williams: Radio Crusader." *Boston Phoenix*, 21–27 October 1988, pp. 6, 24, 28, 31.

———. "Talk Radio's Blue Streak." *Boston Globe Sunday Magazine*, 13 February 2000, p. 16.

Kane, Thomas. "Public Argument, Civil Society, and What Talk Radio Teaches about Rhetoric." *Argumentation and Advocacy*, vol. 34, no. 3, Winter 1998, pp. 154–162.

Kasindorf, Jeanie. "Bad Mouth: Howard Stern vs. the FCC." *New York Magazine*, 23 November 1992, pp. 38–45.

Kempley, Rita. "Rose on the Thorns of a Ratings Dilemma" (Charlie Rose). *Washington Post*, 21 June 1981, p. TV3.

Kennedy, John W. "Mixing Politics and Piety: Christian Talk Radio." *Christianity Today*, 15 August 1994, pp. 42–48.

Kent, Leticia. "For Women Only?" *New York Times*, 30 March 1969, p. D21.

"Killer Joe" (Joe Pyne). *Time*, 29 July 1966, p. 30.

Kipling, Kay. "If You Knew Jerry: There's Much More to Sarasota's Most Famous Resident, Trash-Talk TV Icon Jerry Springer, Than Most of Us Would Ever Imagine." *Sarasota Magazine*, January 2006, pp. 112–114.

Kolbert, Elizabeth. "Political Candidates and Call-In Shows: When the People Want to Be Heard." *New York Times*, 10 June 1992, p. A20.

Kornheiser, Tony. "Stand Up and Be Comic: Jay Leno Rolls into Town with his Late Night Laugh Track." *Washington Post*, 24 September 1983, pp. C1, C5.

Kupelian, David. "Breaking the Rules" (Rush Limbaugh). *New Dimensions*, vol. 6, no. 2, August 1992, pp. 21–23.

———, and Robert Just. "Radio Revolution." *New Dimensions*, vol. 6, no. 2, August 1992, pp. 14–16.

Kurtz, Howard. "A Voice from Above, and to the Left: North Dakota Talker Ed Schultz Is Set to Blanket Washington." *Washington Post*, 10 January 2005, p. C1.

Kurtz, Paul. "A Tribute to Steve Allen." *Skeptical Inquirer*, January–February 2001, pp. 5–7.

Laurent, Lawrence. "Dinah Shore's Comeback." *Washington Post*, 4 August 1970, p. B5.

———. "Talk, Food, Sewing, Art, Music—and Dinah." *Washington Post*, 2 July 1972, p. TC5.

Lee, Felicia R. "Media Man on a Mission: The Whirl of Tavis Smiley." *New York Times*, 10 October 2006, p. E1.

Lichtenstein, Grace. "Last of the Hot Shot Big Mouths" (Barry Gray). *New York Times*, 15 February 1970, p. 97.

Lipton, Michael A., and Jennifer Frey. "The (Far) Right Stuff" (Sean Hannity). *People Weekly*, 11 February 2002, pp. 117–119.

———, and Pamela Warrick. "Funny Man at Work" (Jay Leno). *People*, 6 May 2002, pp. 64–68.

Logan, Joe. "The King of Talk: Remarkable Rise" (Rush Limbaugh). *Philadelphia Inquirer*, 2 June 1995, p. A1.

Lowry, Brian. "Talkers Take Toll on Mere Mortals." *Variety*, 15 January 2007, p. 18.

Lowry, Cynthia. "Insomnia Cure: Les Crane?" *Chicago Tribune*, 8 November 1964, p. S7.

Lynn, Barry. "Dobson's Crusade: Ushering in an Officially 'Christian America.'" *Church and State*, October 2004, p. 15.

Marcucci, Carl. "Don Imus: Telling It like It Is." *Manager's Business Report*, January 2000, pp. 15–18.

Marin, Rick. "Coming Up Roses" (Rosie O'Donnell). *Newsweek*, 15 July 1996, pp. 44–48.

Mark, Norman. "Sex-Talk Radio Shows Get Message." *Charleston (WV) Daily Mail*, 6 April 1973, p. 13.

Maslin, Janet. "In Dirty Laundryland." *New York Times*, 10 October 1993, pp. 1, 7.

Mason, Marilynne S. "The Battle for Carson's Mantle." *Christian Science Monitor*, 21 September 1993, p. 12.

"Maxwell On Radio 15 Years." *Pittsburgh Courier*, 1 February 1947, p. 17.

Mayer, William G. "Why Talk Radio is Conservative." *Public Interest*, Summer 2004, pp. 86–104.

McCabe, Bruce. "AM Radio Heating Up the Airwaves." *Boston Globe*, 10 February 1989, p. 41.

McDaniel, Mike. "Rosie Exit Blamed on Money, Not Mouth" (Rosie O'Donnell). *Houston Chronicle*, 26 April 2007, p. S1.

McNichol, Tom. "Rush Is Always Right." *Titusville (Pennsylvania) Herald*, 25 January 1992, USA Weekend Section, pp. 6–8.

Meisler, Andy. "A Different Voice Comes to Public Radio" (Tavis Smiley). *New York Times*, 21 April 2002, pp. A1, 36.

———. "Tom Snyder as Everyman." *New York Times*, 8 May 1994, pp. H31–32.

Meyer, Thomas J. "The Master of Chin Music" (Larry King). *New York Times Magazine*, 26 May 1991, pp. 20–21, 32.

Meyers, Kate. "Donahue Dawns on Daytime." *Entertainment Weekly*, 8 November 1996, p. 84.

Moffett, Matt. "A Sports Talk Show Prospers by Giving Callers No Respect" (Pete Franklin). *Wall Street Journal*, 29 September 1986, pp. 1, 10.

Moore, Micki. "Driven By Necessity" (Sally Jessy Raphael). *Toronto Star*, 13 August 1990, p. C1.

Murdaugh, Don. "Joe Pyne Saw Tobacco Juice Fly." *Chester (PA) Times*, 22 April 1959, p. 19.

"My Mother Has Always Been an Honest Friend" (Cristina Saralegui). *Hispanic*, May 2001, p. 28.

Nelson, Jill. "The Man Who Saved Oprah Winfrey." *Washington Post*, 14 December 1986, pp. SM30–32, 52–57.

———. "Talk Is Cheap." *The Nation*, 5 June 1995, pp. 800–802.

"New PBS Series by Steve Allen Starts Monday." *Hartford Courant*, 9 January 1977, p. P37.

Nichols, Adam, and Corky Siemaszko. "You're Don For, CBS Tells Imus." *New York Daily News*, 13 April 2007, p. 3.

"Night Call Program Gets Favorable Reviews" (New York). *Amsterdam News*, 29 June 1968, p. 27.

"Nitecap Radio Talk Show a Party Line" (Herb Jepko). *Lawton (OK) Constitution-Morning Press*, 12 September 1971, p. 10C.

Page, Don. "Jackson Learns Lesson in Yank Etiquette." *Los Angeles Times*, 11 August 1963, p. D27.

———. "Night of the Hunter Returns to the Airwaves" (Ben Hunter). *Los Angeles Times*, 15 December 1963, p. B34.

———. "Pyne Answers Final Call on Two-Way Radio." *Los Angeles Times*, 21 February 1969, pp. J1, 14.

———. "Telephone Gladiator in the L.A. Arena" (Steve Allison). *Los Angeles Times*, 16 April 1967, p. C38.

Parisi, Albert J. "Talk Radio Bulldog Is Really Just a Pussycat, Friends Say" (Bob Grant). *New York Times*, 27 November 1994, pp. NJ1, 17.

Passy, Charles. "Talk Radio: The Big Business of Big Mouths." *Palm Beach (FL) Post*, 10 May 2008, p. 1A.

Patnode, Randall. "What These People Need Is Radio: New Technology, the Press, and Otherness in 1920s America." *Technology and Culture*, vol. 44, no. 2, April 2003, pp. 285–305.

Peterson, Clarence. "Radio's Latest Success Format: What Are Your Thoughts, Joe Blow?" *Chicago Tribune*, 6 August 1967, pp. H22, 31, 33.

"Phone Beep Rule For Broadcasts Eased by FCC." *Hartford Courant*, 17 December 1972, p. 27.

Pierce, Charles. "Hot Button Issues." *Boston Globe Magazine*, 18 July 2004, pp. 18–21, 31–34.

"Political Voice Personalities." *Radiolog*, 20 November 1932, p. 3.

Post, J. Y. "Comic, Songwriter, Author Steve Allen Dies; Pioneer of 'Tonight' Show in 1953." *Washington Post*, 1 November 2000, p. B7.

Pothier, Mark. "Sounding Off: Jerry Williams, Boston's Irrepressible Dean of Issues-Oriented Talk Radio, Never Got to Say Goodbye." *Boston Globe Sunday Magazine*, 16 June 2002, pp. 11, 29–33.

Prial, Frank J. "Telling Off the Public: Broadcasters Find It Pays to Be Rude." *Wall Street Journal*, 9 May 1967, pp. 1, 14.

"Price Control." *Time*, 20 December 1943, p. 92

"Price Lauds Press on Self-Censorship." *New York Times*, 9 March 1942, p. 17.

Purcelli, Marion. "Miss Graham Talkative about Most Anything" (Virginia Graham). *Chicago Tribune*, 8 August 1965, p. IND8.

Pyne, Joe. "Call Joe. He Won't Call You." *Los Angeles Times*, 12 September 1965, p. N39.

"Radio Congress." *Time* (20 October 1924). http://www.time.com/time/magazine/article/0,9171,769108,00.html (accessed 27 August 2008).

Rahner, Mark. "Liberal Radio Joins the Bray; Air America Dug in its Heels Despite a Rough Start." *Seattle (WA) Times*, 16 December 2004, p. C1.

Randall, Laura. "Talk Radio: Call In Hosts Revel in the New-Found Popularity of Radio as Public Forum." *Christian Science Monitor*, 25 June 1992, p. 14.

"Recording Phone Talk." *Hartford Courant*, 1 December 1947, p. 8.

"Reds' Friends Run Church Council, Head of International Group Says" (Carl McIntire). *Los Angeles Times*, 27 August 1952, p. 7.

Richards, David. "Confidant of the Call-Ins" (Sally Jessy Raphael). *Washington Post*, 26 June 1984, pp. C1–2.

Rifkin, Janey M. "International Talk-Show Host Exists in a Variety of Worlds." *Hispanic Times Magazine*, March–April 2001, pp. 44–46.

Rivera, Geraldo. "I Was Going to Hell." *Newsweek*, 15 July 1996, p. 48.

Roberts, Myron. "Yackity Yackity Yack about Radio Talk Shows." *Los Angeles Times*, 2 July 1967, p. C7.

Robinson, Alan. "Radio Personality Trucker's Companion" (Buddy Ray). *Charleston (WV) Gazette*, 16 July 1976, p. 39.

Rohter, Larry. "Aqui Se Habla English" (Cristina Saralegui). *New York Times*, 26 July 1992, p. 60.

———. "For 100 Million, He Is Saturday Night" (Don Francisco). *New York Times*, 2 June 2002, p. 32.

Rose, Bob. "Kook-Baiting Pyne Likes Controversy." *Washington Post*, 29 July 1967, p. D15.

Rosen, Joel Nathan. "The Mouth Roars No Longer: Pete Franklin, Sports Talk, and Cleveland Indians Baseball, 1967–1987." *Nine: A Journal of Baseball History and Culture*, vol. 15, no. 1, Fall 2006, pp. 13–26.

Rosenberg, Howard. "Letterman: Waiting in the Wings." *Los Angeles Times*, 23 August 1979, pp. E1, 24.

Rosenfeld, Megan. "Maury Povich: Can He Talk!" *Washington Post*, 9 September 1991, pp. B1, 6.

Roshan, Maer. "Poor Little Rich Boy" (Howard Stern). *New York Magazine*, pp. 34–41, 126.

Ross, Chuck. "Creating a Template for the Syndicated Talk Show: Mike, Merv, Phil and Dinah Help Television Talk Come of Age." *Television Week*, 26 February 2007, p. S4.

Rothenberg, Randall. "Morton Downey Jr. Is Taking His Abrasive Style Nationwide." *New York Times*, 16 May 1988, p. C15.

Ruffin, Kyle. "Now an Outbreak of Sex Talk at Night." *Radio Only*, December 1992, pp. 10–14.

Rust, Michael. "Tuning In to America." *Insight*, 17 July 1995, pp. 11–13.

Rutenberg, Jim. "As Talk Radio Wavers, Bush Moves to Firm Up Support." *New York Times*, 17 October 2006, p. A16.

Schleier, Curt. "Jay Leno: Sometimes Nice Guys Do Finish First." *Biography*, August 1997, pp. 38–44

Schudel, Matt. "Joey Bishop, Mild-Mannered Comedian Grounded Hollywood's High Flying Rat Pack." *Washington Post*, 19 October 2007, p. B6.

"The Secret's a 7-Second Delay For Cuss-Word Cuts." *Chicago Defender*, 7 June 1966, p. 13.

Seidenbaum, Art. "KLAC: Where The Talking is Constant." *Los Angeles Times*, 24 March 1968, pp. B9, B12.

Severo, Richard. "Jack Paar, Unpredictable TV Host Who Kept Americans Up Late, Dead at 85." *New York Times*, 28 January 2004, p. A23.

———, and Bill Carter. "Johnny Carson, Low-Key King of Late-Night TV, Dies at 79." *New York Times*, 24 January 2005, p. A1.

"Sex on the Dial" (Bill Ballance). *Newsweek*, 4 September 1972, p. 90.

Shales, Tom. "Jack Paar: Hamminess and Wry Wit." *Washington Post*, 19 June 1983, pp. H1, H5–6.

———. "Jay Leno Named Johnny's Successor: Letterman Said to Be 'Furious' over NBC's Tonight Show Pick." *Washington Post*, 7 June 1991, pp. C1–2.

———. "Shriek Chic: It's Morton Downey!" *Washington Post*, 6 July 1988, pp. D1, D4.

———. "Tom Snyder Turned Television into a Tete-à-Tete." *Washington Post*, 31 July 2007, p. C1.

———. "Top of the Morning: NBC's 30 Vital, Lively Years of 'Today.'" *Washington Post*, 15 January 1982, pp. C1, 4.

Shanley, J. P. "Night People's Friend" (Jean Shepherd). *New York Times*, 19 August 1956, p. X11.

"Shocking Ringmaster Revelations" (Jerry Springer). *Television Week*, 8 May 2006, pp. 32–34.

"Show Biz-Wise Psychologist Still Old Fashioned Woman" (Joyce Brothers). *Hartford (CT) Courant*, 13 May 1978, p. 13.

Simon, Clea. "The Relationship Doctor Is In" (Joy Browne). *Boston Globe*, 7 September 2000, p. B12.

Smalley, Suzanne. Sarah Kliff, Setodeh Ramin, et al. "Just How Low Will They Go?" *Newsweek*, 9 June 2008, pp. 34–35.

Span, Paula. "The Irreverent Voice. Deejay Howard Stern: Life in N.Y. After D.C." *Washington Post*, 26 December 1983, pp. D1, D12.

———. "Radio Waves: Talk-Show Host Randi Rhodes Joined a New Liberal Network Hoping to Advance Her Career While Shaking Up This Election Season." *Washington Post Sunday Magazine*, 12 September 2004, p. W11.

Squires, Catherine R. "Black Talk Radio: Defining Community Needs and Identity." *Harvard International Journal of Press/Politics*, vol. 5, no. 2, Spring 2000, pp. 73–95.

Steinberg, Jacques. "Liberal Voices (Some Sharp) Get New Home on Radio Dial." *New York Times*, 31 March 2004, pp. E1, 8.

Stengel, Richard. "Midnight's Mayor" (Jay Leno). *Time*, 16 March 1992, pp. 58–62.

Stepp, Laura Sessions. "The Empire Built on Family and Faith" (James Dobson). *Washington Post*, 8 August 1990, pp. C1–3.

Sweeney, Louise. "Television's Talk, Talk, Talkathons on the Late, Late, Late Shows." *Christian Science Monitor*, 8 March 1968, p. 4.

"Television's Most Curious Man" (Dave Garroway). *TV Guide*, 24 March 1956, pp. 4–6.

Thomma, Steven. "On Talk Radio, Conservatives Still Dominate." *Philadelphia Inquirer*, 10 October 2005, p. A3.

Thompson, Bill. "Limbaugh Loves to be Hated." *Pacific Stars and Stripes* (Tokyo, Japan), 20 July 1994, p. 12.

Tiede, Tom. "Talk-Jockey Jimmy Hits Phones" (Long John Nebel). *Galveston (Texas) Daily News*, 4 March 1977, p. 9.

Tresniowski, Alex, and Lorenzo Benet. "King of Comedy" (Steve Allen). *People Weekly*, 13 November 2000, pp. 70–73.

———, Maureen Harrington, and Vickie Bane. "Alone at the End: Long Estranged from Her Daughter, Dr. Laura's Mother Dies Mysteriously." *People Weekly*, 13 January 2003, p. 64.

"Tribune Comptroller Scores on TV Show" (Joe Pyne). *Philadelphia Tribune*, 8 July 1958, p. 2.

Trohan, Walter. "Censor Many Radio Programs. Stations Quick to Comply." *Chicago Tribune*, 17 January 1942, p. 11.

Trombley, William. "LA Turns On to Talk Shows." *Los Angeles Times*, 25 August 1975, pp. A3, 17.

Valdes, Alisa. "Talk TV's Numero Uno: 100 Million Listen as Cristina Saralegui Tackles Latino Taboos." *Boston Globe*, 10 February 1998, p. E1.

Vogrin, Bill. "In 20 Years, Focus on the Family has Grown in Size and Influence." *Colorado Springs Gazette*, 30 March 1997 p. A3.

"Voice of America's Left" (Rachel Maddow). *New Statesman*, 17 April 2006, p. 22.

Von Hoffman, Nicholas. "Topping It Off: Topless Radio." *Washington Post*, 30 October 1972, p. B1.

Waldman, Allison J. "American Pie: The In-Your-Face Success of 'The Jerry Springer Show,'" *Television Week*, 8 May 2006, pp. 26, 31, 34, 37.

———. "History and Highlights" (Jerry Springer). *Television Week*, 8 May 2006, p. 37.

———. "Six Who Shine in Whatever Language" (Cristina Saralegui). *Television Week*, 16 October 2006, pp. 25–32.

———. "25 Years of Syndie Landmarks." *Television Week*, 21 May 2007, pp. 36–37.

Wallsten, Peter. "The Imus Scandal: Political Impact." *Los Angeles Times*, 13 April 2007, p. A23.

"Wally Phillips Brought Class, Not Sass, to Morning Radio." *Chicago Sun Times*, 28 March 2008, p. 29.

Waxman, Sharon. "King of the Trash Heap; Jerry Springer Digs the Dirt On Television." *Washington Post*, 20 January 1998, p. D1.

Wild, David. "Rock and Roll Yearbook: Jay Leno." *Rolling Stone*, 11 January 1996, pp. 76–9.

Williams, Scott. "Springer Foes Talk Trash: Dump It or Clean It, Execs Told." *New York Daily News*, 8 April 1998, p. 5.

Wilson-Smith, Anthony. "Fox News? Bring It On." *Macleans*, 4 October 2004, p. 4.

Wiltz, Teresa. "Spanglish Star: Can Univision's Cristina Translate into Prime Time? Stay Tuned." *Washington Post*, 31 January 2004, p. C1.

Winslow, George. "Talk Much? CNN's Larry King Has Interviewed Almost Everyone." *Broadcasting and Cable*, 19 June 2006, p. A5.

Wolk, Josh. "Stalking Stern." *Entertainment Weekly*, 7 April 2006, pp. 21–25.

Wolters, Larry. "A Man Going Everywhere" (Steve Allen). *Chicago Tribune*, 1 March 1959, p. H16.

Yorke, Jeffrey. "He's Baaaaaaack! Howard Stern's Return Threatens a Ravings War." *Washington Post*, 30 September 1988, pp. B1, B3.

Young, Cathy. "One Man's Culture War" (Bill O'Reilly). *Reason*, January 2007, pp. 16–18.

Zehme, Bill. "Interview: David Letterman." *Rolling Stone*, 18 February 1993, pp. 32–38.

Zoglin, Richard, and Georgia Harbison. "New Dave Dawning" (David Letterman). *Time*, 30 August 1993, pp. 50–57.

———, and Hannah Bloch. "Talking Trash: Ricki Lake and Her Disciples Have Achieved the Impossible: Lowered the Standards of TV Gabfests." *Time*, 30 January 1995, pp. 76–79.

Index

About the Author

DONNA L. HALPER is a well-known media historian with expertise in broadcasting and social history. She has been a guest on the History Channel, PBS, and NPR, and her research has been quoted in numerous publications. She has spent over twenty-five years as an educator and over thirty years as a broadcaster. She is the author of three books, including *Invisible Stars: A Social History of Women in American Broadcasting* (2001).